Herman "Baron" Lamm,
the Father of
Modern Bank Robbery

Herman "Baron" Lamm, the Father of Modern Bank Robbery

WALTER MITTELSTAEDT

McFarland & Company, Inc., Publishers
Jefferson, North Carolina, and London

LIBRARY OF CONGRESS CATALOGUING-IN-PUBLICATION DATA

Mittelstaedt, Walter, 1946–
    Herman "Baron" Lamm, the father of modern bank robbery / Walter Mittelstaedt.
       p.   cm.
    Includes bibliographical references and index.

    ISBN 978-0-7864-6559-0
    softcover : acid free paper ∞

    1. Lamm, Herman, 1890–1930. 2. Criminals — United States — Biography. 3. Brigands and robbers — United States — Biography. 4. Bank robberies — United States — History — 20th century. I. Title.
HV6653.L36M58 2012
364.15'52092—dc23
[B]   2012037183

BRITISH LIBRARY CATALOGUING DATA ARE AVAILABLE

© 2012 Walter Mittelstaedt. All rights reserved

No part of this book may be reproduced or transmitted in any form or by any means, electronic or mechanical, including photocopying or recording, or by any information storage and retrieval system, without permission in writing from the publisher.

Front cover: The Citizens State Bank an hour and a half after a robbery (Indiana Historical Society, M0888); mug shot of Herman "Baron" Lamm (Wikipedia.org); stopwatch and background © 2012 Shuterstock

Manufactured in the United States of America

McFarland & Company, Inc., Publishers
  Box 611, Jefferson, North Carolina 28640
    www.mcfarlandpub.com

In loving memory of Art Hockett,
who took me around.

Difficile est propria communia dicere. — Horace
There was nothing else to do except what we were doing. — *Deliverance*
O God, that one might read the book of fate. — *2 Henry IV*
By the world, I recount no fable. — *Love's Labor's Lost*

Table of Contents

Acknowledgments	viii
Preface	1
An Unarmed Prologue	5
I. Materials for a Death	15
II. Minions of the Moon: St. Bernice, 1924	34
III. Easy Money: Milwaukee, December 8, 1924	51
IV. "We always had our eyes open": Of Hooligans and Vigilance	58
V. Under the Radar at Winston-Salem	73
VI. Death Comes to Lafayette	80
VII. The Simple Art of Bank Robbery — Frankfort, Indiana, December 3, 1930	89
VIII. Clinton; or, The Wheels of Chance	99
IX. "You're out of luck"	125
X. After "the most thrilling manhunt ever staged in this part of the country"	138
XI. The State of Indiana vs. Walter E. Detrich and James Clark, Alias William M. Long	154
XII. Tell the Jury What, If Anything, Happened Then: The Witnesses Speak	163
XIII. The Greatest Escape	192
XIV. Laid at His Doorstep	208
XV. Who Else?	217
Chapter Notes	233
Bibliography	251
Index	255

Acknowledgments

I suppose my first obligation is to those that I've bothered longest. This is readily recognized. For the past four years I've hovered around the reference desk at the Bloomington (IL) Public Library ordering books and microfilm so thickly that they almost needed a traffic light to control the flow and protect innocent bystanders. Chief among that set, having suffered longest, is Amy Richard. I scarcely can pick up a photostat or Dewey decimal notation or a this-and-that among my papers that hasn't its origin with her. To only a slightly lesser degree the same holds true of the others in the Adult Services Department—Marcie Shaffer, Mary Cruser, Natalie La Rocque, Karen Moen, Theresa Denham and Robin Helenthal. Similar not-a-little-indebtedness must go to Jeanne Gordon and Debbie Mattingly of the Interlibrary Loan Department at the library for rounding up countless newspapers and books, some of them bearing inscriptions from their authors. Talk about immediacy...

Many thanks, too, to Mary Tate of the Sidell (IL) District Library. She brought Art Hockett and Merrel Chew to my attention and, after many false starts, my research was thus off and running. My deepest gratitude goes to the people of Sidell and vicinity who kindly took me into their homes and shared stories and showed newspaper clippings to me—Lillian Swiggert, Charles Lyons, Sue Dobson, and Mr. and Mrs. Barry Eakles and their lovable mutt, Whitey.

The Clinton (IN) Public Library provided useful local history information and microfilm. Thanks go to Karen Walker, Sue Vinyard, Theresa Faller and Carol Gudino.

A most grateful shout-out goes to Ellen D. Swain, Archivist for Student/Life Culture at the University of Illinois at Urbana/Champaign, for the transcripts of John Edward Klutas and Fred Samuel Goetz.

The newspaper library at the University of Illinois was a tremendous boon to me in the early stages of my research. It was quite a pleasurable experience for me to be able to sit at a single microfilm reader in one room in one sitting and be able to follow Nellie Bly's dispatches on the "Nebraska sufferers" of 1894–5 and try to pick up the point where Wild Bill left Buffalo Bill in their production of *Scouts of the Plains* in 1874 before getting down to business with Dillinger and Baron Lamm in the Midwestern dailies of a more modern era. It was not a little like the time traveler's ride in the *Time Machine*— quite appropriately, since the original manuscript of H.G. Wells' most cherished book just happens to reside one floor up from the newspaper library.

Many thanks to Vicki Casteel of the Indiana State Archives for information on Joseph Burns, Walter Detrich and James "Oklahoma Jack" Clark.

I greatly appreciate the kindness and long suffering of Susan Sutton and the staff of the William H. Smith Memorial Library at the Indiana Historical Society in dispensing the Cejnar papers and key photographs related to December 16, 1930. I garnered a precious handful of photographs — I wish I had taken them all. They all told a story.

Faith Burdick, Reference Librarian at the Galesburg (IL) Public Library, looked into an old volume for me, hunting for any sign of Baron Lamm, for which, all these years later, I warmly thank her.

Susan Storm, of the Champaign (IL) Public Library, aided my research in the days when I was just about to put pen to paper by supplying dates of birth and death for several people connected with Lamm and Dillinger. I owe her for Hazel Haase and Louella Cloutier and, most especially, for that big guy who wouldn't fit in this book — Grover Cleveland Lutter. Ha! Ha! Susan.

Jack Keefe threw precious tidbits my way concerning Dillinger and our hometown — Bloomington, Illinois. We often work together at the microfilm readers at the library and talk Cubs baseball or Ohio State football while doing so. Jack is one of those people, like Mark Twain and Truman Capote, who seems to have met everybody and have been everywhere. Anyway, he sure has stories, some of which appear in these pages, and I am most indebted to him for them. I never would have come by them otherwise.

Another friend, Pete Rubini, who jogged with me in the old days before Fox Creek got chastened with subdivisions and a golf course, had to hear all about Baron Lamm when I had just unearthed him out of John Toland's pages. It was reassuring to find that Pete was as certain as I was that there was a book in Lamm.

In the final stages of this research, I was highly gratified and greatly encouraged by Kevin Murley's efforts on my behalf and for the expeditious work of the Clerk's Office of the Indiana State Supreme Court in forwarding transcripts that I thought were long since lost to view, if they ever existed in the first place.

My greatest debt — one that I could never repay in a million years of 24/7 — is to Sheryl Hansen. She has been a constant bulwark against self-doubt and inaction since I began writing this book in a serious way four years ago. She has been my Girl Friday, my IT guy, my Minister of Finance and, like Editor Peabody in *Liberty Valance*, she also sweeps out the place. *I can no other answer make but thanks, and thanks and ever thanks.*

Warmest thanks to my family — some, like my parents, now gone — and friends for their support, not only on this project, but countless others, all, seemingly, mare's nests. No one ever tried to shake me off the scent, a quality us headstrong folk always greatly appreciate in our own stock and our friends.

Preface

I came to Herman K. Lamm, "Baron" Lamm, after getting seriously steeped in John Dillinger. That's pretty much the way it must be for any student of Lamm. Lamm is always an offshoot of Dillinger. Nobody ever comes to Lamm first.

My interest in Lamm began about three weeks after I invited myself over to the house of Dillinger's kid sister, Frances, for an interview while she and her husband, Carl Thompson, tried to watch *Wheel of Fortune* and the Indiana State Lottery drawing. Of course, I did not bring up Lamm — how could I, never having heard of him? — and I doubt that John in any of those trips to the homestead in Mooresville, Indiana, told little Frances what he knew of Lamm. What Dillinger knew of Lamm was hearsay, acquired from two of Lamm's henchmen. In any case, Dillinger was in stir throughout Lamm's heyday. Nevertheless, there was a very real connection between Lamm and Dillinger and it is this influence which is a large part of this book.

What did Dillinger learn from Lamm? All the little things. Former gang member Edward Shouse told police that the Dillinger gang rehearsed their robberies — something Lamm did. Dillinger learned, too, the urgency of preparing a getaway plan, honed down to the least detail. He learned, as in the Racine robbery, to plant gasoline cans along the getaway route — improving, perhaps, on Lamm's way of carrying a can of gas in the back of the getaway car. And, finally, only the best late-model cars were to be used in heists. But Dillinger never learned the overarching lesson that he should have learned after reviewing Lamm's career — that things happen.

When I came to Baron Lamm nearly two decades ago, some of the old-timers were still up and around. I got to as many of them as I could over time. Most were kids when Lamm went down, but I talked with two widows in their nineties — Mrs. Everett Helms and Mrs. Leo Moody. Even so, I don't think this book would have gotten off the ground if I hadn't met Art Hockett and Merrel Chew. Art led me to a number of other key interviews and was always just full of hunches. Merrel saw something that gave the whole matter an air of mystery, which to this researcher, more than most perhaps, is a prime ingredient of the writing process.

The record of holdups perpetrated by Lamm and company, unlike that of John Dillinger and Jesse James, is very difficult to pin down. Lamm was no showman. He did not write letters to the editor protesting his innocence after one of his gang's robberies, nor did he, as did Dillinger, tell a young DePauw student to "to take a good look at me, so you'll know me next time." He had to be tracked down by modus operandi and physical description. Once in a great while, as in Lafayette, bank personnel put the finger on him. With Milwaukee, it was that city's police department that not only tagged Lamm with their first daylight bank robbery but identified his remains at McCauley's funeral parlor.

Baron Lamm took shelter under a bunch of aliases (Milwaukee police said seven) — Tommy Wyatt, George Barney, Herbert J. Madsen, Joe Masters and, most famously, Thomas Bell. Even today, researchers sometimes confuse the real name with the ubiquitous alias. But Lamm's World War I draft card makes it clear that he was born Herman Karl Lamm in Cassell, Germany.

In that bygone day, you didn't have to work that hard on an alias. You could get them handed to you for nothing, even if you were upstanding. Thus, in newspaper accounts and court documents, young Roy (Leroy) Gritten appears as Roy Gritton and Roy Griffen. Roy Haase is sometimes Ray Hays and Roy Hays. Homer Hamm transmogrifies into Omer Hamm and Omar Hamm. With scarcely more than one stroke of the pen, he could warp from posse man to the author of the *Rubaiyat*. John Nolan becomes John Noland in at least one account. Mildred Brookbank is sometimes Mildred Brockbank, and her occupation clouds from teacher to head of the Clinton DMV. Her freight varies, too, in that 70-mile drive — from one student to three vigilantes. But this is newspaper stuff — the court records and the inquest don't even know her by any name. They should have. She had a front-row seat for the last stand of the outlaws. We do have her picture and we do know her age — 22. Still, somebody should have talked to her for the record. Most chameleon-like of all is Lt. Rex Resser of the Indiana State Police, who is sometimes Rex Reeser, Rex Risser, Rex Risher and I don't know who all else. Almost every time he's mentioned, he's someone else. With such divergence so often, it leaves you wondering whether one individual is meant or two or even three.

This book is the first book-length study of Baron Lamm. He is no longer confined to supporting roles in a discussion of Dillinger or sentenced to a mere column in a crime encyclopedia. A screenplay has recently come out, so that Lamm, at long last, may make it to the silver screen.

Today Baron Lamm remains a figure more legendary than real. His proverbial genius as a mastermind of crime is much overrated. He was arrested at least a half a dozen times in his career, beginning in San Francisco, December 1, 1914. In Kansas City, Missouri, in July 1918, he was arrested for vagrancy — this just a month after an arrest for a holdup in Superior, Wisconsin. Whatever vagrancy may entail today, back in that day it was merely a way of holding a suspect by the authorities while some heftier charge might be made to stick. George "Bugs" Moran, Al Capone's North Side rival, was always being held in his rapid decline on vagrancy charges (as on December 12, 1930). I sometimes wonder whether if Baron Lamm hadn't gone out so spectacularly, we would have heard of him today.

But if Baron Lamm isn't all that he's cracked up to be, why do a whole book on him? Why not keep him in the footnotes where he belongs? Always before me as I wrote was this special observation, that of all the notable outlaws of the last century, Lamm went out in a way all his own. He may or may not have been the first scientific bank robber, but he certainly departed this earth in the most inconceivable manner possible. You couldn't make it up because you couldn't begin to explain it. I once told Stan Hayes that some of the accounts of Lamm's death were exaggerated. That in itself was an exaggeration. You couldn't exaggerate what happened that day.

When Baron Lamm's demise is discussed, it is presented as a mad dash to try to save his neck. Even the newspapers closest to the story — the *Daily Clintonian*, the *Danville Commercial News*, the *Indianapolis Star* and the *Terre Haute Tribune* — could not — or would not — see that there were light scenes intermixed with those of the most intense drama, like something from the Henriad or *The Searchers*. It was "all excitement there," is how, I believe, posse man Ernest Boetto put it. It was a day fraught with danger and filled with gunsmoke, but it is doubtful if a single one of the participants wanted it that way. No one was to be harmed, if possible — no civilian, that is. Lamm was not sparing of lead when it came to lawmen, but everyday citizens — that was a different matter. Wells Gilbert, the only hostage I know ever taken by Lamm — and that because Gilbert was the only one who could drive his truck — was made to take shelter behind one of the wheels of that vehicle during a firefight. If Gilbert as the gang's driver was necessary to Lamm's survival and thus safeguarded, Gilbert's fellow passenger, Roy Gritten, was let go. At 17, Gritten would have made a fine hostage, and there was room for him in the back "of that old Chevrolet truck," but he was given his freedom with no more endangerment than the command, "Hit the road!" Lamm was not into endangering everyday folks. On this his final day, he surely could have. It is surely astonishing that the thought of taking hostages under such circumstances never crossed Lamm's mind.

But the general populace was not so careful of Lamm. They turned out in droves on his last day to put a stop to it. As many as a hundred vehicles pursued Lamm and his gang across the Illinois line from Clinton, Indiana. Somewhere between two hundred and five hundred vigilantes swarmed into Leo Moody's cornfield to bar the gang's escape. There were forty vigilantes present when Lamm gave up the ghost. That many were that close. This part of the story is not unique. In the twenties and thirties of the last century, it was fairly common to pick up a newspaper and read about bank robbers having to deal with vigilantes, sometimes in greater numbers than in Lamm's case. Crime was to be stopped in its tracks and American citizens were in the forefront of that fight all through those years. It is almost mind-numbing to think of such actions taking place today. Vigilantes were a curious and fascinating part of Lamm's story for me and it baffles me as to why there isn't more out there on the vigilantism so rampant in that era.

This has been a long project. Truman Capote told an interviewer that if he knew what he was getting into when he began *In Cold Blood*, he would have run like hell. From start to finish, *In Cold Blood* took Capote six years. I have escaped much of the frenzy Capote went through, but my task has taken considerably longer — nearly three times as long. Not that I had my nose to the grindstone the whole time. In addition to Baron Lamm, I had other things to think about — I worried an awful lot about what the middle name might have been of Dick Broadwell, a member of the Dalton gang. It seemed like the thing to do. I wondered about all the things that might have happened to Shakespeare's *Love's Labor's Won* to make it disappear without a trace. And I, perhaps uniquely, wanted to know what went on in Jacksonville, Illinois, the night Dillinger made his celebrated wooden gun escape from the Crown Point jail. All these matters went unresolved, yet all deserve my undivided attention and, as Mark Twain says somewhere, "I don't have anything in particular to do next winter anyway."

But all through these years Lamm was never far away, egging me on from the sidelines. I first went to Indiana looking for Lamm on Saturday, November 7, 1992. I combined Lamm with Dillinger on that day and Dillinger netted results, but Lamm did not. At the end of that year, I had much better luck at Sidell, Illinois. From then on, the game was on. Progress was ever slow and useful bits and pieces of the Lamm story, unlike sorrows, came one at a time. I first learned of the Lafayette robbery in December 2003 and finally saw my first picture of Lamm in March 2007. It was at this time that I began my first draft. All these drafts later, I can be certain that I have at least produced the tip of the iceberg.

An Unarmed Prologue

I just want to see where this goes. — Philo Vance in *The Kennel Murder Case* (1933)

At a book sale in Clinton, Indiana, in December 1995, I picked up a copy of an old book called *If; or, History Rewritten*.[1] It's one of those books that seem to come out every year now and are done jointly by a group of scholars who examine key events in history and reverse their outcome. This particular book boasted essays by the likes of Winston Churchill, Hilaire Belloc and G.K. Chesterton, among other notables. One has only to glance at the table of contents to see how much of history turns on a dime. It was most fitting that I should find such a book in Clinton, Indiana, because it was in this town, only a few weeks before the book was published, that Baron Lamm, the father of scientific bank robbery, met his downfall. Today, Baron Lamm is fabled for his perverse genius, but his perverse fate is much more worthy of record. It was uniquely his own.

Bad men, of course, had bad luck before Baron Lamm came on the scene. Lamm didn't invent ill fortune, though on his last day he might have thought about taking out a patent on it. More than half a century earlier in September 1876, Jesse James made the mistake of ranging too far from his graze when he ventured up to the Minnesota country with his gang. In Northfield, the townspeople, armed with squirrel guns, rocks and whatever else came to hand, plugged fellow gang member Bill Chadwell right where he sat in the saddle in front of the First National. When Chadwell gave up the ghost, more or less instantly, he took with him his vast knowledge of his native Minnesota—the only outlaw of the James-Younger gang who had any such knowledge. Jesse and Frank made it out of Minnesota in tortuous fashion back to the familiar haunts of western Missouri, but the rest of the gang, including the three Younger brothers, were either captured or killed in Minnesota.

The Dalton gang, too, blundered spectacularly when they took up bank robbery after a successful run of train robberies. Their initial foray into this trade proved to be their last. Apart from being recognized under their makeshift disguises early on, the gang, because of construction going on, had to hitch their horses much too far from the scene of their business. They had to charge through a hailstorm of lead to get to their mounts. Four of the five didn't make it, though two of them had their morgue shots taken standing up just the same — and the one that did make it, Emmett Dalton, was laid up for months before serving fifteen years in prison. Emmett surely would have been lynched that day, but a physician named Wells assured the mob that under his care the outlaw would probably die anyway.

Some outlaws in the old days were bad judges of horse flesh, but on his last day ever Baron Lamm was a bad judge of horsepower. He was double-crossed by that miracle of assembly-line ingenuity, the American automobile, no less than five times in a single morning. A late-model Buick crossed him first, once right off the bat and once later, just for good measure. Then a second Buick, a bit older than the first, proved just as unreliable as the former. A Chevy truck, for diversity's sake, figured next in the mix. Finally, a Ford topped everything off when the Model-A variety ran short of gas. Lamm's downfall couldn't be thought up by a writer of fiction in a million years because the operations of chance are given so much sway in it. Yet, even for a factual episode, there is much about Lamm's downfall that strains credulity.

Outlaws had been driving cars away from bank robberies since Henry Starr initiated the trend in 1915. But fifteen years later, in committing an act "with no relish of salvation in it," Baron Lamm would have been better off if he had come and gone to the bank by dogsled. If Baron Lamm had been granted nine lives and he had all nine in his pocket at nine in the morning of December 16, 1930, all nine would have been peeled off one by one by noon.

I first read about Baron Lamm in John Toland's *The Dillinger Days*.[2] It was late at night, well past midnight, when curiosity should be ready to tuck itself in. But, for some reason, at this late hour my guard was down and I left myself wide open for new awakenings. It was this book, after all, which hit screenwriters David Newman and Robert Benton (and, perhaps, Robert Towne) right where they live and where we all live. They read the section on a couple of Dallas-area sweethearts who raced around the entire Dust Bowl robbing banks and anything else that stood still long enough in the early thirties. Newman and Benton were completely mesmerized. The rest is screen history. Their inspiration became the 1967 screen classic *Bonnie and Clyde*.

I knew Toland's book from my high school days but had successfully managed, in my brief sessions with it, to overlook something that struck me now. In three quick pages, Toland deals with the life of Herman K. Lamm, notorious as Baron Lamm. He particularly dwells on all the bad luck that attended Lamm on his last escapade. Reading these pages now, I reached for a road atlas to see just how far from my home in central Illinois, Clinton, Indiana — the setting for Lamm's last gasp — was. I was thrilled to see that it was not that far. A three-hour drive at no more than the speed limit would easily do it. In those days, with the right amount of enthusiasm, I could have jogged it.

So, one November day, I went for a drive.

It turned out to be an odd sort of autumn day, the kind on which you can't quite put your finger on anything much. It was cloudy, as most November days are in temperate climates, and should be (according to almanacs), with the sun, a late sleeper, in bed with the covers pulled up over his head. Old Phoebus, "that wand'ring knight so fair," seemed like he couldn't make up his mind about what his job description stipulated and he wanted to take the day off to think it over. It was cool — without being cold — but cool enough to make you want to stay in your car unless compelled to leave it at gunpoint.

Straightaway, I went to a bank with the same name as the one robbed by Lamm and company more than six decades before, but the building looked far too upscale to have been plundered by a robber gang at the start of the Great Depression. That old bank building, as I afterwards learned, was just down the street in a new incarnation housing the Department of Motor Vehicles. I got out of my car and took a snapshot of the modern bank just for the hell of it, which, as we all know, is the best reason of all.

I sought out the public library a few blocks away. I would need to avail myself of microfilm of the local paper to get a fix on the events of that fast-receding day. Since no books had been written on Lamm, newspapers would be the place to start. They always are when books shrug their shoulders.

Here, again, I was stonewalled. The library closed on Saturdays at the three in the afternoon. It was around four when I pulled up. I came so belatedly because, first of all, I naively thought that no library once opened for business on a Saturday would dare close before five that afternoon and, secondly, I had stopped at neighboring Rockville on the way and visited with some folks whose bank in that town John Dillinger and Harry Copeland once robbed. The robbery has only recently made it into Dillinger biographies. And though Dillinger's biographers did not know of it when I first came to Rockville, everyone in town did. I had not been in Rockville five minutes before I became quite convinced that Dillinger had been there on business, even if his biographers hadn't caught up with that fact.[3]

Since I didn't yet know anybody in Clinton and had no idea whom I should know, I had to settle for my success at Rockville earlier (see chapter XII). That would have to get me through the day. As I drove away from Clinton up S.R. 63 to U.S. 36, I glanced at all the hills and woods around me. They were now eerily coated with a late-afternoon orange pallor. I felt like I had wandered into a menthol cough drop and come down with a bad cold. All I had for my trouble on this day, so far as Baron Lamm went, was a picture of the wrong bank.

There would be other days. I would see to that.

Always, whenever I visited Clinton, I was struck by two things time and again. Everyone I talked to, from the Dairy Queen habitués, to the librarians at the public library, to the personnel of *The Daily Clintonian*, the local paper, all knew about the robbery in town way back when. They knew that the whole town was up in arms and that the robbers got the short end of the stick. But, curiously, not a soul from Clinton, Indiana, to Tuscola, Illinois, knew who it was that had caused all the commotion. Their knowledge of the incident seemed almost to be transferred through the genes, like blue eyes, from their parents and grandparents. They were born knowing all about the big bank heist that went wrong. None, however, knew who Baron Lamm was or Dad Landy (even so, all knew about "the old guy who blew his brains out"). None knew of "Oklahoma Jack" or a sharp-looking jerk named Walter Detrich. Of course, no one had ever heard of E.H. Hunter. That would be asking too much of anybody. Hunter makes the least sense of anybody in this whole affair, probably because we know less about him than anyone else in Lamm's gang. He seems to have been a latecomer to it.

There was no one around who had seen Lamm or knew of someone who had. This would change in time, but at first it was slow going. I would not see a picture of Lamm for several more years. Crime annals and encyclopedias have been even more sluggish in handling Lamm. They give a few bare facts but never once does his likeness peep out from their pages. Not even a pen-and-ink sketch. Somehow that seems appropriate. The legendary Clinton robbery was an event without a face.

Interviews in those first days were scarce. Some people were recommended by librarians and local historians and I never got around to them — in time. When, in late December, I got to Sidell, Illinois, for example, local historian Art Hockett recommended that I drop by a nursing home at Chrisman, Illinois, to talk with Ernest Dawson. Dawson was then about to turn ninety and had been for many years a rural mail carrier. In 1930, during the Big Event, he was among the two hundred vigilantes who ran Baron Lamm and his robber gang to ground. I had not been to Chrisman before and as it was a frozen night with no more encouragement to comfort the inmost part of me than a thin sliver of silver-bright moon overhead, I thought it wise to hold off on traveling on any two-lanes that might lead to nowhere in the middle of the night. If I learned nothing else during these days, I learned that there's still an awful lot of prairie in the Prairie State on a lonesome winter night, even when you know what you're doing, and in this case I did not. You soon learn what they mean by "a country mile."

Not only is there a lot of prairie out there yet, there's also a lot of weather. A snowstorm can come at you just as soon as you leave town. You keep going because all that is going on initially are those restless ribbons of windblown snow marching at a last-minute-shopper's pace. A moment more and the pavement is a mere memory and the whole world is quite quiet and quite white. When these storms hit, it is usually at night — not late at night — but the time of night when it usually makes sense to be out. Or if it isn't exactly nighttime, it might as well be as far as visibility goes. In no time on those back roads the center stripe (when there is one) disappears and with it all sense of proportion. For what seems a life span, you wonder which lane is which and what is a road and what a cornfield. The lanes suddenly shift and trade places and then vanish altogether, and you are left wondering why the deuce you ever took up this life. To compound the situation, there is no traffic, either in your direction or the opposite direction, largely because you're the only one foolish enough to be out in this kind of weather, or to be caught in it, rather. If you wander into a small town, it is usually too late to catch anybody open for business, so you keep going. Eventually, you'll come to a four-lane, which in the present emergency becomes a two-lane, and thrill to see a touring bus or a semi and follow it back to civilization with its cable television and transfat and bottled water that costs as much as Diet Coke.

I had spoken earlier with Mary Tate at the Sidell, Illinois, library (who graciously kept the library open beyond its usual five o'clock closing time so that I could get situated in my research). She connected me with Merrel Chew as well as Art. She also showed me a volume or two of local histories (both county and village history) that had something in them about the Clinton robbery and its Sidell aftermath. So all in all, I had a pretty good day of research under my belt and this, combined with the frigid, uninviting weather and late hour, kept me from venturing further on this day. Yet, it was most unfortunate that I felt that time would stand still, because it so rarely does. Before I could get back — two blizzards intervened on successive Saturdays — my traveling days — and talk to Ernest Dawson and hear about the Sidell episode from a vigilante's standpoint, he passed away. I don't know what he took with him. I can only guess. I do know that I'll always regret that I never talked with him.

Now, more than eighty years after the Clinton robbery, none of the principals involved are around. Of the two bad guys who survived the climatic gun battle, Walter Detrich lasted longer (presumably). He died on April 24, 1979, at the age of seventy-four. He had gone straight finally and had no trouble staying that way for a quarter of a century. "Oklahoma Jack," paroled to Kansas in the spring of 1950, was never heard of again. He could have been hanged a thousand times over, but he escaped the noose, perhaps because he once saved a lawman's life.

Despite this setback, things were soon coming together and I was getting somewhere in my research. Most of all, I found myself growing fond of the region and its inhabitants. At a gun shop in Fairmount, Illinois, in the late summer of 1993, I even saw a revolver picked up on the Leo Moody farm after the bandits' last stand. It obviously belonged to one of the bandits since they had had no chance to gather up their belongings when the smoke cleared.

Thrilling as that was, it was an anonymous pistol. No one knew which bandit it had belonged to. So I still had no real fix on Baron Lamm or Thomas Bell or whoever was the instrument behind all the carnage and excitement that day in 1930. Art and Merrel told me about what they saw at the mortuary in the days following the gunfight near Sidell, but I still was not versed enough in the story to be able to distinguish one corpse from another going by their descriptions at this point. My best guess was that the small, bald guy in the tan suit — a professorial type — spoken of by Merrel Chew was Baron Lamm. This turned out to be all wrong. Far from being a member of academe, or Baron Lamm, for that matter, this man was merely the gang's driver, E.H. Hunter.

All through my research, the Ixion's grindstone that confronted me was: Why is not Baron Lamm better known? Outlaws such as John Dillinger, Pretty Boy Floyd and Baby Face Nelson are household names today while Baron Lamm remains in the shadows, a true "gentleman of the shade." These others have books about them churned out regularly, and now and then they appear as the subject of a Hollywood film. Baron Lamm remains as elusive as a full stop in a preface by Maurice Morgann.

But there is a reason why these others are so well known today and Lamm isn't. The reason just may surprise you — J. Edgar Hoover. Neither Hoover nor his field commander, Melvin Purvis, was in on the kill, though it must have seemed to Lamm that everyone else, save for these two souls, was. But Hoover and his Chicago Office proxy, Melvin Purvis, had other fish to fry in 1930.

J. Edgar Hoover had been in the Department of Justice for thirteen years when Baron Lamm was killed. For the first few years, he was perfecting surveillance techniques and whom to use them on. He played a role in the notorious "Red Raids" of 1919–20, seeing Emma Goldman and her lover off personally in their deportation. Then, in 1924, due to a fortuitous set of circumstances, he made the leap from assistant director to director. Upon Lamm's death, Hoover, via the Justice Department's Bureau of Criminal Identification, his pride and joy, confirmed Lamm's fingerprint identification and provided a rap sheet. That was all Mr. Hoover wanted with Baron Lamm.

Even though bank robbery was running rampant all through the twenties, nothing much on a federal level was being done about it. The emergence of vigilante organizations for a decade following 1925 seemed to have had a deterrent effect on bank robbery. The Justice Department was having none of it. That would change dramatically less than three years after Lamm's death.

Around 7:30 in the morning on June 17, 1933, a pleasant Saturday in Kansas City, machine gunners mowed down four officers of the law, one a Bureau of Investigation agent, in the parking lot of Union Station. This brazen attempt to free a federal prisoner, Frank Nash, failed in its mission as Nash, too, was accidentally killed. The nation was horrified by the boldness of this brutal act in broad daylight and demanded immediate action. This, Hoover and his boss, Attorney General Homer S. Cummings, were only too happy to provide. Thus began the War on Crime.[4]

By 1934, under the impetus of new legislation enacted by Congress, bank robbery became a federal crime and the FBI (not yet so designated) was hot on the trail of the likes of Dillinger, Baby Face Nelson and Pretty Boy Floyd. The Chicago Office was the primary agency involved. Its special agent in charge, Melvin Purvis, would be on the scene when Dillinger and Floyd were killed and on the way when Nelson died. If you were a public enemy during the few short years of the War on Crime, people were going to know about you.

The public enemy program caught everyone's attention. Today, Hoover is often accused of engineering this war to build his own reputation. Dillinger, according to this view, was merely an annoying rural bandit until he was pumped up by the Justice Department into the poster boy for the crime epidemic in America in the mid-thirties. Never mind that he helped bust out ten of the worst criminals of that day from the Indiana state prison; never mind that they in turn freed him from jail two weeks later; never mind that he escaped from the Crown Point jail with a wooden gun, locking up eighteen captives of his own, and shot his way out of a trap in St. Paul at the end of the same month; never mind Little Bohemia.

The year following Dillinger's death, 1935, saw the emergence of J. Edgar Hoover as rock star. The Warner Brothers film *"G" Men*, starring James Cagney, cemented Hoover's reputation as America's greatest crime fighter. Though nowhere mentioned in the picture, Hoover's presence is not to be missed. His alter ego calls the shots on the crime war going on in the Midwest. The real War on Crime was still raging at this time, but the film came timely on the heels of the untimely demise of Pretty Boy Floyd and Baby Face Nelson. By then, Dillinger had lain cold in his own grave for nine months. The bandit kingpins, with only minor exceptions, were exterminated or incarcerated. Hoover and, as it turned out, not the attorney general, could not help but see his reputation enhanced by this motion picture.[5] He did not provide assistance in the making of this motion picture, but Hoover had to be inwardly grinning over its release in late April 1935.

Hoover continued to get bigger over the next three decades. It is true that he caught some flack now and then. Toward the end of the War on Crime, United States Senator Kenneth McKellar of Tennessee took him to task, as Dirty Harry might have, for being a big shot in law enforcement and not having made a single felony or misdemeanor arrest in his entire career. Stung deeply, Hoover went after the last public enemy, Alvin "Old Creepy" Karpis, in 1936. After chartering a plane, he caught up with Karpis in New Orleans on May 1.

It was not exactly a picture-perfect arrest, and the organization was already belittled by other police agencies as college kids and pencil pushers. When Karpis was subdued, no one had remembered to bring handcuffs along. Someone took off his necktie and that had to do. For a host of reasons, both personal and professional, the last public enemy would never give Hoover any credit for his capture. He said that Hoover was out of sight until after the arrest was made. But Karpis was ever a man with axes to grind, and he is not the most reliable source in his two books for anything. Hoover was certainly not the first man to lay hands on him that day, but he was hardly in hiding as Karpis would have it.[6]

In recent years, J. Edgar Hoover has come under fire for many other things. He was never a crusader against organized crime and refused, in effect, if not in reality, to recognize its existence. This has bolstered the charge that he catapulted Dillinger and his like into national prominence because it was an easier task to bring them to bay than the Mob. But, then, the Mob may have had an understanding with Hoover. Meyer Lansky obliquely referred to something that the Mob had on the FBI chief.

According to biographer Anthony Summers, Hoover was a cross-dresser and closet homosexual. It may have been compromising photographs related to this rumored aspect of Hoover's personality to which Meyer Lansky referred cryptically. Or it may have been Hoover's alleged addiction to gambling.

Hoover notoriously wiretapped Martin Luther King and others whom he believed to be radicals, and this is always at the forefront when accessing his reputation today. It is ironic, in view of Hoover's relations with Dr. King, that he has been accused of passing for white in a recent book.[7]

Hoover's star would continue to shine brightly after the thirties, first with World War II then the Cold War augmenting his power. He was, if not the most powerful man in U.S. government, one of the most powerful. Baron

Lamm, on the other hand, would begin to be forgotten as soon as he hit the ground in Leo Moody's cornfield. Were it not for Dillinger and John Toland's book on Dillinger, Lamm would be a resident of the dustbin of history today.

So, why isn't Lamm better known today? Perhaps the best explanation and, certainly the easiest, is that given by Janet Margolin in Woody Allen's *Take the Money and Run* (1969). Ruminating about why her husband didn't make the FBI's Ten Most Wanted list, she concludes, "It's who you know."

I

Materials for a Death

The details are naught and anyway it was so awfully long ago. — Henry James, "The Birthplace"

You fit a lot of descriptions. — *The Searchers* (1956)

Not much is known about Baron Lamm. In fact, what isn't known about Baron Lamm, or is wrongly known, would fill a nice folio-size volume in the out-sized section of the public library. Like that "Colossus of Crime," Chesterton's Flambeau, nobody could be certain of anything about Lamm. Police circulars out of Milwaukee and his draft card tell us that he was Prussian, yet few of those robbed by him noticed an accent. Though many crime annals and encyclopedias carry an entry on him almost obligatorily, no book has ever been written about him. He interests us probably because he was good at what he did and because, for all that, so little could be pinned on him. He could be booked but rarely held. He was in and out of jails all over the country and he even went to one state prison for more than a year, but for him rehabilitation was never an option. He was a bad man and he was all business when it came to being bad. He was no Robin Hood. No report has come down to us that describes him laughing or joking or even smiling for the camera with arms akimbo — unlike virtually everyone else associated with him and who, by the way, were just as bad or wished to be.

When he or his gang killed someone, there was never a second's hesitation about it. Killing someone, even an officer, was never a goal of the gang, however. It was on the order of that collateral damage that Timothy McVeigh spoke of following the bombing of Oklahoma City's Federal Building. There is even a good bet that on one occasion someone in the gang shot to wound and not to kill. The victim in this case, quite naturally, was a policeman. If this was Lamm's gang who did the shooting, why did they choose the merciful way out when on at least two other such occasions — one before, one after — they shot to kill with the least possible waste of ammunition?

Baron Lamm was no good, but that hardly made him unique. He might well be overlooked today were it not for the persistence of the legend making him the most scientific of scientific bank robbers and the incontrovertible fact that he did not go to his grave in a straight line. He probably should have died a million times before he actually did and he probably knew it, but he must have resented how it all ended when it came right down to it. His taking off was so completely at variance with the so-called Lamm Method that he had worked so hard to craft. He may well have suspected that he would get shot stepping into a bank or stepping out of one, but he couldn't in a million years have envisioned how it all would end. That end should never have happened and Lamm, if he could have postponed it, could probably have shown you why it should not have happened — reason 1, reason 2, reason 3. But fate doesn't go in much for chalkboard demonstrations.

Certain things about Baron Lamm may be taken as more or less established. He was Prussian because no one ever said that he wasn't — it's hard to argue with that. But even those aware of his Prussian roots called him by his alias of Scottish derivation — Thomas Bell. Gang member Walter Detrich, who should have known all about him, having associated with him for at least three years, called him Thomas Bell — at least, when dealing with the authorities.

No one knows when Lamm left Prussia to come to America. The usual guess states that he left Germany due to an indiscretion — cheating at cards on the eve of or during World War I.[1] But that sounds like something of a reach. You stand people in the corner for cheating at cards, but you don't deport them when your nation is in the middle of a life-and-death struggle, like a world war — the first such in history and one very much in the balance at the time.

That Baron Lamm was in charge of a gang of malefactors is also not to be gainsaid. But did this gang change membership with each robbery, as did that of Eddie Bentz, or did it remain fixed to its Pole Star, as did the John Ford stock company with its "Good Chuck" and "Bad Chuck," or, not to mix metaphors, like the Dillinger gang? Certainly Dillinger's gangs — for there were more than one — retained their membership until death or a police dragnet bid them part.

Once in America, Lamm went from bad to worse. He did time in prison at least once. He now graduated to a higher order of crime. He robbed banks according to a well-thought-out system. This system took place in three steps — planning, rehearsal and the getaway. To Lamm, this last was the most important part of any heist. He may not have originated the Lamm Method, but he probably used it more effectively and more often than anyone else. Unlike the cool, methodical Eddie Bentz, who would not work on more than three bank jobs a year, Lamm apparently worked as often as he pleased. The last two weeks of his career may have seen him participating in no less than four different jobs. One feels that this was typical of the man. At his death, Indiana authorities suspected Lamm's hand in a series of robberies (amounting to, perhaps, two dozen) along the Indiana-Illinois line alone.

Lamm lived in a wild and wooly era—1920s America. Banks, particularly rural state banks in the Heartland, were the easy targets of bandit gangs. In the middle twenties, bandit gangs simply rode roughshod over such states as Indiana, Illinois, Kansas, Oklahoma and Texas. It was during this time that the Dalton gang's aspiration of robbing two banks at the same time was realized. The Cotton Top Walker gang certainly did it in 1927, and others did it later, if not earlier. (Just when somebody first robbed two banks without bloodshed is something I've yet to discover.)

It's hard to make out of such chaos what jobs were Lamm's work and what Harvey Bailey's or that of the Fleagles or Eddie Bentz. All of these gangs believed in rigorous preparation as being paramount in a bank robbery. As a result, it is sometimes hard to tell who did what. Quite often, the various gangs shared the same fences, suppliers and protection, a point well made in the film *Public Enemies* (2009).

The gangs had their own lawyers and their own big guy at the top. The big guy, in Lamm's case, seems to have been someone calling himself "Uncle Ben" or "Uncle Ed."[2] When Lamm and two others were arrested in Winston-Salem in 1927, a Chicago lawyer arrived so fast that it made the local authorities' collective heads swim. This shyster pulled out a fat wad of bills—seven thousand dollars is the usual estimate—to arrange bail for the three men. Chicago, as one might expect, was home to most of the big-time bandits of that era.

Physically, Baron Lamm seems to have been a tall man, but how tall no one knows anymore. He describes himself, at age 27, as a medium-sized man. Latter-day witnesses didn't see him that way. Probably, he was not less than six foot or more than six-four. He was thus quite the biggest man in the gang, usually described as composed of individuals well under six feet. In a robbery, whenever a big man is described as doing this or that, it is almost always Lamm who is being fingered. Usually, the big man is giving orders and waving a pistol.

Ages of bandits, as given by robbery victims, are almost always too young when it comes to Lamm and his adjutant, G.W. "Dad" Landy. In Landy's case, the figure is quite often short by a decade or even two. Similarly, heights, too, are always too short. Rarely is anyone described as being six foot or more in height. In fact, rarely is anyone tallied at anything over five-foot eight. The reason for such discrepancies would seem to be that victims were preoccupied with other things besides note-taking during a robbery—first and foremost, their own survival. Moreover, if any took an especial interest in Lamm's features or Bertillon measurements, they suddenly found themselves pistol-whipped into other diversions, such as staring in rapt fascination at a wall.

When it comes to Lamm's biography, one can summarily dismiss the crime dictionaries and encyclopedias as purely superficial and derivative. Their provenance, almost always, is John Toland's *The Dillinger Days* (1963). There's a pretty good reason for this. Toland did his legwork. He is the first writer to refer to the outlaw as Baron Lamm. The name is apparently an underworld nickname. Toland doesn't identify the source of information for this detail or any other fact relating to the criminal mastermind. On Lamm, as with the other heavies in his book, Toland went to great pains to get at the facts. He devotes only three pages to Lamm, but they are among the most fascinating in the book. The author clearly relishes talking about the outlaw. He discusses the Lamm Method and the older man's influence on Dillinger. He tells how Lamm set out to rob a bank.

First, the targeted bank ("jug," in underworld argot) had to be cased or scouted out. A floor plan was drawn up, showing the positions of the tellers' cages and safes and vault. A robber had to know the bank personnel well enough to know who could get into the vault. The next step was the rehearsal of the bank robbery with some of the gang acting the part of bank employees. The last step, as conceived by Lamm, was the getaway. This had to be accurate almost to the point of being abstruse. The getaway car had to be fast but not too stylish. It had to fit in with the pack. The driver had to be a veteran of the race track or a former rum-runner, or, preferably, both. A chart showing the route by each block with turns to be made was clipped to the sun visor over the dashboard. Practice runs had to take into account all types of weather conditions. It was an ambitious method, designed to take the hit and miss out of bank robbery.

Toland then describes at length where the method went wrong. Lamm simply did not foresee how the best-laid plans of mice and rats "gang aft agley."

Toland, incidentally, mentions the fact that Lamm's last driver, E.H. Hunter, had a hawk-like appearance. Hunter surely did. His picture in the Danville (IL) *Commercial-News* the day after his capture adequately attests to this. Toland had either talked to someone who knew this, such as INS Indianapolis Bureau Chief Jack Cejnar, or he saw the *Commercial-News* photo. Most likely, he came into contact with both. Why not? Random House was paying for all his legwork—and that of his wife, Toshiko, too.[3]

Other Dillinger surveys take up Baron Lamm, too. In 1970, co-authors

Jay Robert Nash and Ron Offen, in *Dillinger: Dead or Alive?*, echo Toland's pages on Lamm, doing so in one short paragraph (p. xi). The dual authors part ways from Toland, however, in a number of areas. They do not believe that Dillinger was involved in a 1934 East Chicago robbery that left a police officer dead. The same is true of a South Bend bank robbery later that year that also took the life of an officer.[4] Most rebelliously of all, they make a case for Dillinger faking his own death at the Biograph Theater. Nevertheless, Nash and Offen heartily agree with Toland in observing an influence on Dillinger by Lamm. The agents of this influence are the two surviving Lamm gang members, James "Oklahoma Jack" Clark and Walter Detrich. These two incorrigibles met Dillinger in the Indiana state prison at Michigan City and unfolded the Lamm Method to him. A grateful Dillinger in turn promised to liberate the pair when it came time for a crash-out.

This little book, quite understandably in view of its theme, carries a letter from J. Edgar Hoover declining a request from the two writers for assistance in their Dillinger research. Hoover, no doubt, had gotten wind of the motive behind the research. It is definitely not a book that would fit snugly in the director's comfort zone. For some reason, *Dillinger: Dead or Alive?* rates an entry in the bibliography of Anthony Summer's best-selling biography of Hoover, *Official and Confidential: The Secret Life of J. Edgar Hoover* (1993). Not only this, but, under its second incarnation, it gets a nod in Summers' text (though the author mixes up the titles and dates of the two editions).[5]

In their coverage of Lamm, Nash and Offen do not cover the matter-of-facts of his life (the stay at the Utah state prison, for example, or the hard luck that befell him on his long ride to Hell). Though Baron Lamm is reduced to the briefest of cameos in it, the book is intriguingly sprinkled throughout with remarks by a number of key people involved in the Dillinger saga. Whatever else this book is, it is certainly a good read.

Three years later, Jay Robert Nash, writing on his own this time, compiled his highly-popular omnibus, *Bloodletters and Badmen*. In this out-sized opus, Nash takes up the story of Baron Lamm in more detail than in the earlier book. Lamm is not accorded a separate entry but does a sustained cameo in the Dillinger entry. Nash's obvious enthusiasm for his subject makes him swerve a little at times from historical accuracy. Lamm's last stand, for instance, is made to last several hours, much too long. Moreover, Dad Landy is given a line or two of dialogue upon his death that is not reported elsewhere. In any case, he did not breathe his last behind the shelter of the getaway car. Landy's age is also a little short of the mark. He was not in his 60s; he was 71. Apart from these errors, the account is reasonably in keeping with what is reliably known of Lamm's damned life and unlamented death. Nash has the gang depart the bank at Clinton, Indiana, with the loot in paper bags.

More accurately, Toland has the loot carried out in one paper shopping bag and the rest in typewriter covers. More predictably, Nash follows Toland's blueprint of the Lamm Method to the letter.[6]

Like nearly everything else, Lamm turns up in unexpected places on occasion. Thus Lamm is the focus of the opening paragraphs of Warren Weith's article on the getaway car in *Murder Ink: The Mystery Reader's Companion* (1977).[7] In this fascinatingly comprehensive symposium on the mystery story, Weith, editor of *Car and Driver* magazine, in his stint takes up the importance of the getaway car in heists, mentioning both Dillinger and Lamm at the outset, with Lamm clearly getting the lion's share of the author's attention. (Even so, of the two, only Dillinger's name appears in the index.)

Of course, Lamm's last getaway is recalled, but not before we are treated to a discussion of the three-step Lamm Method — although only the last step gets due recognition. Nothing much that is new and useful is added by Weith to previous accounts. Weith, however, does indulge himself in some novelties. He has the fateful U-turn that started the gang down the road to ruin made by the driver *before* picking the rest of the gang up. This was done in response to a barber carrying a shotgun. The getaway car blows a tire going over a curb. He also has the gang then rush out of the crippled car to steal another vehicle — a parked one at that — without dealing with their flat. These things didn't happen, though they might as well have; they were no more uninspired than the actual events. Weith also gives us the make of the intrepid barber's shotgun — an Ithaca pump. No other account mentions this. But Weith goes too far when he states that the barber fires that Ithaca pump at the fleeing bandits. He did not, though he more than thought about it. Nor, as a photo taken later that day shows, was the shotgun a pump — it was a double-barrel shotgun.

Such divergences from the standard scoop of what went down that day of doom for Lamm and his gang may have originated out of the print ephemera that appeared after Lamm's death. After all, 1930 was the heyday of the detective magazine, with such titles as *True Detective Mysteries* and *Startling Detective* staying on top of just such misadventures as Lamm's last robbery. In addition, the Indiana Bankers' Association published its own newsletter — *The Hoosier Banker*, which had an account of the Clinton robbery (without mentioning the names of the outlaws). The American Bankers' Association also had its own journal. Other similar newsletters and journals, carrying such information, may have been out there. Weith, like Nash before him, wonders about the origin of the phrase "take it on the lam," and deduces that it owes its origin to Baron Lamm. This seems a reach, as the phrase was likely in circulation before Lamm was out of his swaddling clothes.[8] No matter; Weith's retrospective of Lamm's career and downfall introduced the outlaw mastermind to readers who wouldn't otherwise have heard of him in a million years.

In a 1992 *South Point Magazine* article, Kerry Ross Boren, founder of the National Outlaw and Lawman Association (NOLA) — or more accurately, the founder of NOLA's progenitor, Utah State's National Center & Association for Outlaw/Lawman History — wrote about Lamm's influence on Dillinger. Boren has done some original research and adds considerably to the meager fund of knowledge concerning Lamm's early career. Boren confirms Lamm's Prussian origins, but has him immigrate to America both before and during the First World War.

Boren's Lamm is a real Wild West buckaroo who rides with Butch Cassidy's Wild Bunch, even joining Butch in South America. Boren doesn't say so, but Lamm and Butch led parallel lives. Both died at similar ages — 41 in Butch's case and 40 in Lamm's. Both were arrested a similar number of times — four in Butch's case and six in Lamm's, but with each serving only a brief term in a state prison. Both were probably suicides or "mercy killings" conducted by their best friends.

In Boren's account, Lamm more than rubs elbows with Charlie Birger, a colorful bootlegger in the Egypt section of southern Illinois during the Prohibition era, and Lamm bums around with Utah outlaw Lew McCarty, burgling, mugging and loitering by turns and being anything but upright. Boren has Lamm correctly lodged in the Utah State Prison in 1917 but should have added that he was incarcerated early the year before. He also associates Lamm with James "Oklahoma Jack" Clark and Edward Wilhelm Bentz in Winston-Salem, North Carolina, in February 1927. He has the trio arrested there following a bank robbery in Mooresville, North Carolina. Bentz, as it happened, was not one of the three, nor did their arrest follow the robbery of a Mooresville bank. Lamm and the others were most likely fixing to rob a bank, perhaps the First National in Mooresville, when they were arrested. The charge for which the men were booked was a concealed weapons charge, not bank robbery, and contrary to Boren's information only two of the three jumped bail. The third man, incorrectly identified by Boren, is quite worthy of a book-length study all by himself. He was Dan Morgan. Morgan didn't bother to jump bail to regain his freedom; instead, he jumped head first out of a train window — taking a railroad detective with him.

Much of what Boren has to say is difficult to support — or negate. Baron Lamm's involvement in the Denver Mint robbery (a misnomer, as Boren knows, since a Federal Reserve truck was pilfered and not the mint itself) makes sense on the face of it. Boren sees Lamm and Harvey Bailey and perhaps ten others as behind this job. Bailey, indeed, was a kindred spirit of Lamm and it is tempting to see them working together. Methodical and cunning, Bailey would be just the type that Lamm was looking for on a heist. And while it is true that Charlie Birger was a member of a cavalry unit in Montana, documentation that he rode with the Wild Bunch or that he ever knew Baron Lamm is lacking. Lamm's association with the Weaver gang, like that of his association with Butch Cassidy and Charlie Birger, should not to be thrown out of court, by any means, but it does require further substantiation. Boren estimates Lamm's date of birth as 1880, and such a date would allow Lamm time to associate with Cassidy as an ingénue and hone his skills. But we now know that Lamm was born in 1890, and that leaves little time for Lamm to associate with Cassidy in the U.S. and makes him 18 at Cassidy's death in South America. The odds are very much against Lamm riding with Cassidy at any time in his career.

In the same category is Boren's unsubstantiated assertion that G.W. "Dad" Landy rode with the Daltons. Born in 1859, he was certainly old enough to have been such a long rider, but one feels instinctively that had Landy ridden with this outlaw gang for any length of time, he wouldn't have lasted long enough to be dubbed "Dad." Again, more proof is needed before going too far, though Nash, in *Bloodletters and Badmen* (without documentation) has Landy's career going back to "stagecoach days."[9]

More recently, Bryan Burrough takes Lamm's measure in *Public Enemies: America's Greatest Crime Wave and the Birth of the FBI, 1933–34.* Burrough mentions the connection between the Hole-in-the Wall gang (Butch Cassidy's gang) and Lamm. This detail escaped the notice of Toland in his account and was probably taken from Boren's article, which seems to be the first to mention it. Burrough's debt to Toland is likely the meticulous "git" or roadmap used in making the getaway. Burrough sets Lamm down quite succinctly as a "quasimythical figure." No description of Baron Lamm, pithy or verbose, could hope to improve on this. Indeed, one may research Lamm for a dozen years or two dozen and come away with no more certainty about him than what this epitome affords. It is as though Baron Lamm sat for a miniature by Nicholas Hilliard.[10]

Motion pictures producers have always had a soft spot for the likes of Baron Lamm and John Dillinger. Since Lamm is usually found in books and articles about Dillinger, it may be useful to see if Hollywood handles the pair in tandem, too. Lamm had four years to molder in his grave before Hollywood ever thought about Dillinger. But Dillinger was anathema in those early days following his death in July 1934, and Lamm was not about to ride on his coattails. The Hollywood Code said so in no uncertain terms:

> No picture on the life or exploits of John Dillinger will be produced, distributed or exhibited by any member [of the Motion Picture Producers and Distributors of America]. This decision is based on the belief that the production, distribution or exhibition of such a picture would be detrimental to the best public interests.[11]

Lamm died just at the start of the gangster picture cycle initiated by Paramount in *Underworld* (1927) and, more emphatically, by Warner Brothers in *Little Caesar* (1931). In the four years that followed the latter, such notable gangster films as *Public Enemy* (1931), *Scarface* (1932) and *"G" Men* (1935) came out. Except for the first and last, Al Capone and Capone's Chicago are the subjects of the films. Indeed, screenwriters such as Ben Hecht and Charles MacArthur brought their intimate knowledge of the Chicago underworld with them to Hollywood to use in pictures like *Scarface* and *The Front Page*. Likewise, W.R. Burnett. These men, or others like them, might well inject a Lamm character into their screenplays.

"G" Men inaugurated a new fashion in the gangster film. It takes a notable screen tough guy, James Cagney, and makes him an agent of law enforcement. The reason for this turnabout had to do with the tremendous disfavor the early gangster films elicited from Catholic organizations, concerned about their effect on American youth, and the International Police Chiefs Association (IPCA), concerned about the depiction of law enforcement personnel on screen.

What *"G" Men* recounts is the hunt by the FBI (not yet so called) for John Dillinger, Baby Face Nelson and Pretty Boy Floyd (none of the three called by their real names in the film), all recently deceased. Neither the Department of Justice nor the Bureau of Investigation endorsed this picture, but Warner Brothers made it just the same. Big fans of FDR and the New Deal, anything they could do to assist the War on Crime waged by the attorney general and the Department of Justice, the Brothers Warner were only too happy to do.[12]

Besides, gangster pictures were good money.

Liberties with the facts were taken in the picture. The trio of heavyweight heavies are part of the New York mob in the film, whereas all three were actually part of the great crime wave in the Heartland. Nevertheless, the Chicago Office of the Bureau of Investigation is the primary agency involved in rounding up these bad guys just as in real life, but things did not go all that well for the forces of Good.

The film depicts the battle at the Little Bohemia lodge with just the right amount of atmosphere. One can even see an officer's breath when he talks. The incident at Little Bohemia took place on a cold Sunday in late April 1934 in the North Woods of remote northern Wisconsin. *"G" Men* generously departs from the facts in having the gang wiped out, save for the Dillinger character (played by Barton MacLane). A bit earlier, the Union Station Massacre in Kansas City is staged. It's extremely well done with only a couple of things out of historical step. The scene takes place late at night instead of early in the morning (around 7:30). Also, in the movie the prisoner is freed and not, as in reality, killed, most likely by an accidental blast from a special agent's shotgun.[13]

Now, in all this is there any likelihood of finding a Baron Lamm character? Probably not. There is an older man named Mac McKay, who is the big crime boss, but he doesn't rob banks. Neither his right name nor his alias — Joseph Lynch — suggest Lamm. He is Cagney's benefactor and having a change of heart about the rackets, decides to get out. This results in his death in the gunfight in the North Woods. What the crime boss represents is a father figure more than a mentor to Cagney. The relationship is not Lamm-Dillinger but is quite the most intriguing business in the film. Oddly enough, Cagney is the one who kills the crime boss — quite mistakenly — as the gang uses the boss as a shield in making their unsuccessful escape from the lodge.[14]

There is, however, a robbery of a Federal Reserve truck in which a guard is killed. This is definitely an allusion to the notorious Denver Mint robbery of December 18, 1922, in which both Baron Lamm and James "Oklahoma Jack" Clark are sometimes said to have had a hand. Even so, it is not Lamm's name that comes up in connection with the robbery but that of the Pretty Boy Floyd character, Danny Leggett. Pretty Boy Floyd is about the only outlaw alive at the time not accused of the Denver Mint job. At eighteen, he was just too young and inexperienced to be this bad.

The next year another Dillinger-inspired film appeared, this time starring Humphrey Bogart. *The Petrified Forest* was made by Warner Brothers not surprisingly and, besides Bogart, starred Bette Davis and Leslie Howard. Bogart's Duke Mantee, "world-famous gangster," is straight out of the Dillinger playbook, even wearing the outlaw's Crown Point vest. But there is no Lamm to be seen in this picture.

Bogart again has a go at Dillinger in *High Sierra* (1941). This motion picture did what *The Petrified Forest* almost did — made Bogart a star. The role was turned down or passed over by all the other Warner gangsters — Robinson, Cagney, Raft and Muni (the latter actually turned Warner Brothers down, not the part) — and put Bogie in the driver's seat for the plum role of Sam Spade in *The Maltese Falcon* a few months later. In *High Sierra*, Bogie plays a "famous Indiana bank robber" (three guesses as to who is meant). This was the first film to mention Dillinger's name, even though he is not a character in the film. In the screenplay, he is merely Johnnie, but in the completed film, he is Johnnie Dillinger.

Dillinger and his alter ego (Roy Earle) spend about the same amount of time in prison and, like Dillinger, Roy Earle takes a trip out west which has unfortunate consequences — Dillinger wound up in jail in Tucson and Earle gets killed on a mountain top.[15] This film does have a crime boss named Big

Mac, but there is little in this bed-ridden, burnt-out Cavalier Shift to suggest Baron Lamm, except that Bogie's character reveres him.

In 1945, Lawrence Tierney played Dillinger in a film of the same name, the first explicit screen portrait of the public enemy. This time, Warner Brothers stepped aside while a Poverty Row studio, Monogram Pictures, took a stab at a gangster film. Chicago was still smarting from the outlaw's impact for such diversion in 1945, so the movie didn't play there for a full year after its release. Philip Yordan's screenplay is pure hokum as far as anything true to life is concerned — even the wardrobe and hairdos are straight out of the forties. For his part, composer Dimitri Tiomkin, for once, is totally at sea in a picture, probably because there isn't a romance worthy of the name. Tierney would later play the ill-fated Sheriff Jess Sarber in the 1991 TV bio-film *Dillinger*, starring Mark Harmon.

In the 1945 film, there's a veteran bank robber, supposed to be the best there is when it comes to robbing banks — Specs Green. Apart from his nefarious genius, there isn't much to remind anyone of Baron Lamm. Dillinger meets him in prison and they work together until Dillinger gets too big and gun-crazy. Before Green can rub Dillinger out, Dillinger gets him. There isn't much danger of over-glamorizing criminals in this film, and maybe that's why it drew an unlikely Academy Award nomination for its script.

Any film made before 1963, the year Toland's *The Dillinger Days* came out, would not have been likely to have Lamm or someone based on him in it, as his influence on the public enemy was not then generally known. Of course, screenwriters bring their own special input to their work, as, for instance, screenwriters John Bright and Harvey F. Thew brought their knowledge of Capone's Chicago to *The Public Enemy* (1931). After the publication of Toland's book, however, Lamm would be expected to play a part in any film made about Dillinger. Toland was the first to point out this influence of Lamm on Dillinger. Any in-depth look at Lamm would have been most unlikely by the time Dillinger was a name to be reckoned with, and this attitude continued through the following decades. When Toland's book hit the stores, something indeed did happen, but it did not concern Dillinger.

As mentioned above, Robert Benton and David Newman read *The Dillinger Days* and were mesmerized by Toland's pages on Bonnie and Clyde. Long before dealing with Bonnie and Clyde in his book, however, Toland dealt with Baron Lamm and his spectacular death. These pages apparently did not register with the screenwriters, and Lamm stayed put in oblivion while Bonnie and Clyde became silver screen legends in a breakthrough film. Perhaps this was as it should have been, but one has to wonder how anyone could have been immersed in Toland's book and not come away itching to film Lamm's downfall.

In 1973, Warren Oates appeared as Dillinger in John Milius's *Dillinger*. This film fudges on almost all of its history, but one scene is spectacularly poetic. When the outlaw's kid sister sees Dillinger pull up in his car on the outskirts of the family homestead and dashes off the back porch into the bright sunshine across a pasture in an attempt to catch him, "Red River Valley" plays on the soundtrack. We are forcefully reminded of Dillinger's love of family and home in a scene worthy of John Ford. It is a truly great moment, among the best in any gangster film. Quite a few historical characters appear among the dramatis personae in this picture but no Baron Lamm or anyone resembling him.

The same is true — only more so — of the Mark Harmon *Dillinger* (1991). This 96-minute film was the most ambitious and most accurate Dillinger film up to its time. Not that it is devoid of quirks. Both Dillinger and his opposite, Captain Matt Leach, refer to big-time hoodlum "Handsome Harry" as Pierpoint, while Dillinger's sweetheart, Billie Frechette, and early accomplice, Harry Copeland, call him Pierpont, as indeed they should. While Mark Harmon makes no attempt to get into the outlaw's head and we do not get Dillinger's philosophy of life, *Dillinger* is amazingly accurate at times. The Daleville and the Indianapolis Massachusetts Avenue bank robberies, for example, are absolutely right on. As noted above, there is no hint of Baron Lamm in this picture, and its one chance to mention Lamm cohorts Walter Detrich and Oklahoma Jack Clark goes for naught when it reduces the number of Michigan City escapees from ten to four. Typically, Hollywood swerves away from the chance to get at the Lamm story every time one rears its head. The film is notable, though, for a cameo by real-life Dillinger gang hostage Ursula Patzke, in what must certainly be a screen first.[16]

Finally, in *Public Enemies* (2009), starring Johnny Depp as Johnny Dillinger and based on Bryan Burrough's book of the same name, Baron Lamm's influence on the outlaw receives recognition. There is still no Baron Lamm afoot in motion pictures, but now at last we have a hint of him. Walter Dietrich (spelled thus) — the first film appearance of his character — imparts the Lamm Method to Dillinger while both are behind bars (all off-camera and inferred solely by the well-versed). Dietrich is older than Dillinger and seems to be a composite of Detrich and Lamm. In any case, Dillinger really looks up to Dietrich, which was probably not the case altogether with Detrich and Dillinger, the former being a year younger than the latter. Oddly, Dietrich is killed during the Michigan City break, forty-six years before the historical Walter Detrich died owing to natural causes in St. Louis. As a later chapter will make clear, there are plenty of things the film could have done with Walter Detrich in that prison delivery besides kill him. He may have died because there was too much of Lamm in him.

While *Public Enemies* overlooks Lamm as a film character, it does boast more historical figures than any other Dillinger or gangster film. It may be a turning of the tide so far as Baron Lamm is concerned. Maybe — just maybe — his fantastic story and his incredible downfall will hit the big screen one day. Nevertheless, as of this writing, Hollywood has a ways to go before it catches up with Baron Lamm. Of course, if Lamm's story ever made it to film, who would believe it? The commentary by director Michael Mann, as a bonus feature on the DVD of *Public Enemies*, mentions Herman K. Lamm as such and not as Baron Lamm or as Thomas Bell. Mann covers Lamm's method of bank robbery quite well without going into his fateful demise. The commentary on Walter Detrich is less exemplary and one has to wonder why, since this film is the most authentic yet made on Dillinger. The fact that a character named Walter Detrich is even in it confirms this point.

As of 2010 a screenplay dealing with Lamm called "Baron Lamm" by Paul Peterson is on the Internet but not yet filmed. In flashbacks, Peterson covers a sad love affair between Lamm and a patrician lady in the midst of Lamm's service on Germany's behalf in World War I. There is the cheating at cards and his being drummed out of the German army. He is seen on the road gang in America. All this is sandwiched in between the fatal Clinton robbery framing-story. Later gang members Oklahoma Jack Clark and Dad Landy are on the road gang with Lamm, alias Frank Smith (though I know of no historical accuracy to this alias). Peterson has done extensive research on Lamm in the west and I look forward to seeing the finished film.

It's funny to think so, but the closest approach to putting Baron Lamm on film to date just may be the "Fritz" character in Woody Allen's *Take the Money and Run* (1969).[17] This film came out just a few years after Toland's book on Dillinger was published and the film is rife with Dillinger undertones. Writers Woody Allen and Mickey Rose may have been influenced by Toland's book and even heeded the three pages on Lamm. In a hilarious scene having two gangs rob the same bank at the same time, a washed-up German filmmaker from the silent days is on hand to film the whole operation. His thick accent derogating the bank robbery that is taking place is remarkably apropos. It sounds very much like John Nolan's recollection of Lamm's announcement at the beginning of the Clinton robbery: "Achtung! Achtung! This is a bank robbery." Whoever Fritz (Marcel Hillaire) is supposed to represent — Baron Lamm or Erich von Stroheim or both or neither — Woody Allen accorded this minor part third billing in his first picture as film director and star.

The printed record proving so unavailing, and the celluloid imagination proving even more barren, one naturally turns to the unprinted record for assistance in uncovering traces of Baron Lamm. On numerous occasions from late 1992 to 1997, I spent time visiting people in Clinton and St. Bernice, Indiana, and in Catlin and Sidell, Illinois, discussing Baron Lamm. I never once told anybody I was coming before an interview because, knowing how whimsical I can be, I never like to set up something that I may not be able to follow through on five minutes later. Also, my transportation was never the best. It was sometimes more whimsical than I am.

But whether in a rented car, a friend's truck or on my own, I was out there every chance I got. At Sidell, I talked many times with Art Hockett, though only once on tape — the last time we would ever get together, as it turned out. Art was the nephew of Wells Gilbert, the stock dealer whose truck Baron Lamm borrowed at pistol point on that wild day when nothing in the world was right side up — or so it must have seemed to Baron Lamm. Gilbert's truck was as crazy as everything else. Imagine running for your life with a radiator with no more moisture in it than it would take to wet a rich man's tongue in Hell! That last time I was with him, Art introduced me to Fenton Williams' brother, Carroll. It was Fenton Williams' Model-A Ford that carried Lamm and his gang to their final rendezvous. Carroll told me about meeting two members of Lamm's gang — James "Oklahoma Jack" Clark and Walter Detrich, when they were locked up in the calaboose in Newport, Indiana. For two and a half years, these two men would be locked up with John Dillinger at the Indiana State Prison in Michigan City.

Harold Frist was a good telephone interview. Certainly, he had heard things over the years. He was a good friend of John Nolan, a bookkeeper in the Citizens State Bank the day Lamm robbed it. His grandfather, Jediah Frist, was the first man whose car was hijacked by the desperate men in their hour of need. Old Frist had told the men in effect, "Fine, take the car, if you've a mind to, but don't you dare break that crockery in the backseat!" Needless to say, Harold, Art and Carroll each imparted things not found in newspapers, magazines or books.

There were other interviews. Walter Stout, of St. Bernice, and I puzzled over where Joe Walker had been killed. One summer day, we traced what we thought was the getaway route before the bandits hit U.S. 36 near Dana. At Clinton, I talked twice with Margaret Helms, widow of former Clinton chief of police Everett "Pete" Helms. She gave me her side of the matter about that day her husband came home with forty bullet holes in his coupe — well, not exactly his coupe — it was borrowed from a garage down the street! She had known the slain deputy Joe Walker "to speak to" — the only person I ever met who did.

Leo Moody's widow, Dorothy, at Tilton, Illinois, told me about that day she went to her brother's place to can meat and returned home to find that all hell had broken loose on her farm. She gave me a couple of juicy tidbits about Leo's capture of Walter Detrich. Some additional details about the aftermath of the final shootout and Leo Moody's personality came from Stan Hayes of Catlin, Illinois. Hayes was the Moody's son-in-law.

Charlie Lyons, of Sidell, told me about seeing the bandit car drive past his school when he was out at recess trying to make a donkey bray to the point of splitting the welkin. He remembered seeing the bandit in back of the Model-A coupe cradling a machine gun. He later saw the bodies of the bandits at the McCauley funeral parlor in Sidell. His description of one of the dead men makes it clear that he saw Baron Lamm in death.

Merrel Chew, of Sidell, also saw the dead bandits. The funeral parlor was the central attraction in that village for kids of eight or ten and they often would look in on the deceased on their way home from school. Young Merrel saw something one bright December morning outside the funeral parlor that made him wonder whether some of the gang got away.

These people kindly allowed me into their homes and talked as far as their knowledge would stretch. Sometimes I recorded them and sometimes I scribbled notes. Sometimes, as with Art Hockett, I just kept coming back and going over it all again. Behind the wheel, when we retraced the bandits' steps between Sidell and Scottland, Illinois, Art was not sufficiently mindful of his age in the least. This was a drive that had me biting my knuckles. Those roads probably hadn't seen that kind of action since that December day when Baron Lamm kept up his fifty-mile running fight to the bitter end.

From the unprinted record of the interview, we must turn to the last resource available to the researcher — unpublished material. This category includes dissertations, monographs and manuscripts too long or too short for their target audience — books, magazines and journals. In this category, there is a 71-page typescript at the Indianapolis Historical Society called "The Jinx That Stalked the Outlaws." It was written sometime between January 1931 and October 1932, that is, between the trial of the surviving bandits, James "Oklahoma Jack" Clark and Walter Detrich, and the date on which their bid for an appeal was turned down by the Indiana Supreme Court. Its author was Jack Cejnar, who in his eighty years of life had illustrious careers both in journalism and as American Legion publicist. Cejnar knew the Lamm story, at least in its final phase, better than anyone is ever likely to know it again. Without Cejnar's study of the Clinton robbery and the photographs in his collection, my own study would amount to little more than juvenilia in its embryonic state.

Cejnar and his wife accompanied some of the lawmen involved in the manhunt, along with other reporters, as they went over the route taken by the bandits from Clinton to Sidell. They talked to those who had participated in or witnessed Lamm's downfall. This was three days after the Clinton robbery took place. The Cejnars and the others were treated to a fine meal afterwards by a Danville restaurant owner who had once been a resident of Clinton.

Cejnar is of interest to Dillinger students as well. Toland lists him as a source for information about Dillinger's big Greencastle robbery. Cejnar had a deal with banks such as the Central National in Greencastle, Indiana, whereby if their bank was robbed, they would notify Cejnar before anyone else, including insurance companies or police. In return, Cejnar would allow them exclusive access to the report that would appear in newspapers under the International News Service imprint.

Besides being Johnny-on-the-spot, Cejnar possessed a memory capable of almost total recall. His supply of remarks made by holdup victims and, at times, rare bits of Lamm's conversation, is invaluable, to say the least. Lamm is probably the least quoted of all the Depression-era outlaws and one has to comb a great many newspapers to come away with a fraction of the conversation given in Cejnar's account.

Excellent as Cejnar's account is, one cannot help being struck by an oddity in it. Long after he should have known better, he continued to call Lamm and Clark by their aliases, Bell and Long. No doubt these were the names that kept coming up when he went over the ground that the outlaws had traveled that fateful Tuesday morning. They must have become ingrained in his thinking through countless repetitions, but how he could associate someone named Bell with a Prussian background is beyond comprehension.

One further thing about the Cejnar account: It is largely Clinton police chief Everett "Pete" Helms' version of events. Immediately after the Clinton robbery, Chief Helms also gave accounts to the wire services, and these must be compared with Cejnar's write-up in order to get at the facts. The earlier reports, however, often show signs of being half-baked. They are confused and downright wrong in places. Compared to Cejnar's version, they are like a rough draft. Yet they cannot be tossed aside because they sometimes speak with the voice of authority. They just need to be taken with a grain of salt where they conflict with other accounts, especially the as-told-to account he gave to Jack Cejnar.

Of all the people mentioned in Cejnar's account of the Clinton robbery and its aftermath, only one lived long enough to be interviewed by me. This was Virginia Gilbert, Art Hockett's "Auntie" Virginia. Art took me to her home in Chrisman, Illinois, on that cool June 4, 1996, and we talked briefly on her porch before Art took me down the Ocean-to-Ocean Road to walk in the shoes of the bandits, as it were. When I met her, "Auntie" Virginia was 93, as Dillinger would have been had he been law-abiding, and as Bob Hope then was. I think that the guns of the posse and the pursued must have been popping pretty close to her home in 1930, but I wasn't smart enough to know that when we talked. I was smart enough, however, to listen to what she described concerning the bed of her father-in-law's truck and the emotions that ran like lightning through him that afternoon when he came to his nephew's home to telephone his wife and advise her of his well-being.

John Toland almost certainly read Cejnar's account of Lamm. How he could have read it and settled for so little is more than I know. It makes the same amount of sense as playing the lottery just hoping to buy a day-old donut all at once.

A little hard-nosed sleuthing only just now turned up a transcript of the trial of Walter Detrich and James Clark, the two survivors of Lamm's gang. My initial inquiries into this document's whereabouts had led me to believe that it did not exist. Two years later, I tried again and learned that it probably did exist but was bundled away in a box and uncatalogued somewhere in the Indiana State Supreme Court clerk's offices. Finally, when the deadline for this book approached, I tried again and this time struck gold. Needless to say, this discovery worked havoc on my original deadline, but it was worth its weight in gold. Is it the most important evidence regarding Lamm's last day? Maybe. All that I can say with certainty is that it bears studying and re-studying and, taken in conjunction with Cejnar's excellent account and some personal interviews, it gives as complete a portrait of the fatal Clinton bank robbery as we're ever likely to have at this late date, short of a séance.

One other item of evidence concerning Baron Lamm has only surfaced in recent years—a PBS American Experience documentary makes use of it, seemingly, in its gallery of Depression-era gangsters, as do at least two works in progress (a biography of Harry Pierpont and the screenplay mentioned above). This item is Lamm's draft registration card, dating from June 5, 1917, when he was an inmate at the Utah State Prison. Apparently neither Toland nor Cejnar were aware of this item. It is something that doesn't jump to the forefront of the investigation since, if Lamm was German, he wouldn't be expected to have registered for the draft in the U.S. in the middle of the Great War. As he states on the card, Lamm, by 1917, was a naturalized citizen of this country. The card was accepted and stamped January 30, 1918, when the Great War was in full swing. By then, Lamm had been out of prison three months and was apparently living in San Francisco.

In his own handwriting, Lamm tells us a number of personal details. He has blue eyes and dark brown hair. He describes his height as medium, in contrast to eyewitness descriptions from his various bank robberies where he is often thought to be a big man. He has a bad heart, he says, so he shouldn't be considered for the draft. He was born on April 19, 1890, and at the time that he was filling out his draft registration card, he was twenty-seven. He

Lamm's World War I draft card in his own handwriting (Ancestry.com).

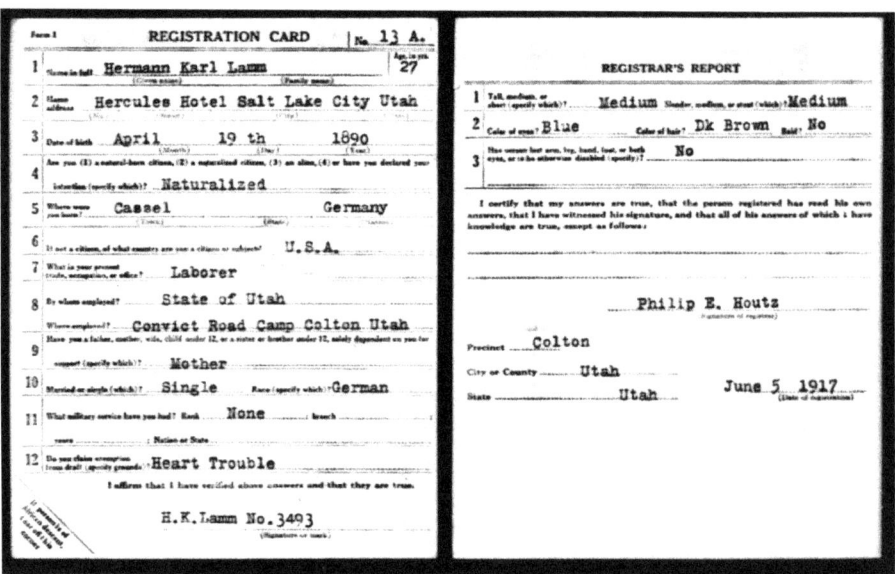

Lamm's World War I draft card with first name misspelled (Ancestry.com).

was born in Cassell, Germany, in the northern province of Prussia. His profession was laborer and, at the moment, he labored for the convict road gang at Colton, Utah.

If the 1890 birth year he lists is correct, it would almost definitely rule out Lamm's association with Butch Cassidy and the Wild Bunch. Butch and Sundance were killed in Bolivia in the autumn of 1908; Lamm would then have been a youth of eighteen. When Butch and Sundance went to South America at the beginning of 1901, Lamm would have been a mere ten years old, much too young to have had any association with the iconic pair of outlaws, even as a relay horse holder.

The draft card is a vital piece of information. From it, we learn those things that we take for granted in the cases of better known outlaws—Jesse James' striking blue eyes and sandy-colored hair; Dillinger's gray eyes, facial moles and cleft chin—now, at last a picture of the man emerges. Physically, he didn't stand out from millions of others. He was of medium height (or could he have been understating his size in order to avoid fighting in a war against the Fatherland?)[18] and had dark brown hair and blue eyes. Thanks to the draft card, we know his full name, as with Jesse Woodson James and John Herbert Dillinger. Lamm was Herman Karl Lamm. His mother was dependent on him, and her alone. He had heart trouble and that would get worse, much worse on December 16, 1930.

II

Minions of the Moon: St. Bernice, 1924

"Convey" the wise it call. "Steal!" foh! a fico for the phrase!—*The Merry Wives of Windsor*

Spring 1924 was a charming, idyllic time in America. Baseball was in full swing and Babe Ruth played an exhibition game in May in Indianapolis. He autographed three baseballs (no doubt, using his impressive Epsilon "E") for a doctor, who then gave each to a friend. Babe Ruth's annus mirabilis was yet three years off, but he was already a kid-swamped legend. In this 1924 season, Ruth would hit only 46 round trippers, but no matter he was still "The Bambino." Mrs. Lydia M. Henry of New York and Mrs. Helen M. Barrett of Michigan, two Daughters of the American Revolution members, were literally just that. Their fathers, nearly a century and a half before, had served with General George Washington. In view of the requisite advanced age their fathers must have enjoyed at their conception, one looks twice to see if these were not *granddaughters* of the American Revolution.

On June 8 of this year, George Leigh Mallory and A.C. Irvine met their deaths trying to scale Mt. Everest. Mallory's last words were, "We expect no mercy from Everest." Seventy-five years later Mallory's body was found, remarkably preserved. No one knows whether he made it to the top or not.

The Civil War had not yet passed from memory in 1924. Many veterans of that internecine conflict were yet up and around, and those Hoosiers who had fought on the Union side came for a Grand Army of the Republic reunion to Frankfort, Indiana. In Frankfort, where we shall soon set our scene, John Dorsey on 136 Henry Street, the youngest Union veteran (he had been a drummer boy on the Union side, aged ten years, one month, when he enlisted) was alive and well at 71.[1] The *Frankfort Evening News*, among other papers across the nation, carried a story about the pursuit of the commandeered

Confederate locomotive *The General* by Southerners in another locomotive across northern Georgia in April 1862. The story, first told by Lieutenant William Pittenger in 1863, would now captivate first gag-man Clyde Bruckman, then Buster Keaton, and become the basis for the 1926 cinema classic *The General*.

Lindbergh's historic flight loomed three Mays off, but history was in the air just the same. The sinking of the *Lusitania* nine years earlier was remembered across the country on May 7. History lay all around in that May of 1924, abundantly enough to trip over.

It was the month of May in this year of 1924 that introduced a triumvirate of outlaws to the Lamm saga who have long gone unsung and who were among the most remarkable outlaws of that or any other era. Each is worthy of a volume in himself. Two certainly worked with Lamm and the other probably did. All three were hard to incarcerate — one because he had a Teflon coating; the other two because no jail could hold them — or, at least, no sentence could contain them. Just as in Lamm's case, what we know of this trio of "crossbyters" is just the tip of the iceberg.

G.W. "Dad" Landy surfaces for the first time in the annals of crime on May 21, 1924. The evening of this particular day saw the first of all those "crimes of the century" with which the twentieth century, from beginning to end, was so afflicted. It was then that Nathan Leopold and Richard Loeb killed young Bobby Franks outside of Chicago. Being a two-hour's drive southeast of Chicago, Landy had nothing to do with this horrific crime, but he found himself booked that night just the same — for a much more venial crime. Before this arrest, apart from the burglary about to be discussed, nothing is known of him, though plenty of things have been posited by those in a position to know.

A very rudimentary biography of Landy has him living in Logansport, Indiana, before removing to Pennsylvania. Since Lamm is known most usually as Thomas Bell of Pittsburgh, the two are thought to have met some time in the mid-twenties in Pennsylvania. Upon his first and only verified arrest, Landy gave his address as Cincinnati. Following his release from the Vermillion County jail in 1924, he went to Logansport. He is said, not too convincingly, to have spent time there working for the Pennsylvania line. The Pennsylvania Railroad did, indeed, go through Logansport, but that Landy was employed by the railroad as a worker in his mid-to-late 60s, after a much-publicized brush with the law, is unlikely.[2]

What is more certain is that he was in bad company. Tall, vicious Dan Morgan was with him. Morgan, at twenty-eight, was already a veteran of five Illinois bank robberies and at least four gas station robberies in Indiana. Shorter in height and shorter-fused than the others (if such a thing was possible), Charles Norman was the third member of this triple pillar of the underworld. Norman was known in the West as James Woodruff, and Arizona authorities were after him for burgling some oil company offices and exchanging pistol shots with a watchman. Norman struck a Walton, Kansas, bank to the tune of $140,000 early in 1924 and then had the audacity one winter evening, about 8, to have his wife, Ona, and a chosen few blow up the jail that housed him (and gave him three squares a day) with nitroglycerin. Deputy Jack Snyder bounced off the ceiling in the process. Norman's wife, arrested with him, either was let off altogether or paid a modest bail — she continued to visit Norman (always thoroughly searched beforehand) until his abrupt, unlooked-for departure. Bail came to $20,000 and was a bit much for prisoners Charles Norman and Pat Carroll, alias J.B. Ross. The two were left in a position where their only solace was just one rubber ball between them to beguile the time until, that is, the night the jail door was blown off.

One assessment — and one alone — can charitably be made of Morgan and Norman: each was worse than the other. They were said by Sheriff Carl Adams, of Walton, Kansas, to have been part of a Chicago gang led by no less a rowdie than Terrible Tommy O'Connor,[3] a man who so cheated justice in 1921 that Chicago eagerly awaited his return with open arms and a hemp necktie for nearly sixty years thereafter. Terrible Tommy disappeared forever after his aborted execution. Norman, under his right name — Clyde H. Nimerick — went to Alcatraz in the '40s, but Morgan disappeared into a Virginia forest one late-winter midnight and was never seen again.

At his arrest, Landy, aged 65, was in a most indignant mood. "I have not been convicted of a crime. You have no right to take my fingerprints until I have," he told Sheriff Dan Power and Deputy Ross Allen. Someone, probably Power, told him that an officer had a perfect right to take the fingerprints of anyone in his custody.

Landy objected strenuously. "I tell you, you have no right to do this." He comes across as a man much imposed upon by the unswerving routine of law and order. Landy's utterances on this occasion imply that he has never before been arrested. It is difficult to believe that someone like Dad Landy could go for sixty-five years without being arrested for some offense. But no one gave him the lie that night and, until further evidence comes to light, he must be understood to have cherished an unblemished record until late in life.[4] In any case, Landy and the other two were fingerprinted that night, and their mug shots were taken the next day and sent around to various police departments across the country in the hopes that some information concerning their identities could be established. The *Frankfort Evening News* carried an amusing account of the procedure.[5]

For his part, Dan Morgan was most obliging when it came to posing for his mug shot. The result would appear six years later in the *Frankfort Morning Times* (formerly, the *Evening News*) the day after the Farmers Bank robbery, when it was thought that Morgan had returned to Frankfort to do a little business. The photograph had also appeared in February 1927 when Morgan was temporarily in custody in North Carolina. In the shot, Morgan looks like a dangerous man but a contented one for the present. He is dressed casually. Dad Landy also put his best foot forward on this occasion. He is even dressed formally, apparently so outfitted when arrested that cool May midnight. Landy is quite the businessman. He looks dapper and sports a gray mustache as sturdy as a cow catcher on a locomotive. He wears a pair of horn-rimmed spectacles — the same kind, though not so damnably unusual, perhaps, as those that led to Loeb and Leopold's undoing that same night when they were dropped in another Indiana culvert. Landy looks, for all the world, like he belongs behind the counter of a bank, working an adding machine, instead of in front of it, pointing a hog leg at a cashier. Landy's poses, frontal and profile, also appeared in various newspapers following the Clinton robbery, the *Morning Times* publishing the former on their front page on December 17, 1930, along with Morgan's picture.

Norman's sitting was a different matter altogether. He was a most unwilling subject. He resisted having his picture taken with a will, comporting himself as intractably as the urchin who bites photographer Bob Hope's finger for daring to take his picture in the film *My Favorite Brunette* (1947). Only the threat of brute force could make Norman take a seat in front of the camera. Even so, he then shut his eyes most resolutely and would not open them no matter how much coaxing and encouragement he received from the sidelines.

We are told that no ruse was overlooked to get him to open those hermetically-sealed orbs, but nothing availed. Norman's mug shot from Frankfort never appeared later, unlike Landy's and Morgan's, even though it was first suspected that he and the other two men were in on the aforesaid Frankfort bank robbery. One regrets that Norman's likeness didn't make it into the paper with the article describing the portrait sitting. It really should have.[6] The picture must have been a corker, perhaps rising to the level, as Mortimer Brewster might have it, of one of those pictures that children use to frighten grown-ups with. Handsome Harry Pierpont's Indiana State Prison mug shot, which shows him looking more dead than alive, perhaps registers the closest approach to the missing Norman/Nimerick mug shot at Frankfort.

Landy was arrested two miles northeast of Frankfort, Indiana, in league with two much younger men, for having burgling tools and safe-blowing equipment. A handbag with a couple of guns made them even more suspicious. A number of area banks had been burgled and their safes blown that spring. Moreover, just a couple of nights before, Dan Morgan knocked over a Standard station in Frankfort, followed by another gas station in Lebanon, Indiana, the same night. Morgan was dressed as he was at Frankfort, in a brown coat and bib overalls with the suspenders over the coat. He was quoted in the Lebanon robbery as saying to his victim, "I don't want your money, only the company's."[7] Morgan wore a phony mustache in both robberies.

This arrest, our first glimpse of Landy, was not an easy task. Dan Morgan took a shot at Sheriff Power, and Norman and Landy tried to drive off. All three failed in their goals just as Sheriff Power and his deputy failed to hit Morgan with two loads of buckshot out there in the dark, but the local paper called it a gunfight, nevertheless. Morgan had the good sense to fling his pistol in some bushes — where a short time later it was found, unfortunately for the outlaw.

Following a tip from a farmer, Ben Beisel, the sheriff and a posse that included six members of the Indiana National Guard, among them a lieutenant colonel and a major, had staked out a culvert in rural Frankfort. They thought that they were looking for moonshiners. In the first years of Prohibition, alcohol was on everyone's mind, almost to the exclusion of everything else, save the Klan, Fundamentalism and Teapot Dome.

The "ambuscade" (again, the local paper) froze its collective toes for three solid hours awaiting their prey. Though late May, a light frost was beginning to coat the ground. Finally, about midnight, headlights appeared in the distance. A late-model Jewett stopped on the horizon and three men got out. They built a campfire and heated up some coffee. They poured the coffee into a thermos. Then one got back in the car and the other two started walking toward the culvert.

"Back the car up. These things are heavy," one of the two men on foot ordered — either Landy or Morgan. When the driver started backing up, the band was jumped by the posse.

On the occasion of his arrest, Landy was described by a reporter as "rather dignified in appearance."[8] His hair was quite gray but still abundant. His glasses made him look half-way respectable, but his Wicked Witch of the West leer meant that he was a man to be no more trusted than "adders fanged." His height is rather hard to get at. He was shorter than young Morgan, but taller than young Norman, both, incidentally, thought to be around 25 years of age, though the former stated his age as 24 (falsely) and the latter was then 29 as suggested by his World War I draft card and the cemetery records of Jefferson Barracks in St. Louis. Landy probably stood around five-foot ten.

This unholy alliance was riding in a Jewett with Illinois plates. Morgan said that it was his. The truth of this statement came from the Illinois State Automobile Department, which had registered the car under the name of Dan Morgan.

Two curious things happened while the three men were in jail at Frankfort. Two days after their arrest, a jail employee found a hacksaw only a slight distance from the cell block where the men were locked up. The hacksaw was in good shape, showing only a trace of rust. Was it simply dropped by someone? Various garages in the neighborhood were visited by the Clinton County Sheriff's Department in the hopes of finding the owner of the hacksaw, but, understandably, no one claimed it.

Oddly enough, Sheriff Power dismissed the significance of a hacksaw's presence so close to three rowdy prisoners. The sheriff probably reckoned that some worker had dropped it some time back quite innocently.

The next development, however, was seized upon by the good sheriff with more conviction. Some of the prisoners' clothes had been sent to the jail from a Chicago dry cleaner's and when searched, a shiny new dime was found in one pocket of a jacket and two pristine toothpicks in the other. This time Sheriff Power suspected an escape plot. Surely, the dime and toothpicks were a secret underworld code alerting the prisoners to the imminence of a jail delivery. Thereafter, the guard was doubled until the trio went to Delphi for trial.

Did Lamm have anything to do with these two incidents? The hacksaw seems a little crude for an evil genius of Lamm's reputed magnitude. The hacksaw, if intended for an escape, was most likely left in place by a girlfriend of Morgan. It seems a bit amateurish for a gang of this stripe and more in keeping with the melodramatic leanings of a sweetheart desperately trying to free her man in the heyday of Pauline Frederick, Tom Mix and his wonder horse, Tony, and all those Saturday matinees.

The code, on the other hand, seems more in keeping with Lamm's style. It would be a very good bet, indeed, that Lamm, or someone close to him, signaled the three prisoners by this means. Just what the code reflected is open to question. It may have meant that an escape attempt was forthcoming or it may have been a game plan as to how best to deal with the present situation, perhaps indicating a likely "mouthpiece" or crooked lawyer who would represent the three men then behind bars. Indeed, the poor trio of prisoners must have felt abandoned by their underworld colleagues in the early going. What issued from them when it was announced that their Chicago attorney, one Donovan, would not be in town to represent them any time soon was, as with Huck Finn's Pap when he stubbed his toe on a bucket, "all the hottest kind of language."

That the latter interpretation may have been the case is evidenced by the appearance of three friends of the cellmates arriving in Frankfort on a Monan passenger train on Monday morning, May 26. Their names went unrecorded and, sadly, their physical descriptions went unnoted. The liquor on their breath was noted, however, but curiously brushed aside. After being frisked for weapons and hacksaws, the three, joined by two local attorneys, met with the three prisoners. The mystery men then left money with the attorneys " to take care of our friends."

The three mysterious strangers later had a meal at the Midway Café in town and paid for it with trimmed money, that is, money whose edges had been carefully sheared off so as not to reveal that it once had burnt edges. Burnt edges indicated safe-blown origins for the currency. Such money, indeed, had been found on Landy and Norman at the time of their arrest on May 21. A safe bet, as we shall soon see, is that all such money came from one source — the American State Bank in St. Bernice, Indiana. Before this incriminating information reached the Frankfort police, the men had gone on their way.[9]

The problematic code of toothpicks and pence came a week after the visit by the three underworld types. If it meant anything at all, it was probably no more than reassurance to the prisoners that legal help and phony witnesses were on their way.

More than a month after the arrest of Morgan and his two cronies, two young people signed an affidavit saying that they saw the robbery at the Standard station for which Morgan had just been convicted. The man they described at the station was a man who was over six feet tall with a full face and red or sandy whiskers.

Whoever the man was, he wasn't Dan Morgan. The youths signed themselves as James Williams and Richard Eubank (or Ewbank). The affidavit was part of an effort by defense attorneys to get a new trial for Morgan, as Morgan wasn't so tall, and had dark hair and a long face.

Certain things about this effort raise questions. Why did these youths wait more than a month to step up to the plate? If they knew that Morgan was the key suspect, erroneously suspected, why did they not come forward before or during the trial to say so? The assistant prosecutor wondered why the youths had gone on if they knew a robbery had just been committed. This last point is not so strong as the others because the youths did not report a gun in the hands of the man they saw and thus did not know a robbery was being committed when one of them looked in the window. The defense said that the youths were willing to testify on Morgan's behalf at a new trial. But would they have been just as unsubstantial as the eight or ten witnesses that supposedly had been booked to show during Morgan's trial that Morgan was in Chicago at the time of the filling station robbery in Frankfort, and who failed to show up? One may reasonably doubt the existence of James Williams and Richard Eubank (Ewbank), as neither of these names appears on either the 1920 or 1930 Clinton County censuses, either as family heads or sons.

Moreover, Williams is a surname not unfamiliar to Baron Lamm. He could be Herman Williams for a need.[10] Lamm could in fact be a good many things. He seemingly tried on just about every alias and pseudonym, whether off-the-rack or tailor-made.

During Morgan's trial in late June, an intriguing query was brought up by the defense that yet goes unanswered. Just before a heated exchange between the state and the defense (which, by the way, went against the defense), it was asked why Morgan would bother to rob a filling station for ninety dollars when a short time later he reckoned that he would get his hands on a thousand burgling a bank. Why, indeed? Anyone studying the actions of Dan Morgan has to wonder why he robbed filling station after filling station, often on his own, when he stood to make more looting banks with perhaps less risk to his freedom.

Fred Baker, the gas station attendant robbed by Morgan in Frankfort, signed an affidavit stating that the robbery occurred on May 26, 1924, fully eight days after it actually took place. When asked by the defense why he signed this false statement, Baker replied that the prosecutor told him that the exact date did not matter so long as it was within two years of the actual date![11]

In fact, a whole not-so-heavenly host of questions arise concerning Dan Morgan. When did he first take up with Baron Lamm? Why did he hit filling stations throughout Indiana in 1924 at a time that he was involved in a number of bank robberies in Illinois, with or without his chum, the nebulous big shot "Danville Danny." Was Morgan alone in the Standard station robbery or was someone with him in a car? Morgan was seen on foot just before the robbery, but he called out to someone in a car during that robbery, either to keep them at bay if they were customers or to reassure them if accomplices. He must have had a ride at some point that night because less than an hour later, he was identified as a Lebanon filling station robber. Lebanon is fifteen miles from Frankfort. Finally, when, where and how did Morgan come to his end?

At the end of June 1924, Dan Morgan was convicted of robbing the Standard Oil station in Frankfort and sentenced to 10–21 years at Pendleton Reformatory. A few days before the trial, a young lady had visited Morgan at the Carroll County jail. It was assumed that she was the prisoner's wife. When she attended the trial subsequently, she said that Morgan was not her husband, only that she had thought so earlier. As to why she attended the jam-packed trial, she said that she was merely concerned. Not improbably, she may have been the source of the mysterious hacksaw found near the jail.

Morgan was seen at the trial reading the story on Charles Norman that appeared in the *Frankfort Evening News* on June 23. He appeared to be quite absorbed in the story. It has to be wondered how long the two had worked together. Possibly the article had some things to say about Norman that Morgan hadn't known. Still, that seems unlikely if both men were associates of Terrible Tommy O'Connor in Chicago. Another point here is that Norman could not have reached Indiana before early May 1924 since he was locked up most of that year previously. If the two had worked together in the old days, why had they separated? The fact that Morgan was avidly reading about Norman during his trial suggests that their acquaintance was a recent one.

Charles Norman was held in Delphi until after Morgan's trial. Though Kansas wanted him, no requisition papers were honored by Indiana governor Forrest Branch until it was clear Norman wouldn't be needed at Morgan's trial. Norman then hopped a train back to Kansas, accompanied by the law, of course, including the aforesaid Deputy Snyder, now a little hard of hearing owing to the explosion that had set Norman at large a few weeks before. Norman was lodged in the Newton, Kansas, jail under heavy guard. Nevertheless, as reported by the *Daily Clintonian* on July 7, 1924, Norman escaped upon his return to Kansas and, according to the *Frankfort Morning Times* Norman and Morgan were still at large at the end of 1930.[12] As it happened, the *Clintonian* was dead wrong, but the *Morning Times* was probably right. Norman was sentenced to twenty years in the Kansas State Prison in early November 1924. He apparently was out by 1932, if not 1930, because he was wanted for a bank robbery in the latter year. He had a habit of breaking out of jails and would in two decades end up in Alcatraz for bank robbery with force and be classified as an "escape risk." By then he was no longer known as Charles Norman but Clyde H. Nimerick, his right name.

When Dad Landy was removed to Newport in expectation of a trial in Vermillion County for burgling a bank in St. Bernice and facing another trial in Clinton County for hoping to burgle banks in Frankfort and Michigantown, his response might almost be described as mild-mannered (if one didn't know any better). "Boys, you don't need to handcuff an old man like me. I wouldn't even walk away from you."[13] Never mind that Landy had been apprehended a month earlier trying to *drive* away from the "boys." Vermillion County sheriff Harry Newland, who would see Landy a final time in six and a half years at the climax of the running fight from Clinton, sagely replied, "Better safe than sorry." The old adage was well observed.

Landy was arraigned in Vermillion County on July 31, 1924, and held at Newport, awaiting trial for the St. Bernice job. In the end, he was let off. The Prosecution felt that the evidence was too weak to get a conviction, especially after the Defense got certain items in the defendant's possession when arrested—an oxygen tank valued at $25 stolen at Kokomo, for one—ruled out by the judge. Shortly beforehand, the prosecutor had tried to strike a deal with Landy. If he pleaded guilty to possessing stolen burglary tools from a

Kokomo resident, he would get a one to fourteen-year sentence. Landy didn't go for it.

A satchel containing two pistols from the American State Bank of St. Bernice figured to be the leading piece of evidence against Landy. The satchel was found in the culvert the day of the trio's arrest. The satchel wasn't needed for Morgan's conviction for the robbery of the Standard Oil station in Frankfort, as there were plenty of witnesses to identify that worthy for his involvement in this and several other Indiana filling station robberies. Apparently, the satchel with its hardware, namely, two pistols, wasn't enough to point the finger specifically at Landy.

On November 11, 1924, attorney Frank Pryor, who had defended Morgan in Delphi and would have handled Landy's defense in the upcoming trial, received word from Newport that Landy had been released for lack of evidence. The day before, the *Frankfort Evening News* heard from Kansas authorities that Charles Norman had just received a sentence of twenty years in the Kansas State Penitentiary. Landy had been in jail — at Frankfort, Delphi and Newport — awaiting trial almost six months. This taste of time in stir, apparently, would weigh heavily on him the last day of his life.

When Lamm and Landy met their ultimate fate, E.L. Osborne, chief of Indiana's Bureau of Criminal Identification and Investigation, stated that Landy was from Pennsylvania and had met Lamm there. No one knows when this was or quite what it led to — merely how it ended. It does seem a good bet, though, that Landy, Morgan, perhaps Norman, and probably Clark were working with Lamm by 1924. For such an assumption, we have certain things to go on.

The trail that led to the arrest of Landy, Morgan and Norman at Frankfort on May 21, 1924, started six weeks earlier in the little Vermillion County town of St. Bernice, just on the Indiana side of the Illinois-Indiana line. In the early morning hours of Thursday, April 10 (the day, incidentally, that Indiana governor Emmett Forrest Branch was sworn in), after a lodge meeting ended atop the American State Bank, somebody burglarized the bank vault.

It was a clever piece of business, but it was almost curtailed at the outset. Four young people returned from a date at a quarter past twelve to find a group of men standing by a car parked two blocks west of the bank. The young couples thought that the men belonged to an anti-horse-thief detective organization and didn't think anything more about it until one of the men came over to their car and shined a flashlight on the driver. The driver told the man that he was pretty fresh, shining a light in a guy's eyes. The man muttered something that quite escaped the historical record and walked back to where the others were standing. The young people couldn't furnish any particulars about the men they saw except that they were sure one of the voices that they heard was that of a foreigner.[14]

It would have been interesting if the young people could have given a ballpark figure as to how many men they encountered because the burglary of the bank was a real piece of work. Twelve or thirteen husky men, it was later demonstrated, could not roll the spherical, screw-lid safe outdoors without taking advantage of a slope. Nor could so many men fit in the vault or position themselves in such a way as to allow passage for safe out of the vault. A hand truck must have been used and possibly a hand-cranked crane in order to lift the safe, once it was out of the vault, onto the bed of a truck. Experts looking at tire tracks figured that a touring car, probably a Dodge or Hupmobile, and a REO Speed Wagon were used to take the safe eight miles out to some woods near Cayuga, where it was made to yield its treasure.

Visiting cashier John Straw of the First National Bank of Clinton (which provided funds to shore up the American State Bank) examined the scene that morning. Straw, who would be held up by the notorious Harvey Bailey four and a half years later at the First National and would fire the only shots in that robbery in the hopes of arousing the populace, mentioned that a crowbar had been found in the vault. He said another crowbar had been found three years earlier in the vault following another robbery when the bank went by another name. This time, Straw noted, the crowbar did not leave so much as a scratch. One has to wonder about that earlier robbery and, while one is at it, a later one![15]

Another mystifying detail about the burglary concerned the fact that the safe was too wide for the door of the vault. In other words, the safe was placed inside the vault before the door was put in. Yet the safe somehow went out of the vault and left without a trace.[16] The safe held the payroll for the local employees of the Chicago and Eastern Railroad overnight. The 11th was supposed to be payday. This fact alone suggested to the authorities that the job was carefully planned.

Investigators traced the truck used in the robbery to Danville, Illinois, and that, for a time, is where matters stood.

The robbery of the American State Bank in St. Bernice stands a good chance of being Baron Lamm's handiwork and, if so, for the first time it places him squarely in Indiana, where so many of his crimes from then on were committed, including his last. This job was a burglary and that may be what Lamm did mostly up until this time.

Upon his death in 1930, the Federal Bureau of Criminal Identification provided a Lamm rap sheet, and some of the holes in his life can be partially filled in. He was arrested December 1, 1914, for robbery in San Francisco. He did a year and a half in Utah State Prison from March 3, 1916, to November 1, 1917, for grand larceny. On June 2, 1918, he was arrested in Superior, Wisconsin, for a holdup. A month and a half later, on July 11, he was arrested in

Kansas City, Missouri, for vagrancy. In St. Joseph, Missouri, he was arrested for burglary at the end of 1920. Though arrested many times, he seems to have done hard time only once — his term in the Utah State Prison. As was learned upon his arrest in Winston-Salem, North Carolina, in February 1927, when he was going around as Herbert J. Madsen, Lamm was arrested many times, but nothing stuck. Except for his year and a half at the Utah State Prison, Lamm seems to have been periodically in and out of jails — no sooner in than out. The federal rap sheet is our only record of virtual certainties concerning Baron Lamm until the 1920s and St. Bernice.

The burglary of the American State Bank the night of April 10/11, 1924, may have been a milestone in Lamm's criminal career. It may have been Lamm's first Indiana crime. It might well be the last burglary he ever committed. The St. Bernice caper is not quite a certainty for Lamm's involvement, but because of the presence of Lamm's associates, G.W. Landy and Dan Morgan, and the fact that one man was described as having a foreign accent, it is a very good fit.

When a farmer, living northwest of Frankfort, Indiana, saw men with flashlights on his farm six weeks later, he was sure that it was a moonshine operation. He reported the suspicious activity to Sheriff Power the next morning and a trap was set that night — May 21. After the trio of safe blowers had been reined in, it was soon learned that one of them — Dan Morgan — could be identified by several oil station attendants as the lone bandit who had robbed them. Norman and Landy presented more of a problem to investigators. It wasn't until their mug shots were disseminated around the country that a sheriff from Kansas put the finger on Norman as the man who had escaped from jail in Newton, Kansas, following his arrest in Denver. Norman went by the name of James Woodruff at his arrest in Denver in March 1924 and, as mentioned above, his real name was Clyde H. Nimerick. Norman and a man named Ross (or Roff) were jailed in Newton after they failed to make bond. Four men and a woman had been arrested in all and two men provided bail. The woman was likely Norman's wife, and she was let off on her own recognizance.

As for Landy, he, too, was wanted in Logansport, Lafayette, and Crawfordsville, Indiana, apparently for jobs with the other two men, though if Norman was an active member of this threesome, he would have had to work fast as he broke jail in Kansas on May 2 and was arrested again in Indiana on May 21. This is not to say that Norman did not work with Morgan and Landy in the old days before 1924. Most likely, he did.

Toward the end of June 1924, Charles Norman was identified by the sheriff of Harvey County, Kansas, for the rascal that he was and was taken back to Kansas. The officer knew Norman as both James Woodruff and Clyde Nimerick.

Dan Morgan went to trial on June 24 and was convicted on the 26th. At his trial, Morgan was identified as the man who, in Frankfort the day of his arrest, had bought a pair of brown overalls for, as he said, "a particular purpose."[17] That purpose, no doubt, was to allow him to resemble a filling station attendant or, perhaps, a truck driver, while he robbed the station. During the robbery, Morgan had stooped down, Colt automatic in hand, beside the station attendant, twenty-eight-year-old Fred Baker, as he worked the combination of the safe in back.

Baker missed the first try. "I haven't got all night. I'm not going to monkey with you," Morgan remonstrated. Baker did much better the second time.

An interesting twist was brought up at the trial that was not covered in the newspaper coverage of the robbery when it occurred. Before leaving the Standard station after the robbery, Morgan actually waited on a local physician, pumping gas and giving him, presumably, the correct change when he was paid through the car window. The good doctor noticed that the man who waited on him wore a fake mustache and had long ears, close to the head, which turned inwards at the top.

The man Morgan shot at in vain the night of his arrest, Sheriff Dan Power, brought him to Delphi in Carroll County for his trial. Power told Morgan that he was going to have to testify against him. Morgan replied simply, "Tell the truth. That's all you can do."[18] When Power delivered Landy to Newport to stand trial for the St. Bernice burglary on July 7, Landy shook hands with him and said that he treated his two cohorts and him fine. Sheriff Power, furthermore, was "a real man," Landy said. At Delphi earlier, Morgan and Norman jokingly told Sheriff Power to look them up when he got to Chicago. Power would see Landy a final time at Sidell six years later, identifying his body at the McCauley funeral parlor in Sidell. The bright July sunshine and the fading vitality of "Dad" would be no more than a memory then.

Power did tell the truth at Morgan's trial and the jury bought it. Morgan got a term of 10 to 21 years in the Indiana Reformatory at Pendleton. The reformatory accommodated men between the ages of sixteen and thirty. Morgan, apparently, was twenty-eight.

Morgan hoped to appeal his case; this would involve eight witnesses who would swear that at the time of the Sunday night robbery of the Standard Oil station in Frankfort (9 P.M.), Morgan was in Chicago. One just has to wonder if Baron Lamm would have materialized among these witnesses. Along with the octave of doubtful witnesses were the two joy-riding youths mentioned above. In any case, the appeal came to nothing.

Nor, as it turned out, did Morgan mind. His term would last just over a year. On September 21, 1925, he and two other prisoners, George Brown and James Jennings, escaped through the reformatory's ventilating system. All three were rounded up in a few short months by the law in three different states—Illinois, California and Texas. Morgan, the first of the three to be caught, was bagged in Texas. But he quickly regained his feet, jumping bond, in San Antonio in January 1926. In a year (if not sooner), he would be working with Lamm and James "Oklahoma Jack" Clark.

On January 14, 1927, Texas governor Miriam A. "Ma" Ferguson held a press conference. She was just four days away from the expiration of her term. Ferguson had signed a record number of pardons, and she was catching some heat for it from political opponents and the press. One of the things the governor had to sting her opponents with was none other than Dan Morgan. Morgan had jumped bond in San Antonio almost exactly a year before (January 24, 1926). How, the governor asked, could anyone like the authorities in Bexar County come down on her when Morgan had left town without even paying his bond? This must have come as news to someone—Morgan paid $3,000 before skipping town.[19]

It may be interesting to take a look at Morgan's short stay in Pendleton. He arrived on July 6, 1924. As he assured a visiting party from Frankfort at the time, he was behaving himself and working in the prison chair factory.[20] Two and a half months later, John Dillinger was sent to Pendleton, at age 21, for the botched mugging of a small-town grocer. The two men were part of Pendleton's prison population for almost a year. Dillinger, however, worked at one of the other reformatory's four industries—manufacturing manhole covers.[21]

The question is: Were Morgan and Dillinger acquainted and, if so, did they discuss Baron Lamm?

While it can only be strongly inferred that Lamm was part of the bunch that robbed the American State Bank of St. Bernice along with Landy and Morgan, in view of their later association, it is much more than a moot point. If the two inmates discussed Lamm, it would have been six or seven years before Dillinger and Pierpont heard about him from Oklahoma Jack Clark and Water Detrich in Michigan City. Dillinger thus may have heard from Morgan about Baron Lamm when Lamm was very much in his heyday.

Dillinger's reformatory records, however, show no trace of Morgan. Dillinger tried escaping on Christmas Eve, 1924, but the unsuccessful attempt seems to have been a solo foray. Nothing in the records indicates who, if anyone, might have put the bee in his bonnet. When it came time for Morgan to make his break several months later, he did so with two others, neither of whom was a big shot then or later. But the breakout plan was not hatched by Morgan. He merely went along for the ride. James Jennings is said to have arranged the escape. So, if Morgan was not the leader of the three escapees, he may not have had any say-so in who went along. In short, we just don't know if Morgan and Dillinger ever met. If the two did meet, it would be an earth-shaking discovery, for then and there Dillinger might well have made his mind up to be a bank robber, long before anyone ever suspected that his mind ran along these lines.

In the late autumn of 1924, Morgan was locked up at Pendleton and Landy had just been released from custody at Newport. Lamm did not work with either of these men in his biggest caper — the robbery of the Northwestern National Bank of Milwaukee on December 8, 1924. Landy would have been considered too "hot" or too preoccupied to take part in this operation. Morgan, of course, was incarcerated. Oklahoma Jack Clark is sometimes said to have been in on this job, but even his presence is doubtful. The gang that robbed the Northwestern National was a disparate and cold-blooded bunch not otherwise associated with Lamm. Were it not for the certainty of the Milwaukee Police that Lamm was a member of the group, it would be easy to dismiss his involvement in the robbery.

None of the descriptions of the robbers given by eyewitnesses fits Lamm. In fact, such specifics as can be gleaned from eyewitnesses point away from Lamm, Landy and even Clark. The leader was around 5'8", seemingly too short for Lamm, and the others in the gang were thought to be shorter than the leader and younger than his supposed thirty-two years. (In 1924, Lamm was thirty-four.) The leader's dark blue coat and felt hat suits Lamm — along with a million others. Clark's height, as given on his prison identification booklet, is no longer discernible. He was less than six foot but probably not much more than an inch or two less. If Lamm and Clark were in on the Northwestern robbery, one can only assume that early descriptions are apt to be off the mark as far as accuracy goes and not to be taken too seriously. Nor, if Lamm was the bandit leader that day, is there any mention of his foreign accent. The leader was said to be gruff but not especially foreign. The language he indulged in the most may have been that "pedlar's French" of a bygone day — the kind that needs to be pardoned, if not paroled. But that was nothing. Every bank robber spoke this language fluently. Bank robbing decorum seemed to demand it.

What to make of Lamm and Landy is a question that must dog the investigator at every step. How did they meet and when? Landy knew western and central Indiana like the back of his hand. Lamm was also probably thoroughly familiar with this area. But he may have wanted Landy less as a tour guide than as an experienced yegg. Landy probably burgled more banks than he robbed; that is, by profession, he may have been a burglar, not a holdup man. If accusations mean anything, Landy had been in Frankfort in May 1924 sizing up the American National Bank for a burglary, and in the afternoon of the day he and the two others were arrested northwest of Frankfort (May 21), he had been seen in the People's Bank at Michigantown, Indiana, no doubt doing the same thing. That burglary was the method involved is indicated by the equipment the bandit trio of Landy, Morgan and Norman had secreted in the culvert and were in the act of extracting at the time of their arrest. Two small oxygen tanks and one large one, in addition to safe-cracking tools and a traveling bag housing a Smith and Wesson revolver and a Colt automatic, were among the booty. (The officers, by the way, removed these weapons, while replacing the traveling bag in the culvert.) Lamm almost certainly was in on the project, though he managed to steer clear of the moonlight arrest for some reason. Perhaps he moved on to other projects, leaving the Indiana-Illinois line to the trio.

It is odd, too, that Dan Morgan seems to have hit filling stations without assistance. As a matter of fact, the first thing he did upon breaking out of Pendleton was to rob a garage and filling station at Scircleville, Indiana. The next day, he looted a hardware store and restaurant in nearby Kempton. He and another man were surprised in the act of burgling a bank in that same hamlet in the early morning hours by workers leaving the graveyard shift at the local canning factory. The two men fled without resistance. Someone — suspicion pointed to Morgan — did better burgling a Standard station in Frankfort just three days after the Pendleton break.

If Morgan did this, it was ironic, for it was the stickup of another Standard station in Frankfort that got him sent up fifteen months earlier. But if Morgan did in fact blow the Standard station safe, his hopes would have been soon dashed, especially if he had partners in the operation. There was only fifteen dollars in the safe.

On Sunday night, September 27, an odd incident occurred just south of Frankfort on the Maish road. An Indianapolis man, driving with his wife and friends, was about to come back to Frankfort by way of the Boyleston concrete when his car acted strangely. The man got out of his car to see what the problem was. Five or six men stepped from the shadows at the side of the road and one asked brusquely, "What are you doing stopping here?" The Indianapolis man explained. One of the men then said, "Well, I am a state highway officer and you can't stop on this road." The Indianapolis man happened to be a fireman and was used to emergency workers. This man did not strike him as this type and he said so. Fortunately, prudence soon set in and the man drove off. He drove by the spot later that night and shined a flashlight along the road. He saw quite a bit of straw scattered along the side of the road, which he believed had concealed some hooch. That seems to have always been everyone's first thought in that day when confronted with a pile of straw or a hole in the ground. But it may have been that the men had dug up a cache of weapons or burglar tools.

None of this brings Baron Lamm to mind, but if anyone notorious was present that early autumn evening, it may have been Oklahoma Jack Clark. The belligerent officer was dressed in overalls and a sheepskin coat with the collar pulled up to hide his features. Five years later Clark would be dressed nearly identically at the Clinton fiasco. Clark had been booked in Aurora, Illinois, in March 1925, following a burglary, but he was out and about long before autumn of that year.

During this same week, a farmer out harrowing his field had been dragged to death by his team of mules. It is a curious juxtaposition. On the one hand, a man was berated for stopping on a roadway where parking supposedly was not permitted, foreshadowing a more auto-congested day when ramps leading to interstates are off limits to even emergency parking by vehicles. On the other hand, plowing a field with a team of mules in 1925 indicates just how rural the nation still was at this time. Indeed, one can drive from Frankfort, Indiana, to Rantoul, Illinois, even now and be overwhelmed by how much prairie yet exists in a world of urban sprawl in the populous Midwest. That prairie grows even more immense when one is negotiating it late at night after the sidewalks are pulled up or during a snowstorm at any time of day.

III

Easy Money: Milwaukee, December 8, 1924

How do you get like that? — Erwin Balman, innocent bystander

BANDITS WERE NICE TO GIRLS, AT LEAST

Thus proclaimed the *Milwaukee Journal* in its coverage of that day's bank robbery in Milwaukee, the first in the city's history.

The robbery of the Northwestern National Bank on December 8, 1924, might well have been Lamm's finest moment in his chosen profession. Not a shot fired, no one seriously hurt and nearly $300,000 worth of bonds and cash taken. In the wake of it all, people all over the city could only shake their heads and wonder — as they always must in such cases — just what this world was coming to. The colorful robbery had everything except a wild chase between cops and robbers. Lamm had been too slick for that. The getaway Studebaker, with side curtains drawn, was seen for no more than a block. Its license plates could not be discerned to be Wisconsin or Illinois plates — or any plates at all, for that matter. The descriptions of the robbers themselves were just about as vague. About the only details proffered that were worth their weight in day-old donuts were the descriptions of the hats — two slouch hats, four caps. Such a detail ought to have been worth something to some detective somewhere. Philo Vance might have made something of it if he had had Captain McTavish alongside and a running time of six reels. Unlike the part played by Nathan Leopold's hornrims in the apprehension of Loeb and Leopold earlier this same year, the headwear yielded no information as to anyone's identity.

The local newspapers couldn't get enough of the story, for it was an undoubted first, and the dailies savored what details were immediately available. Extra editions hit the streets by noon.

A closer look at the robbery, however, reveals that, far from being the perfect caper, there were some flaws — about thirty-five thousand of them. Ten thousand dollars had waltzed out the door when young Eric Digman transferred a satchel full of money from the Northwestern National Bank to its sister bank, the Marine National Bank, in Milwaukee. The gang had dillydallied too long in striking the bank that morning. Business had been going on for nearly a half hour when the robbers struck. Worse yet, Lamm got a wrong answer from cashier and vice president Henry A. Digman, and accepted it as currency of the realm, thereby costing the gang another twenty-five thousand dollars. All of this absconding money was cash and, though the total from this haul would approach $300,000, only $10,000 of it was in cash.[1]

Just who led this robbery was not altogether clear in the beginning. The physical description of the leader — never mind the absence of a foreign accent — is at variance with what we know about Lamm. It was thought to have been Matt McNeil, a thirty-year-old ex-con who had done time for manslaughter in a hijacking in the Minnesota State Prison at Stillwater. McNeil, who shared Lamm's hard, no-nonsense demeanor, hadn't been out of prison a year when the Northwestern robbery took place. The reason for the initial confusion is probably owing to a common failing of human nature — to make the one giving you the orders the exact center of the universe, or, at least, the particular universe you are in, as well as to the fact that none of the men measured up to Lamm's six-feet-plus height, which topped the heights mentioned by witnesses by the altitude of a size-12 chopine.[2]

The Northwestern National Bank, a two-story, elaborately-carved limestone structure, stood at the corner of Northwestern Avenue and Forty-Seventh Street. Four employees and a patron (another would walk in while the robbery was in progress) were in the bank that Monday morning when six men entered the front door at half-past nine, half an hour after the bank opened. The robbery would take a whopping twenty-five minutes and it is surely surprising, in view of its leisurely pace, that not more customers walked in on it.

The four employees were busy at their positions at their desks or in the tellers' cages, using adding machines or working over columns of figures by hand. Cashier Henry A. Digman, a lean, mustache-suave man whose face bore the important air of a man who knew his business at all times, looked up from his desk to see someone wearing a gray felt hat place his hand on the railing that separated the west end of the bank from the foyer and leap over. The man then covered the cashier with his revolver and announced a stickup. Two other rakehells quickly leaped the railing and got behind Digman. Two more men ran to the back and began rifling the tellers' cages at the north end. Another stood guard in back, covering two patrons and three employees. The man dealing with Digman was none other than Baron Lamm, the biggest and gruffest of the outfit, and his business was with the vault — while the cages were being cleaned out of $10,000 cash.

The robbery of the Northwestern National Bank was a piece of work. Lamm may not have improved on it in the six years he had remaining to him, although his penultimate effort at Frankfort, Indiana, was a similar criminal masterpiece. No shots fired; no one seriously hurt — on his side or the other — and a very large haul. The only thing wrong with the effort, from the bandits' point of view, is that it may not have been nearly as profitable as the net take made it sound. As mentioned above, only $10,000 cash was taken; some $285,000 in securities made up the remainder, and these may have become worthless before they could be fenced. The bonds, mostly public utility bonds, were registered and of short maturity. They may well have expired before they could be cashed in.

The day after the robbery, Walter Gaulke, of the Wisconsin Bankers' Association, said, "This job was done by experts, I am convinced. To prevent the sale of the stolen bonds, every bonding house in the United States and Canada has been notified of the serial numbers of the bonds. This will prevent any turnover of the bonds."[3] Gaulke was open to an offer by the bandits to sell the bonds. His reputation as a man of his word was well known and he expected such an offer within thirty days — with a request for immunity. Nothing came of the offer.

Apart from Lamm's customary gruffness in a holdup, the gang seemed in particularly good spirits for a bank robbery. This is not to say that the requisite amount of swearing done to strike the most memorable terror into the hearts of those in the bank was not indulged in. It was. One teller in fact regretted that ladies had to be subjected to such tokens of fire and brimstone, though one strongly suspects that such language might be equaled pound for pound in the ordinary table talk enjoyed by diners in any first-rate fast food restaurant today during normal business hours with no more excuse than that two or three were gathered together.

A customer, who it was deemed did not walk fast enough, had his ears boxed and his face slapped — protocol rigidly enforced by Dillinger nine years later at Racine. But there were less menacing moments as well. The women employees and customer Gertrude Hahn were treated, as the *Journal* gleefully noted, most cavalierly, with all the magnanimity of a prizefighter retiring to a neutral corner after a knockout blow, and the ladies, to a one, were only too happy to call attention to this aspect of the robbery.[4]

What the Milwaukee job may have produced in unusual abundance, so far as newspaper coverage goes, were quotes from Baron Lamm.

After jumping the railing that separated Digman's desk from the foyer,

Lamm growled, "Put up your hands and do as we tell you and do it quick, or I'll drill you." Digman was forced back to the director's room where three employees and two customers (a third would soon join them) were being held. Digman was told to keep his fingers over his eyes as the two marched to the back. After stepping into the director's room, Lamm had second thoughts.

"Get into this side room. There might be a burglar alarm in this director's room. We don't want any police interference."

Not satisfied with the cash take, Lamm fumed, "There's more than this around. Get busy and show it to us."

Digman protested that there wasn't any more money to be had.

"There's more around here some place and we want it now."

Digman was marched to the back to where, just under the impassive clock on the north wall, the huge vault was located. The bandit leader grabbed the cashier and shoved him into the vault, holding a pistol directly behind his ear. It was here that $285,000 worth of securities were added to the loot. But, Lamm, his black satchel ready to burst like a plump melon, was still a man easily provoked.

Suddenly, Lamm struck the cashier a heavy blow with his revolver, either because his touching a desk was taken to be an attempt to reach for a burglar alarm or because he lowered his hand from his face and thereby took in too much territory with his sweeping gaze. Either pretext would serve for a bandit potentate trying to maintain discipline among his subjects.

"Don't look at me, you," Lamm growled. "Keep your hands to the side of your face." (It is rather paradoxical to find outlaws like Lamm and Dillinger, who never wore masks in their holdups, so touchy whenever someone took a good look at them. Digman's photo in the next day's *Journal* shows his head tightly wrapped with a bandage as he talks with the bank's president and an interested bystander. Although the bandage is secure and brightly immaculate, blood has dripped all over Digman's shirt collar.)[5]

Digman dropped to the floor, but Lamm wasn't through with him yet. The bandit yanked the cashier to his feet.

"What's in that?" Lamm referred to a currency chest in the vault.

"That's the president's private strong box," Digman said. "I haven't the combination and can't possibly open it for you."

Lamm thought it over for a second, then said, slowly, ominously, "I think you lie."

Digman must have quaked in his shoes for he was lying through his teeth. There was a hefty $25,000 in that box just waiting to be pilfered by the best or the worst and he could have gotten to it in a wink.

The bank man wasn't believed and was made to try to open it. Twice he tried and twice he failed — on purpose. Fortunately for him, the bandit leader finally believed him. Digman had waited him out. He later told reporters that had he been asked to open the chest a third time, he would have complied, for he knew the combination.[6]

To the cashier's immense relief, Lamm told the others that it was time to go.

The six bandits now hastened to the front door but as they reached it, they slowed down and walked in a more stately fashion, just like so many businessmen. It was a good move for it fooled all who saw them leave the bank.

Typical of most of those who saw the bandits depart the bank was Max Lanoff. "I saw them come out and paid no attention. They looked like businessmen and were not in a hurry. They all got into the automobile without haste and I saw them move away on North Avenue."[7] But car painter William F. Teske saw the departure differently. The last three bandits, as he saw it, had backed out of the building and, while this made him wonder what was up, the thought of a bank robbery did not enter his mind. This was, after all, Milwaukee's first daylight bank robbery.

A reward of $5,000 for each of the bandits was posted by the Milwaukee Clearing House Association the day of the robbery.

Six bandits had gone inside the bank. Another remained at the wheel of the getaway car parked in front of the bank. The six inside men were all white, but the driver may have been African American.

This robbery was not without some amusing incidents, which the *Milwaukee Journal* relished in its coverage. The first concerns Gertrude Hahn, a twenty-year-old cashier working for a building and loan association next door to the bank. Miss Hahn entered the bank to deposit some checks. The robbery was in progress when she got to the bank, and she was made to stand against one wall.

"They were not unnecessarily rough," Miss Hahn reported. "They just drove me back against the wall and one of the bandits stood there on guard with his revolver pressed against my back. I stood there, sort of looking around to see everything I could, but the robber didn't like that. 'You'll have to cut that out, girlie,' he told me. 'I ain't never had to shoot a woman yet, and I sure would hate to start on you.' I took the hint and kept my eyes shut from then on."[8]

Sixteen-year-old Erwin Balman, an employee of a nearby market, was on his way to the bank to make a deposit. He found his way blocked by a man standing at the door with his back to him. Balman could get nowhere with hints that the man should kindly move, so he asked, "How do you get like that? Turn around?"

The man — one of the gang — with a plain tale put young Balman down.

"Listen, son, we're bank robbers and we can't stop to answer foolish questions while we are busy robbing a bank."[9]

Balman subsequently found himself surveying the same wall that Miss Hahn and another patron, along with four employees, had been facing for several minutes.

Milwaukee police soon produced a working scenario about how it was that daylight bank robbery came to Milwaukee. By 1924, with a murder a day, Chicago was gaining quite a lurid reputation for crime, especially after the "hand-shake murder" of Dion O'Bannion in November. The Chicago police had recently done a cleanup operation in their city, and this resulted in a diaspora of rogues throughout the Midwest. Some of these undesirables naturally would drop in on Milwaukee businesses for their future transgressions as Milwaukee is less than eighty miles from Chicago. The police considered two theories initially. One involved a bandit gang that had long been raiding rural Wisconsin banks. When one considers that Lamm had been detained for questioning for a bank job at Superior, Wisconsin, in 1918, the idea becomes intriguing.

The other theory is equally appealing. The gang, police theorized, operated out of Chicago. No doubt, of the two theories, this one was the better one to follow up on. Judging by the locations of the banks in Lamm's best-known robberies, Chicago would seem to have been the epicenter for these operations.

It wasn't long, however, before interest centered on the usual fall-guy city of that era — St. Paul. St. Paul would in time become the robber's roost of numberless gangsters, ranging from John Dillinger, Baby Face Nelson and Homer Van Meter to the Barker-Karpis gang. Corruption was rife in the city, and this had been going on since the turn of the century. Bribes and palm-greasing here were the order of the day for the first three decades of the twentieth century. Homer Van Meter was killed here on August 22, 1934, quite possibly having been betrayed by a corrupt city official.[10]

On the weekend following the robbery, police in the Twin Cities rounded up thirty-two police characters. Miss Marian Landisch, one of the employees at the Northwestern National, looking at a rogue's gallery, identified Matt McNeil as one of the bank bandits a week earlier. Another man, unidentified, known as a habitual criminal, had been seen in Milwaukee the day following the robbery. His trail led to Chicago, but nothing came of the lead. Just when Baron Lamm became a suspect in the Northwestern National robbery doesn't appear. He may have been the unidentified incorrigible seen in Milwaukee the day after the robbery. Most likely he was fingered when McNeil and another participant were captured.

In any case, ten days after the Clinton robbery, Lamm was identified by the Bureau of Investigation, as well as Milwaukee police chief J.G. Laubenheimer, as the leader of the gang who had robbed the Northwestern National Bank on December 8, 1924. But Lamm, according to these authorities, was an alias, like Tommy White, George Barney and Herbert J. Madsen.[11]

Of the known members of the gang that had hit the Northwestern National Bank, Lamm was the only one at large in 1930. At the time of Lamm's death, Matt McNeil was back in Waupun Prison and Dutch Kanner, identified by Milwaukee police as another member of the gang that robbed the Northwestern National, was doing time in Leavenworth for post office robberies. Another Northwestern robbery suspect had died in a shootout following a bank robbery in New York. This number, however, is short three of the number of bandits that hit the bank as given in the *Milwaukee Journal*. The gap leaves open the question of whether Oklahoma Jack Clark was one of the three unidentified bandits.

IV

"We always had our eyes open": Of Hooligans and Vigilance

> We knew that Summit couldn't get after us with anything stronger than constables and, maybe, some lackadaisical bloodhounds and a diatribe or two in the *Weekly Farmer's Budget*. So, it looked good.—O. Henry, "The Ransom of Red Chief"
>
> "Get a rope!"— Heard on the streets of Frankfort, Indiana, May 1924.

On a cold, bright afternoon in January 1927, a young man walked into the First National Bank of Secor, Illinois. In his left hand was a red traveling bag. He stepped up to the teller's booth and asked for change for a five. As the cashier counted out five ones, the young man pulled a pistol out of his brown herringbone overcoat and announced, "Hands up!"

The bookkeeper was just about to step out the front door en route to the post office when the robbery began. The young bandit ordered her to get back of the counter. She assumed that he was joking.

When he pointed his pistol at her, she gathered the full import of what was taking place. Just as the young man set about to sweep the tellers' cages clean of their cash, a Lutheran minister entered the establishment with his brother. The robber pointed his gun at the pair, telling them that a holdup was in progress. They, too, thought that the young man was joking. Whether the robber straightened the two out with a terrific oath or whether he chose to be civil despite the extreme provocation is anyone's guess. Certainly he had to be asking himself why he wasn't getting any respect on this particular day.

In any case, the four innocents were soon taken back to the vault, told to lie face down and locked inside. The robber scooped up just over a thousand dollars in cash and put it in his satchel. He was in a hurry. Small town or not, anything could happen during a bank robbery, and he was going it alone. He did not bother the safe. Indeed, all he wanted from the vault was a place to deposit people for safekeeping.

The robber fled the bank on foot, going up the street three blocks to where his new Ford sedan was parked. This was perhaps the young man's worst mistake. The getaway car was parked too far away from the bank. He could have been stopped by half the town if, as so often happened during a bank robbery, the hue and cry had gone out immediately.

The occupants of the vault, meanwhile, were in no serious danger since the vault could be opened from the inside. The cashier was the first one out, and he went for his gun. It lay under the counter. When he reached the door, he could see the robber getting into the sedan. The cashier fired three rounds from his pistol at the car as it pulled away. One shot hit the right rear fender, but the robber was able to drive away unhurt.

The bank was equipped with an alarm system that alerted all the businesses in Secor when a bank robbery occurred. These businesses in turn alerted nearby towns in all directions of the event, and roadblocks were immediately set up on all the arteries leading away from Secor.

Out on the street, the bank cashier flagged down a friend, one of Secor's town guards, and together at a speed of 65 miles per hour on slick January surfaces they followed the young man in the Ford sedan.

The bandit car weaved in and out of traffic so that no shots were fired either way as the chase made its way east to El Paso. At the intersection of Routes 2 and 8, Dr. A.C. King, a physician and part-time Woodford County deputy, set up a roadblock. No sooner had he done so than he saw the bandit car approaching. He waved his double-barreled shotgun at the driver in an attempt to show him how hopeless his situation was. Suddenly, King saw the driver lurch forward, his arms thrust high, and then he saw the car overturn into the ditch in an outburst of smoke and snow and dirt. King thought the young man had been shot by his pursuers. However, when the dead man's revolver was examined, it was found that only one round had been fired. He had ended it all rather than bear the disgrace of imprisonment.

In this unheralded episode from the Jazz Age, there is something of an epitome of what went on in mass at the time. Bank robbers very often had to face not only the resistance of law enforcement personnel but the wrath of armed citizens as well. Though it was not yet the era of the big-name bandits — John Dillinger, Bonnie and Clyde, Pretty Boy Floyd, Baby Face Nelson — bank robbery in the late twenties seemed as easy as it was colorful. You go into a small town with no more than a small-caliber automatic and waltz out with a couple of thousand dollars. Where's the constabulary? Where's the police? So many small towns had to do without a police department or so much as a constable.

Township constables, in any case, were often ill-trained in enforcing the law and in the methods of criminal investigation. Serving summons about sums up their usefulness. Such office holders usually worked as constables only part of the time, and the pay was low. Ostensibly, this elective post existed for the benefit of the sheriff, but very few sheriffs ever had a good word to say about their assistance.[1]

Small-town banks, of which there was a terrific flowering in the years just ahead of the Depression, had to look to the nearest big town for protection. While no one ever knew what made garage mechanic Henry Smith, twenty-six, a husband and father of a six-month-old son, and a resident of Chippewa Falls, Wisconsin, turn crook and attempt the easy pickings of a small-town bank so far from home, they did know what ended his outlaw career before it had effectively begun — an aroused populace.

His misfortune happened to be that he was the second one to hit that same bank in tiny Secor, Illinois. The first ones to rob it had done so nearly three years before and had gotten away clean. They were the Joseph brothers of Peoria. The brothers were later captured, along with sundry accomplices, when their string of bank robberies had run its course at the end of 1924. Today, no one knows the first thing about them.

In the three-year interval between the two robberies at Secor, the Woodford County Bankers' Association, in league with the Illinois Bankers' Association, started offering rewards for bank robbers as well as organizing vigilante groups.

Henry Smith came to Illinois expecting it to be more of Wisconsin. There was as yet no pervasive vigilante presence in the "Badger State."[2] On the wall of the bank Smith robbed was a poster advertising a thousand dollar reward for bank robbers — dead or alive. Whether or not Smith saw the poster, it was his death warrant. Dr. A.C. King and the cashier split the reward once Henry Smith's body lay cold in Evergreen Cemetery in nearby El Paso.

Henry Smith's misadventure was but a portrait in miniature of what took place after the ill-fated Clinton robbery by Lamm and his gang. Both Smith and Lamm hit towns that had recently had bank robberies, and the citizenry was in no mood for encores. Also, the communications systems in the immediate area of the bank robberies was state of the art and, therefore, not easily outrun. The hue and cry in both cases was more deadly than volleys of lead.

Smith hadn't been much of a bandit, but his funeral was better than most of those who were good at it. Probably because he was so lousy at bank robbery and was not to the manner born, he received plenty of respect from total strangers in that January cold when they carried his casket to the grave. He quite escaped the black pine box of the pauper's ditch that would gape wide for Baron Lamm and his henchmen.

IV — "We always had our eyes open"

There are some interesting parallels between Smith's fatal misadventure early in 1927 and that of Herman K. Lamm almost four years later. Apart from the fact that only a bare handful of vigilantes went after Henry Smith and the number that pursued Lamm were numerous as the grains of sand in the desert, both men struck towns that had been robbed successfully in recent memory. In both cases, things couldn't have been worse if they had walked into a hornet's nest. Furthermore, suicide played its decisive role in the final hand dealt both men. In Smith's case, we are left wondering, why Secor? He had cased a bank in Oakwood, Illinois, a few days before, but he went into Secor without a dry run first.

Lamm and his confederates talked over their prospective hit and finalized plans at a Danville hotel the night before the robbery, but going to Clinton and casing the bank preparatory to robbing it was not done.[3] The organizing genius of Baron Lamm, with its legendary meticulousness and detailed planning, took a day off in the Clinton operation. The only thing that he did that day that fit the legend was to depart the bank after only a few minutes.

State banks were much more numerous than national banks. In Indiana in the twenty years between 1916 and 1936, state banks outnumbered national banks 3 to 1 on the average and sometimes more than 4 to 1.[4] Banks, particularly rural state banks, were easy targets, situated as they often were in the hinterlands where police and township constables were scarce. Because law enforcement seemed to so many to be understaffed and crime so rampant, banks and bankers' associations organized vigilante groups to stamp out what must have seemed like a crime pandemic.[5]

The vigilantes were unpaid volunteers who were furnished pistols, shotguns and high-powered rifles from bankers' associations, either county or state. They were appointed special deputy sheriffs and were to be prepared in the event of a bank robbery or any other emergency that called for plain dealing. The vigilantes, also known as bank guards and town guards, served under the sheriff of each county. Sometimes the sheriff appointed a county chief to act as supervisor of the vigilantes. Vigilantes were also insured by the bankers' associations to cover the sheriff's department against any lawsuits engendered by their actions.

"We always had our eyes open," Roland Goheen, of South Bend, Indiana, said in 1991. Roland had been at a neighboring bank when John Dillinger, Baby Face Nelson, Homer Van Meter and two others robbed the Merchants National Bank at high noon on June 30, 1934, and shot up the town, killing a policeman. He could hear all the shooting. "[And] I was the secretary and treasurer of the St. Joseph County Vigilante Association. I bought seventy-five Smith & Wesson .38s on .45 frames. We had about sixty farmers deputized. The idea was that if we had a robbery in South Bend, we'd call up all the farmers leading — on roads leading — out of South Bend to tell them what to do. They were trained to shoot and if they saw the car coming, why they would fall in the ditch and shoot it after it passes. [And] I was in charge of teaching them how to shoot a gun. We had target practice once a week. [Now,] that was all a side issue of Dillinger, but it was all caused by Dillinger running around robbing banks."[6]

To keep performance up among vigilante organizations, marksmanship competitions were organized annually at the county level. Typical of such competitions was that held in Pontiac, Illinois, by the Livingston County Town Guard Organization in October 1930. About sixty of the county's seventy-four vigilantes competed in a pistol competition and then a rifle shoot. Sheriff J.R. Scarrat presided over the contest as officer-in-charge.

Just to the south, in McLean County, Illinois, that same month, a more elaborate event took place. There were five different competitions. The first involved the vigilante's use of his own firearms. The second tested his skill with weapons furnished by the bankers' association. The third event rated slow-fire shotgun accuracy on a clay target at fifty yards. The fourth event was the same as the third, except this time rapid-fire accuracy of the weapon was tested. The fifth was a pistol shoot, using .38- and .45-caliber revolvers at twenty yards as well as a .45-caliber automatic. All this was topped off with a trap shoot competition and, for a select few vigilantes, training was provided in the use and history of the Thompson submachine gun by Sheriff Walter Nierstheimer. The good sheriff did not know as yet that two years earlier, that Tommy gun might have come in handy as the notorious Kansas outlaw Jake Fleagle (using the name of Frank Barrett) was then a resident in the county seat of Bloomington for three weeks.[7]

In Mason County, Illinois, that October, town guards had their shoot under the auspices of the Mason County Bankers' Association, with Sheriff Ernest Kramer in charge. In this case, even police, sheriff's deputies, bankers and bank clerks were in on the action, along with the requisite town guards. In Mason County, town guards were equipped with riot guns (sawed-off shotguns) and were told to shoot to kill when they had need of them. They were also reminded of rewards for bandits taken dead or alive. The shoot was followed by the usual banquet at the local club in Havana.

Each county made note of its best score, and the state gave an award to the county with the highest score. Prizes were also handed out at individual events, so that attendance seems to have been no problem. Such competitions had been going on in Illinois since 1925 when town guards were first organized.

Much the same thing went on in Indiana. By June 1925, ninety-eight of the state's one hundred and two counties formed vigilante organizations.

(Of the four that did not, most interestingly in light of this book, the notable holdout was Vermillion County.)[8] In the state, nineteen bank robberies took place in the first half of the year. Between June 1 and September 1, 1925, only two bank robberies were committed. Things were looking up for Indiana's war against bandits. Indeed, all eyes were on Indiana as a sort of test case for the vigilance movement, so far as bank robberies were concerned.

The *Frankfort Evening News*, for September 3, 1925, noted that in some Indiana counties greater rewards were offered for dead bandits than live ones. Five years later, Iowa would put a bounty of $500 on each dead bank robber killed in the act of robbing a bank.[9] This seems to have been standard practice in those states making use of vigilantes to fight crime.

In Indiana, vigilantes numbered between 25 and 50 per county. Like their counterparts in Illinois and other states, they were trained in the use of firearms and held competitions regularly. Weapons were provided by county bankers' associations and, ultimately, the U.S. War Department.[10]

The impetus for the recurrence of the vigilante movement in this period occurred in Iowa in 1923 with the abrupt taking-off of one Hank Hankin in a bank robbery. His whole bunch — Harry "Canada Yellow" Dean, Bill "Lop-eared" Davis, Freddy "The Kid" Martin, Scar-faced Hogan and Nervy Allen — went to the penitentiary for life. Iowa could breathe easy once more, though journalists must have missed those Runyonesque gangland handles. Bank holdups, which numbered more than fifty a year before Hankin's departure (as swift as unlamented), dropped to only three a year later. Bank losses went from $210,000 to $2,600 in the course of that year. Out of 1,000 Iowa towns, 781 enlisted vigilantes. Statewide, there were 3,876 vigilantes and $110,000 worth of reward money to be paid out for bandits, whether dead or alive. A total of 3,740 firearms and 712,000 rounds were purchased from the U.S. government.

Illinois liked the sound of all this. Former Des Moines chief of police Roscoe C. Saunders came over to Illinois to offer some tips on setting up a vigilante program in the spring of 1925. Soon, vigilantes took root all over the Midwest and beyond — Indiana, Missouri, Oklahoma, Texas and Kansas. Along with setting up vigilantes, there was a push to stiffen laws dealing with bank robbery.[11] In some states, too, there was a call to oversee gun laws so that there would be a corresponding restriction of gun sales.[12]

Going into the year 1925, when the vigilante movement really kicked in, two-thirds of all bank robberies took place in only eight states — California, Kansas, Illinois, Indiana, Michigan, Missouri, Oklahoma and Texas. Addressing the Executive Counsel of the American Bankers' Association at Pinehurst, North Carolina, in May 1926, the manager of the Protective Department, James E. Baum, pointed out that in the six months previous to February 28,

1926, daylight bank robberies in these states went down from 85 to 53 and burglaries dropped from 49 to 14.[13]

In Illinois, 73 bank robberies were committed in 1924, some of which, according to the Illinois Bankers' Association, were committed by Dan Morgan, a Lamm associate on occasion and quite possibly on these occasions. Illinois, therefore, took up the vigilante movement with a vengeance. In many counties, the town or bank guards were complemented by the horse, cattle and chicken thief detectives, unpaid volunteers whose job it was to guard against poultry and livestock theft. In addition to the manpower afforded by these organizations, there were telephone exchanges that could notify households and law enforcement personnel with remarkable efficiency.

All of this came into play in the final chapter of the Lamm saga. Five states hard-hit by bank bandits, which chose to organize vigilantes, reduced the national bank crime rate by eighty percent. These five states were Illinois, Indiana, Iowa, Kansas and Oklahoma.[14] In Oklahoma, in early September 1925, bank personnel were taken to the famous 101 Ranch and taught the "trigger squeeze" and other tricks of the gunman's trade. Even before this move on the part of the banks, six bandits had already been killed attempting to rob banks in the state during the previous eight months. Oklahoma was definitely getting a grip.

Undoubtedly, vigilantes made a dramatic difference in the number of bank robberies committed and losses suffered by banks in the first few years of their existence. In Illinois, for example, bank robberies went from 73 to 15 in three years, while losses dipped from a whopping $347,945.10 to a more civilized figure of about $15,000 in the same three-year period.[15]

But, alas for Indiana, the vigilance committees made little difference in the number of bank robberies in the state over time. Between January 1, 1930, and December 16, 1930, forty bank robberies were committed. This is almost exactly the average annual figure for bank robberies occurring in Indiana in the wide-open days before June 1925 when the vast majority of counties took up arms against bank robbers, the erstwhile "gentlemen of the shade" and "minions of the moon."[16]

Vigilantism, then as now, did not always involve masses of vigilantes. Individuals — men, women and youths — went after the bad guys when occasion demanded.

In December 1924, a young wife in Memphis, Tennessee, Mrs. J.W. Buchan, got suspicious of the boarders in the room next to hers, so she tapped the phone. She overheard plans to rob a bank that very day. The young lady grabbed a shotgun and when bank robber Hart Austin came to the boarding-house to gather his confederates, she captured him. Austin was a big catch, being wanted all over the Southwest and Ontario.

IV — "We always had our eyes open"

In Seattle that same month, a high school youth hit a store robber in the head with a rock as he fled the grocery, fatally injuring him. In Boston, two youths attempted to rob the Salvation Army headquarters. One was temporarily overpowered by Anne Fuller, a Salvation Army employee, before fleeing, and the other was held at bay by her until police arrived.[17]

In Portland, Oregon, in November 1927, a sixteen-year-old named Louis Emanual made a flying tackle at a would-be robber at a lunch counter. Emanual was fired on three times but emerged unscathed. He escorted the malefactor to police headquarters in a taxi. Ironically, the youth who could tackle a robber under fire could not make the football team.[18]

Again in December 1930, this time in Los Angeles, a service station employee suddenly saw three men robbing a branch of the Security National Bank. He wounded the driver and after chasing the two fleeing bandits on foot, loaned his gun to a bystander. The bystander then collared one bandit. The remaining bandit was later captured nearby by other citizens. Filling station personnel, just as much as bank personnel, kept guns on the premises in the old days. They were expected to know how to use them. This was in a day when gas was barely twenty cents a gallon.

Next to banks, gas stations — or as they were usually called then, filling stations — were the favorite targets of desperados, particularly the younger set or those just beginning freebooting careers.[19] In August 1930, just a few months before Lamm went down in that same region, a gas station robbery led to a massive vigilante action. Three youths held up the Rawley filling station, a few miles east of Brazil, Indiana. They picked the wrong one. This one had been staked out by vigilante farmers who were perched on top of the station, bunched up in a cornfield across the road and seated in a car near the station. As the gang drove off, the farmers opened fire, killing the driver, the son of the county road commissioner. The car went into a ditch and overturned. The other two youths got behind the car and made a stand for a time. When one caught a slug in the leg, the battle ended.

A bank job at Madison, in southeastern Indiana, in that same month came to an abrupt conclusion. The robbers, after shutting bank personnel and patrons in the vault, did not secure the door. The alarm went out immediately. A construction crew soon got wind of the robbery. They promptly put up a barricade across the road on which they had been working, and when the three outlaws came upon it, the men were seized by the road workers, who, somehow, were furnished with firearms in time for the capture. It would almost seem that there were no innocent bystanders in these stirring times. Certainly, there were no inert ones.[20]

Banks armed their employees in many cases, men and women alike. A photo on the front page of the June 1927 number of *The Hoosier Banker* shows five comely bank tellers trying their level best to squint ruthlessly and point their pistols directly into the camera.

As with the robbery of the First National Bank in Secor, Illinois, mentioned above, tellers made sure firearms were available in the event of a robbery. At Monroe, Ohio, on January 5, 1931, two young men and a 19-year-old girl walked into a bank bent on making a significant withdrawal. One of the men stood at the door with a submachine gun. The girl approached the teller and said, "Come up with it." Instead of coming up with the cash, he came up with a revolver. He fired on the girl and missed. She returned the fire and missed just as much. The getaway car wrecked in a culvert and the three took to their heels. A farmer saw them in his field and called the Middletown Police. The gang was captured without incident. The girl told police her husband, one of the robbers, was unemployed and that they needed money for the baby. The judge had heard that one before and doubtless would again, though not always from such kids.

Clyde and Buck Barrow might well have met their doom in Lucerne, Indiana, on May 12, 1933, had they elected to go into the vault where some employees had scrambled during a bank robbery attempt. A shotgun was kept in the vault as a matter of course and no doubt someone inside knew what to do with it.

Alice Hockett, a cousin to the Art Hockett who appears in these pages so often, was engaged to be married to a young bank teller in 1936. He worked at a bank in Bloomingdale, Indiana. One day, as the couple returned to the bank from lunch, a robber emerged from the bank. The young teller was armed, as so many tellers were in that day — armed by the Indiana Bankers' Association itself. The bandit and the teller both fired at the same time and both died. At the bandit's wake, the body lay exposed from the waist up so that the school children could see the gaping wound in his chest as they passed by the casket. Indeed, it was mandatory that the kids view the dead bandit. A sad footnote to this incident is the fact that Alice Hockett would never marry in the course of her long life. In one crackling, unthinking instant during a lunch hour, two lives ended and a third was altered forever.

One week after Dillinger was paroled in May 1933, Culver, Indiana, saw a vigilante action that left one bank robber dead and the rest of the gang in custody. Some five hundred vigilantes took part in the capture. In December 1921, Culver had been visited by bandits and a teller was killed. Joseph Burns got sent up for the crime. He would be among the dirty dozen who unsuccessfully tried to break out of Michigan City in 1930 and one of the ten inmates who, with Dillinger's help, successfully fled the prison in September 1933. The vigilante action at Culver, if Dillinger knew of it (and he almost certainly did), seems to have made no more impression on him than the likely seminar by Walter Detrich and Oklahoma Jack Clark on the absolute hell that followed the Clinton robbery.[21]

For Dillinger, once he was out of the pen, the future was written in letters of fire. He would rob banks and he would die because of it. It was only a question of when. It probably didn't matter to him whether a vigilante's bullet outran him or a cop's. Baron Lamm, if he was indeed a suicide, seems to have minded how he died. It would be on his terms.

Other outlaws, unknown outlaws, would die on their own terms when cornered by vigilantes.

A particularly tragic case of a bank robbery gone wrong took place over three northern Illinois counties in January 1935. The robbery instantly brings to mind two other notorious robberies gone wrong — one of which, the Clinton robbery, is largely the subject of this book. The other catastrophic robbery was that of a Lamar, Colorado, bank in May 1928. Three bank personnel were killed by the Fleagle gang and a doctor was kidnapped and murdered. The crime outraged the nation, and the lust for vengeance did not cool until three members of the gang were hanged and its leader shot down just a few weeks before the death of Baron Lamm.

The parallels between the 1935 robbery and the Clinton robbery, just over four years earlier, suggest a paradigm symptomatic of such incidents. Bank personnel are assaulted when they give the wrong answer or killed when they try to interfere with the robbery. An inexperienced or headstrong officer of the law falls prey to the firepower of the bandits after they lure him into a trap. Cars are hijacked and hostages taken. Civilians are engaged. Shootouts follow, with a climactic battle taking place in the countryside — in these two cases in a cornfield still full of standing corn in the dead of winter.

It all went down in this way. In Lenore, Illinois, a town of five hundred in La Salle County, four men rode through town the morning of the robbery, attracting the attention of the president of the State Bank of Lenore as he walked to work. The nearest police department was ten miles away at Streator, and he called it before opening the bank. His misgivings were confirmed by other bank personnel who were reporting to the bank. When the bank was opened three of the bandits, who had entered the bank through a coal chute, took the men inside to the rear of the building. One of the bandits remained in the stolen getaway car.

When the three bandits came out of the bank, they found the driver and getaway car gone. Apparently, people were quickly getting the idea that the State Bank was being robbed and made the driver jittery. He had fled the scene; but not for long. Eighty rods outside of Lenore, his car broke down. The bank president and a bank guard were able to capture the unarmed bandit as he ran into a cornfield. The two men — the president had thwarted a robbery two years before with his bare knuckles — were able to quickly bag the bandit. But then, a car commandeered by the remaining bandits pulled up and shot and killed the president and wounded the guard. The four bandits drove southwest with a car salesman and a boy as hostages.

By this time, the word was out, and lawmen from nearby counties were speeding to the vicinity of the robbery. The bandits were quickly overtaken by the Marshall County sheriff and his deputy. The getaway car pulled over. One of the outlaws stepped out of the car and raised his hands, pretending to surrender. When the sheriff got out of the pursuing vehicle, he and his deputy were gunned down through the busted-out back window of the bandit car. The deputy survived.

The bandits were eventually run to ground at a farm near McNabb, Illinois, only a few miles from where the day's events began. A large posse of lawmen and vigilantes converged on the farm of Jake Loger on the heels of the bandits. Loger's wife and daughter were alone when the bandit car pulled in the drive. Having heard of the robbery, Mrs. Loger ran out to meet the men in the car, thinking they were deputies. Two bandits went into the farmhouse with the women while the other two took off into a cornfield. The posse was easily able to capture three of the bandits, even though those in the cornfield had taken a submachine gun with them. One of the bandits in the cornfield killed himself with his pistol.

The Lenore bandits were more cold-blooded than Lamm and his gang, but not so cold-blooded as the Fleagle gang. The Lenore bandits let their hostages go. Before it was all over, one of them had said to Mrs. Loger, "You remind me of my mother. I wish we had never done this. I have a wife and children."

Of course, not all vigilante actions succeeded. Sometimes, as with Harvey Bailey at Clinton, Indiana, and in the January 1931 robbery of the Albany State Bank in Albany, Indiana, the bandits simply outran their pursuit. Bailey got away. So did the Albany State bandits — for a day. The Albany bandits were not smart. They defiled their nest. They robbed banks in Delaware County, their own turf. They were young, under thirty-five, and they didn't know their business. They needed a Fagin. Two were immediately apprehended, and all four were identified within two days. The arrested bandits each received a sentence of fifteen years within three days of their arrest.[22] The Depression had no patience for thinking things through. If prosperity was always just around the corner, retribution was a whole lot closer.

Another illustration of justice not standing on ceremony in the Depression occurred just a fortnight before the Albany robbery. The weekend after the demise of Lamm Incorporated, four men robbed the Seward Bank of Burket, Indiana, of $250. One of the gang was killed by vigilantes after a chase and the rest were captured. Two days later, they were hauled up in front of a judge and the leader got thirty years. Two brothers got thirty years between them. Nor was this swift justice exceptional. Justice was meted out by the multitudes, and when suspects survived posses, a similar no-nonsense justice was parceled out by the local courts. In Indiana, bank robbery drew a minimum ten-year sentence and a maximum life sentence.[23]

Justice in Michigan following the robbery of a Battle Creek bank and subsequent murder of a state trooper on October 14, 1930, was even swifter than that dished out to the Burket bandits. For the first time in Michigan, a state police radio system came into play, and immediately thirty-five patrol cars were summoned to the Sturgis area. Within four hours, the robbers were caught and, within twelve, all were sentenced to life in prison. Justice may have been blind, then as now, but in those days she at least wore sneakers. It is said that this state police radio system in Michigan kept the Dillinger gang from operating there.[24]

Organizing state police forces was the beginning of the decline of vigilantism. State police are as old as the Texas Rangers, but in the first two decades of the twentieth century, a number of eastern states, particularly Massachusetts, Connecticut and Pennsylvania, organized state police units along modern lines. State police and highway patrol agencies sprang up with the rise of motorized bandits and interstate highways.

Their duties included training new recruits when other police agencies were unable to do so, regulating traffic, setting up roadblocks and criminal investigation, and assisting the American Bankers' Association. Typical of state police activities is this itemized list from the fall of 1930 in Illinois. There were 107 types of crime and infractions — 64 relating to highway laws and 43 covering anything from bad checks to murder. The highest number of arrests concerned failure to obey traffic signs — 4,364 arrests.

Overweight trucks accounted for 1,815 arrests. Intoxicated drivers and persons under the influence on a public highway brought in another 441 arrests. Up to October 15, six bank bandits had been arrested.[25]

In that year, Baron Lamm had little contact with any state police agencies until the climactic chase, but John Dillinger and his gang would have to shake the Indiana State Police a number of times following the prison break that set Oklahoma Jack Clark and Walter Detrich at large in the autumn of 1933.

In September 1925, Chicago was trying out armored shields for police in order to fight bandits. Captain John Stege, later to be the leader of the fifty-man Dillinger squadron, was the primary spokesman for this device. In Elkhart, Indiana, in March 1927, the St. Joseph Valley Bank installed something called the "pillbox" to fight bank robberies. This device consisted of a five-foot steel frame, 36 inches square, with bullet-proof glass apertures.

It was suspended from the ceiling where it could overlook the lobby and the tellers' cages. Three employees in the accounting department were trained in pistol and rifle marksmanship. They would take turns in manning the pillbox. While Lamm probably did not deal with such pillboxes, Dillinger had to overcome one in Mason City, Iowa, seven years after Elkhart took up the innovation.[26]

Along with these measures went a wave of technological advances, such as sophisticated locks, screw-top, spherical safes and burglar alarms. Perhaps the most important of the innovations was the state police radio system, mentioned above in connection with the Battle Creek robbery, which would turn out to be among the principal reasons for the disbanding of vigilante organizations. In 1930, police radio was still in its infancy, but by the end of the decade, it was in use throughout the country in all municipal and state police departments and highway patrol organizations throughout the land.[27]

The fight against crime coupled technological advances with a corresponding shift of political philosophy. Vigilantes needed the supervision of the local authorities. And local government in turn was subordinate to the state government. Bureaucracy and a system of checks and balances can do a lot toward curbing the primal instincts of a surge of vigilantism. With the beefing up of police departments and the organization of state police forces, trained professionals were on the scene to meet the emergencies formerly handled by vigilantes. Of course, a rifle in the hands of a pheasant hunter on the wrong side of the law in an upper-storey window can be pretty deadly even to trained professionals, as happed at the Battle of Ingalls in September 1893 and the so-called Young Brothers massacre in January 1932.

But no doubt the primary reason for the decline of vigilantism in the middle 1930s was the fact that bank robberies just did not decline in number with the rise of vigilante organizations over time. True, most Midwestern states reported decreases in bank robberies in 1925, but the trend was short-lived.[28]

Yet, as late as 1933, R.C. Saunders could claim:

For the past twelve years vigilante organizations have been built up in five middle western states under the direction of the sheriffs in the various counties, by the bankers associations, and in all of those states, as long as interest was maintained in the vigilantes, bank robbery continued to be reduced. In two of those states it showed a reduction of about 90 percent at the end of three years over the years before the organization was attempted.[29]

Sadly, Indiana did not seem to notice this progress — or, at least, its outlaws didn't.

In 1930, there were forty bank robberies in Indiana up to the Clinton robbery on December 16, a number on pace with the usual number of bank robberies in the state before the advent of vigilante groups five years earlier. By the end of 1931, the *Hoosier Banker* soberly noted that Indiana bank robberies had increased that year by fifty percent.[30]

In the first week of January 1931, the Indiana Bankers' Association listed the Frankfort Farmer's State Bank robbery as Indiana's biggest bank robbery of the previous year, announcing that the actual amount taken had been $140,000. There was no doubt about which robbery had been the most spectacular in the last year. The total number of bank robberies and bank burglaries, furthermore, was stated to have been forty-five. The month of December, alone, saw twelve robberies in the state. Losses from these robberies — or, rather, all but the last five — amounted to $245,000.

Vigilantes swarmed after outlaws by the hundreds, but they rarely saw any action. Theirs was a supporting role; they backed up sheriffs and deputies. Rarely were they killed and rarely did they kill. Sometimes, indeed, they were outflanked, as in Brazil, Indiana, on July 18, 1930. When three suspicious strangers were seen hanging around a bank, locals kept a vigil on the bank. The three men robbed a general store instead. Vigilantes could simply be outrun, as when Harvey Bailey vanished into midair after his Clinton robbery in 1928.

Going into a job, bank robbers didn't expect to deal with vigilantes in any substantial way, just as robbers didn't expect to deal with life imprisonment or capital punishment in any substantial way afterwards.

Perhaps not coincidentally, the decline in vigilantism went hand in hand with the decline of the big-name Public Enemies enumerated by the Justice Department in the mid-thirties — John Dillinger, Pretty Boy Floyd, Baby Face Nelson and, lastly, Alvin "Creepy"(or "Old Creepy") Karpis.

The idea of a Public Enemies program began in Chicago during the Capone era in the warfare between mobsters, like Capone, and the Chicago authorities. The Department of Justice caught onto the idea five years later and named John Dillinger as Public Enemy Number One nation-wide on June 22, 1934, a day that just happened to mark the outlaw's thirty-first birthday. It was to be the worst and last birthday present he was ever to have.

Dillinger would remain on top for exactly one month, until his death at Chicago's Biograph Theater. The vacancy was filled by Charles Arthur "Pretty Boy" Floyd until his death on an Ohio farm exactly three months after Dillinger was killed. Baby Face Nelson came next. His death a little over a month later resulted in a curious replacement.

The Bureau of Investigation had been on the lookout for John "Three-Finger Jack" Hamilton just as soon as Dillinger was laid in his grave. They would seek Hamilton longer than any other public enemy. The reason the hunt went on so long is that Hamilton had been killed before it started. Only belatedly did his death come to light. He had died following the infamous gun battle at Little Bohemia in northern Wisconsin in April 1934 and was buried by Dillinger, Nelson and others in a gravel pit near Oswego, Illinois. So, thus laid low, Hamilton could effectively lie low until mobster Volney Davis' girlfriend, Edna "The Rabbit" Murray, revealed his unusual hiding place.

The likes of John Dillinger, Baby-Face Nelson, Pretty Boy Floyd, Homer Van Meter and others saw the last of their ilk captured in New Orleans on May 1, 1936, when Alvin "Old Creepy" Karpis was arrested by FBI agents, with J. Edgar Hoover, himself, in attendance. It was a good job, though Karpis crabbed about it for decades, and though the agents forgot to bring handcuffs so that a necktie had to be appropriated to bind the felon's wrists, instead of the customary "bracelets." After Karpis' arrest, there were no more high-profile public enemies, and the FBI's War on Crime, waged since the Kansas City Massacre on June 17, 1933, shifted to a lower gear. The big shots were mostly dead or on the Rock by 1936. The "G" Men had been in on the kill of all the deceased public enemies, including Ma Barker and son Freddie in January 1935.

And where the FBI was in those days, there was the Chicago Office and its head, the ubiquitous Melvin Purvis, right up to the arrest of Volney Davis in Chicago on June 1, 1935. The 1935 James Cagney film *"G" Men* celebrated the Bureau of Investigation, soon to be the FBI, as America's answer to Scotland Yard, encompassing all the action it could think of, though not always accurately. America's greatest crime wave was licked by 1936 and farmers, for the most part, could go back to farming. The eradication of the public enemies by the FBI changed how the nation would deal with crime.

As Bryan Burrough writes: "The manhunts for Dillinger and his peers introduced America to an idea that we take for granted today: that the federal government bears the ultimate responsibility for the nation's law and order."[31]

V

Under the Radar at Winston-Salem

> I'm always peaceful, Marshal, when there ain't no use doing nothin' else.—*Rio Grande* (1950)

It was apparent to just about everyone in law enforcement in Winston-Salem, North Carolina, that a most important arrest had been made in the "Twin City" in the early morning hours of February 21, 1927. The only problem was: Who was arrested and what had they done? Three men had been picked up at the Robert E. Lee Hotel in town at six in the morning. Officers busting through the door of their room got the drop on them before they could reach for their guns under a pair of pillows. The men called themselves James M. Clark of New York, Herbert J. Madsen of New York and Robert E. Willard of Chicago. Willard was a tough monkey and the authorities were sure that he was not who he claimed to be. Nor, for that matter, were the others likely to be what they claimed to be — bootleggers running hooch from Pensacola up to New York City. They seemed to be yeggs, at the very least. Nevertheless, the trio were treated like bootleggers and their bonds were set at $1,050 each for Clark and Madsen and $5,000 for the belligerent Willard, who in spite of his handcuffs had taken a sock at an arresting officer.

James M. Clark was, of course, Oklahoma Jack Clark, who, for the only documented time in his life, gave his real name before he gave any others. Herbert Madsen was Baron Lamm. It is the third party whose identity presents a problem. He was a six-footer and tough to control. He gave a couple of names—Ed Stein and Robert E. Willard. He could have been anybody.

Writing in 1992, outlaw historian Kerry Ross Boren identified the third man as Edward Wilhelm Bentz.[1] There are plenty of things to bolster the identification. The suspect was a tall man, around six foot. Bentz was six feet tall. The man, as we shall see, seemed on the verge of a heist when taken.

Bentz was a big time operator by 1927, rubbing elbows with only the best in the business. Another factor supporting the idea that Bentz was the third man is that he never liked to work with the same bunch over and over again. If the man was Bentz, this is the only time we find him with Baron Lamm. Like Lamm, Harvey Bailey and the Fleagles, Bentz was meticulously methodical in his work. He planned his robberies to the least detail. Most importantly, he had to know his getaway route for many miles. Lamm could have used a man like Bentz, a man very much after his heart.

Edward Wilhelm Bentz was born in Nebraska in 1894 and was raised in Seattle. He started his life of crime at an early age, stealing scrap metal and bicycles. Between 1916 and 1926, he was a two-time loser six times. Like Baron Lamm, Bentz spent his jail time productively. He did a lot of reading while in stir. This passion led to his taking up book and coin collecting when he was on the outside. He seems to have had something of an aversion for too many jobs per year. Three bank robberies per annum seems to have been his limit. He didn't believe in tempting fate — too many outings would eventually lead to capture. Like Lamm, Bentz had a rap sheet to verify his theory. Both men had their fair share of arrests. Bentz is probably best known for his plundering of the People's Savings Bank of Grand Haven, Michigan, in August 1933, with his young protégé, Baby Face Nelson. Grand Haven was a wild, noisy affair, which by sheer luck saw all the bandits, save one, alive and still on the loose at the end of it.

The idea that Bentz teamed up with Lamm and Clark is intriguing, as they would naturally have gravitated to each other. Boren's account states that the three men robbed the First National Bank in Mooresville, North Carolina, just prior to their arrest in Winston-Salem. Boren also says that Lamm, Clark and Bentz jumped bail. As far as I can discover, Boren is certainly wrong on the second of these counts and probably wrong on the first. Only two of the three men jumped bond — Lamm, alias Herbert J. Madsen, and Clark. The third man had tried to escape and punched a police captain. His bond was set higher than that of the other two and in time it was revoked altogether, since it was learned that he had broken out of the Indiana State Reformatory, and there could be no bail for a fugitive from a penitentiary. And, as a matter of fact, as we shall soon see, this escape artist would escape yet again to the shock and disbelief of Winston-Salem, Pendleton, Indiana and San Antonio.

Neither the First National Bank of Mooresville, North Carolina, nor any other bank in the area was robbed at this time.

Wherever Eddie Bentz was in February 1927, he certainly wasn't in Winston-Salem. A much better fit than Eddie Bentz as Winston-Salem's third man is Dan Morgan, a.k.a. Robert E. Willard. We first met Morgan at Frankfort, Indiana, three years earlier when Dad Landy, Charles Norman (that is,

Clyde Nimerick), and "Young Dannie," as he was sometimes called, were arrested for concealing safe-blowing paraphernalia. Morgan, it will be remembered, had fired a shot at the arresting officer, Sheriff Dan Power, on that occasion. Fortunately for both men, Morgan's shot went awry. Morgan was tried for a Frankfort, Indiana, gas station robbery committed on Sunday night, May 18, in a sensational trial at Delphi, Indiana, at the end of June 1924. The jury took less than an hour to reach a verdict. He was sentenced to from ten to twenty-one years at Pendleton Reformatory. He was not yet thirty, so he skirted the state prison at Michigan City. On July 6, 1924, Morgan found himself at the start of a long sentence at Pendleton. On September 21, 1925, a little over a year into his sentence, it was abruptly terminated. Morgan escaped through a ventilator shaft with two other inmates. All three were rounded up within nine months, but Morgan forfeited his $3,000 bond in San Antonio in January 1926. He was gone before the Indiana authorities could dispatch a man to pick him up. Morgan remained free until his arrest just over a year later at Winston-Salem, in league with Oklahoma Jack and Baron Lamm.

That arrest came about purely by luck.

Two Forsyth County deputies were driving down the Belews Creek road on Sunday night, February 20. They saw a sedan bearing Indiana plates, suspiciously parked at the side of the road. One deputy got out of the car to do a stakeout while the other drove down the road to turn around. Somehow, three men got to the abandoned sedan and drove off before the other deputy returned. The deputies got a good description of the car and reasoned that one of the garages in town would have it. Flashlights in hand, the two deputies looked around in the woods and discovered a hole that had been freshly filled in. They suspected moonshiners. Digging up the loose dirt, the deputies soon found an automatic shotgun, a sawed-off shotgun, four pistols, packets of ammo and large-headed roofing nails.[2] Such large heads would have made the nails stand upright when thrown on the roads during a getaway. The deputies gathered up this contraband and went calling on the garages in town. The second garage they came to harbored the sedan with the Indiana plates. Someone in the garage informed the officers that the occupants of the car were staying at the Robert E. Lee Hotel in town. The two deputies added the chief of police and a police captain to the arresting party and went to the hotel. There, they were told that the men had requested a wake-up call for six that morning. The officers told the staff not to bother; they would see that the men got up on time.

Punctually at six, the four officers knocked on the door. When it was opened, the lawmen pulled out their pistols and took command of the room. Pistols were found underneath the pillows on the bed. Lamm and Clark were taken to the police station, while Morgan was taken to the county jail in an effort to separate the men for interrogation. Lamm called himself Herbert J. Madsen of New York City and Clark was James M. Clark also of New York. (As usual, there is no mention of Lamm's German accent.) The third man said his name was Robert E. Willard of Chicago. Lamm, apparently, was the one who offered an explanation for his actions. He was a booze runner—a noted booze runner—running booze up from Pensacola to New York. The booze could be bought for $35 a case in Florida and sold for three times that amount up north. Clark denied knowing both the other men, insisting that he was merely a simple farmer. The *Journal*'s reporter wryly noted that Clark's hands showed no trace of having worked either a hoe or a plow.[3]

The three men said that the car bearing the Indiana plates was not theirs. They said they had ridden in a car with Alabama plates. Authorities confirmed that such a car had been picked up off the streets before the other car was spotted. Inside the car with the Indiana plates was a spade caked with fresh dirt and, more sinisterly, a bloody handkerchief.

As their story didn't ring true and the three men looked to be up to something big, the Winston-Salem officers asked police agencies all over the country for assistance. They were sure that they had taken some big-time operators in the stand-and-deliver way and not just mere bootleggers. Nothing could be found on Clark or Madsen (Lamm), but an investigator found that Willard's prints were a match for that of an Indiana fugitive named Dan Morgan. So was his photograph.

From Illinois, detailed information came in a letter to police chief J.A. Thomas from W.E. Rowens, Jr., of the Illinois Bankers' Association. It singled out Willard as Dan Morgan.

> Dan Morgan is known to us as "Young Dannie" and was a member of one of the worst bank robbery gangs that has ever operated in the Middle West.... We have had Morgan identified in connection with numerous bank robberies in this state which occurred during the years 1922–23–24. He was a very close pal of "Danville Dannie," whose identification we have never been able to establish.[4]

Obviously, the identity of Danville Dannie was as much an issue with the Illinois Bankers' Association as the apprehension of Dan Morgan. Indeed, the identification of Danville Dannie, like the bruited association of Lamm with Butch Cassidy, is one of those fascinating loose ends with which the rise and fall of Baron Lamm is replete. No light even now can be shed on the mystery, though one may toss a few names into the ring—Baron Lamm, G.W. "Dad" Landy and, possibly, E.H. Hunter. Hunter is the least likely, in view of his seemingly late arrival into the Lamm fold, though he could have worked in a gang with Morgan apart from Lamm's gang. Lamm and Landy, though familiar with Danville, Illinois, did not hail from there, and the sobriquet implies long-term residence. Most probably Danville Dannie was a thug of only local reputation.

When Willard was presented with Dan Morgan's photograph, he nearly choked. After he regained his composure, he denied any connection with the other man. He stated his wish not to be rude to the officers as he paced his cell, but he had nothing more to say. All in all, a very telling moment. Willard *was* Dan Morgan. Morgan was looking at two and a half years on a North Carolina chain gang for slugging an arresting officer, besides a concealed weapons charge,[5] but Indiana wanted him back in the pen. Morgan told the judge that he would much rather stay in North Carolina on the chain gang. The judge wasn't sure he had heard the young man aright. No one had ever volunteered for the chain gang before. The judge said that things must have changed since he had been around a chain gang. This observation brought a grin to Morgan's face, which he quickly concealed with his hand.

A round of legal battles loomed. Morgan would fight extradition with all the power within his means. Nevertheless, by week's end, Morgan was headed back to Indiana to serve out his 10- to 21-year sentence, owing to a gas station robbery. Instead of the reformatory at Pendleton, however, Morgan would be going to the state prison at Michigan City because he had turned thirty since breaking out of Pendleton and thirty was the cutoff line for admission to the reformatory.

Morgan's arrest was big news in Winston-Salem. A Chicago gangster — no matter where he claimed residence — was something to marvel at in this region. His every utterance, his every visitation would be chronicled by the papers. The dailies overlooked the fact that Baron Lamm, quite incognito, had gotten away with only a loss of $1,050 — the bond he gladly forfeited — as did Clark. Lamm and Clark were viewed by the authorities as most likely a pair of baddies, but they would certainly leave the state — and that was that. Good riddance to bad rubbish — so long as it was in somebody else's yard. An attorney from Chicago hired the law firm of Wallace and Wells to represent the three prisoners at a habeas corpus hearing. As nothing much had been found on Madsen (Lamm) and Clark, their bond was set at a beggarly $1,050. Morgan's bond came to a whopping $5,000, before being revoked altogether by Superior Court judge T.B. Finley upon discovering that Robert E. Willard was Indiana's Dan Morgan, a fugitive from the state reformatory.

As for Baron Lamm, the *Winston-Salem Journal* could only say this:

> So far as is known, Clark and Masden [*sic*] are not wanted at any point for anything.... So far the two men are not under suspicion for any crime, but the one in which they skipped in this city. Where they are at this time is not known. Masden has been under suspicion at various points, but has never been convicted, according to the records.[6]

No one could know it then, but the clock was already ticking on Baron Lamm. He had less than four years to live.

On Sunday, March 6, the *Winston-Salem Journal* ran this Pollyanna editorial under the caption, "I Was in Prison and Ye Came Unto Me":

> Robert E. Willard, escaped felon from the penitentiary at Indiana, will probably always remember his short stay in Winston-Salem. Part of this time he was a prisoner in the city jail awaiting extradition, but it is not this fact alone which he will recall vividly. He has been in jail before — in fact, many times, and in many places, but during his residence in the Winston-Salem jail something extraordinary happened — two things really. He was visited by a Christian and he learned to pray. Shortly after he was placed in jail, a minister of the city came in to see him ... and ... ministered to his soul. As a result, the criminal's conscience, which he long thought dead, awoke.... A great burden was rolled from his shoulders and he knew again a bit of "the peace that passeth understanding."

The next day's headlines in the *Winston-Salem Journal* sang a different hymn[7]:

WILLARD ESCAPES FROM OFFICERS IN WEST VIRGINIA

Saturday afternoon, March 6, at 1, a Norfolk and Western passenger train left Winston-Salem, bearing Dan Morgan and two Indiana parole officers, Peter F. Stoner and J.H. McCafferty. At Roanoke, Virginia, George M. Calloway got on the train to assist in taking Morgan back to Indiana. The Indiana State Prison in Michigan City was the ultimate destination. In the early morning hours of Sunday, March 7, 1927, the four men were sitting in a stateroom when the train stopped at Vulcan, West Virginia, to take on coal and water.

Morgan seized this moment to gain his liberty. Being heavily shackled, he asked that his shackles be removed so that he could use the washroom. This was done and detective Calloway accompanied him into the smoker. As soon as Morgan got through the washroom door, he spotted a window and dove through it, glass and all. Calloway grabbed him by the heels but was propelled by Morgan through the window. Calloway suffered multiple cuts and broke his right arm in two places.

The train apparently was still stopped when the escape occurred. Since the detective who clung to Morgan was hurt badly from the dive, it was thought that Morgan must have sustained injuries. This, however, does not seem to have been the case. The engineer of an oncoming passenger train saw Morgan running down the tracks and then turning into the woods. West Virginia State Police and Norfolk and Western Railroad detectives scoured the surrounding hills but came up empty in their search for the elusive fugitive. This was the second time Officer Stoner was caught holding the bag with

Morgan. A year earlier when San Antonio detectives announced that they had apprehended Morgan in their city, Stoner was on his way to round him up. When he arrived in San Antonio, he was too late. Morgan had skipped town.

Morgan's flight from the freight train at Vulcan, West Virginia, is the last certain record we have of him. But that he went on to work with Lamm again is likely.

The authorities in Winston-Salem heard the news of Morgan's escape in shocked disbelief. They had some questions. Foremost among these was the presence of detective Calloway on the train. What was he doing there? And, secondly, why were all of Morgan's shackles loosened when he went to the washroom?

These pointed questions were suspended in mid-air, unanswered, but they nevertheless implied that Chicago money — the same pocketbook that had gotten Madsen and Clark off the hook — was at work in Morgan's daring escape.

Two days after the sob sister editorial appeared, the *Journal*'s editorial page was a bit more worldly-wise:

> Crime and criminals in the United States are far better organized and far more efficient than are the law enforcement agencies. Witness the fact that when the news of the arrest of the three men, including Willard, by the local police was given wide publicity a lawyer from Chicago arrived in the city with $7,000 in cash to make bond for them and $2,000 was actually put up to liberate the two against whom there was no specific charge of a highly serious nature. It is only fair to suppose that this money came from the headquarters of the ring of which these men were members in "good and regular standing." Such organizations actually exist and maintain their corps of lawyers to "protect" their members and to liberate them by putting up bond whenever they are arrested. In such emergencies the average bond is of no avail to hold them because they have plenty of money for this very purpose and their associates are far more active in their behalf than is the average citizen to see that the law is enforced.[8]

Today, Baron Lamm and Dan Morgan are largely forgotten in the region where they busied themselves the most in their nefarious trade. But Winston-Salem, with only a nodding acquaintance with the outlaws, found it a real education.

VI

Death Comes to Lafayette

If one's got your name on it, there's nothing you can do.—Sergeant York (1941)

Only Lamm's final robbery compares with the robbery of the Tippecanoe Loan and Trust in Lafayette, Indiana, for the inexplicably bizarre. First, this robbery was bizarre for the way it was handled by Lamm and his gang. Second, it was bizarrely handled by the police. One has to wonder whether the Lafayette robbery wasn't a case of Baron Lamm gilding the lily with too much planning. Or, perhaps, somebody in the gang on this occasion acted on his own initiative and forced a gunfight. Whatever the explanation for the events that happened on this day, it remains unfathomable so many decades later. Like the Clinton robbery, the Lafayette job led to the death of a brave lawman. It may have led to the death of one of the bandits as well. It was all needless and, as with the latter robbery, bandit cunning took a wrong turn.

This tragedy took place on Tuesday, November 1, 1927. The Tippecanoe Loan and Trust had just opened its doors for business at nine and, a few minutes later, five men came in. They were well-dressed and two were wearing spectacles. All five brandished revolvers and meant business. Three started for the tellers' cages, while one stayed in the lobby. Another stood at the door.

Stenographer Helen Cheney had just been to the post office. As she got back to the bank, she saw police captain Charles Arman, dressed in street clothes, just ahead of her. The two exchanged brief greetings. When Miss Cheney went on to ask why the captain was in such a hurry, he did not respond. Instead, he stepped silently, resolutely into the bank. Helen Cheney followed, bewildered. Crossing the lobby, she went inside the railing to go back of the tellers' cages. As she did so, she felt an odd sensation. It was too dark in the bank during business hours even for the first day of November. She brushed by someone standing at the counter. This, too, made no sense. There shouldn't have been anyone standing there — no one she couldn't identify, at least. In the dim light, she turned to look back as she continued walking. It was then that she saw the men and knew that she had just walked into a robbery-in-progress. She gathered up her skirt and ran up the stairs that led to the mezzanine floor.

The next moment would appear to defy all reasonable explanation. Arman was recognized by the bandits immediately. Even though he was dressed like the usual bank patron of that day with a cap and business suit and did not display a weapon, he was recognized as a lawman at once by the bandits.

James "Oklahoma Jack" Clark, a.k.a. William Long (left) and Walter Detrich (right) (courtesy the *Daily Clintonian*).

Someone among the bandits behind the cages north of the narrow passageway that led from the lobby spoke out in a way that surely froze the officer's blood. That certain someone spoke in spare phrases, shorn of any trace of civility but steeped to the hilt in all the scorn of those casting lots on Golgotha. The greeting must have torn asunder the heart and soul of a man doing his level best to blend in with the wallpaper.

"Oh there you are.... We'll get you. We know who you are!"[1]

If Captain Arman was petrified, he did a fine job of not showing it. He had been a cop all his life and had also served valiantly in the Great War. His sinews stiffened as he instantly sprang into action. He fired five rounds from his revolver at the bandits in the cages, one of whom was later identified as Walter Detrich. When he ran out of shells, he flung his weapon at the men and then rushed them. He joined them in close combat, knocking the hat off one bandit and the eyeglasses from two others. His own cap, too, was knocked off onto the floor. But the odds against the officer were overwhelming and he fell with a gunshot wound to his face. He died within seconds.

Mrs. Claude Smith was just opening the door of the bank when she saw Captain Arman drop to the floor. Two bullets whizzed past her, one piercing the screen door and the other lodging in the copper plating of the main doors. Mrs. Smith was too badly shaken to talk to reporters afterwards.[2]

Miss Cheney watched with horror from the mezzanine floor above. She wasn't sure who had fired first, but she saw that Captain Arman stood his ground to the last.

And when the end came, he fell without a sound. The bookkeeper thought that perhaps ten shots were fired in the exchange.[3] But she could not — would not — count them. Besides the fatal wound, Arman had been shot in the thumb and groin. The slugs were from a .45.

Miss Cheney ran up another tier of stairs to the office and began to shout out the window for help.

The bandits did not waste any time. They scooped up a thousand dollars from the cages, all the cash that was on hand. At length, one of the men, probably Lamm, grew uneasy. He said, "Let's get out of here. This is a trap."

A moment later, the bandits were seen by those on the street assisting one of their number to the getaway car. The wounded man was bleeding from the head. It may have been no more than a cut caused by the officer's fist shattering a pair of eyeglasses, but a witness all but put a nail in his coffin when he described the stricken bandit as seen later in the getaway car resting his head on his buddy's shoulder.[4]

Before the shooting started, the bandits corralled everybody in the building and shut them up in the vault. There were seven employees and one patron in the bank when the robbers entered just after nine that Tuesday morning. Margaret Cheney, sister of Helen Cheney and a secretary/treasurer of the bank, pressed the burglar alarm while in the vault working on the combination of the safe. After pressing the alarm, she worked very deliberately as she knew help would be on the way. Oddly enough, she was under the scrutiny of one of the robbers, who must have seen her press the alarm but did not retaliate for her action.

When Fred Goodman, bookkeeper of the Heywood Pulp Company, tried to enter the bank, one of the robbers barked, "You get out of here!" Goodman thought that sounded like good advice. He promptly turned on his heels and went elsewhere — any elsewhere would do.

Another pedestrian, Louise Deventer, caught sight of the gang making their exit from the bank. Baron Lamm seems to be the one singled out for description: "As far as I could see there were six men in the car. The man next to the driver was just closing the front door and was about six feet tall, I should say, a real big man — had on a dark suit, black or dark gray hat and an overcoat — he was waving a gun."[5]

The bandit car backed away from the curb on Main Street. In doing so, a door handle came up flush against the door of another car and locked horns with its handle. The door of the bandit sedan flew open. One of the men inside had to hold the door shut as the car drove on.

The getaway car, a late-model Buick or Hupmobile straight-eight sedan[6] (with most witnesses favoring the latter), went north on Main to Third Street, continued north to Fourth and Brown Street over the levee. It was believed that the bandits went northeast a jaunt before turning northwest and going to Chicago. Word of mouth had it that the gang came from Calumet City. Not a bad guess, as it happened. Most of the big shots in this line of work did — Harvey Bailey and Fred "Killer" Burke, to name two of the most active.

At West Lafayette, Herman Schmitz of the Soldiers' Home caught a glimpse of the sedan with the damaged passenger door and, by his count, the five occupants inside. One of the men in the back seat, as has been said, had his head lying on another man's shoulder.[7]

Strangely enough, someone had penned an anonymous letter telling the police department that another bank in town, the Fowler National Bank, would be robbed the Thursday before the robbery. Chief of police A.G. Eversole ordered all his traffic cops to work in the bank district the few days before and the few days after that Thursday, October 28. He cautioned the banks to have no more cash than necessary in the tellers' cages. As a result, the gang got no more than the minimum amount of money needed to do business that morning — a thousand dollars. All in all, a very odd robbery and one hardly worthy of the legendary father of scientific bank robbery.[8]

Captain Arman was the only member of the Lafayette police force to respond to the robbery. When the burglar alarm had been set off by Margaret Cheney, Arman and another officer, Sergeant Frank E. Burghby, were present in the police station, but only Arman answered the call. Incredibly, when Arman went out, Burghby had no idea what was afoot. The police captain must have made it seem like a false alarm. Apparently, his plan was to catch the bandits by surprise, and he deemed that this could best be done alone — all alone and out of uniform. A number of other officers were then at the courthouse dealing with disorderly conduct (public intoxication) cases, but Captain Arman did not summon any of them. One has to wonder just what he thought was going on at the bank.

Maybe he just didn't know what he was getting into.

One policeman, Charles Weaver, in the wake of the robbery actually chased the bandits in a Ford truck but was badly outdistanced and gave up after a short distance. He was criticized at first for not firing on the bandits as they fled the bank, but attorney John Randolph and others vouched for his behavior, saying that he had had no opportunity to fire on the robbers.[9]

If extra officers were placed on the street, owing to the threatened robbery of the Fowler National Bank, they were not aware of the ruckus that erupted at the Tippecanoe Loan and Trust. Nor was anyone on the streets keen to get involved. There was no vigilante effort directed at the robbers nor any murmur from the ranks of those "pain-in-the-ass, innocent bystanders," spoken of in *The Godfather* (1972). The robbery must have transpired very quickly indeed. The gunfight and Lamm's gesturing with his revolver afterwards out on the street should have provoked some kind of response from the general public, given what happened at Kincaid, Illinois, on September 27, 1924,[10] and at Boley, Oklahoma, on November 27, 1932.[11] Yet nothing happened. Pursuit had waited to get organized, but the bandits did not stick around for it to materialize. Less than sixty miles away, Chicago beckoned.

Chief Eversole and Prosecutor Mark L. Thompson led a posse that took off west out of town, then headed north toward Wolcott. Meanwhile, Dr. A.C. Arnett, commander of the American Legion Post No. 11, high school football coach James Phelan, Eph Caster and Edwin Lyman sped west to the Dixie Highway.[12] Nothing would result from these expeditions, but Detective William Weinhardt of the Weinhardt Detective Agency called from nearby Chalmers, saying that he had picked up "a meager clew [*sic*]." The clue probably had to do with the gang's ultimate destination after leaving Lafayette, a foregone conclusion for any detective over the age of ten.

The next day a number of officers came to Lafayette to investigate the robbery. Harry Webster represented the Indiana chapter of the American Bankers' Association. Joining him were four members of the newly-formed Indiana Bureau of Investigation and Identification. They were Chauncey A. Manning, Albert Schofield, G.P. Wright and Forrest Huntington.[13] The first man would be on hand when the culprits who killed Captain Arman met their bloody end three years later. The fourth man, Forrest Huntington, by then would take a position as an investigator for the American Surety Company. A further three years would pass when he would be involved in the hunt for John Dillinger. A spectacular chase down Irving Park Boulevard in November 1933, involving the bandit and his girlfriend and a number of Chicago policemen, would result from a stakeout set up by Huntington and a stoolie. The ambush failed, but to Huntington's credit, it was activated against his wishes.

That afternoon, Chicago detective chief William O'Connor dispatched a detective squad, known as 21 B, to Lafayette. This high-profile squad specialized in investigating payroll and bank heists. The idea behind this move was that if Chicago was the headquarters of the gang that had hit Lafayette, the detective squad would soon get to the bottom of their identities.

The two pairs of spectacles dropped on the floor of the bank seemed like the best evidential bet, and these were seized on eagerly by investigators. If these were prescription glasses gotten in Chicago, they might well provide the identities of their owners, precisely as Nathan Leopold's eyeglasses had done three years earlier in the famed Loeb-Leopold matter. Apparently, the glasses did not furnish any immediate leads. Indeed, the only real leads lay in eyewitness descriptions of the bandits and associating these with the huge mug books in Chicago.

The bandit trail, predictably, led to Chicago. Employees of the Tippecanoe Loan and Trust were taken to the Windy City to look over five suspects brought in by three crack detectives. The suspects were released after the bank employees failed to identify them. Thereafter, the trail grew cold. For three years, nothing would develop in the case until the horrible events that followed the Clinton robbery.

Captain Arman, 41, was a veteran of the Great War, serving appropriately as an MP in the 309th. A Lafayette native, he had been brought up a blacksmith. After World War I broke out and America entered the fray, Arman resigned from the Lafayette police force to fight in France. He returned to Lafayette after the war and resumed his career as a policeman, becoming a patrolman in 1919. For the next six years, he worked in that capacity. He rose to the rank of police captain on January 4, 1926.

Flags in the city were flown at half mast for Captain Arman's funeral on the 4th. Paul V. McNutt, former commandant of the American Legion in Indiana and then head of the Indiana Law School, was in Lafayette a week after the robbery. He lauded the fallen police captain for his valor. McNutt in six years' time, then Indiana's governor, would be unfairly stigmatized as the man who paroled Dillinger in May 1933.

Captain Arman was eulogized in the resolution of the Transfer Center Merchants Association:

> We ... hereby desire to express our admiration of the gallant conduct of Police Captain, Charles W. Arman, who met death on the field of duty Tuesday morning, 1 November, while battling with desperate bandits robbing the Tippecanoe Loan and Trust Company.
>
> Captain Arman died a hero's death and every resident of Lafayette should feel that the brave police officer gave his life for the community. He not only did his full duty, but displayed rare personal heroism in entering that room of death where the odds were so heavily against him.[14]

The Tippecanoe Loan and Trust Company donated a thousand dollars to Arman's widow, Rose.[15]

What about the anonymous letter that warned the police of an upcoming robbery taking place on October 28 at the Fowler bank? Was this just a juvenile prank lost in the sands of time? After all, Halloween was fast approaching. Or did Lamm himself pen the letter to decoy police into concentrating on the wrong bank at the wrong time? Naturally, after the 28th came and went, police in Lafayette would lower their guard and get onto other things. That may have been the purpose of the letter.

Or it may have been sent by an informer, after a contretemps of some sort with the gang, who happened to get the time and bank wrong; things changed after the split, perhaps.

One intriguing possibility that would explain much of what went on in this robbery has to do with the unidentified bandit who was seen leaving the bank bleeding from the head. Could this man have been a Lafayette native who knew most of the police force in town by sight? If so, this would explain how it was that the robbers knew Captain Arman, despite his being dressed in plain clothes and packing no obvious weapon. That things did not go the bandits' way altogether in this robbery is shown by the manifest haste they made in their departure — leaving two sets of eyeglasses and a hat on the floor. Two bullet holes were found in the wall behind the tellers' cages. These holes were obviously made by bullets from Captain Arman's revolver. But Arman had fired all five rounds from his .38 at the robbers. Three shots, then, must have found their mark.

Did these three shots hit the unidentified robber? If the two men — officer and robber — knew each other due to some previous hostile encounter, this would be all the more reason for the captain to single this man out in the fusillade that erupted in the bank. It is hard to resist the conclusion that Arman got his man. Besides the report of Herman Schmitz about the dire condition of the bandit in the back seat of the car, there is the mute testimony of the hat belonging to one of the bandits that was left at the scene. The hat was picked up off the floor of the bank by a reporter within minutes of the robbery. It was blood-soaked.

That the wounded robber was familiar with Lafayette may have been the case, but, if so, no one who saw him leaving the bank, nor Herman Schmitz, who saw him later in the fleeing getaway car, recognized him. Still, it must be said that, though none of the bandits were wearing masks, it is not likely that a man with a wound to the head would be in full view of bystanders, not to mention the difficulty in making out his appearance while slumped over in the backseat of a speeding car.

The funeral of the fallen officer was held at Lafayette on Friday, November 4. More than five hundred mourners had to be turned away from St. Boniface, where the funeral was held, because there wasn't room for them. Two hundred and sixty-seven cars were in the funeral cortege. It was attended by delegations from police departments and railroad police from across the state of Indiana. Most of these, whose names duly appeared in the *Journal and Courier* for that day, are not names which jump right off the page at you. One of them, however, does — that of Lieutenant Matt Leach, of Gary, Indiana.

When Dillinger first emerged on the scene in 1933, Matt Leach, now

Captain Matt Leach, Indiana State police captain, would become nationally famous. He will turn up in these pages later in connection with Walter Detrich.

Captain Arman died in one of the most fabulous years in American history. What was most notable about 1927 had come to pass by the time of his death on the first day in November, so that he probably discussed at least some of the following events with his brother officers ad nauseam.

Charles Lindbergh had become the first person to fly across the Atlantic in May. The papers were full of Colonel Lindbergh for the rest of that year — and, indeed, for the next few years. Lindbergh was the kind of hero that comes along once in a blue moon.

A sports legend, Babe Ruth, at 33, had his greatest year ever in 1927. He hit 60 home runs, a record for that time and one which would not be assailed until Roger Maris had his own annus mirabilis in 1961, hitting 61 home runs in a season a bit longer than Ruth's.

Boxers Jack Dempsey and Gene Tunney dueled once again for the heavyweight title in September. In round 7, Dempsey had Tunney down for the count but waited too long to go to a neutral corner. As a result, Tunney was able to regroup and hold onto the title.

Crime, too, reared its ugly head spectacularly in 1927. In Hollywood on April 26, a love triangle gone wrong resulted in the death of musical comedy star Ray Raymond after a drunken brawl broke out between actor Paul Kelly and him over the affections of Raymond's wife, Dorothy MacKaye. Both MacKaye and Kelly served time but were able to resume their careers and marry within a few years. The episode made the front pages for a fortnight in May.

On the 18th, Matthew Kimes and eight other bandits did what the Daltons and Henry Starr had failed to do in their criminal careers — rob two banks at once. Robbing two banks at once had been the unholy grail of bank robbers ever since the Daltons initiated the idea and were wiped out at Coffeyville, Kansas, in 1892 in pursuit of it. Kimes and his bunch — the Cotton Top Walker gang — robbed the First National and Farmers National banks of Beggs, Oklahoma. A gunfight of forty-five shots erupted during the latter robbery, resulting in the deaths of a lawman and a woman caught in the crossfire. Kimes was arrested the following month.

On the same day as the double bank robbery, in Bath, Michigan, farmer Andrew Kehoe, unhappy with the local tax situation, blew up a consolidated school, killing thirty-eight children and six adults. The horrific crime had no equal in mass murder in the U.S. for seven decades, until Timothy McVeigh blew up the Federal Building in Oklahoma City on April 19, 1995.

That spring also brought the nation a sensational love triangle gone wrong — the Ruth Snyder–Judd Gray murder case. A corset salesman killed a magazine editor for the love of his wife — and the deceased's insurance policy of $96,000, complete with a double indemnity clause. The trial took place in May. The following year Ruth Snyder and her paramour were executed. Mrs. Snyder died at Sing Sing Prison in New York in the electric chair, and one of the New York papers carried a photo of her snapped at the moment of her execution — a photo as famous as it is grisly. The case was handled rather distantly by James M. Cain in a successful novella *Double Indemnity* (1935), and most brilliantly by Billy Wilder and Raymond Chandler in the celebrated film of the same name, released in 1944.

More sensational than any crime of 1927 was the execution of anarchists Sacco and Vanzetti, on August 23, 1927. The case still fuels controversy concerning the nature of the evidence used against the pair on the one hand and a number of damning statements made by both the trial judge and defense attorney on the other. Riots all around the world followed the execution of the two men.

The year 1927 was also a watershed for Baron Lamm and his gang. It would be the first year that they killed an officer in a bank robbery.

A curious incident took place three days after the Lafayette robbery. The Indiana Bankers' Association received a tip that the West Baden Springs Hotel Bank was going to be robbed. The tip was passed along to authorities. West Baden chief of police Claude Worley dispatched five officers and a state trooper to the bank to keep an eye on it all the next day. The bandits didn't show up. Chief Worley felt that the gang involved was the same that had hit the Tippecanoe Loan and Trust, though on what information that belief was held does not appear. Just the same, one cannot help wondering what was going on with Lamm and his men at this particular time. In this case, as with the Lafayette robbery, there was a tip informing on a proposed bank robbery. In neither case was the tipster identified. The tipster may have been making an effort to mislead authorities in one or both cases, or he or she may have been someone who grew disenchanted with the gang and turned on them in this way.

An interval of barely a week separated the two tips. If the tips were meant to deceive authorities, it is hard to see what was gained in the latter case.[16] Late that Friday afternoon (November 4), Chicago police raided an apartment on Drexel Boulevard, acting on yet another anonymous tip.[17] They took in four suspects to be viewed by eyewitnesses to the Lafayette robbery. The four men, whatever their vices else, were innocent of any complicity in the Lafayette robbery.

VII

The Simple Art of Bank Robbery — Frankfort, Indiana, December 3, 1930

A swell lot of thieves. — The Maltese Falcon (1941)

Clinton County, Indiana's first daylight bank robbery took place in the oldest banking institution in the county, one covered by a plump $125,000 loss policy from the American Surety Company.[1] The robbery of the Farmers' State Bank on the south side of the square in Frankfort, Indiana, remains after eight decades a masterpiece of its kind and the largest Indiana bank robbery loss of its day, more than double the $67,500 of initial reports.[2] The robbery commenced shortly after 2:30 on the afternoon of December 3, 1930, a half-hour before closing time, with no less than twenty-two people in the bank. The robbery took scarcely ten minutes. The robbers went through their paces as though everything had been rehearsed. They seemed to feel that time was on their side and nobody who behaved, said they, need worry.

Just how many robbers were involved varies with each wire service account — six, seven, eight. Not a soul was hurt and not one shot was fired, even though each robber brandished two pistols while "threat'ning the world with high astounding terms." The language, as usual in such operations, was scabrous, and virgin ears, if such found their way into the bank, were violated. Specifics of physical description were almost altogether lacking, despite the fact that none of the men wore masks. Much change escaped their canvas bags and even gold, when it dropped to the floor, was left where it fell. Only a well-disciplined bunch of bad men could leave gold behind, even when guns were sounding in the distance. Only a careful plan would allow for such departures from the norm in a Depression-era bank robbery. Only a criminal mastermind could inculcate such a plan among his subordinates. Their coolness and professionalism did not go unremarked.[3]

At least four and perhaps as many as six men entered the bank. The robbery that was now in progress was announced to bank personnel and patrons in these words:

"Hold up your hands and go to the back and lay down."

The first man through the front door was about 50 and more than six feet tall. The next man was portly, around 65, and called "Dad" by his fellow bandits. These are the only specifics given by those inside the bank. "Portly" made its way from man to man, as did "middle-aged." Somebody waited outside in the getaway car parked in the alley behind the bank. It may have been one somebody or it may have been two. One or both, as the case may be, looked foreign ... that is, Italian ... that is, Chicago ... very, very Chicago. And Chicago was equal to "foreign" always, downstate and next door to downstate. The car itself, as described by a number of witnesses in and out of town, was a black 1929 Buick with yellow wheels and a trunk on the back. It bore Indiana plates, the first three numbers reading "488." A woman may have stepped into an already crowded getaway car when it took off. Or it may have been another man. No certainty here either. More certainly, but rather inexplicably, a man, wearing a hat and overcoat and chewing on a stogie, left the Buick while it sat in the alley and stepped briskly across the street to the Broadlick and Booher bakery. He peered in the window, then went back to the Buick. This man was a lookout. His job was to keep traffic out of the alley where the Buick was parked behind the bank. This he did by walking along the sidewalk and waving off any traffic that tried to approach the alley while the robbery was in progress. We may surmise that the stogie gave him the requisite authority for such an office. A cigar bobbing up and down in such a man's countenance was as good as a handgun in his hand when it comes to diverting uninvited curiosity.[4]

Inside a phone booth in the bank, cashier Harry Cosner was on the phone making a long-distance call when the men walked in. One of the bandits yanked him out of the booth, and the receiver fell, dangling in midair. "Come on out of there. This is a bank robbery."[5] Thus learning the mission of the men as they stepped towards her, a lady with a check offered it to them. It was politely declined with the explanation that cash — the bank's — was what the gang had its heart set on just then. Employees and patrons were hustled to the hallway connecting the counting room and the bookkeeping department. There they were told to lie down and not to look up on pain of death.

The big man grabbed bank clerk Grover Sims and demanded the combination of the vault from him. Sims said that he didn't know it, indicating that cashier Clarence Masters did, however. His attention compelled by a

VII — The Simple Art of Bank Robbery

pistol at his neck and punctuated with a blow to the ribs, the thirty-eight-year-old Masters was marched back to the vault. Masters must have had a word or two under his breath for Sims.

The big man spoke: "Open the vault and be damned quick about it. Or I'll blow your damned head off."

Masters opened the vault, but he made a mistake in his first effort to open the strongbox full of specie, some of which was gold held for the Christmas holidays. The big man jabbed the gun barrel harder against Masters' neck and barked, "You better get it right this time or it will be just too bad!"[6]

With this irresistible incentive, Masters managed to open the strongbox. He was then made to lie down on the floor in front of the vault. In the narrow space between the vault and the tellers' cages, people were being rounded up from every part of the bank. The robbers were intent on making their escape through the bank's back door. To that end, two of the robbers emptied the back office of a bookkeeper and clerk. The man who had looked in the bakery window and who had earlier waved traffic away from the alley was seen to tear a screen off the back door. He stood waiting for the gang to emerge from the bank.

Meanwhile, customers kept entering the bank while the robbery was in progress. One man with a fist full of money offered it to a robber. The robber merely told him to get in back with the rest of the crowd.

Shortly after the Frankfort robbery, Tippecanoe County sheriff Arthur G. Eversole (Lafayette chief of police at the time of the Lafayette robbery three years earlier) passed a Lincoln sedan carrying six men near Lafayette. Two coupes followed the Lincoln closely.[7] A little later, Eversole got word of the robbery and the escaping black Buick. As he was looking for a Buick, he didn't worry about the Lincoln until later. By then, he was almost certain he had overtaken the bandits without knowing it, since at this point, if these were the robbers, they were not traveling in a black Buick any longer. If he did glimpse the bandits, the Frankfort job had been a much larger operation than anyone suspected. When Sheriff Eversole and the Lafayette police got to State Road 52, there was no trace of the black Buick or Lincoln.

Syndicated Hoosier newspaper humorist Kin Hubbard heard about the Frankfort robbery down in Indianapolis and wasn't impressed with either the gang or the penal system. In his column, "Abe Martin," syndicated across the country out of the *Indianapolis News*, Hubbard had this to say: "The car load of 'ole, fat, gray-haired outlaws who robbed the Frankfort bank to the tune of $67,500 prob'ly had jest been paroled to spend their last days with loved ones."[8]

Two striking anomalies present themselves in boldface in connection with the robbery of the Farmers' State Bank. The first has to do with how daring it was for four or five or six men to march into the bank after being let out of the Buick in front of the bank in broad daylight. Such a thing in itself would have been enough to alert passersby that trouble was afoot. Yet no one noticed the men at the peak of the business day. Secondly, the action inside the bank could have been seen by anyone who happened to look in, as there was a prominent plate glass window in the bank's façade, not to mention windows on either side of the door. The door itself was hardly opaque, being largely made of glass. That plate glass window should have troubled the gang, but it seems not to have. Their only measure against the danger the window presented was to herd everyone in the bank to the back just as fast as possible and have them lie down. Even in this they were untroubled, as evidenced by the fact that one old-timer had difficulty getting down on the floor as quickly as the threat seemed to imply. One of the bandits, seeing this, displayed patience unparalleled among the bank-robbing set. "That's all right, buddy," said the bank robber. "There's no hurry. We have plenty of time." One would give a king's ransom to know who this bandit was!

Nevertheless, the robbers were evidently on a schedule, following a prepared plan, and that plan called for entering by the front door and emerging from the back door, something Dillinger tried to do without success at Rockville three years later. But the Dillinger gang knew what to do with large plate glass windows. When they robbed the American Bank and Trust Company in Racine, Wisconsin, in November 1933, gang member Leslie "Big" Homer pasted large posters urging support for the American Red Cross over the front windows. No way of telling whether Dillinger and Harry Pierpont thought of this stratagem on their own or whether Oklahoma Jack Clark and Walter Detrich ran it by the two men while taking tea in their prison issue at Michigan City.

Assuredly, if Clark and Detrich were at Frankfort, they would have noticed those imposing, inviting windows at the front of the Farmers' State Bank, perhaps to the extent of discussing them with other like-minded individuals. They may have mentioned them just long enough to point out that they had good luck on a day when they shouldn't have.

But for those of us looking at the robbery of the Farmers' bank over a span of eight decades, the most baffling problem connected with the robbery has to do with the failure of bank personnel to identify any of the culprits. This almost defies all earthly explanation. Clarence Masters, assistant cashier, who was strong-armed into opening the strongbox inside the vault, traveled to Vermilion County, Illinois, the day after the gang met disaster there. At this time, the Frankfort robbery was, after only two weeks, very much in the air because of the large amount taken (that is, admitted to). Along with the robbery of the First National in Peru the year before, the Frankfort robbery rated the highest among Indiana bank losses in recent memory. Both capers may have been Lamm's. Or it may be that he only did one or the other of the pair. Then, again, both jobs may have been someone else's. Fred "Killer" Burke is sometimes credited with the Peru robbery.[9] A good gambler would give you odds on Lamm for both jobs.

In Danville, Masters saw Detrich very much alive; in Tilton, he saw E.H. Hunter very much dying; and in Sidell, he saw Lamm and Landy very much deceased. But the physical state of the men didn't much matter. He never saw any of these men before in his life. Or so he said.

And so it might have been.

But, then again, one can think of a very compelling reason why it might not have been so.

When Masters made his rounds in the Illinois-Indiana border country, he would have seen that five bandits were accounted for — just five. Yet two weeks before, as many as six or even eight bandits had hit the Farmers' bank. If the gangs were the same, possibly three outlaws were yet on the loose. Masters may have figured that it was best for his safety's sake to draw a blank when endeavoring to recognize the bandits, at least in front of the authorities.

Here, again, there is another complication. Why did not the other bank personnel finger anyone?

Clarence Masters was the only one from the bank's personnel to travel to Illinois in order to identify the fallen bandits. But others in the bank were given the opportunity to finger suspects when Ollie Wright, of the Indiana Bureau of Criminal Identification and Investigation (the last part of the name is usually omitted in newspapers of the time), came to Frankfort from Indianapolis lugging volumes of mug shots under his arms. This was the day after the robbery of the Farmers' bank — December 4.

Whose mugs were in those books is anybody's guess, but one would think that Lamm and Landy and Clark, all put in the jug at some time or other, would be in them. But, just possibly, they weren't. Neither Lamm nor Clark, so far as is known, did time in Indiana for any crime, and Landy had only been arraigned for — but not convicted of — burglarizing the American State Bank in St. Bernice more than six years previously. The charge against Landy was dropped and he did not serve hard time. Even so, it's hard to believe at this late date that Lamm's mug shot was not available to the bank personnel of the Farmers' bank, since the bureau had a file on Oklahoma Jack Clark at this time, as evidenced by an article in the *Indianapolis News* two days after Clark's apprehension in Sidell, Illinois, and just two weeks after the Frankfort robbery. Clark, so far as is now known, did not get busted in Indiana before the Clinton raid.

Immediate suspicion pointed to a gang from Ft. Wayne, possibly Ray Caldwell and his associates.[10] This may have been the focus of the investigation early on, and Lamm and Landy may have been an afterthought brought about by the Clinton robbery. What is certainly odd is that Landy would have shown his face in a Frankfort bank six years after being a ripe subject for a lynching there, and that then, after having shown his face and having his nickname uttered amongst his fellows in that bank, no one immediately thought of him as a suspect.

Who was in on the Frankfort job? A most likely nucleus of the gang which committed this robbery consists of Lamm, Oklahoma Jack Clark and G.W. "Dad" Landy. Detrich probably should be included as being part of this nucleus, too, though he seems to have been something of a wallflower that day. No witness observed this strikingly handsome man. That big man, about fifty, with sandy hair and blue eyes who acted as the leader — at least, of those bandits inside the bank — was most likely Lamm, but it may have been Oklahoma Jack Clark. Except that the age is overripe for Clark, the rest of the description fits. There can be little doubt that the "Dad" among the bandit crew was G.W. Landy, yet even here he passed for a man somewhat younger than he was.

The outside man parading up and down the sidewalk, chomping on the cigar, just may have been Lamm. He may have felt that a supporting role for this particular robbery needed his special talents, trusting Clark, or some other worthy surrogate, to handle things on the inside. Or it may have been the other way around. Clark may have taken the outside gig and Lamm may have commanded those inside. It's just that the sandy hair doesn't seem to fit Lamm. Nor does the age of 50, though the height of six feet does. Lamm's photographs, in so far as they have anything at all in common, suggest dark hair — probably dark brown. This is supported by Lamm's own statement, made on his draft card in 1917, that his hair was dark brown in color. In the end, one just goes with one's instincts — that and the fact that witnesses described the two outside men as being dark and about 45 years of age. Both traits do suit Lamm.

A $2,000 reward was offered for the arrest and conviction of each member of the gang. Half of this was to be paid by the Clinton County Bankers' Association and half by the American Surety Company, the company which insured the Farmers' State Bank.[11]

A curious incident occurred two days after the Frankfort robbery at Stockwell, Indiana, a small town eleven miles east of Lafayette. Around ten at night, two men entered the residence of Oscar Hamilton, a bank cashier. He and his wife were tied to chairs in the living room. A daughter of 15 and her two younger brothers were upstairs asleep in their bedrooms while this was going on. The older daughter, Helen, 19, walked in on the home invasion when she came home with her date. They, too, were tied up. The bandits were chatty. One called himself Butch Bishop, and said, "We are here for money. Times are tough and we cannot make it honestly." But what is most certainly strange is the lack of communication between Butch Bishop and his partner(s). Mrs. Hamilton said that Butch had initially called out the door for someone named Mike. Mike did not instantly appear on the scene. In fact, Mike never showed up. After twenty long minutes, someone calling himself Smitty came in. Unlike Butch Bishop, Smitty wore a mask. It was he who bound everyone, either with belts or scarves. The younger daughter heard the noise below and investigated. Seeing what was going on downstairs, she decided to go to a neighbor's for help. She climbed down a wooden trellis, which gave way under her weight.

The resulting thud rattled the two invaders. Little did they know that the girl would not have any luck raising the alarm until she tried three different neighbors, and then that neighbor would have to drive her eleven miles to Lafayette to summon police. Unaware of the girl's plight in summoning help, the two men deemed it time to go but took Helen along with them. They had originally planned to take Oscar Hamilton to the Stockwell State Bank in the morning and clean it out. But this idea was quickly abandoned upon the flight of the younger sister.

More discrepancies turn up at this point. Helen could only be sure of the presence of two men on this caper, but the Lafayette *Journal and Courier* reported that a third man was on the porch and that a long car picked them all up.[12]

In any case, the two thugs got in a blue Ford sedan with their hostage and drove north to Hammond, as Helen remembered, "as fast as the car would go." In Hammond, where they stayed off the main thoroughfares, they were yet cautious enough to ask Helen to stay down so she wouldn't be seen. Apparently, the two men had more things on their mind than robbery. One of the men — the one calling himself Butch Bishop — made advances to her, but Helen backed him up with a simple "no." At some point, the men mentioned working for Capone. If they did work for Capone, then or ever, a safe bet is that this particular misdeed wasn't part of the job description. The two miscreants decided that the place for Helen was Chicago, in particular the East Chicago Avenue Police station. They seemed not to know Chicago than Hammond, twice having to ask taxicab drivers for directions to the police station. The men thought that the boss wouldn't be too happy that the bank robbery didn't come off, and they reckoned they'd have to try again later. They thanked Helen for not giving them any trouble, but, in the same breath, added that she was to meet them at various places near or in Stockwell the next Monday evening at 7:30 or she would be killed. She was let out in Chicago, was given fifteen cents to hop on a bus to take her to the police station, and was home at the end of that day.

The incident could be easily dismissed as a botched job by a couple of amateurs (with obvious delusions of grandeur), were it not for two things. First, the two men boasted of having been among the bunch that robbed the Farmers' bank a couple of days earlier. They were described as being between 35 and 38 years of age, which is a pretty good fit as far as the Farmers' bank bandits were concerned, though one of the men bore a prominent scar on his face.[13] Second, at least one of the men was armed with two pistols, as was each of the Frankfort bandits. Third, a machine gun was also among their arsenal. Machine guns (in this case, a submachine gun was meant) were the especial tool of the professional underworld, whose headquarters were always taken by crime commissioners and the public alike to be Chicago.

One today can only wonder who these two men were. Had they really been among those who cleaned out the Farmers' bank? They might have been freelances brought along for just one job, perhaps with talents suited to home invasion. Baby Face Nelson worked as a freelance for much of his career. Nelson "made one" on just such jobs as the Stockwell caper. In Mazzon, Illinois, in October 1930, four men (one of which may have been Nelson) held a banker and his family hostage overnight, taking him to the bank the next morning to make a sizable withdrawal.

That there were more men involved in the Stockwell affair is also possible. Helen Hamilton couldn't be sure, but she thought a car was following them as they sped to Chicago. And, as mentioned above, more men than just the pair who rode with Helen were mentioned in some reports. But that Lamm or Landy or anyone who knew their business was numbered among the occupants of the second car is most unlikely.

Whoever else was behind the abduction of Helen Hamilton, no known member of Lamm's gang was ever brought to book for it.

It may be significant that a day or two following the deaths of Lamm and Landy, at a time when Landy, at least, was thought to have participated in the Frankfort robbery, the Stockwell State Bank offered a $100 reward for the abductors of Helen Hamilton. Apparently, the bank did not consider the case over with the death and capture of the Clinton bandits, who were thought to have also committed the Frankfort robbery, a robbery her abductors boasted of to Helen Hamilton.

Just the day after the Hamilton abduction, a far more fitting scenario for Lamm took place in Chicago. Five men robbed the State Bank of Clearing, one of Chicago's community areas on the southwest side, smack up against Midway Airport. It was Saturday morning and just three days after the Frankfort robbery. On this occasion between thirty and forty people were in the bank at the time of the robbery. All were herded to the back and made to lie down on the floor or stand against the wall. The drawers were cleaned out in the tellers' cages, but the vault was left undisturbed. A safe deposit box yielded $50,000. Another one just below would have yielded another $60,000 but was overlooked by the bandits, even though they struck some as professionals. Certainly, the fact that this money was part of a payroll told investigators that this was an inside job.

One line of conversation was recorded. Assistant cashier W.L. Duerr was approached by one of the gang who said, "Give me that dough in there," motioning to the drawer with his revolver.

As with Frankfort, the robbers impressed their victims as well-prepared. They were cool and knew their business. The leader wielded a submachine gun. As with the Milwaukee robbery six years earlier, after leaving the bank, the bandits walked casually to their car — a blue sedan with yellow wire wheels.

One incident occurred during the robbery which was halfway amusing and possibly illuminating. A doctor walked into the bank while the robbery was in progress. The bandit at the door suddenly assumed a drunken gait and bumped into the doctor. He then stuck a pistol in his ribs and announced a robbery. Could this man have been Oklahoma Jack Clark? It was his style.

Was this job the work of the Lamm gang?

The authorities did not number it among his depredations. The day after the robbery, employees of the bank identified the robbers from mug shots. Just who was identified was never made public (though one name, that of a police character, was leaked to the press), but a few days later when Lamm and his gang were wiped out, there was no mention of their being suspects in the State Bank of Clearing robbery. Downstater Glen Nichols and his gang were, however.[14]

Lamm was, however, suspected of a much more modest effort made that same day and right in the same neighborhood.[15]

At 6:45 that same Saturday evening, five men paid a visit to the State Bank of Mundelein, a village thirty-three miles northwest of Chicago. Their motives were not aboveboard. They drove up to the bank in "a high-powered car." Four men got out. Three went inside. One remained out front on the sidewalk. The driver waited at the wheel.

Three bank personnel and two customers were locked in the vault after a teller opened the safe.

A young man was about to enter the bank with a deposit from his father's hardware store. He was intercepted by the outside man and told to get in the getaway car. The youth ran off to get help. He soon returned with the village police chief and a squad of deputies, but by then the robbers had fled. Just over $3,000 was taken from the safe. The investigation into this robbery was ongoing ten days later when Lamm was killed and Lamm, rightly or wrongly, was the main suspect.

The number of robbers involved was the same as would be used at Clinton. The modus operandi differed only in shutting the innocents in the vault — something not done in any of Lamm's four best-substantiated bank robberies — Milwaukee, Lafayette, Frankfort and Clinton. Also, the amount taken was pretty meager for a Lamm robbery. Considering that Frankfort and Peru, if the latter was indeed his handiwork, netted Lamm and his gang well over $200,000 between them, the Mundelein jackpot seems out of character. It can only be accounted for if one assumes that Lamm was expecting a larger haul such as a payroll stored in the safe.

And whoever heard of robbing a bank at 6:45 on a Saturday evening, even during the Great Depression? That it was an unusual thing to do doesn't exactly point away from Lamm, but it was certainly something that no big-time outlaw ever did. The odd time suggests an outlaw gang not among the forefront of bank robbers. Lamm was a bank robber who observed bankers' hours. As Virgil Starkwell observes about crime in the film *Take the Money and Run* (1969)—"The hours are good." Lamm probably didn't even bother banks on the weekend, unless, of course, he did the aforesaid Clearing job, which isn't likely.

The State Bank of Mundelein was hit two other times in the thirties, on both occasions by the same gang. The gang's method was to hit the cashier's home first, then drive with the cashier to the bank. Three of the four culprits were caught before they could strike the bank a third time.

VIII

Clinton; or, The Wheels of Chance

So much can happen in a year —
So much can happen in a day. — *Hail the Conquering Hero* (1944)

And yet new *Hydraes* lo, new heads appear
T'afflict that peace reputed then so sure. — Samuel Daniel (1594)

So utterly at variance is Destiny with the little plans of men.
— *The First Men in the Moon* (1901)

Changes tend to throw you. — *Giant* (1956)

Tuesday, December 16, 1930, began as frigidly cold. At 7 A.M., under cloudy skies, the temperature was 14 above in Terre Haute. Further west, as the day wore on, the sun would peek through the clouds and the temperature would reach 25 by noon and 30 by 3 P.M. Surprisingly, considering the time of year, snow cover was practically nonexistent. Snow would not fall for another two days. On the whole, the 16th was a very even-tempered day, fine for diving into a ditch and ducking machine gun fire.

Clinton, Indiana, over on the western edge of the state, just above Terre Haute, was a coal-mining town and largely a melting-pot of central and southern European stocks. Fifteen thousand people — two thousand of them coal miners — made it their home. Since half of the town was of Italian extraction, Clinton was nicknamed "Little Italy." For many years, until well past mid-century, Columbus Day, with its colorful parade, was the big event each year. Apart from an occasional store robbery or mugging, non-support was about the only crime that kept the court dockets occupied in nearby Newport.

In the days just before Baron Lamm and his gang hit town, there had been a rash of burglaries and thefts in Clinton. The public was advised to keep an eye peeled for suspicious-looking strangers. Indeed, there should have been plenty of watchfulness from Clinton's citizens. As it turned out, there were some strangers staying in Clinton just then. There were five of them — four men and a woman. The five stole a handbag at a boarding house, and groups of five should have come under suspicion. As for Lamm, if he prepared for the Clinton robbery in the textbook manner he himself patented, he would have been in town about the time everyone was on the lookout for strangers. What is little short of amazing is that no suspicious-looking parties were reported in town; that is, if the Lamm gang was hanging around. Perhaps the woman confounded the vigil. People were looking for a party of five, but not precisely five men.

There had been a big bank robbery at the First National in Clinton almost exactly two years before, but the town seemed to be getting over it at long last. Harvey Bailey and his bunch came to town on December 20, 1928, made a haul of some forty thousand and left almost without incident. A teller got a shot off at the fleeing getaway car, but Harvey Bailey, in 1973, didn't even see fit to recall it. Vigilantes took up Bailey's trail, but once the gang reached the first paved road beyond the Wabash, it was all over. Bailey and company disappeared.

The robbery must have made an impression on Baron Lamm. He probably heard about it soon afterward from Bailey himself in Calumet City. Lamm probably licked his chops as he heard how easily Bailey had walked off with forty G's. Lamm had worked the area before for much less — unless, of course, you take it in the aggregate, as probably you should. He put Clinton on the back burner until things cooled off in that town. But Clinton, at a different bank, must always have been on his short to-do list.

The population of the United States in 1930 amounted to 122,775,046 souls. On this Tuesday in December, the five worst drove up to the Citizens State Bank at 141 South Main in Clinton just a few minutes past 9 A.M. The bank had opened its doors at 8:30 and would close at 4 that afternoon. The bandits must have had a motive for coming this early in the business day. It may have been a coal mining company's payroll. The gang was in a black 1931 Buick sedan bearing Lake County, Indiana, license plates.[1]

The next five minutes would be crucial, as Lamm must have known, but he could not possibly have foreseen how they would cut short his life. Nobody could have. These five minutes would lead to more than a dozen different decisions by the gang that morning and every last one of them would be resolved all wrong.

There were five employees and one customer in the bank when the gang struck. Arthur V. Hedges, the bank's cashier, was 65. He happened to be in the washroom when the robbers walked in. Two bookkeepers were on hand — Louella Cloutier, 27, and John Nolan, 24. Also present were a teller, Lawrence

VIII — Clinton; or The Wheels of Chance

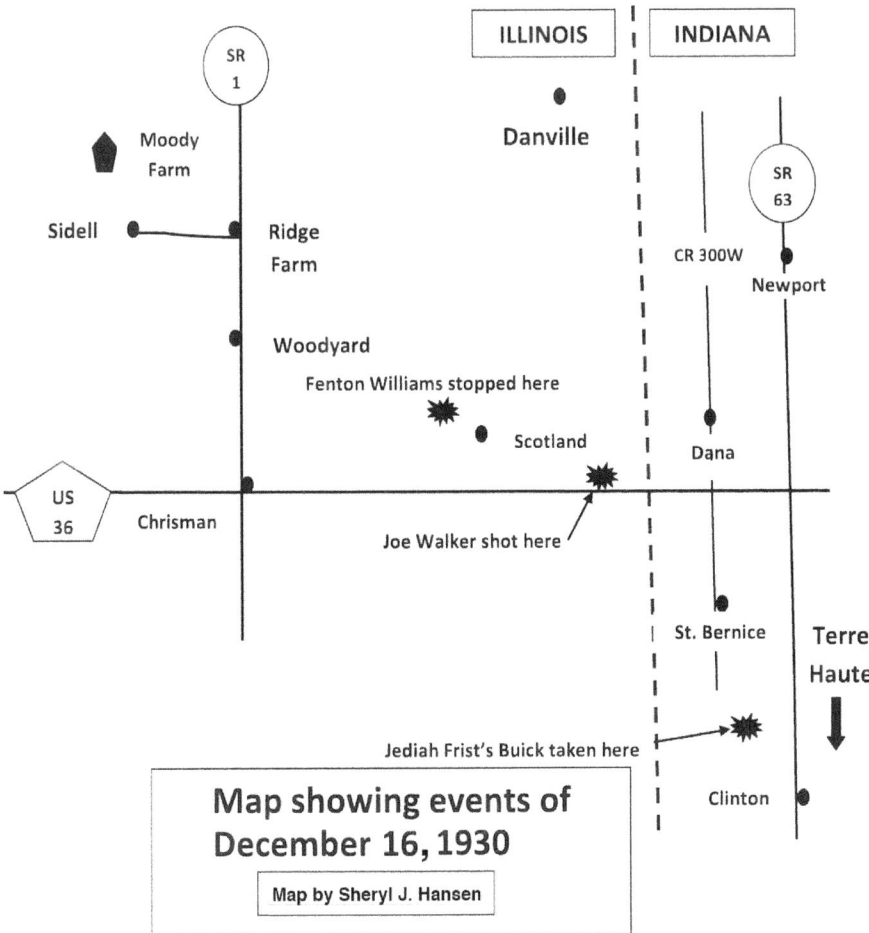

Map showing events of December 16, 1930

Map by Sheryl J. Hansen

Jackson, 26, and assistant cashier Pete Voto, 36. Of the five employees in the bank, four would talk to the newspapers and would later testify at the trial of the two surviving bandits. Louella Cloutier neither talked to the papers or testified. We do not know a thing about how she was treated by Lamm and Detrich in the bank when the male employees were made to lie on the floor and received some rather harsh language as incidental music to accompany the robbery. Odd as it must seem that Miss Cloutier could keep her feelings bundled up in her heart, it may not mean much. Of the three customers in the bank before the robbery was completed — all were male — only one was asked to testify at the trial two and a half weeks later.

Customer John Moore, a shoe repairman whose shop was just down the street, was at Lawrence Jackson's window making a deposit when the robbers

The Citizens State Bank an hour and a half after the robbery (Indiana Historical Society, M0888).

entered. There were four of them. After they disembarked from the black 1931 Buick on the other side of Main Street from the Citizens State Bank, the four bank bandits split up into pairs. Baron Lamm and Oklahoma Jack Clark entered the bank from the north from the Rosenblatt corner just up from the bank. A minute before, Dad Landy and Walter Detrich had stopped to talk briefly before entering the bank from the south.

Inside the bank, Clark stopped at the door. In the center of the lobby, Lamm stood with his hand in his overcoat pocket. His coat was unbuttoned and loose enough to reveal the brown-checked suit coat underneath. Detrich stood beside him, glancing nervously in turn at the one customer and the bank employees.

Landy flanked Lamm on the other side. Were it not for their restless eyes, they could have been ordinary businessmen up to this point, dressed as they were in Fiske felt hats and stylish overcoats, the kind that in *42nd Street* would surely have begged a walking stick tucked under one arm. Clark, however, wore bright blue bib overalls and a lumberman's coat. This attire, no doubt, was scripted so as to make him blend in with the working class. But it would take a lot more than this to make Clark look like an honest man, locally or otherwise. For one thing, he should have begged, borrowed or stolen some calluses. Though his paws were as big as catcher's mitts, they were hardly those of a hard-handed man unused to study.

Lamm now took the podium for the final time.

"Achtung! Achtung! This is a holdup. Go to the back and lie down!"[2]

Lamm, as always, headed for the gate in the railing separating the desks of bank personnel and offices from the lobby. Cashier Pete Voto looked up and saw the bandit leader storm through. Voto took him to be a bank examiner, with an ax to grind. Right behind the large outlaw was Landy. Voto could scarcely believe his eyes. In Landy, he saw a hoary-headed man of seventy-one with the countenance of a death's head and the disposition of a dreadfully-attended diva. When Landy saw the cashier observing him with reportorial regard, he quickly nixed the notion. "Shut your eyes!" he growled, raising his .38 revolver.

Landy herded the employees and Moore to the back, where they were made to lie face down. Such folk constituted the "floor brigade" because they were to have no more temperament than a rug. Landy kept a close eye on them just in case somebody effervesced. As a first-rate yegg, Landy was totally wasted in this capacity. He could have taken the bank all alone some unhallowed midnight with nothing more than an acetylene torch, a crowbar and a pair of tennis shoes, all borrowed, of course.

Not the man to overlook little things, Lamm checked the washroom. Hedges, being more present than he might have wished, was marched to the back and gathered among those prostrate with the need for survival.

There were now six people on the floor beneath the gaze of Landy's watchful revolver—five men and a woman.

Sizing up the huge vault in back, Lamm looked around for someone to open it. The bandit leader pulled teller Lawrence Jackson to his feet, probably because Jackson was in the process of taking money when the bandits walked in. Jackson told the outlaws that he wasn't able to open the vault as a time lock was in place. Lamm doubtless expected to hear such a reply, but that did not make him like it any better. He promptly lashed out at the teller with the butt of his revolver. Jackson went down in a heap, dazed and bleeding from the forehead.[3]

"Don't you strike that boy!" Arthur Hedges shouted, not sufficiently valuing his own skin. "Neither he nor anyone else can open that vault for you now."

Hedges was permitted his two-cents' worth, probably because Jackson groggily offered to prove that the vault wouldn't open. He grabbed a large iron crank lying beside the vault and slammed it hard against the lock on the vault. Nothing happened. This exhibition was apparently convincing. Lamm and Detrich then cleaned out the tellers' cages. Next, Detrich with his huge hog leg prodded Jackson up to the small safe in front. Money needed to get through the day was taken from the vault and placed in the safe at the start of each day.

This time Jackson was able to be of some service. The take from the small safe and the cages, counting securities, amounted to $15,567. The mining payroll was either in the vault under the spell of the time lock or non-existent. A take of less than $16,000 strongly suggests that the payroll was not part of the haul. In Kincaid, Illinois, six years earlier, a bank held a mining payroll of $60,000. It is such numbers as these that one expects from a payroll job. The problematic payroll could only have been tucked away in the vault. Lamm must have been aware of such a turnabout, and yet there is no evidence that he had a plan B other than grabbing up all the money outside of the vault.

Initially, the money was put in paper bags, but as these began to give way beneath their illicit burden, dark typewriter covers were substituted. As mentioned above, a mining payroll was to figure in this loot. If there was anything to the payday angle, it was obviously the reason the gang hit the Citizens State Bank on this particular day. In fact, fear of losing the payroll during business hours may be the reason the gang struck just after the bank opened its doors instead of at the end of the day, a strategy which had brought them such good luck two weeks earlier at Frankfort.

Two more customers walked in during the robbery. They were greeted by Clark and then made to go to the back. The first man was C.N. Hawley, a Clinton telegraph operator. When he heard Clark say, "Now I've got you," he responded with, "Oh, no, you haven't." He thought Clark was joking. The desperado's revolver told him he'd better not laugh until he got home.

The second patron, Harry Call, an insurance man of forty-six, was to play the part of the gang's Achilles' Heel.[4] Harry Call was the last man on earth that should have gone to the bank that day, if four lives were to be spared. Call was one of those people who followed a routine at the start of each working day. As soon as businesses opened, he would go to the bank, hand the cashier his bankbook and deposit, then cross the street and go to the post office. Afterwards, he would return to the bank and pick up his passbook. On this particular day, too, he had something to deliver to Willis Hedges at the bank.

Not only did Call have a daily routine, but he had a friend who counted on his observing that daily routine. You could almost say that he banked on it. Barber Ed Vansickle had a shop a block down from the Citizens State Bank, and through his front window, he could see everything that was hap-

Barber C.E. Vansickle. On the back of this photograph of barber C.E. Vansickle, newsman Jack Cejnar wrote, "Would you run this gauntlet if you were a bank bandit?" (Indiana Historical Society, M0888).

pening on Main Street.⁵ His barber shop was next to the city jail and city hall at 142 Mulberry Street. Vansickle saw Call go into the bank but did not see him come out. His vigil went on for several minutes. In itself, this may not have occasioned much concern in the burly barber, but he had also seen two sets of strangers enter the bank just ahead of Call. Such numbers might add up to a bank robbery. Suspicion was augmented by the knowledge in recent days that the Frankfort Farmers' Bank, hit less than two weeks earlier, had been cleaned out of $140,000, not the $67,500 originally reported. Bank robbery was in the air just then. The Frankfort robbery was the largest of the year in the state, if not the largest haul ever in Indiana.

The barber voiced his suspicions to a young employee and a friend, who had stopped by for a visit. Growing more suspicious by the second, Vansickle kept his eyes glued to the bank.

The robbers had about scooped up what money was available to them when Clark, standing at the door, mentioned that the black Buick had returned. This prompted a wisecrack from Detrich. As he watched Jackson pulling bags from the safe, he shouted, "Shake it up. We're double parked outside!" It is not a matter of record whether or not anyone looking down his gun barrel enjoyed this irregular humorist's levity. Generally, God or the Fates, or whoever runs that dicey department, likes someone with a sense of humor, but not today. On this day, a good attitude and a sense of humor availed nothing. The bandits' hard fate had been set in stone.

The contents of the safe and the cages would have to do. As Baron Lamm knew, the clock was ticking. The gang had been in the bank more than five minutes. The vault was too big a job for daytime safe cracking. For his part, Landy must have yearned for a chance to give the vault a whirl some other time when he had a pair of roughnecks like Danny Morgan and Charlie Norman (Clyde Nimerick) to assist. But there would be no burglaries today; Lamm knew it was time to go. So far, he was on top of his game. Things had gone so swiftly that neither Voto nor Hedges would be able to finger Detrich and Clark at their trial two weeks later. Whatever was missed in the vault was no sweat if the safe and the cages were true. The robbery had been going on long enough.

Vansickle decided to head up to the bank. In his car parked at the curb in front of his shop, Vansickle had a double-barrel shotgun. He was a man who liked to hunt, and he kept a gun in the car quite often this time of year. The barber loaded the shotgun as he walked. He had something more than just a notion that he'd need it.

One of those surreal moments occurred now that always seems to accompany matters of life and death. As the barber walked up the street, a man who was a part-time merchant, part-time auctioneer and full-time busybody saw the shotgun and wanted to do a little horse-trading.[6] He had a pooch in hand. How, he asked, would the barber like to have a first-rate hound? Vansickle, without taking his eyes off the bank, put the man off with, "No, thanks. Don't need a dog for what I'm hunting today." The busybody kept after him, wondering what he was up to. Vansickle went on in silence.

"Just what exactly are you hunting today?" inquired the busybody.

"Bandits," Vansickle returned, grimly.

It was at this point that Lamm, Detrich and Landy hustled out the little door of the bank. Lamm had his right hand in his overcoat pocket and his left hand clutched a shopping bag full of loot. Detrich and Landy maintained the same posture, only grasping typewriters covers in their left hands. Pulling away from the curb slowly, E.H. Hunter picked the three men up. They climbed in back.

Somewhat belatedly, Oklahoma Jack Clark came bounding out the door of the bank with a dark bag full of loot. Hunter threw open the passenger door of the Buick and Clark slid in front.

The Buick was headed south on Main when Hunter spotted the approaching barber, double-barrel in hand. He quickly jerked the vehicle left into a U-turn at Mulberry Street and struck the northeast curb, resulting in the "dreadful thunder" of a blowout. The right front tire had blown. The back door on the passenger side flew open on impact and a large gasoline can flew out, grumbling its way down the sidewalk. Probably no one in the car or out of it yet knew what that meant. It was the clanging of Baron Lamm's death knell.

One thing alone was clear. This was no time to stop and remedy the situation. The Buick kept going. Apparently Dad Landy had an idea where things were headed, for he rose up in the back seat and lunged at Hunter. Those on the street could see Detrich and Lamm, on either side of Landy, trying to restrain the old freebooter. The busybody, now devout in Vansickle's take on the bank robbery, lifted up his voice, "trumpet-tongued," and proclaimed the alarum — "Bank robbers! Bank robbers!"

Heads turned and curtains were pushed back. There was a whiff of burnt rubber in the air.

Vansickle withheld his fire as the Buick went past because he was still not sure that a bank robbery had taken place. For their part, no one inside the Buick fired on him either. When the Buick, now going north, went up on a curb as it turned to go west on Vine Street, Vansickle thought it time to fire on the vehicle. Probably the car by now was too far away for a shotgun to do any real damage. In any case, the weapon did not fire. In all the excitement, the barber had forgotten to release the safety on the shotgun. This was to be the last break Baron Lamm would ever get.[7]

Clinton chief of police Everett "Pete" Helms (courtesy the *Daily Clintonian*).

Clinton day patrolman Walter Burnside (courtesy the *Daily Clintonian*).

The gang now headed west; first to Seventh Street, then to Ninth Street. Apparently, the original getaway route was to go straight out of town south on Main, then get on U.S. 41 and head to Terre Haute. That plan had to be ditched since they were now going west and would need to go south or east to connect with the finest paved road in the area — U.S. 41. A new plan had to be devised. This one, as the *Clintonian* somehow divined, was to get on State Road 63 and head up to Danville, Illinois, where the gang had stayed at a hotel the night before.[8] At the moment, nobody was chasing them and Danville must have seemed like a good bet. First, though, they would have to change tires.

C.N. Hawley, the telegraph operator among the captives in the Citizens State Bank, waited until the coast was clear, then got on the phone and called the Clinton Police Department. There were six officers in the department, four of which worked the night shift. Only two officers were on duty at this time. They were sitting by a stove and talking to their favorite locals — an attorney, a reporter and a judge. These two officers were chief of police Everett "Pete" Helms, 31, and day patrolman Walter Burnside, 39. Helms had the face of a dark-haired cherub and an ironclad sense of duty. Burnside, though still in his thirties, was a kindly, grandfatherly type. Both officers tore out of town less than two minutes after hearing the news of the robbery. Their cruiser was in Hershel Cheeks' garage being serviced this particular morning, and Cheeks had obligingly loaned the department an Oldsmobile coupe.[9]

At the Bell Telephone exchange in Clinton, the operator who made the connection from the bank to the police department notified the head operator,

25-year-old Hazel Haase, that something was up at the bank. In no time, Miss Haase was calling police departments and constables in all communities that might be crossed by the bandits in their flight. Her persistence in alerting businesses and law enforcement personnel throughout the region on this day would earn her, among other things, a medal from her employer and fifteen minutes of fame in the *Hoosier Banker* the following month, a publication that scrupulously avoided naming the outlaws concerned.

As the bandits went down Seventh Street at high speed with the right front tire bumping along, they drew the attention of a young car salesman named Charles Clark. Clark was on his way to work at the time, but he followed the suspicious Buick for four blocks until it hit the Fairview Road going seventy. All the roads in this area were still unpaved in this day. Only U.S. 36, eight miles to the north, and U.S. 41, just to the east and south, were paved. Hunter's job, therefore, driving on the rim and going seventy on such roads, was a remarkable feat — as Helms later observed. Clark decided to continue on to work, which was a car lot three blocks down from the Citizens State Bank. There he would spread the word about what he had encountered on the way. Clark's employer, Ernest Boetto, owner of the Boetto Motor Company, a Dodge Brothers dealer, was in his office when Clark brought word of the bank robbery at about 9:30. He immediately had a high-powered Dodge-8 sedan ready to go in pursuit of the bandits. Boetto was a special deputy sheriff, appointed by both the Indiana Bankers' Association and Sheriff Harry Newland. He was also a crack shot. He had been in the Great War and, as everyone vouchsafed, was quite the best marksman in Vermillion County. He grabbed a .30-.30 rifle, a .38 revolver and a bag of shells. Clark, who could drive like a bandit himself, got behind the wheel.[10]

It was 9:30. A chase that would encompass some seventy miles of running battles was underway. Just moments before, Helms and Burnside, in the Oldsmobile coupe, went to the bank where a crowd was gathering. They were told that the bandits had gone north. They took Sixth Street north out of town in pursuit of the bandits.

They knew they were looking for a car with a flat tire and five or six men in it. One news account says that the Clinton lawmen first saw the bandits at the old covered bridge on Ninth Street.[11] Once out of town, they dared not take hills too casually.

It was near the Summit Grove schoolhouse, just

Dodge dealer Ernest Boetto (courtesy the *Daily Clintonian*).

north of town on S.R. 63, that real contact between lawmen and bandits was made. Here Lamm and his men decided to replace the spent tire. All but one of the bandits were out of the Buick. Two of them kept their eyes on the officers while another put on a spare tire. The fifth, Lamm, stood by giving orders and gripping his trusty revolver tightly. While this work was being done, the two sentries, using a submachine gun and a pistol, fired on the approaching Oldsmobile. Helms turned right down a side road, just in front of a hill on top of which stood the Harlow Frist farm. Helms and Burnside had gotten too close.

"Get the one in uniform!"

Suddenly, bullets rained on the Oldsmobile and one bounced off the passenger door handle into Patrolman Burnside's Sam Brown belt, bruising one of his ribs. As day patrolman, Burnside was the one wearing his uniform. Chief Helms pulled over and got Burnside out of the car. Burnside had passed out. Helms took his pistol. He then fired over the hood of the Oldsmobile at the bandits, first with his own pistol, then with Burnside's. One of his shots, Helms would learn later, parted Walter Detrich's hair.

A car now turned down the side road coming toward Helms. The bandits fired on the car and the driver kept going. Helms could not identify this driver, and he does not otherwise turn up in the record.

Harlow Frist had heard all the shooting while preparing to feed his livestock. From a bluff overlooking the intersection, he watched the action from a vantage point not totally immune from the bandit machine gun. A stray bullet pinged and sent Frist devoutly to the ground. The sheepskin-lined denim coat that Frist was wearing now sported a bullet hole. Frist breathlessly spoke to Helms a moment, then went to telephone for help.

In a few minutes, the tire was replaced and the bandits sped on. But Lamm's hard fate continued, too. In little more than a mile, the new tire gave out. It may have been weakened by one of Helms's bullets. Whatever caused the flat, the bandits got off the road and pulled into the yard of the Thomas McWethy farm home.

The bandits had used their spare and needed a different car. They were in luck—a fool's gold kind of luck. A 1927 Buick master-six sedan, dark blue with black trim, was coming down the road from the west. The driver was 71-year-old Jediah Frist, an ex-farmer now living in tiny Dana and father of the aforementioned Harlow Frist. He was heading south from Dana to the old homestead, currently occupied by his 38-year-old son, Harlow. Guns trained on Frist, the five bandits besieged his car.

Walter Detrich pulled Frist out of his car, gently, as Frist said afterwards. Clark came up on him with the machine gun. It nudged Frist's chest. Lamm explained to the old man, as they stood on the side of the road, that the car

VIII — Clinton; or The Wheels of Chance

Jediah Frist and his 1927 Buick (Indiana Historical Society, M0888).

was needed but that Frist would be paid for its use. A headstrong man, Frist gave the orders as the men removed sacks of sugar and flour and an empty gasoline can from his backseat. The bandits did the unloading — or, at least, two of them did; Hunter, Landy and Lamm were more concerned with getting the Frist Buick turned around. The bandits then put weapons and loot in the new car. Frist was given $500 in gold by the men. The gang also left a lot of silver in the original Buick, being in too big a hurry to gather it up.[12]

No shots were fired here — by the lawmen. Helms and Burnside, who had now come to and was spoiling for a fight, did not want to endanger anyone in the McWethy home. The bandits, however, kept up a steady stream of submachine gun fire on the lawmen just to keep them honest. This action took place on the Fairview road, a bit to the west of the Summit Grove elementary school.

Ensconced and probably bubbling over in their new Buick, the bandits went west. Before long, though, they would realize that something was not as it should be.

A moment after the outlaws departed, the two Clinton officers stopped at the McWethy place long enough to tell the owners to call Hazel Haase at the Clinton exchange and alert her as to what the bandits were driving just now and the direction they were headed in.

The speedometer of the Frist Buick quickly climbed up to 30–35 and then would go no more. The bandits deep-searched one another's faces. What trick had fate played on them now? Unknown to the gang, and probably to Frist as well, Harlow, as one of his concerned five sons, had installed a governor on the automobile to keep the old man from endangering himself and others on the highway. A block of wood under the accelerator and a rotary clip had done the trick.[13]

The bandit Buick, with the machine gun firing sporadically at the two pursuers, continued west at a snail's pace. Nevertheless, Helms had to slow down every time they came to a hill because of a possible ambush by the bandits on the other side. Clark had busted out the back window of Frist's Buick so that he could fire the machine gun at them. The bandits weaved in and out of back roads trying to lose their pursuers, but their speed was too slow for that.

When the Buick got to State Road 71, it proceeded north. The gang may have wanted to make Danville even now, but with yet another crippled Buick, they could not hope to outdistance pursuit. It was to be rolling with the punches and flying by the seat of the pants from here in.

For their part, Ernest Boetto and Charles Clark were coming into the picture after the switch at the McWethy farm. They could easily spot the tracks in the unpaved roads made by the first Buick before its abandonment at the McWethy farm. Chunks of rubber from the blown-out tires and chunks of the rim lay here and there along the side of the road. When they got to the McWethy place, a number of men bearing shotguns stood around the overwrought bandit Buick. At first, the two possemen wondered who these armed men were. Cautiously, they stopped a hundred feet from the farm home. A couple of the men walked up to their car, telling them that bandits had stolen Frist's Buick. Frist was nearby, hovering over his groceries with clenched fists and bellowing about what this world was coming to. Boetto and Clark were told by the McWethys what had taken place and that the chase was headed west.

Meanwhile, back at the telephone exchange in Clinton, Hazel Haase was busy informing police and sheriff's departments in the area that a bank robbery had taken place and that the bandits might be coming their way. She called Sheriff Harry Newland at Newport right off, and he in turn got in touch with Joe Walker. Joe Walker had been a Vermillion County deputy sheriff until the spring primary when he ran for sheriff and lost to his old boss, Newland. The incumbent went on to beat his Republican opponent in the November 5 election, five weeks earlier, by a thousand votes. For the past eight months, Walker had worked as a mechanic at the Chevrolet garage in Dana and moonlighted as a detective for the Indiana Bankers' Association. As if these duties weren't enough, he was also a volunteer fireman for Dana.

Walker, 31, was battling the bug on this day, but when Newland called, he responded like a whole man — no easy task in a time which still vividly recalled the 1918 flu pandemic. He grabbed a revolver and a .25-.20 rifle and enlisted two others "of the boys," Harold "Pete" Scott, a Dana merchant, and Homer Hamm, a Dana store manager. Hamm drove his Ford touring car. Both Walker and Scott brought along .25-.20 rifles, Walker tucking one pistol in his belt and Scott setting a .45 and a .38 beside him on the seat.

Walker may have been out to prove his mettle once and for all. Harvey Bailey had gotten away clean after a Clinton bank robbery two years before when Walker was a deputy under Sheriff Harry Newland. That wasn't going to happen again, if Walker could help it. Whether he had designs on a future election or was just hell-bent on rounding up bank robbers that had violated his turf, it is plain that he meant business.

Joe Walker (courtesy the *Daily Clintonian*).

In 1993, Margaret Helms, the widow of Everett Helms, remembered Joe Walker: "Joe Walker wasn't tall and he wasn't real heavy. I would call him a medium-sized person. I don't think he'd be quite six feet tall. I knew him when I saw him to speak to. I just was never around where he was to any extent. Of course, he was probably up around the jail and I wasn't there very often. He was a really nice person."

When asked if Walker could be fearless to the point of being foolhardy, she replied, "Reckless, that's really the word." It is also the word that the local paper used to sum him up at his death.[14]

Walker and the other two men drove south from Dana in the Ford touring car. Walker was on the left running board. The Dana men came to Tillotson (sometimes called Tillson) corner, an intersection five miles south of Dana. Hamm went to the Tillotson house to get in touch with the telephone exchange in Clinton to get the latest news on the bandits. He was told that the bandits were headed that way in a Buick that belonged to Jediah Frist. Before Hamm was back in the touring car, the Frist Buick went by the intersection. The Dana men knew Frist and recognized his car. They followed it immediately.

Apparently the bandits were not disturbed by the presence of the Ford touring car following them. The bandit machine gun did not spit out its venom at them. The Dana men must have been stalking the Buick and nothing more. Scott was not shooting his rifle just yet. Probably each side was waiting for the other to shoot first so as to declare who they were and what they were up to.

After two or three miles, Helms and Burnside caught up with the Dana men. Helms had been tailing the Buick a discreet half-mile back. The impetuous Walker was motioning with his arm at the Clinton men.

"Come on, you yellow sons of bitches, follow me!"[15]

"Stay back," Helms shouted to Walker. "Don't get too close. They have a machine gun!"

As Walker and the others seemed to pay no attention to his warning, Chief Helms repeated the information about the machine gun. He also mentioned that Burnside had been wounded by the bandits. Helms advised going slow and taking potshots with a rifle. There would be others on the road ahead to assist in overtaking the gang. Helms then allowed the touring car to take the lead in the matter, hoping they would exercise due caution.

The gang decided that pursuit was growing too onerous now and that their getaway car had taken them as far as they cared to go in it. They looked

Stock trader F. Wells Gilbert and his Chevy cattle truck (note the bullet hole in the windshield) (Indiana Historical Society, M0888).

VIII — Clinton; or The Wheels of Chance

around for another ride. The bandits were now on a paved road, U.S. 36. They could be sure that somebody would be coming along shortly who would be just what they needed. That somebody was Wells Gilbert, a 68-year-old stock trader from Dana, who was going west to Scotland, Illinois, to do some hog trading. He was riding in his black Chevy (Carmack) cattle truck. His driver and assistant was 17-year-old Roy Gritten, also of Dana.

Just moments before, Gilbert had been at a Dana garage — just possibly the one where Walker worked — having a new tire put on his truck. Somebody at the garage mentioned the Clinton bank robbery. Gilbert chuckled. "I'll have to hunt me some bandits, I guess."

Now the bandits were hunting him, and no doubt about it. And in Gilbert's truck, happening along at this instant, Heaven was ordinant.

Or Hell was.

The bandit Buick had gotten on U.S. 36 near the Illinois line. They had only driven west long enough to reach Edgar County, Illinois, when they caught sight of Gilbert's truck. Three intersections down U.S. 36, near the Roy Wimsett farm, about two miles into Illinois, the gang blocked the road, parking the Buick crossways. Walter Detrich was the first man out of the car. Waving a pistol, he ordered young Gritten out of the truck. "Hit the road!" Detrich bade the lad. Gritten wasted no time in lighting out.

Lamm took charge of Gilbert. Leveling his pistol at the cattle broker, he shouted, "Get the hell out of there!" Gilbert, however, was not a good subject for the bandit chieftain. He gripped the steering wheel with all the resolve of two men of five and twenty. Lamm then grabbed his feet and, with terrible fury, yanked him unceremoniously out of the truck on his backside.

At this moment, Walker and the others came on the scene. The Ford's brakes were faulty, and it barely pulled to a stop two telephone pole lengths short of crashing into the barricade, consisting of the Gilbert truck and the Frist Buick. Lamm told Gilbert to get down behind the right front wheel of his truck — the one with the brand new tire.

There was silence now — the loudest kind of silence. Nothing was uttered, nothing understood. For a moment, the whole world was void and soundless and each one in it, with wondering eyes, eyed his neighbor. It was a dreadful, pent-up silence that might erupt without warning and cast a soul into eternity.

Everyone stood with fixed gaze on what might lie ahead. The two groups of men were like so many stone images. Motion was something that had happened in the past. The pale light, the slanted light, came out of the brooding sky tentatively, as though awaiting a sign. Finally, Walker, watching for that first movement and holding his pistol at the ready, walked out into the road toward the bandits. Hamm and Scott, not yet out of the Ford, stayed back, lying low.

Walker spoke an order to surrender to the outlaws, but it quickly became a moot point, lost in the whirlwind of shots that rang out. Those opening shots must have sounded like sonic booms in a public library. Walker was hit instantly, grievously. He managed to gasp, "Give 'em hell, boys, I'm shot."[16] He went down in terrible agony but, somehow, he was able to fire three shots before crawling in back of the Ford.

Probably the gang fired first, but not even this much is certain. What is certain is that the shooting stopped as abruptly as it started. From out of nowhere — it must have seemed to all of those present — a team of horses pulling a wagonload of hogs bolted into the path of the gunfire, and both sides stopped shooting on the instant. The horses whinnied and strove wildly to break free of their harness for one taut moment. Van Daily, an employee of the highway commissioner of Prairie Township, grabbed the horses' reins and was somehow able to get the wagon clear of the combatants' wrath. Shooting broke out just as soon as the wagon was cleared and, before it was all over, some twenty-five shots had been fired. Walker crouched down behind the Ford, vomiting.[17]

What the casualties amounted to in this skirmish is unknown. According to one report, Joe Walker took three machine gun bullets in his stomach and groin. According to another, he was hit twice — weapon unspecified. Yet a third report states that he was shot once by a .38 special fired from a machine gun.[18] In any case, he got off three rounds from his revolver. The gang's driver, Hunter, may have been hit. Scott fired some shots after Walker was hit and saw somebody drop a bag of money on the pavement. One thing only is certain. Though Hunter began the day as the gang's driver, he did not end the day as such. Either he was wounded at some point in the running fight that morning or he was given a pink slip and replaced. Duress or wounds or both would have made him less than apt as a driver. The Clinton job may, in fact, have been his baptism by fire.

Helms and Burnside were watching the action from a distance when Boetto and Clark drove up. Helms asked Boetto if he had his rifle. When told that he did, Helms told him to open fire on the gang. With shots splattering all around him, Gilbert hugged the right front wheel like a long lost friend — or like a brand-new tire that he had shelled out for only moments before. It was almost as though he wanted to take the hit himself rather than risk his new tire getting a puncture.

Somebody removed the loot from the Frist Buick onto an overcoat spread on the ground. If Hunter wasn't wounded, this was probably he. Grabbing up the four corners of the overcoat, he tossed the bundle into the back of Gilbert's truck. Some of the bills flew back into the Buick. The bandit got into the back of Gilbert's truck. This made three in back — Lamm, Landy and Hunter.

Location on U.S. 36 where Deputy Joe Walker was shot (Indiana Historical Society, M0888).

Lamm asked if anyone in the gang could drive Gilbert's truck. No one could or would. Lamm pulled Gilbert to his feet and shoved him back into the cab. Detrich got in beside Gilbert. The young bandit now pushed the gas pedal down and nearly flooded the engine. Gilbert, in a knee-jerk reaction, pushed him away. "Here, let me try it," he said, half amazed at his sudden grace under pressure.

"Drive, old man, drive!" Detrich shouted, sticking his revolver in Gilbert's ribs.[19] As the truck moved ahead, Detrich shot out the window next to Gilbert just in case the law got too close, especially when it came to turns. The truck took off west on U.S. 36.

Walker lay crumpled over on the side of the road when Helms and Burnside arrived. He was still conscious. "Get them!" he told Helms.

The fallen deputy was placed in Hamm's car and driven to Dana, where he was attended by Dr. W.C. Myers.[20] According to Dr. Myers, Walker had taken a .38 special fired from a machine gun in the right side. It penetrated the liver in two places and the stomach in two places. It made a lateral tear of eight inches in the intestine. After receiving first aid, Walker was taken by the McMullen and Woodard ambulance to St. Anthony's Hospital in Terre Haute, just over a half-hour's drive from Dana.

Helms and Burnside, with Scott on the running board, took off after the Gilbert truck. Boetto and Clark were already tailing that vehicle.

Wells Gilbert had not filled the truck's radiator with water that morning. He always drove less than twenty-five miles an hour out on the road and usually did not go far in his rounds. Besides, the weather was cold. The radiator didn't need much water to cool the engine at a slow speed.

But a slow speed is the last thing Lamm and his men desired on this morning. Lamm wanted to shake off the pursuit, and now that one of the posse had been shot, that pursuit would be more numerous and more dogged than ever.

Going west in this region, a mighty leveling of the land takes place. The proverbial hills and hollows of Vermillion County are gone. For weary mile upon weary mile, now, there is nothing reminiscent of Spenser's Arlo Hill or Old Father Mole or the monumental Mittens of John Ford's West. There are no vast red mesas, overseen by far-reaching blue buttes. Here and there, a grain silo, painted at one time, stands out, or a lonesome windmill, groaning with age, in a distant field. The sameness is there to be reckoned with all the way down 36 from Dana to Tuscola, and then half way to Morgan County. It is December now. Cornfields still tall with corn, their stalks bearing uninspired yellow-brown leaves and wizened ears, resist the rain.

It is all of a piece, this land. No place to hide; no place to run, no place to shoot it out.

Where was the gang going after crossing into Illinois? Were they headed somewhere in particular? What did they intend to do when they reached whatever their destination was?

As to all this, Art Hockett, Wells Gilbert's nephew, had two notions. He believed that the outlaws were racing to get to State Road 49 and head up to Chicago. State Road 49 was a quick drive down 36. It was also a highly visible one in a country swarming with vigilantes on the watch. If getting to State Road 49 was the intention of the bandits under these heightened circumstances, they would have done well to go over back roads to get to it. This is pretty much what they did. They seem either to have taken the Woodyard Road west or to have gone west out of Ridge Farm.

Art's other idea is less likely. He thought that the gang may have been headed for a limestone quarry in Fairmount, Illinois, north of Sidell. While the gang, no doubt, was familiar with eastern Illinois, the quarry would not have been likely to impress itself on the imagination of any member of the gang. Moreover, it is doubtful that Baron Lamm, at any point in his long

VIII — Clinton; or The Wheels of Chance

flight, was interested in making a last stand anywhere. The last thing he would have had in mind was a last stand. Like Warren Beatty's Clyde Barrow, he probably wasn't headed anywhere; he was just running from.

In Tuscola, America's second oldest radio station, WDZ, the home of future Gene Autry sidekick Smiley Burnette, suspended regular programming full of grain markets and country music to send out regular bulletins about the bandit trail and where it tended. Hundreds of farm homes heard the messages and suddenly rural life — quiet, routine, isolated, with heads most often turned towards the sky — now broke into passionate resistance, not for, as one might expect, an acre of ground, but to safeguard the life of a bank that held the mortgaged life's blood of farms far away. The farm lads did not know which bank had been robbed. They did not know any officers of that bank or even anyone who did business with the bank. There were at least six degrees of separation between them and the bank that was robbed. The farm folk knew only that it was not their bank. Yet they acted, immediately, sidestepping the customary country-wise way of thinking on the morrow. Shotguns were grabbed in have-at-'em fashion, and automobile engines were made to race.

This region boasted one of the best vigilante organizations in the state. A handful of telephone operators at an exchange in Tuscola could reach a network of hundreds of vigilantes in mere minutes. Government-armed or self-armed, the vigilantes were not slow to respond to a call-to-arms. They came alone and they came in bands and they came from all directions at once. Homer and Allerton, Broadlands and Longview, Sidell and Fairmount, all yielded their best and bravest to the present emergency.

The outlaws were on very thin ice, indeed.

Now, four miles from the intersection where Joe Walker was shot, the Gilbert truck began to heave and shake, becoming altogether impossible to handle. The water in the radiator had been low enough to begin with, but racing along as they were, the engine now was smoking. Plainly, Gilbert's truck was about to blow its top.

Gilbert's nephew, Art Hockett, had this to say in 1996:

> I think he [Wells Gilbert] got out to the crossroads there on the old Ocean-to-Ocean Highway just by Scottland. And their car gave up [so] they would take that old truck. There wasn't nothing else to get ahold of but Uncle Wells' truck. They just throwed that old machine gun and everything in the back end. Down that Ocean-to-Ocean Highway they come to Scotland. Of course, that poor old Chevrolet truck wouldn't make only about thirty miles an hour. I think they run it so fast that when it got to that there intersection, why it just blew up. They had to get them another car.[21]

Art Hockett's take on this part of the story is interesting in that he brings up a note not usually sounded about the Gilbert truck. In Art's mind, the amount of water in the radiator was never a factor. It was the condition of the Chevrolet truck and the reckless handling of it by the bandits that made it so problematic that day. And certainly it does seem odd that a man going to make his rounds for a dozen miles or more would not fill his radiator, even on a cool day—and this on a day when he had stopped at a garage before leaving town. After all, he had a mechanic put on a spanking new tire. Why not check the radiator? What Art's statement implies is that the fate that overtook the bandits on this day was at least partly owing to their own stupidity and recklessness. The radiator, low on water, may have been a detail added by someone other than Gilbert to make a good story even better, with fate as the general theme.

Now, passing by Scottland, the outlaws headed west again. They were just north of U.S. 36, crossing the Ocean-to-Ocean Highway (old 36), an unpaved road. The bandits looked around for another set of wheels. It came in the form of 22-year-old Fenton Williams' 1930 Model-A Ford. Northwest of Scottland the switch was made. Williams had only just left his home in nearby Ridge Farm. He recognized Gilbert's truck and slowed down.

Sixty-six years later, Fenton's younger brother, Carroll, recalled this part of the action:

> Fenton was a-coming south, you know, there on the Cullen Road. He knew Wells' truck. He saw somebody waving him down, so Fenton just thought it was Wells. Well, right then, they unloaded. It just scared Fenton to death. He hopped out and laid down in the ditch and laid down in all the shooting. That's the way they got Fenton's car. That's where they traded Wells' truck for my brother's car. I forget how many there was of them, but they took the lid off the rumble seat and threw it out in the ditch ... and took off. Fenton was scared to death. He wouldn't even talk about it. He was afraid they'd come back after him, see, and he wouldn't talk about it. He was scared to death for a month.[22]

Apparently, Ernest Boetto was within range at this point. Chief Helms, Patrolman Burnside and Harold Scott were probably shooting, too.

"That old guy [Landy] wanted to shoot it out right there in the road," Carroll Williams marveled all those years later. "According to what Fenton said, he was going to shoot it out with that machine gun. But the others told him, 'Come on, if you're going with us.' So, he got in."

Landy crawled into the space in back left by the discharged rumble seat (actually, a lid covering a compartment in the back). Oklahoma Jack got in back, Indian-fashion, holding the machine gun in his lap.

Fenton Williams' Model-A was headed south when intercepted by the bandits. The bandits wanted to go north and this presented a problem. In turning the vehicle around, they would be exposed to Boetto's rifle fire on their flank. Boetto's rifle was a long range weapon and could outshoot even the machine gun. The about-face left the bandits practically as sitting ducks until they got moving. And the worst case scenario for them was executing such a risky maneuver.[23]

Boetto took full advantage of the bandits' temporary predicament and poured round after round into the Ford. The car stopped for one long moment before completing the move.

Wells Gilbert, meanwhile, remained behind one of the wheels of his truck at the behest once more of Baron Lamm. Gilbert later would say that the Ford had stalled and that is why it stopped abruptly. Chief Helms thought differently. He was pretty sure that Hunter, the driver, had been hit by Boetto and that Detrich took over behind the wheel at this point. Much later and much out of context, Detrich brought up a fact that may bear on this part of the chase. When told that the posse blew out the windshield of one of the getaway vehicles, the twenty-nine-year-old ex-con objected: "During the chase, one of our men became excited and fired a shot from the machine gun through the windshield." Very likely, this incident took place when young Williams was waylaid.

No one knows anymore what really happened. One would think Gilbert must have known what went on in the Ford at that moment — unless, that is, he was facedown against Mother Earth the whole time. In any event, poor Gilbert lost his brand new tire. One of the posse's bullets had punctured it. He would eventually get the truck going and make it to his nephew's house near Scotland. There in a wild-eyed state, he would exclaim over and over, "The robbers has had me! The robbers has had me!"[24]

With the addition of the Ford coupe, the chase began anew. More and more carloads of people were taking up the pursuit and even two airplanes were overhead, loaned to the effort by the Indiana National Guard. The chase was much too high-profile for a nondescript cracksman like Baron Lamm. What had begun with Helms and Burnside, augmented by Boetto and Clark, approached a train of one hundred vehicles at the finish line.

It probably came as no surprise to Lamm and the others when they learned that the coupe was low on gas. About twenty-five miles' worth of gasoline was all that remained in the tank. Still, the bandits kept up the desperate pace — seventy, seventy-five, up. They had to get out of range of Boetto's rifle. They may have crossed Rt. 1 at Woodyard and gone west down the Woodyard Road. (Chief Helms, in testifying during the trial of Detrich and Clark, made it a bit further north at Ridge Farm.)

It is not at all clear what they did after they crossed the north-south running Rt. 1. The movements of the bandits from this point until they drove through Sidell are a blur. Though the bandits were never out of sight of the pursuit, the shooting must have come at intervals, instead of as one constant running fight. No report in any of the area dailies has an account of the bandits after they crossed Rt. 1 until they were seen nearing their final rendezvous. In time, they passed the Ross Barnett one-room schoolhouse a mile and a half south of Sidell. Down to their last gallon of gasoline and down to their last few miles, Lamm must have been thinking, "My kingdom for a horse!"

A jackass — and not a horse — was the only thing on young Charlie Lyons' mind at this moment. Charlie was in the seventh grade at the Ross Barnett School and at recess when the bandit car went past his school — one of the 215 one-room schoolhouses in the annals of Vermilion County.[25] With thumbs poked in his ears and fingers spread wide apart and waving wildly, he stuck out his tongue at the animal. *Hee-haw, hee-haw, hee-haw.* He had been making faces at the jackass quartered in the pasture next to the schoolhouse for most of the recess, hoping to get a rise out of it. He was in the mood, as only a thirteen-year-old with time on his hands could be, for some industrial-strength jack-assing. When, finally, he turned around, he saw the bandit car drive past with Clark cradling the machine gun in his lap. At this time, there was a large gap between pursued and pursuers, and no shooting could be heard. It was recess in more ways than one.

It wasn't long after Charlie went back inside that there came a kind of official knocking on the schoolhouse door. His teacher, small, spinsterish and bespectacled, led a tall man in uniform into the room. The man may have been a highway patrolman or he may have been an Indiana State trooper. Most likely, he was Deputy Razz Foltz. Foltz and Sheriff Harry Newland had made a wrong turn on the way over to Illinois, possibly owing to an erroneous bulletin from Hazel Haase, and were well behind the rest of the posse as a result. The officer in front of Charlie's class was almost certainly one or the other of these two men.

Had anyone seen anything out of the ordinary, the officer wanted to know. Well, certainly a machine gun this far outside the Chicago city limits was extraordinary. Charlie might have suggested that five grown men and a water-cooled machine gun in a coupe must have been some kind of record — even for bandits on the run.[26]

The bandits were now well away from civilization. Cities were nonexistent, towns few and far between, villages and hamlets, occasional. What the outlaw crew needed in this area with little traffic was not a different car (which might turn out to be worse than the others) but a filling station. If they had been near one, they might well have placed the machine gun out in the road with Clark and Landy behind it and made a mini-stand in order to fill up. But there was just too much prairie where they were to even dream of such a thing.

VIII — Clinton; or The Wheels of Chance

This raises the question: Did the bandits go through Sidell on their way to oblivion? It seems that they did, though no written report has ever said so.

Little Hattie Drummond, the daughter of a Sidell village policeman, was in the third grade at the Sidell Grade School when she looked out her classroom window and saw the Ford go by with its five occupants and deadly machine gun. The sight of the men and the knowledge of what was shortly after to occur disturbed Hattie so much all her life that she would not consent to be interviewed about it decades later.[27]

And, apparently, the law went through Sidell, too. Eddie Smith, 31, was standing on a corner when a car with two men in uniform pulled up. Smith was asked if a car full of bandits and a machine gun had gone by. Smith said that he heard that they did and that was why he was out on the street corner trying to catch sight of them.

"Get in," one of the men said. "We're making you a deputy."

Smith must have remembered the part about the machine gun. "The hell with that!" he said. The long arm of the law was shorter by one Edward Smith that day.[28]

Going north on Chicago Street out of Sidell, the bandits passed a Danville bond salesman, Winchester W. Rogers, driving a new Chrysler coupe. Interested in putting miles between the posse and themselves, the bandits hardly eyed Rogers as they went by. Rogers, however, eyed them. He couldn't miss that machine gun sticking out of the back of the coupe. He was ruminating about this situation when he saw two men up ahead on the road frantically waving him down.

Boetto's Dodge-8 had just run out of gas. He and Charlie Clark got out and started walking. Suddenly Rogers hove into sight, and the two excitedly flagged him down. They explained the situation and Rogers agreed to drive them in pursuit of the bandits. He quickly turned the car around. Rogers may not have known what a high-speed chase could mean to the finish on his Chrysler. At this point, the posse must have been far behind, even Helms and Burnside and their Olds with the forty-odd pock marks.

The bandits really should have stopped Rogers. The Chrysler's full tank would have gotten them to Chicago or very near it and would have enabled them to outdistance pursuit.

By allowing Rogers to get by, Lamm had sealed his doom once and for all. Without Rogers' Chrysler, the pursuit would have been in a bad way. Boetto's Dodge-8 was out of gas and Helms' Oldsmobile was down to a gallon or two. Without Boetto's keen eye and firepower, the pursuit would have been severely crippled. With Boetto out of the action, it would have been a demoralizing blow to the posse, to say the least.

The bandits were very likely trying to make Illinois Route 49.[29] They had just past the Jamaica intersection and, at the first road going west, they made a left turn. There was a farmhouse in sight and this must have looked to the gang like the one big break of the day. It wasn't. It was to be more of the same. But for the last time.

IX

"You're out of luck"

Then come the farmers.—Ignazio Silone

Just rushing towards death.—*High Sierra* (1941)[1]

Die the way you lived—all of a sudden.
—*Manhattan Melodrama* (1934)

We had a lot of bad luck.—Walter Detrich

The farm belonged to Leo Moody and his wife, Dorothy.[2] On this morning, Leo Moody was at home with his mother. Dorothy, just moments before, had taken the family automobile down the road to Leo's older brother William's place to can meat that morning.[3]

Leo Moody was a big, strapping, boyish-looking thirty-two-year-old. Like Lincoln and John Wayne, he stood six-foot-four without trying. At nearby Georgetown, he had played football in high school. In fact, the school took its nickname from him—the Buffaloes.

Big as he was, Moody was something of a teddy bear. He could be easily imposed upon. Tools borrowed from him and not returned rarely brought from him any kind of retaliation. All too often, others had to light a fire under him to get him to reclaim what was rightfully his. Yet, withal, it was said that he could knock a bull off his feet with one punch.[4] Like most farmers, Moody had a rifle on the premises. He needed it for killing livestock, in his case cattle and hogs. He never had time to hunt. "Hunting is for city folks," he'd say.

Whoever was driving the Ford coupe was driving it for all it was worth. He made the driveway a bit wide of the mark and a line of oil drums fell victim to the crazed arc of the raging vehicle. The din from this mishap alerted Moody, who was out in the barnyard slopping hogs at the time, that company had come calling. He came around from behind the board fence to confront the intruders. All five of the bandits bolted from the coupe with guns drawn. According to Moody's statement to the press that afternoon, all the bandits

Leo Moody, on whose farm this wild day ended (Indiana Historical Society, M0888).

Detrich drove into these oil barrels when pulling into the Moody farm (Indiana Historical Society, M0888).

confronted him. Apparently, if Hunter had been wounded in the running fight, he was holding up well at this point.[5]

"Buddy, you've got to help us out. We need your car," someone in the gang said.

"You're out of luck —." Moody was about to inform them of where things stood with his car when Lamm took the conversation in a new direction.

"Get busy," he snarled, shoving his pistol under Moody's chin. "We want your car."[6]

Moody saw that it was no use trying to sell the men on the absolute truth, so he decided that they might be in the market for an outright lie. He told them that his car was in the barn and that he would go in the house to get the keys.

Lamm stayed put as did the other men. Once again he had come to a fork in the road and had chosen the wrong path. But this time either fork would have been wrong, no matter which he chose. The time for being right was over. Even had Lamm gone into the house with Moody and kept him covered (as well as Moody's mother) and watched his every move, he would not have been able to stop the inevitable. The inevitable had now arrived and was parked along a stretch of road alongside the farm, armed to the teeth.

Moody's mother, seventy-year-old Mary Moody, was in the kitchen. Moody warned her about the men in the driveway. "There are some bad men out in the barn lot, but don't worry. Go down to the cellar. I'll take care of it."

Not good at following orders even in an emergency, as her son grabbed a .22-caliber rifle, Mrs. Moody went straight to the telephone and called the Sidell Village Police. Moody now emerged from the house shooting. But, by this time, everyone else had arrived. Across the road, vigilantes were streaming through a cornfield to the northeast of the Moody farmhouse. Helms and Burnside were on the road that ran in front of the farmhouse. So, too, were Boetto and Clark. All were looking for a shot at those who fled on foot across the barn lot toward the cornfield.

Seeing such overwhelming numbers against them, the bandits dispersed. Moody was shooting from his doorway. Boetto took a shot at the fleeing men and hit someone — possibly Hunter, possibly Lamm. Whoever it was, he went down to his knees, let slip a five-dollar bill and then got up and went on. Three of the men went over the fence into the pasture and about a hundred yards later reached the cornfield. These men were Lamm, Landy and Clark.

The Moody farmhouse (Indiana Historical Society, M0888).

As ever, Lamm was giving the orders as the men headed to the field full of five-foot-tall corn stalks.[7] Backing up, he was looking at the fast-approaching army. Landy, not daring to look upon "the swelling scene," stumbled onward into the corn. Clark clutched the machine gun tightly, wondering when to make a fight of it.

Boetto had but three rounds left in his rifle when he came on the scene. The first one went into either Lamm or Hunter. If Lamm was the target, he had strength enough to make it into the cornfield. If Hunter was his victim, he managed to crawl out of sight into a hog house, somehow avoiding the notice of a large band of vigilantes as well as Moody. Boetto's second shot was the stuff of legend. At the distance of a football field, Boetto fired on Clark and knocked the machine gun out of his hand, disabling the weapon. Clark froze in place, completely stupefied by the unerring aim of a garage man who seemed to be a scion of Adam Bogardus or perhaps Pardner Jones himself, settling for the next best thing to a clay pipe in a Hollywood extra's mouth. Boetto's last shot, somewhat anticlimactically, like Gehrig's homerun after the "called shot," merely tore up the dirt between Clark's legs.

It is not clear whether or not the bandits fired back at this point. All three men in the cornfield carried revolvers, but these, of course, were no

Leo Moody found the satchel of bank loot near his barn (Indiana Historical Society, M0888).

match for a high-powered rifle. The machine gun must have been their last hope of making a last stand. It had range, and once it began to speak its piece, you could be sure that it would find an attentive audience. An oddity about this final part of the long-running fight has to do with the two submachine guns later found near the barn lot fence. Why were these weapons left behind? Maybe the bandits didn't wish to be encumbered anymore with their weight, but more likely, by this time, they were just out of ammo.

Detrich separated himself from the rest as soon as the posse was seen by the men. He went to a large outbuilding that was used as both a cob and a coal shed. He grabbed hold of the window ledge six feet above the ground and climbed through. He got down in a pile of corn cobs and buried himself for dear life.

Hunter, wounded in the stomach and liver, sought refuge in a hog house south of the farmhouse, near the barn. He had a pistol but was hardly in the mood to use it. He had been shot, probably more than twice and possibly by more than one man.[8] He hid the pistol and the ammo in the straw all about him.[9]

Boetto, seeing that his rifle was out of shells, went up to a truck just arriving on the scene and borrowed a shotgun from a vigilante. The scatter gun would be suitable for the close-quarters work ahead.

Now that the three outlaws had gone into the cornfield, which even at this time of year was full of standing corn, it was hard to locate them. Chief Helms, at one point, and Moody, at another, had climbed up on a windmill tower and signaled to the posse about the movements of the trio in the cornfield. Meanwhile, an endless stream of vigilantes was surrounding the cornfield, so that there was no hope for the bandits of making an escape.

How dire were their circumstances the three men must have known. At this point, once more, all certainty vanishes. Clark made his way over to a fence bordering the road that the bandits had traveled to get to the Moody place. Burnside and others saw him and were about to pop him when Helms urged caution first. Although he must have seen Boetto's crack shot, he thought it best to make sure that Clark was the man down in the cornfield before anyone started shooting. Burnside called on Clark to throw up his hands, an order with which the bandit was only too happy to comply. Burnside bound his wrists with rawhide.

As for the other two, the rest is worse than silence, it is a mass of contradictions. Anything could have happened. Some things, however, can be assumed with reasonable certainty. Lamm went first. Just how he departed this world is open to question, natural causes and heart failure from the excitement of eating an orange being the only options safely ruled out. He may have shot himself in the heart. There were powder burns that said so, at least in some reports. He may have been shot by Ernest Boetto — Chief Helms and many in the posse said so.

The bullet that took his life passed clean through him. That was reason, as Chief Helms saw it, to believe that Boetto's long-range rifle did the job. Then, too, Lamm may have been shot by Landy. Some in the posse thought so, as given in some early newspaper accounts.[10] Then again, more than one of these scenarios may have occurred. Lamm may have been shot in the barn lot or pasture by Boetto or some other member of the posse and then received the fatal wound in the cornfield either by his own hand or that of another. If, on the other hand, Landy did, in fact, shoot Lamm in the cornfield, what made him do it? Was it out of anger, or was it a mercy killing? The newspaper account, without saying so directly, leaves the impression that Lamm was killed out of mercy. It may be that Lamm and Landy had arranged a suicide pact.

By this time, Clark was out of the cornfield and could not have overheard anything the two elder statesmen of the underworld said. Maybe nothing was said, nothing that made any sense. Maybe both men knew that what was about to come was written down long ages ago and would not now be gainsaid. In any case, no one could ever have figured this ending at the start of the day. Both Lamm and Landy were well dressed and did not belong in a muddy cornfield. But as so often happened in those days that bank bandits transacting business in an urban setting at the start of the day leap into eternity from a cornfield at the end of it.

Certainly if Lamm died by his own hand, it is odd that he shot himself in the heart. People stab themselves in the heart, but they shoot themselves in the head. But, no doubt, a man in his final moments may go against the percentages a bit and shoot himself in the heart, whatever actuarial tables suggest. Perhaps that was why Lamm's shirt was torn open; he didn't want anything to even slightly impede the bullet's course to his heart.

In his account written up by Jack Cejnar, Helms claims to have been present in the last moments of both Lamm and Landy. The two arch-rogues were separated by about fifty feet of corn rows. Lamm had a gaping wound in his chest as he lay on his back gasping for breath. Helms could hear the death rattle as the gang chieftain breathed his last. Lamm's future, like Hank Quinlan's, was all used up. The bandit leader's shirt was either torn open or blown apart. He died without saying anything, staring up at a futile gray sky on a day completely out of step with his marching orders. He died right in front of Helms, a man who probably didn't figure one bit in Lamm's thinking that morning as he left the Danville hotel on a job expected to be a breeze.

Landy was fifty feet away from Lamm when Helms and Boetto happened up on him. He was very much alive but completely unnerved by Lamm's death. Somewhat ingloriously, the old gentleman's coat was pulled up over his head as he lay face down in the cornfield. When called upon to surrender, Landy raised up. His .38 revolver was in his hand. Helms and Boetto must have shuddered for what must have seemed a lifetime. Both had their fingers at the ready, wrapped around the triggers of their weapons — Helms with a pistol; Boetto with a shotgun. But, instead of firing on the two men, Landy put the gun to the right temple of his head and fired. He died instantly. Thus, the "sphinx of gangdom" departed this world, leaving no clue as to why he had chosen to go in this manner. Unlike Lamm's death, there was never any doubt about how Landy came to die.[11]

The dense clouds parted and the heavens brightened as the sun looked down triumphantly. The armed men all around wondered at their shadows.

Oklahoma Jack, in the custody of Walter Burnside, was brought to where the bodies of Lamm and Landy lay. Clark's hands were bound behind his back with rawhide. Helms now replaced the rawhide with a pair of handcuffs. Clark looked on the dread scene impassively. His gods lay shivered all around him.

But some of the vigilantes, contemplating not Lamm but Clark, wore their hearts on their sleeves.

"Get a rope," someone said. There was a sudden swell of lynch-mob justice surging through the rural minutemen. These men were probably new to the conflict, having been summoned from towns and hamlets like Sidell and Fairmount, Longview, Allerton and Broadlands, Homer and Ogden — all in the immediate area. Some of these communities had banks that had lately been the victims of Glenn Nichols and his coed bunch and, as Nichols had not yet been apprehended, these citizens were chafing at the bit. They may well have surmised that Lamm's gang had been the ones to rob the Allerton bank just down the road in October. Clark's role as machine gunner must not have endeared him to the pocket militia either, especially if they had heard, as was likely, anything about the Walker shooting.

More and more people were pouring into the cornfield; some just curious, some ready to wreak vengeance. Before the final conflict, Boetto had dispatched Danville salesman Winchester W. Rogers to Sidell for all the help he could get, and that help had quickly surrounded the farm. The shooting now having come to an end, people were coming up for a look at the dead bandits and the living one. They were looking for loot and weapons and anything else that might be lying around. They were on the prowl for other bandits, too.

Near Sidell at this point in the day, Carey B. Hall, manager of the Danville Transfer and Storage Company, was out hunting. His gun was loaded for rabbits and not for the bank robbers that report said were in the area. Hall happened to be a good friend of Wade Holton, president of the Sidell National Bank. Hall immediately repaired to Holton's bank and demanded that cashier Don Lewis hand him some suitable shells. Hall suddenly found himself staring down the barrel of Lewis's pistol. Lewis, not being as acquainted with Hall as his bank president, drew his gun first before he ascertained anything at all. It was a day unlike any other in the region — ever.

Oklahoma Jack Clark was placed in the custody of Sheriff Harry Newland and Deputy Raymond "Razz" Foltz. He was expedited to Newport, Indiana, for his immediate safety. That safety was soon found to be not safe enough, so Clark spent the next twenty-four hours in the Vigo County jail at Terre Haute.

The thing to do next was to determine just who these bandits were. To that end, their clothing was searched. One of the bandits, probably Lamm, had a passbook with the name H.D. Wilson on it. Another had a wallet with several names and addresses in it. This wallet disappeared before long, to the great loss of anyone trying to get to the bottom of the case.[12] Police circulars on Fred "Killer" Burke had made the local rounds, and soon a strong resemblance between the big guy with the gaping wound in his chest and Burke was noted. The news went out that Burke had been killed at Sidell. It was a national sensation, especially interesting to the Toledo, Ohio, authorities and those in Chicago, both of whom had sought the former St. Louis Egan's Rat for years. If Burke had been curtailed, some of the other "American boys," as Big Al called them, may have been present, too. Somehow, the idea got around that Landy was someone named Ziegler, probably Shotgun George Ziegler, another of the "American boys." The Burke identification (of, presumably, Lamm), and the Ziegler one (of, presumably, Landy), were way off, but it would take the arrival of Chauncey A. Manning, of the Indiana Bureau of Criminal Identification and Investigation, to put a nail in that coffin. Ziegler (Fred Goetz) was in reality nearly four decades younger than Landy, but nobody on the premises would have known that.

It was just about high noon when the fight in the cornfield concluded the morning's sixty-mile-plus running battle. Two bandits were dead and another was in custody. All this time, Hunter lay in hiding in the hog house, a somewhat bigger structure than one might suppose from newspaper reports. But his blood had dripped all over, inside and out. Danville town guard Mace Smoot noticed blood at the entrance of the hog house. He called two other vigilantes over and then ordered Hunter to come out. Hunter had lost so much blood from his wounds that he was too weak to comply, even if he had wanted to. Smoot hauled him out by the collar.

Things only got worse for the wounded man. He was driven to the Vermilion County Police station at Danville eighteen miles away and questioned before finally being taken to the Vermilion County Hospital at Tilton. Here, if Hunter was in any condition to look out the window, he was able to see the cemetery across the road where he and the others would be interred shortly thereafter.

Nobody, at least among the forces of good, seems to have done any counting. The plain fact of the matter is that the posse did not know how many bandits they were chasing. With Hunter in custody, the tally came to four, with two bad men dead and two in custody. Almost immediately following Hunter's capture, many of the posse left. There were still plenty of bystanders hanging around and most of the Indiana lawmen as well. Two airplanes, courtesy of the Indiana National Guard, had landed in the pasture after the shooting stopped.

These planes had kept a vigil from the air on the bandits for most of their mad dash to nowhere. A pilot from neighboring Ogden had also kept an eye on the scene from above. It is not clear whether he landed at any point or flew back to Ogden when those on the ground signaled that all was well once again. A fourth plane from Champaign also landed on the Moody farm not long after the fighting. The carnival-like atmosphere would continue for most of the day.

Now that the shooting had stopped and some of the crowd was dispersing, Mary Moody, the farmer's mother, ventured into the coal shed where Detrich was hiding She may have gone in for coal to stoke the furnace or out of sheer curiosity. Apparently, her curiosity wasn't thorough enough to see Detrich under a pile of cobs, so coal must have been the attraction that took her to the shed. She must not have been aware that the numbers just didn't add up as far as the gang was concerned. One report says that she took her daughter with her to the coal shed, so she must have not have been concerned about unaccounted-for outlaws hanging around. Another report says that someone among the posse had inspected the shed. If so, this was likely in advance of Mrs. Moody and her daughter.[13]

Whatever Mary Moody knew or didn't know about the number of outlaws who had come to the farm, Leo Moody knew that he had dealt with five—five men pointing guns at him. He explained this circumstance to the lawmen who were trying to piece the whole story of the day's events together. After at least an hour, Moody's .32-caliber rifle was yet under his arm. He decided to go into the coal shed and have a look for himself. Even though some vigilantes and lawmen stood around the building and even though his mother and sister had just been in the shed, Moody wanted to see for himself. At some point well after Hunter's capture, Moody grabbed his rifle and went into the cob shed for a look. At the same time, Harold Scott clambered up the back of the building to look through the window, which, suspicion told him, should not have been up.

Clutching his rifle tightly, Moody entered the shed. Though now well beyond noon, it was always dark in the coal shed. He tried to adjust his eyes to accommodate the dim light. He was quick to look for any sudden movements. His ears were attuned to the slightest noise.

After a moment or two, Moody thought that he could make out a form lying among the old corn cobs. It was a man. The young farmer could not make out whether the man was armed or not, but he could wager on what he thought. Catching his breath, Moody held his rifle at the ready. His rifle wasn't the appendage it is with some farmers. He used it only occasionally for slaughtering cattle and hogs, some of which had provided the meat which had been canned by his wife at his brother-in-law's that very morning.

"Hunting is for city folks," he'd say. "Farmers have enough to with crops and livestock."

Moody trained his rifle on the prostrate form and spoke with the authority that his full height avouched.

"All right, you, get up out of there."

The form could have been lifeless, it was so still and quiet.

"Come out with your hands up."

Detrich toyed for a moment with the idea of making a run for it. But his better angel assured him that that would be foolish. The game was up. After all, that old hog leg beside him was empty, and the man standing there so imperially was carrying a rifle and was as big as a bull moose. It would take a Sharp's big-bore carbine to increase his understanding to the right metric. Detrich knew that his empty revolver wasn't going to move mountains — or man-mountains. And judging by Moody's countenance, there was no use for the outlaw to even attempt to bluff his way to freedom. Besides, another vigilante, Roy Haase, now came through the door.

At last, Detrich spoke up.

"All right. Don't shoot. I'm coming out."

The mouthy bandit, now reduced to a becoming silence, was taken over to the sidelines by Harold Scott and two other vigilantes, Roy Haase and Roy Maddox. Two weeks later at Detrich's trial, Haase remembered that when Leo Moody stepped out of the coal shed with his prisoner, he held a gun to his head. Leo's mother walked alongside, saying, "Shoot his head off, Leo." Haase urged caution. It was decided to put Detrich in Maddox's car and take him to the Danville jail. The prisoner was accompanied by Maddox, Roy Haase and Harold Scott. On the way, Detrich would not give his name, saying only that had the gang had a fast car, they would have gotten away. When Haase remarked that Detrich seemed too smart and too good-looking to be a bandit, Detrich merely shrugged.

After depositing his prisoner in the custody of the three Dana men,

Moody came upon a rather startling discovery. His rifle was out of shells! He had fired what rounds were in the weapon when he rushed out of the farmhouse. Both outlaw and captor were out of shells when the test of wills ensued, and neither knew it.[14]

Unlike the feeling among the vigilantes toward Clark, there was not any talk about lynching Detrich. Either tempers had cooled down or Clark, for some reason, was singled out as particularly guilt-ridden. When they hauled Detrich away, Moody simply said, "Nice-looking chap."

Nobody seems to have paid any attention to those first reports that mentioned six outlaws. Even just five outlaws looked like a stretch for most of the morning. When one considers the outlaws' last getaway vehicle, the Model-A Ford coupe, five does seem like the maximum limit, unless, of course, the running boards were utilized. As we have seen, Clark stood on the passenger side running board on Gilbert's cattle truck. But nobody has ever said that the outlaws boarded the running boards on the Williams' coupe. With Boetto's rifle barking at a reasonable range and bouncing bullets off the car as it turned around outside Scottland, it would have amounted to suicide.

In any case, everyone, including Leo Moody, thought that all the bandits had been collared by this point. After some further discussion, people started going to their cars. Moody watched them for a moment, then went back to watering the hogs.

Just when everyone thought they had seen it all, that "there's nothing left remarkable beneath the visiting moon," there was something.

Apparently one meddlesome individual was not quite sure that the bandit gang had been rounded up altogether. In 1993, Stan Hayes shared another of those unpredictable moments that seemed to be about the only kind that went on that day.

> I heard [the Moodys] talk about how they had cars lined up from their house clean down to the pavement and then a quarter of a mile down that way. Of course, back then people didn't think anything ... they all left their keys in the car. And when it was all over with, the people went back to their cars — and no car keys! Some guy got the idea that these guys would get a car and take it away. So he took a hat and went around and took everybody's car keys out and just put them in that hat and when it came time to go — I guess they had an awful mess — people trying to pick their keys out — which is a comical side. I've heard Dad [Leo Moody, Hayes' father-in-law] talk about that.[15]

In 1993, Margaret Helms recalled how she found out about all the excitement that she missed out on that hectic day: "I think I was at the bridge club and I didn't know about it until somebody called here. They heard that Pete had gotten killed. I'm not one to get excited. I mean, I realize that you don't always have the story. I didn't even know anything was going at all."

Over the decades Mrs. Helms was able not only to forgive the caller dishing out this horribly infelicitous report but also to forget just who the caller was.[16]

About the time of the Citizens State Bank robbery, Mike's Motors, a car lot in Clinton, featured an auto constructed by joining the back ends of two Chevrolet coupes together with two front ends sticking out. This anomaly seems to have been the one thing on wheels that Lamm overlooked in his haste to make a getaway.

X

After "the most thrilling manhunt ever staged in this part of the country"

And do not stand on quillets how to slay him.—*2 Henry VI*
You win for a while, but you lose bad in the end.— Ralph Fleagle
Nice-looking chap.— Leo Moody

Around noon, Woody Freese, teller of the First National Bank of Champaign, Illinois, and pilot Andy Tate flew to the Moody farm. They stayed long enough to learn that two bandits had committed suicide there. Tate was not the only pilot who flew to the farm. Three other pilots had been paying close attention to the overland flight of the bandits all morning — all of the planes had been flying directly overhead while the bandits were in flight. Two were in the service of the Indiana National Guard. The third plane was that of a private citizen from nearby Ogden, Illinois.[1]

Dorothy Moody was with her brother-in-law and mother-in-law a few miles down the road when someone telephoned her and told her what was afoot on her place. When she arrived at the farm, she saw the bodies of Lamm and Landy being carried off on stretchers. Oklahoma Jack Clark, handcuffed, was in the custody of Vermillion County sheriff Harry Newland.

The bespectacled, soft-spoken Newland looked more like a 9-to-5 insurance salesman than a man-hunter. He performed his job well enough to have won election to a second term the previous month. Sheriff Newland pondered his chances of taking Clark to the jail at Newport, the seat of Vermillion County, Indiana. But the Danville authorities were the ones calling the shots just now. The mortally-wounded Hunter had just been taken away by Danville town guard Mace Smoot and friends in his car to the Danville police station.

After taking some time to reassure his wife, mother and sister of his well-being, Leo Moody wondered whether all the bandits were spoken for. When they had approached him not quite an hour earlier, he had been sure that they were five in number. Three dead or dying men were accounted for and another, very much alive and strangely unmoved, stood by watching his dead comrades being loaded into an ambulance. Another healthy bandit had just been found in the coal house by Moody and three Dana men. That made five. Five seemed about the right number. Maybe, Moody thought, just maybe, he could relax now.

Sheriff Newland and Sheriff Ward had to decide what to do with the uninjured pair of prisoners. Given some time and only a little encouragement, there very well might be trouble. Only four months before and a hundred miles to the east, two black youths had been taken out of the Marion, Indiana, jail and lynched for the murder of a white youth and what was, at first, thought to be the rape of his girlfriend. The lynchings made headlines across the country.[2]

And when Landy and two others had been captured after firing an errant shot at the arresting officer near Frankfort, Indiana, six years earlier, there was a lynching mood in the air. The Judge Lynch talk probably was fueled, not illogically, by rumors that other hooligans might come to bust the trio out of jail. The feeling was much the same now.

In the end, the bandit gang had killed Deputy Joe Walker (though at this time he was still fighting for his life in St. Anthony's Hospital in Terre Haute). As some might see it, only the lynching of the two men, who gave their names as Long and Martin, would clear the air. Lest "public feeling manifest itself in a great sensation," it was deemed the best course to take Clark to the Vigo County jail at Terre Haute until tempers cooled somewhat. Detrich would remain at Danville in the Vermilion County jail. The decision to split the pair up, of course, lessened the likelihood of either being lynched. But was there a specific reason for Clark's being taken to Terre Haute?

All those miles would, of course, make Terre Haute safer for Clark, so far as any incensed vigilantes were concerned. Clark may have fired some rounds at the vigilantes during the last stand down in the cornfield and almost certainly had operated the machine gun in the bandits' flight, perhaps mowing down Joe Walker, and, so, he most particularly needed to be locked up some place far away. Detrich had long since made himself scarce when the last stand occurred and seems to have been rather mild-mannered ever since the gang spilled into the Moody farm.

But the authorities were not concerned about the Illinois vigilantes, stiff-necked and murmuring as they might be. They were worried about feeling in Dana, Indiana. Some there had threatened the pair. Vigilantism taken up to assist authorities in rounding up a gang of hooligans was one thing, but lynch mobs were quite another. How imposing a mob could be when aroused in tiny Dana was a good question. But they just might be dealing with much of Vermillion County. No chances were to be taken. Detrich would go to Danville for the time being and Clark to Terre Haute until authorities could see what was in the wind — or until some better move could be reckoned.[3]

In all, there were at least two hundred vigilantes and law enforcement personnel gathered at the Moody farm. Most did not do any shooting whatsoever. Many of the vigilantes had been out that morning rabbit and pheasant hunting and, hearing word that bank robbers were in the area, responded to the emergency. They had come from Broadlands and Allerton, Homer and Longview, Fairmount and Sidell.

Officers from the largest area community, Danville, Illinois, also hustled to the scene. Most of them missed the fireworks, but they came regardless of the defused situation. Chief Robert H. Swift, no spring chicken anymore, stayed behind and coordinated his personnel's movements. Chief Swift was in constant touch with Clinton Bell operator Hazel Haase, who, for the police chief's money, was the heroine of the chase. Chief Swift was not the only one who thought so. Hazel Haase, soon to be Hazel Cunningham, would receive the Bell Telephone Silver Medal, $250 in cash and the Theodore N. Vail Award recognizing her service during an emergency.[4]

All roads leading into Danville from every direction were blocked. Vermilion County (IL) sheriff F.W. Ward and numerous deputies did go to the site of the final fray.

Stan Hayes was a youngster in 1930. He knew something of law enforcement's third-degree treatment as practiced in that day. His father, Ora, had been a bank teller at the State Bank of Allerton when, on October 10, 1930, three daring young bandits robbed it. They took Hayes hostage and, after driving a mile, dropped him off in the country.

Sixty-three autumns later, Hayes remembered the long arm of the law as it was practiced by some practitioners back in the day. Thirty-two-year-old bank robber Glen Nichols hit nine Illinois banks in 1930, including the State Bank of Allerton. Stan Hayes recalled what happened after Nichols was arrested in late December 1930:

> I'll never forget [my father] talking about [when] they took him back to where [the suspects] were. They had a police chief — I believe his name was Barry — and this Barry told my father, "Now, you don't say a word. You let me do all the talking." And he took him back to where these two young farm boys were and said, "Do you know this man?" And they said, "Yeah, that's the man we robbed down at Allerton." So he took him back to see [Glen] Nichols and they had him back in what is called the bull pen. He was a pretty rough character. Chief Barry

had thirteen locks of hair on his gun belt, my dad said, and he asked him what that was for. And he said, "That's how many men I've killed." So he asked Nichols if he knew this man and Nichols didn't even look at him. He asked him about three times. No answer. He told the turnkey or jailor, "Unlock that cell." And he said he went in and got that guy ... and crammed his head into the bars and said, "Do you know this guy?" And he said, "Yeah." You know, things like that stick with you.[5]

Nichols, in fact, became gratifyingly talkative, and all of his ill-gotten gains were recovered beneath the floorboards of his attic.

Chief Barry was actually Lieutenant Andy Barry, who took the Nichols gang almost single-handed from start to finish. He was apparently a man well-schooled in "the Chicago way." There were others like him in that tough-as-nails day.[6]

In the five years between 1925 and 1930, Vermilion County, Illinois, saw eight daylight bank holdups. Of these, seven were solved.[7] All were small-town robberies. One bank robbery was foiled by a merchant with a rifle. The holdup pair, fleeing the scene, pushed a hostage out the door in front of them. Another time-honored ploy, cherished by Depression-era bandits, was to lock bank personnel in the vault while making their getaway. It was around this time that banks started putting catches in the vaults that enabled them to open from the inside. Both hostage-taking and vault-confining were used at times by Dillinger in his fourteen months on the run, but neither practice seems to have entered into Lamm's game plan. F.W. Gilbert, it will be recalled, was taken hostage by the gang before it met its final rendezvous, but the reason for this had more to do with his ability to drive his truck than his value as a hostage.

Most of the aforesaid robberies were open-and-shut cases, routine detective work. And, while it may be tempting to think that some Lieutenant Barry, with his strong-arm approach to problem solving and his rather definite ideas about the care and feeding of bank robbery suspects, was most responsible for retrieving loot and bringing suspects to book, former Danville chief of police William Ryan, a likable man who didn't take scalps, seems to have been the county's lead investigator in the prosecution of these crimes. All in all, a pretty good batting average in handling bank robberies in the county.

If anyone extracted any information from Detrich or Clark by the short-fused, two-fisted approach of the Chicago manner or whether by indirection directions were found out, cannot now be determined. Howsoever it was, they were up against the clock. Both prisoners would soon be taken to Newport, Indiana. Neither would so much as divulge his real name until his fingerprints gave him the lie.

Down in Terre Haute, Clark seems to have said nothing, apart from lying about who he was. He was William Long of Moberly, Missouri, and that would have to do. And for the next few weeks, it did.

At his grilling, Detrich was the soul of brevity. After being asked at Danville police headquarters what his name was, Detrich played the hardhead.

"That's your business. That's what you're being paid for. Find out for yourself because I'm not telling you anything."

Detrich then claimed his name was William Martin.

Chauncey A. Manning, of the Indiana Bureau of Criminal Identification and Investigation, got fingerprints from Police Chief Swift, and a short time later Detrich's whole story came out. "What's the use of denying it now?" a sullen, slumping Detrich said as he sat in his chair gazing down at the floor. When told that Bell (Lamm) and Landy were dead, he became slightly philosophical. "If they are dead, it doesn't look like they'll be on any more jobs." Asked where Bell and Landy were from, he answered, "I'm going to be frank with you. I don't know where Landy's people are and I don't know where Bell's people are." Pressed further, Detrich said, "I've done enough talking."

The authorities got absolutely nothing out of Detrich worth the having. It was the gangster's code of silence, only with a touch of jibber-jabber sprinkled in. Lieutenant Barry obviously wasn't consulted.

Reporters took photographs of the scene of Lamm's final escapade. A submachine gun used by the bandits, probably when Walter Burnside was

A member of the posse points to the bullet holes in Fenton Williams' Model-A coupe (Indiana Historical Society, M0888).

wounded early in the chase, appeared in the *Danville Commercial-News* the next day. The last vehicle commandeered by the bandits, the 1929 Model-A Ford belonging to Fenton Williams and complete with bullet holes in the back, was also photographed.

Chief Helms and the borrowed Oldsmobile coupe, with the earmarks of dozens of machine gun bullets in it, graced the next day's edition, too. One of the posse, car salesman Charles Clark, found his photograph prominently placed on page three of the *Commercial-News* for the 17th. He was typical of the hundreds who responded to the hue and cry, seemingly without a thought about the morrow. He and Ernest Boetto were in the vanguard of the hydra-headed posse that tailed the bandits for so many miles. He had piled out of his boss's car when it came time to chase the bandits through the cornfield. No one ever said what he was armed with or whether or not he did any shooting, but he was there when the smoke cleared.

With his matinee-idol looks, Walter Detrich, under the alias of William Martin, made the front page that same day. On the far right of that same front page, a photograph of Deputy Joe Walker dressed in his uniform appeared just beneath a shot of a submachine gun. The mortally-wounded Hunter's picture also appeared on the front page to the left. He was yet alive when photographed and that in itself was something of a miracle. Lynch mobs need not threaten his existence. Bureaucracy was enough in itself as noted above. After being hauled out of a pig pen by his coat collar by Mace Smoot and three others, Hunter was taken first to the Danville police station before being taken to the county hospital outside Tilton. At Danville, $625 was found in his clothing. Hunter would finally succumb two days later.[8]

In the vanguard of the hundred-vehicle pursuers of the bandits were a twenty-two-year-old Clinton woman, Mildred Brookbank, and her charge, a fourteen-year-old youth. She was said to have had a ringside seat for the action in the cornfield, but, unfortunately, no reporter thought to interview her or

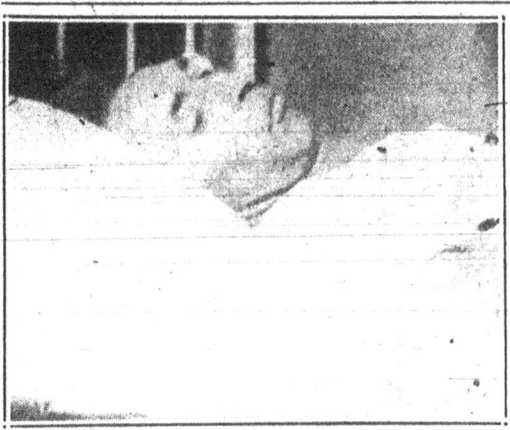

E.H. Hunter breathing his last at the Vermilion, Illinois, county hospital (*Danville* [IL] *Commercial-News*).

the boy who accompanied her, though her picture appeared in the newspapers. Nor was the lady or the lad asked to testify at the coroner's inquest four days later.[9]

No one knew with whom they were dealing. Certainly none of the vigilantes had any idea who the men were that they had run to ground.[10] An account book found in Lamm's coat pocket gave a Chicago address. From this, and the fact that the men had automatic weapons, it was assumed that the deceased were Chicago gangsters.

The chain of reasoning seems to have really taken off at this point. The account book gave the name of H.D. Wilson, along with a Chicago address, but this ruse was quickly seen through. Wilson was not his right name.[11] How could it be? No gun-toting hoodlum from Chicago was Anglo or a Scot — they were all Italians or Sicilians, "made-men" — so this line of reasoning went. Just look at the big man who died out in that cornfield next to him. He could be "the big guy" himself, Alphonse Capone — that is, if the latter weren't busy just then attending the wedding of a relative.

Dark and sinister-looking, this man, if not Big Al, must be Fred "Killer" Burke, wanted at this time all over the nation for being the lead triggerman in the notorious St. Valentine's Day Massacre the year before, as well as for killing a Michigan cop. If Lamm was Burke, then Landy/Wilson must be his cohort, Shotgun George Ziegler. Decades later, some of the old-timers still spoke of Landy as Ziegler. It is little short of amazing that Landy was, in so many reports, taken to be a man more than thirty-five years his junior.[12] No one thought of him as a seventy-one-year-old, though his morgue shot, perhaps understandably, shows him owning up to every one of his seventy-one years.

E.H. Hunter's identity was definitely established by the initials tattooed on his left forearm, "E.H.H," just as Dillinger gang member John "Red" Hamilton had his initials, "J.H.H.," tattooed on his forearm. Who shot Hunter and when was not so readily established. Hunter was thought to have been shot by Deputy Walker in the gunfight that claimed that officer's life. He was also thought to have fallen victim to Ernest Boetto's .30-.30 when the bandits piled out of Fenton Williams' Ford or perhaps earlier in the exchange near Scotland. Boetto was a Great War sharpshooter and it's hard to think of him not scoring a bull's eye somewhere in the running fight, since he was among those in the vanguard of the chase. He was down to just three rounds when the last battle took place and was, therefore, likely to have made his shots count.

By his own admission (and by Clark's and Detrich's, as well), Hunter was a booze runner from southwestern Indiana. He may even have been from Clinton, but Terre Haute seems more likely, or, at least, more credited. Detrich wanted it known for some reason that their booze-running friend had driven only at the start. If true, then it may be that Deputy Walker made good on at least one of his shots at the gang.

Hunter lay dying in the county hospital while Superintendent E.A. Church and Coroner John Cole questioned him.

"Two of your buddies are already dead and we would like to get some information concerning them, so we can send their bodies home," Cole said.

"Yes, I know and I guess I'll be the next to go and when I do there will be somebody show up to take care of me," the bandit assured the officials.

Hunter was all through with cooperation when the superintendent spoke again. The superintendent wanted to know something about the two dead men.

No response.

"I noticed the scar on your side. Where did you have the operation?"

When Superintendent Church went on to inquire about the bank robbery, Hunter snapped, "What are you — a doctor or a detective?"

He then turned over on his side. A dying man and well aware of it, he adhered to the gangster's code of silence to the bitter end. The *Commercial-News* was impressed.[13]

When Chauncey A. Manning of Indiana's Bureau of Criminal Identification and Investigation arrived at Sidell, he pegged Lamm as Thomas Bell, age 42, of Pittsburgh. Herman K. Lamm was his alias, one of many, according to Manning. He was wanted for more than a score of bank robberies in western Indiana alone. No word about whether or not he was wanted elsewhere.[14]

No word, either, about his being originally from Prussia.

As for the two surviving members of the band, James "Oklahoma Jack" Clark and Walter Detrich, both were going by the names they gave out upon their capture — William Long and William Martin.

Dad Landy in death (left); Herman K. Lamm in death (right) (*Danville* [IL] *Commercial-News*).

Detrich lied to his captors about his name, but told the truth about his age—26. Clark's age was given as 32, which also seems about right. Nor did anyone question it. Clark gave his residence variously as Moberly and Kansas City, Missouri.[15] Three years before, at Winston-Salem, it had been just as various, being either South Bend or New York City. His occupation remained consistent, however. He was a farmer.

It was said that the gang was pretty much a predator along the Illinois-Indiana line. Oklahoma Jack, it is true, was wanted in connection with the Denver Mint job—as the mastermind, no less—working as one Mike Burke, alias Jimmie Wilson—but no one had worried about him of late because it had been reported that he was dead. He had been reported killed following a Seminole, Oklahoma, bank robbery in 1928. Clark may well have participated in the bank robbery, but his death as a result of it must have been news to him.

"We are positive the bandit known to the authorities that now have him in custody as William N. Long is Burke," wrote the Denver police chief by letter to Danville chief Robert H. Swift. The felonious Clark, however, never made it to Denver, nor did anyone else in connection with the Denver Mint job. No one was ever brought to book for the robbery of the Federal Reserve truck on December 18, 1922, though most of the $200,000 stolen that day was recovered and several suspects killed or imprisoned for other crimes. Clark, however, was identified by fingerprints and photographs as one of the men wanted in the Denver job. He was ID'd by Rowland E. Goddard of the U.S. Secret Service. Clark was going to be tried for bank robbery and murder in Indiana and/or Illinois. He would get life—or worse. The Denver authorities simply let it go at that. Still, the fact that Clark was so close an associate of Baron Lamm and that he was suspected of involvement in the Denver Mint robbery suggests that Lamm may well have had some role in the crime. In this case, there is plenty of smoke, whatever there is of fire.

Before his rise to gangster stardom, Oklahoma Jack may have been a farmer; at least the Muncie, Indiana, authorities thought so. If Oklahoma Jack was a farmer, he couldn't have been one for long because he seems to have gone bad at an early age. He had been arrested for horse stealing in Wichita in April 1919, when he was in his early twenties. One can't help but suspect that, if anything, "farmer" was more likely to have been an alias than an occupation for someone named Oklahoma Jack.[16]

Arrested for horse stealing on April 30, 1919, James M. Clark was sent to the Kansas Reformatory at Hutchinson. He broke out, and the next time we hear of him is the Denver Mint robbery. Just over two years later, he was arrested in Aurora, Illinois, for burglary. So, for one brief moment in time—the spring of 1925—both Clark and Danny Morgan were in stir. A short time later, both were found in the company of Baron Lamm—again in the lockup.

As for the younger of the two survivors, Walter Detrich, St. Louis authorities were terribly interested in him. For one thing, he had a reward on his head of $6,000 to be paid by the Employers' Liability Assurance Company and the Proctor & Gamble Soap Company. The reward stipulated that Detrich and a companion in crime upon capture be convicted of the robbery of the soap company's payroll in St. Louis. Chief of police Joseph A. Gerk filled in Clinton police chief Everett Helms on more of Detrich's history. Detrich was born in 1904 and was thus 26 at this time. His career of crime began in St. Louis with vandalism on June 5, 1918, when he was fourteen, or almost. Latterly, he was wanted for a robbery at a Los Angeles theater on July 15, 1929. His biggest known robbery was the aforementioned Proctor and Gamble payroll job in St. Louis on March 5, 1929. He obtained a whopping $10,000 from that heist.[17]

Furthermore, that month's number of a four-page monthly magazine, published in St. Louis, called the *National Police Officer*, spotlighted Detrich (among others), mentioning, in addition to the Proctor & Gamble caper, a hotel robbery at Jefferson City, Missouri.[18]

Between them, Chief Gerk and the periodical exposed, at the least, the tip of the iceberg when it came to St. Louis' native son.

The bodies of the bandits were taken to the McCauley funeral parlor in Sidell. Lamm and Landy were unceremoniously laid out in their long johns. They had been stripped of their other clothing by mortician F.M. McCauley on the battlefield. When the bodies and clothing were brought to the undertaking parlor in Sidell, $165 was found in one of the bandit's clothes . This amount was in addition to the $150 to $200 found on one of the pair in the cornfield and the $625 found on Hunter.

When Hunter died of his wounds two days later, his body was brought to McCauley's also. All three bandits were now decked out in their Sunday best (or someone else's). Lamm was dressed in a dark blue suit with red tie. Landy wore a dark brown suit and green tie and Hunter, looking more like a professor emeritus than a rumrunner, had on a tan suit and yellow tie. Poor Dad Landy had placed cardboard in his shoes to cover up the holes in the soles.[19] So much for crime paying.

Six years younger than Art Hockett, Merrel Chew was a boy of eight in 1930. The funeral parlor was an object of supreme interest to him, as it was to every other boy in Sidell.

"We used to slip in on the way from school, see, and we'd lock other kids in there and hold the door on them, you know."[20]

Stan Hayes, a youngster, also eight, from nearby Allerton, saw the dead bandits when his folks took him to Sidell. His father, Ora, had good reason to take young Stan to the McCauley funeral home. He had been held up just

The McCauley Funeral Parlor in Sidell, Illinois, where the bodies of Lamm, Landy, and Hunter lay on canvas cots for a week (Indiana Historical Society, M0888.)

two months earlier at an Allerton, Illinois, bank and the robbery still was unsolved. No doubt, Mr. Hayes wanted to see if these men were connected with the earlier robbery. In 1993, Stan recalled seeing the bodies in Sidell:

> I lived at Allerton. I went through school at Allerton. My father worked at a bank there. If I remember right, they either killed three — one shot himself and they killed a couple of them and they laid them out in the funeral home down there in Sidell on the canvas cots and the whole countryside went through and looked at them. Now you can't imagine anything like that today, but I mean it was something I'll never forget in my life. It stuck with me... In those days, people didn't have much to do and they walked through and looked at them. It sounds gruesome. I mean that one guy was shot in the heart. And another one was shot in the temple, I believe, and you could see where they were shot and you went over and they'd let you look at them.

Late Saturday afternoon, December 20, Vermilion County coroner John D. Cole, held an inquest at McCauley's funeral parlor in Sidell. Cole had promised that the inquest would be short and sweet. Only a few witnesses would be called, none of them from Indiana. This was done evidently to spare the Hoosier people the inconvenience of making a long journey in the dead of winter to corroborate what could be handled definitively on the premises.

Four witnesses, consisting of Sidell village policeman Martin Drummond, Sidell banker Wade Holton, Sidell postmaster Joe Ackerson, and Kemp C. Catlett, cashier at the State National Bank in Homer, Illinois, were examined. Drummond had been foremost among those who closed in on the bandits during their last moments in the cornfield. It was his belief that Lamm and Landy both had committed suicide. The others concurred implicitly.[21]

It is curious that all the witnesses for the state in Detrich and Clark's trial came from Indiana. One might have expected Van Daily, an Illinois resident, to have something to say about the gunfight that followed Walker's death. Daily was not even subpoenaed. Leo Moody, another Illinois resident, was subpoenaed but did not testify.

When Milwaukee authorities got wind of the gunfight in downstate Illinois, they wondered whether the elusive Thomas Bell was involved. Bell had slipped away from them in 1924, after Milwaukee's first daylight bank robbery, and they wanted to know his fate. They notified Danville chief of police Robert H. Swift not to do anything with the bodies until they sent representatives to have a look at them. Also, to the local authorities, it seemed like a good idea not to bury anyone before word had got out to relatives of the bandits.

So it was that it was more than a week after the bank robbery that the three bandits were buried at Songer Cemetery, just across the highway from the county hospital where Hunter died, on the outskirts of Tilton, Illinois. It was the morning of Christmas Eve. A short service was held at graveside. Only a bare handful of people were present, unlike the scene at the funeral parlor where throngs came day after day for nearly a week. As with Dillinger's funeral three and a half years later, information about the time of the burial was indefinite to keep the crowds down. In this case, at least, the ruse worked.

The Rev. Harmon Kelly, of the Methodist Church in Sidell, spoke on the wages of sin. If he had been of an cynical turn of mind, the Reverend Kelly might have observed of the deceased that they would "fill a pit as well as better." While the preacher spoke, F.M. McCauley, Sidell mortician, and Roy Houghton, a Georgetown undertaker, lowered one casket after another into a single grave. The grave containing the three caskets remains unmarked.[22] Even among aficionados of Baron Lamm, few know that Songer is the final resting place of the trio. In the Vermilion (IL) County cemetery records, Lamm is listed as Thomas Bell. Landy and Hunter are listed by their proper names.

After the fatal skirmish between lawmen and bandits on Route 36 in Edgar County, Deputy Joe Walker was taken by ambulance to St. Anthony's

End of the line: Songer Cemetery outside Tilton, Illinois, where Lamm, Landy, and Hunter were buried in an unmarked grave (Sheryl J. Hansen).

Hospital in Terra Haute. He was on the operating table just after noon and underwent surgery for two hours. Three bullets had hit his intestine, liver and groin. Because his condition was so weak, it was thought best not to give him a blood transfusion. Walker held on until nine the next morning, the 17th.

Deputy Joe L. Walker's service, in contrast to that of the bandits, attracted multitudes to the Dana Methodist Church on the afternoon of Friday December 19. Masons and members of the Indiana Firemans' Association filled the church pews almost to capacity. Fire chaplain Raymond F. Koon of Gary, Indiana, officiated at the service. Businesses in tiny Dana were closed from 12:30 to 2:00 P.M. that Friday so that people could pay their respects to the fallen deputy without competition from worldly concerns. Walker was thirty-two at the time of his death. He left behind a sister, a brother, his mother and his widow, Florence Jones Walker. She was given $2,475 by the banks of Vermillion County (IN) and the Indiana Bankers' Association as commiseration for the loss of her husband.[23]

State of Illinois Standard Certificate of Death 5185, describing the death of Thomas Bell, was issued by Vermilion County coroner John D. Cole and witnessed by Vermilion County sheriff F.W. Ward the day before the bandits' funeral, December 23. It is a modest, self-effacing document. What it doesn't say would fill a book. Bell's, that is, Lamm's, date of birth was unknown. His parents' names and their occupations were also unknown. Bell's own occupation was unknown, but one feels that a judicious estimate of this could have been made without undue exertion.

Bell's age is approximated — 45. He was thus born "about 1885." He was a white male. Furthermore, he was a white male who packed an alias, although just what that alias was happened to be left blank, probably because there were too many to choose just one. His military service, too, was an unknown quantity. Apparently, Lamm's full-blown legend, complete with the cheating at cards, had not yet reached the authorities at Danville.

As one might expect, there was a cause of death: "Bullet wound through heart self-inflicted when surrounded by armed posse following a bank robbery."

Despite the assurance of the coroner's inquest and the death certificate that Lamm/Bell was a suicide, some of the posse felt differently. Ernest Boetto was sure that he had shot someone at the Moody farm. He may have shot Hunter running through the barn yard for the cornfield. The local paper credited Boetto for certain with downing someone among the bandits in the cornfield. If so, it may well have been Lamm. The *Commercial-News*, however, forgot about Boetto after the inquest.

Lamm may not have been either a suicide or a victim of Boetto's rifle. It's possible that Landy had used his .38 revolver on Lamm before he used it on himself.[24] This would explain the powder burn evidence remarked by those first on the scene. We'll never know for sure because the vigilantes and F.W. McCauley, the Sidell mortician, removed the bodies, the clothes from those bodies and the bandits' weapons before the authorities could make a determination.[25]

Late Wednesday, the day after the robbery, the two prisoners, giving their names yet as William Long and William Martin, but who, of course, were really James "Oklahoma Jack" Clark and Walter Detrich, were reunited in the jail at Newport, Indiana. Newport is the county seat of Vermillion County and is about equidistant from Danville and Terre Haute, where the two men had been held until the evening of the 17th. At Newport, the prisoners were housed in a two-story red brick structure that still stands.

Fenton Williams' younger brother, Carroll, had a close look at the two surviving members of Baron Lamm's gang. In 1996, he spoke of it:

> For some reason, somebody mentioned, "Let's go up and see the boys." So, we took off to the jail — Ray and I.... It was right at noontime or a little after noontime. We asked if we could talk to them. The warden — he didn't seem — no big

deal. So, we talked to them a little bit. Something was brought up about the late meal and this Clark spoke up and said, "Well, it don't make any difference. Don't think we're going any place anyway." He had on a pair of overalls. The other fella [Detrich] I don't remember too much about. I don't think he had much to say. Pretty dressy, wasn't he?"[26]

It is interesting that Carroll and Ray Bishop got in to see the prisoners so easily in light of what the *Daily Clintonian* had to say on December 22: "Clark and Detrick [*sic*] are being held in separate cells in the county jail at Newport. Utmost care is being taken to guard the men and only persons who are known to Sheriff Newland are admitted into the jail."[27] On the 26th, the same paper noted even more imposing conditions: "After the arraignment, Judge Wait ordered Sheriff Newland to maintain a 24-hour guard over the jail by a special detachment of deputies."

Maybe Sundays didn't count. Sundays cost the county more money.

This interview took place on what was probably the last Sunday the two prisoners were at Newport — the 28th. Clark and Detrich were locked up in separate cells on the second floor of the jailhouse. If only one jailor was present at the time of Williams' visit, security had obviously let up since the early going following the capture of the two bandits. That would change when the pair went to trial.

The sheriff's house and jail in Newport, Indiana. Detrich and Clark were here for two weeks.

Detrich was a bit more fortunate than Clark when it came to visitors. On Tuesday, the 30th, a comely young lady paid him a visit at the jail. What the two talked about no one knows. What her relationship with Detrich was is also unknown. All that anyone could gather about her was that she was from St. Louis — logically enough, as this was his hometown and the town where he died.

The "boys" were lodged in the Newport jail for two weeks before going to trial. The trial would take two days, and one wonders why. They didn't have much representation and what little they had was all bluff.

XI

The State of Indiana vs. Walter E. Detrich and James Clark, Alias William M. Long

> How many does it take to make twelve?—O. Henry, "The Ransom of Red Chief"
>
> Aw, they look like a passel of pallbearers.—*3 Godfathers* (1948)

For a time, it wasn't clear which county in which state would be prosecuting Walter E. Detrich and James M. Clark.[1] The bank robbery, of course, had been committed in Vermillion County, Indiana, but there were numerous auto banditries that could be prosecuted, the last two of which were committed in Illinois counties. Most seriously of all, Joe Walker, a native of Edgar County, Illinois, had been mortally wounded in that county.

Which crime stood the best chance for conviction?

Vermillion County prosecutor Homer Ingram had been away in the South on his honeymoon when the Clinton robbery took place, so his colleague, deputy prosecutor Willis A. Satterlee, was at the helm for Vermillion County's bid for the outlaws—something always assumed by the newspapers as a fait accompli. Over in Edgar County, state's attorney Charles Tym would study the situation and render a decision on whether or not his county would prosecute a murder case by Monday, December 22.

Since conviction of bank robbery in which a first degree murder had been committed carried an automatic death sentence in Indiana, Tym gladly turned over all aspects of the prosecution to Satterlee. Nevertheless, no murder had been committed during the bank robbery, and Walker's death came as the result of a gunfight with the robbers in his state and county. Moreover, three rounds had been fired from Walker's .38-caliber revolver. Walker had been slain, but he was certainly not murdered in cold blood.

Tym, no doubt sensing that the bank robbery charge had the best chance to carry a conviction and knowing that Walker's death would stretch the sentence to the limit, waived his county's right to prosecute the two men. On the 22nd, Tym merely offered his desire to prosecute a murder case against Detrich and Clark if Vermillion County failed to secure a conviction on the bank robbery charge. If convicted of bank robbery in Indiana, under a new law, the two would be looking at 10 years to life, with life the more likely sentence in view of Walker's death.

Just in case Detrich and Clark tasted freedom too early, an Edgar County grand jury indicted the pair for the murder of Walker on February 9, 1931. By this time, the two had been in Michigan City at the state prison a month, serving a life sentence for bank robbery. Detrich, in view of his tender years— only 26 years of age — really should have been incarcerated in the reformatory at Pendleton.

After his arrest, Detrich had told Danville authorities that his name was William Martin and that he was from Chicago. His fingerprints were taken and sent to the Indiana Bureau of Criminal Identification and Investigation on a card that he signed as William Martin. His true identity was revealed immediately and, for the most part, thereafter, he was referred to as Walter Detrich in the newspapers.

On the morning of the 18th, Detrich was driven from Newport to Terre Haute by Deputy Raymond "Razz" Foltz to have his mug shot taken. Clark, the evening of the 16th, underwent questioning by members of the detective bureau. No doubt Detrich came in for the third degree while at Terre Haute. Both men seem not to have yielded anything but the most rudimentary information, as false as it was thin. They clung steadfastly to their aliases, William Long and William Martin.

Clark had claimed either Moberly or Kansas City, Missouri, as his residence, though which isn't clear. His address was apparently meant to convey an image of being a Missouri farmer; presumably rural Moberly or rural Kansas City was implied. And, as mentioned earlier, the Muncie, Indiana, police department accepted Clark's avowal of being a farmer. At Louisville, following one of two arrests in February 1927, he had claimed New York City with no mention of farming as an occupation. Now, however, Clark was just trying to pose as a simple farmer from Missouri. Detrich was reunited with Clark in Newport after his grilling. The two would remain in the Vermillion County jail there until after their trial in January.

Detrich and Clark apparently asked local lawyers for representation. They also applied to Chicago firms. Neither local nor out-of-town attorneys, however, would touch their case when it was clear that they had no money. The men were lacking in funds, perhaps, but did they really lack connections?

This brings to mind two things. First, what about "Uncle Ed" or "Uncle Ben?"[2] By one or the other of these names, this gentleman from Chicago was the source of a gala Christmas dinner for Detrich and Clark. He obviously was someone whom it would pay to know if you were an underworld figure. Why, then, did he not do more for the pair? Why did he not, then and there, furnish legal counsel for the two men? And, second, when Dad Landy was arrested in May 1924, in league with two other yeggs with a Chicago background, counsel from the Windy City was forthcoming so swiftly that the Clinton County, Indiana, authorities were sore amazed. Indeed, the latter were at a loss to account for how the news of the capture had reached Chicago so quickly. Landy and the others had been snared in the wee hours of the 22nd, and that afternoon a Chicago lawyer named O'Donnell called, volunteering his assistance. None of the trio had made any calls to Chicago. Plenty of calls had come out of Chicago, however.

What this incident seems to point up is that Landy had connections, owing to a nefarious past, most probably burgling banks — the reason for his arrest on the night of May 21/22, 1924, outside Frankfort, Indiana. It makes one wonder whether Landy belonged to a bank-robbing syndicate. The two with Landy went to prison, but Landy was let off, owing to lack of evidence. This development, too, sounds like the work of a typical syndicate lawyer.[3] Given his arrest in Frankfort for having burgling equipment, it would seem that Landy had a history of bank burgling and that he may have thus been valuable to a bank-robbing syndicate in his bank-burglar capacity. Nor was the aged felon above shoplifting. Landy, in tow with a lady friend, had swiped a ladies' coat a day or two before Christmas, 1929, at the Kadner-Bach department store in Terre Haute. The next day, Christmas Eve, again accompanied by the lady, Landy looked at women's coats at the Samuel Smith department store in Terre Haute. Landy made a scene over the price and stormed out of the place. That night, the store's safe was relieved of nearly $10,000.[4] Landy was definitely wasted at Clinton. He could have taken the bank singlehanded — but only after midnight.

Colonel C. Sawyer, public defender or pauper attorney for Vermillion County, and the junior half of the law firm of B.S. Aikman and C.C. Sawyer, was assigned Detrich and Clark's case by Judge William C. Wait. Sawyer was only twenty-three and had just seen his salary increase by $300 a year for his gig as pauper attorney.[5] He was the son of Herbert Sawyer, county recorder for the past eight years. Colonel, by the way, happened to be his Christian name and not a title, honorary or otherwise.

Sawyer knew that the men didn't have so much as a wooden leg to stand on, but he did come up with a colorful feint. He met with Clark in conference the afternoon of the 18th and when they emerged, reporters were told that they had been preparing "a mystery defense." Reporters were intrigued, and they naturally asked the lawyer and his client what this stratagem amounted to. Clark seemed more than happy to impart some details, but no sooner did he begin his explanation than he clammed up, owing no doubt to Sawyer's presence. Reporters were not to be enlightened; not then, not ever. The so-called "mystery defense" would remain exactly that—a mystery.

Was there anything to it or was the "mystery defense" mere sham? Probably there was nothing more to it than hot air. But if there was anything to it, it might have taken account of the fuzziness of so much of the evidence against Clark and Detrich.

How many men were in on the robbery? Fuzzy math there. Clark was one of a group of five, it was determined, but a number of reports said that there were six men in the robber band. How many getaway cars were there? More fuzzy math. Some reports indicated that there were two or even three cars carrying the gang. How much loot was taken from the Citizens State Bank and how much was recovered? If any money was missing, how was that to be accounted for?

Clark was unhappy about the fact that he and Detrich were to be tried together. It was his wish that they have separate trials and this, too, may have been part of the "mystery defense." Probably Clark was just trying to enlist public opinion on his behalf by making it appear that Detrich was the more incorrigible of the two, with a lengthy rap sheet to prove it.

The facts are otherwise. Clark made Detrich look like an amateur when it came to crimes attributed to him, both in number and seriousness. If Clark had had anything to do with the Denver Mint robbery, Detrich would have had to go a ways beyond simple extortion and theater and payroll robberies to be mentioned in the same breath with him.

In any case, whatever Clark's motives, there was never any strain evident in the relationship between the two men, and they went to trial together without a whimper. And they went to prison together without a whimper. And they broke out of prison together without a whimper.

While the two were in jail, they had their fair share of visitors. Even before being jailed together at Newport, both were questioned by a delegation of Frankfort lawmen and Clarence Masters, assistant cashier at the Farmers' State Bank. This took place while Detrich was still at Danville and Clark was at Terre Haute. Masters, by the way, was the only member of the Frankfort delegation that had actually been in the Farmers' bank during the robbery of December 3.

Then, a few days later, the prisoners were viewed by a delegation of bank and law personnel from Lafayette, who put the finger on everybody killed or taken at Sidell with the exception of Hunter, the driver. Landy, too, according to most accounts, was not identified with the Lafayette robbers.

Lieutenant Rex Resser of the Indiana State Police was most likely the one who put the bug in the ear of the Frankfort people. He had flown in one of the two Indiana National Guard airplanes used to track Lamm and his gang in their flight from Clinton. Resser was convinced that Landy was one of the Frankfort bandits (a view not supported by patrons of the Farmers' bank) and so, by extension, were the others who had been killed or captured near Sidell. Former Clinton County sheriff Dan Power, who had arrested Landy, Dan Morgan and Charles Norman/Clyde H. Nimerick outside Frankfort on May 21/22, 1924, also identified Landy at Sidell.

Just what led to the Lafayette delegation doesn't appear. Perhaps it was no more than simple thoroughness on somebody's part whenever a robber band had been run to ground in the area to see if anyone who had been in the Tippecanoe Loan and Trust when it was held up could identify anyone in the gang. Just how many of the Lamm gang were fingered by Lafayette personnel also isn't clear. Clark and Detrich are always fingered in newspaper accounts. In the Lafayette *Journal Courier* coverage, Lamm is prominent, but Landy is omitted. On the other hand, Landy is mentioned in the *Danville Commercial-News* write-up of the visit and nowhere else. This might seem like simple inconsistency among newspapers of the region if it were not for the fact that more than any other area newspaper, the *Danville Commercial-News* was on top of the story.[6]

What was there about Landy that made him so hard to finger? He almost certainly was at Lafayette, yet scarcely anyone said so. He was even more certainly at Frankfort, yet no one but law personnel felt up to placing him there.

Clark's presence at a Lamm robbery is never a surprise, since he was something of a constant in Lamm operations, at least after Milwaukee in 1924. Detrich, too, was something of a Lamm regular in the closing years. The major question is whether or not Landy was at Lafayette. If so, this would place him with Lamm three years before the Frankfort robbery, their first undoubted daylight collaboration, thereby raising the question of just how long their association went back. Of course, it is up for grabs how long Lamm's acquaintance with any of the other bandits at Clinton went back, but Landy's case is somewhat different. Landy was an older man, old enough to be Lamm's mentor, in fact. As we have seen, the two probably worked together at St. Bernice a month before Landy's six-month incarceration.

While the idea that Landy rode with the ill-fated Dalton gang has nothing to support it, except his age — no Dalton authority knows him — he may have been somebody well respected in the holdup industry. He had Chicago connections who were ready to go to bat for him following his arrest in 1924. The fact that Landy was at Lamm's side during their final moments seems significant. He may have been the man Lamm depended on most. Lamm may even have asked Landy to do him in.

On December 23, Detrich and Clark were arraigned at the Vermillion County courthouse before Judge William C. Wait. The courthouse was two blocks down from the jail where the men were being kept in separate cells. When Judge Wait asked how they pleaded, both men pleaded, "Not guilty." Realizing how astronomical it was, Clark laughed abruptly when their bonds were set at $100,000 each. He may have wanted to cry when he recollected how paltry his bond had been in Winston-Salem, not four years earlier, when he and Lamm skated out of that town without leaving a forwarding address.

But to most observers, Detrich appeared the more jovial of the two. Clark struck those in the courtroom as being nervous for the most part. Their differing attitudes would remain much the same throughout the trial, except that Clark sometimes appeared more studious than nervous. He would hang on every word spoken at the trial, even finding an unlikely time to chuckle.

Judge William C. Wait, who presided over the trial of Detrich and Clark (Indiana Historical Society, M0888).

The trial date was set for 9 A.M., Friday, January 2, 1931. Judge Wait would preside. Homer Ingram, back in Vermillion now, would take the lead in the prosecution of Clark and Detrich, being assisted by deputy prosecutor Willis A. Satterlee. The trial would take place at the Vermillion County courthouse in Newport, Indiana. There would be tight security, undoubtedly with two aims in mind: not to let two certain someones out of the courthouse and not to let anyone worse in.

On December 29, Sawyer, Clark and Detrich went before Judge Wait to ask for a continuance of the trial, which was just four days away. They stated that they needed more time to prepare their defense adequately, which, of course, was true. The crime with which Clark and Detrich had been charged was not even two weeks in the past.

Robberies in those days committed on one side of a weekend could see justice meted out in a big way on the opposite side of that same weekend. The first day of a twenty-year sentence in the state pen was often served by mid-week.[7]

Their next objection concerned the media coverage, newspaper and, presumably, radio, which they said had whipped up public feeling against them.

The Vermillion County Courthouse, Newport, Indiana.

To see how valid this point was, it is only necessary to examine one or two scant items from area newspapers.

The same article in the *Lafayette Journal and Courier* for the 29th that covers Clark and Detrich's motion for a continuance, due to "false newspaper reports" tending "to work up prejudice against them," opens with these remarks: "Two of the *bandits* are left to face trial at Clinton. They are Long [that is, Clark] and Detrich. Both were held in connection with the death of Joe Walker, Dana, Ind., garage-man and former deputy sheriff, who was fatally wounded by the bandit mob as they fled away from the Clinton robbery" (italics mine).

A randomly-picked item from the *Indianapolis News* one week before categorically describes "James Clark, age thirty-two, and Walter Dietrick [*sic*], age twenty-six, *two surviving members of a bandit gang of five* which held up and robbed the Citizens Bank here a week ago" (italics mine).[8]

It would almost seem that nobody ever did anything *allegedly* in those days; they just plain did it and everybody for miles around knew it, except, of course, the accused and, most especially, their counsel; although in this case, the youthful counsel seems to have known it, too.

Attorney Sawyer's motion to quash the indictment on the 26th was itself quashed by Judge Wait as out of order. It had been filed five days too late. (Nevertheless, Sawyer would make another futile attempt to quash the indictment in the opening moments of the trial, as well as requesting a change of venue. Both motions would be turned down.) The best that Clark and Detrich could hope for now would be a continuance. With the trial set for the second of January, there wasn't much hope of that.

If it was any comfort to the pair, a lot of other bandits fared worse when it came to trial dates. Clark and Detrich had had more than two weeks to put something together. All they could do in this time was stall, hoping for some real assistance, probably out of Chicago. As it was, they didn't have a penny to bless themselves with, nor a shred of evidence to suggest that they hadn't been inside the Citizens State Bank on the morning of the 16th.

Still, one is left wondering why Sawyer did not ask for a change of venue — before it was too late. Whatever the media coverage of the incident might suggest, there was very real sentiment against the men in the area. Clark, after all, had been taken to Terre Haute and Detrich was held in Danville because feeling in Dana, Joe Walker's residential town, was so intense that there was talk of lynching the men if they were held anywhere close to Dana. Although Clark and Detrich must have pressed him with some urgency, Sawyer did not move for a change of venue until the first day of the trial.

The trial of James M. Clark and Walter E. Detrich began on Friday, January 2, 1931, at 9 in the morning as scheduled. Security was tight. Guards with machine guns were stationed around the courthouse as well as inside the courtroom and in the lobby.

An overflowing crowd of spectators filled not only the courtroom but the lobby and courtyard as well. The prisoners were brought in shackled with an escort of four heavily-armed lawmen. As with their arraignment eleven days earlier, the two prisoners had ambled (as best they could) handcuffed and shackled the two blocks from the red brick county jail on the corner of Market and Main Street. Deputy Sheriff Razz Foltz held onto a long chain attached to the men's shackles. Chief Helms, Sheriff Newland and Court Bailiff Roy Ingram accompanied the prisoners to the courthouse.

The trial would not take long — part one day and part of the next.

XII

Tell the Jury What, If Anything, Happened Then: The Witnesses Speak

Yes, sir, and shot a lot, too. — F.W. Gilbert

Prosecutor Homer D. Ingram swore two counts against Walter Detrich and James Clark. The first count was larceny with threatened injury to the five employees of the Citizens State Bank who were present on the morning of December 16, 1930. The second count was for burglarizing the Citizens State Bank in the daytime with attendant threats of physical harm to the five employees of the bank present. The death of Joe Walker was not part of either count. The defendants were up for bank robbery, pure and simple. A murder rap was waiting in the wings should the bank robbery charge fail.

The first day, Friday, January 2, 1931, began promptly at 9 A.M., with jury selection. This took up an hour. Then the state made an opening statement. The defense declined to make one. Three witnesses testified before the noon recess. The afternoon session would see no less than thirteen witnesses take the stand. In all, a very full day.

The procession of witnesses followed a more or less chronological pattern. The first two witnesses were bank employees. The next two were men who happened to be on the street, or looking out on the street, when the bank robbery occurred. Then, two more bank employees and a patron in the bank at the time of the robbery testified before witnesses outside of Clinton and law enforcement personnel took the stand. The fullest testimony came from, predictably enough, Clinton chief of police Everett Helms. On the other hand, some testimony occupied no more than a mere moment or two.

No single witness saw everything in his sphere of reference. Dad Landy, for example, may as well have stayed home on the 16th, for all the good or bad that he did. No one saw him as a living, breathing thing—no one on the witness stand, at any rate. If any did see him, they kept it under wraps when testifying. As the oldest member of the bandit band, by decades, he should have stood out like a sore thumb.[1]

Cashier Arthur V. Hedges was the first of the eighteen witnesses summoned by the state. By the time the jury had been selected and Prosecutor Homer D. Ingram made his opening remarks, it was after ten thirty in the morning. Asked by Prosecutor Ingram to recount the events of the 16th, Hedges responded:

> Well, it was, I presume, a little after nine o'clock. I had gone back to the lavatory and I heard someone hollering or calling, "Open that door." I didn't know they were calling to me and a man opened the door and took a revolver and waved it around in front of me and said, "Come on," and he took hold of my shoulder and gave me a pull and said, "Come on and come outside." And he took me in the front room and told me to lay down. I saw several people on the floor there and I started to lay down and he said, "Lay on your face," or some such remark as that, and I lay down with my head on my arm and laid there.
> Want me to continue?

Prosecutor Ingram did, indeed, want Hedges to go on, but, for our purposes, we will do as well by going directly to the testimony of assistant cashier Pete Voto, who covers much of the same ground, with the exception of the amount of money taken—$15,537. Voto followed Hedges on the witness stand, the second of three prosecution witnesses to testify the morning of the trial's first day.

> Well, we opened up that morning and I judge it was along about nine or nine ten. I was working on the books of the previous day. I was back at the last desk,—there are three desks there,—the front window and second and third and I was at the third window posting up the daily books,—previous day's business. Mr. Jackson was right at the side of me waiting on a customer at the Christmas Savings window. After a little bit I heard a shuffle and happened to look up and I seen a bunch of men filing in through the door. They said, "Get back there and get your hands up." So we got in the back part of the back room there and had our hands up and they said, " Shut your eyes or I will bust you," or something to that effect and they made us close our eyes and made us lay on the floor. I heard one them say, "Which one do you want to open the safe?" They must have pointed or something and they got Jackson up. They told him to open the safe, and he said it was a time lock on there after he made an attempt to open it, and said he couldn't open it. One of these fellows hit him with a revolver and cursed at him for a little bit and told him to open that safe. He told him that he couldn't, that there was a time lock on it and it couldn't open until four o'clock. At that time Mr. Hedges spoke and said that safe had a time lock on it and nobody could open it. So they let him go and sent him up in front to open the other safe. They went in the vault. They evidently thought there was a

XII — Tell the Jury What, If Anything, Happened Then

safe in the vault. They came back and he opened the front safe up near the door where they came in and I suppose they got the money that was in there. We lay there awhile and I could hear them talking to themselves, asking if they got this and got that and have you looked here and have you looked there. After a little bit everything was quiet and one of the fellows said, "I guess they are gone," and we got up then.

In another moment, Ingram asked the witness if the man who talked to him during the robbery was one of the defendants.

A. No, sir.
Q. Did you find out afterwards who that man was?
A. Yes, sir.
Q. Tell the jury who that man was.
A. It was a fellow by the name of Bell. I made a trip over to Sidell and recognized him there.

Curiously, Pete Voto said not a word specifically about Dad Landy in his testimony, yet in his remarks made to INS Bureau Chief Jack Cejnar in the days following the robbery, he clearly described Landy. It was Voto and Voto alone who placed Landy in the bank. But it must be remembered that no witness in the bank saw more than two robbers — and all agree that at least three robbers were present. Bookkeeper Luella Cloutier certainly was in the bank at the time of the robbery, and we don't know a thing about her. She is merely listed by two witnesses, not described. She was no more substantial than a politician's platform.

The Prosecution now went to the street for its next two witnesses before returning to the bank for three more. Why this was done is anybody's guess. Possibly, the Prosecution wanted to avoid the monotony of too many witnesses speaking from the same perspective — five such. We shall hear from the street in due time, but two more bank employees and one patron need to be heard from first to flesh out how Baron Lamm operated during his bank-robbing swan song.

Following the two witnesses from the street were bookkeeper John Nolan and bank teller Lawrence Jackson. Nolan described Jackson's encounter with Detrich and Lamm from the vantage point of a man with his eyes glued to the floor. He went on to mention something Lamm told Detrich, but here the defense objected to Nolan's relating statements made by the bandits, instead of describing their actions. Nolan saw only one bandit — Thomas Bell (Lamm). Nolan was examined by Prosecutor Ingram.

Jackson described opening the safe in front after an unsuccessful attempt to open the vault in back. He makes it clear, as did Nolan, that on his last day Lamm was anything but a master cracksman. Describing "what, if anything," happened in the bank the morning of December 16, Jackson responded:

... they went through all the drawers looking for money, got all the money out of the same. I presume it was all gone and they couldn't find a sack. And one of the fellows went in the vault and came back out and they were going around trying to find something to put the money in. And I was laying in the door at the back then and one of the men went to the rear, and took a paper off the electric fan that we had out there and brought it up to the front.

Q. How many of these men that were in the bank did you get a clear and distinct view of?
A. Two of them.
Q. Do you know at this time who they were or who they are?
A. I know by the name[s] they go by. Mr. Bell. I went over to Sidell and saw him laying in the morgue.
Q. Which one of these men hit you over the head?
A. Mr. Bell.
Q. And who was the other man?
A. Detrich.
Q. And if that man is in the court, point him out?
A. Right there he is. He is the one that was standing up in front and he called the other man by name and said, "Have him open that safe," and he took about two steps with me and we went to the front and opened it.

Apparently, Jackson is saying that Lamm was the one who told Detrich to have him open the safe up front after Lamm had struck him for not getting into the vault in the back. Jackson's pronouns sometimes step on the toes of his meaning, but the above interpretation can be the only accurate one of his remarks.

Q. How was he [Detrich] dressed at that time?
A. He had on sort of a tan top coat and cap and I mentioned to the fellows after he went out, he was dressed very nice and was a nice-looking young fellow.

The next witness was insurance man Harry C. Call. He happened to walk in on the robbery that morning. While bookkeeper John Nolan saw only Thomas Bell/Baron Lamm during the robbery, Call did not see him at all. That's how focused witnesses were while the robbery was in progress. Call was examined by Prosecutor Homer D. Ingram.

Q. ... state if you went to the Citizens Bank that morning?
A. Yes, sir. I had a paper for Mr. Hedges that I was supposed to deliver to him the first thing that morning and I went down a little after nine o'clock ... nine ten, something like that.
Q. And went in the bank there?
A. Yes, sir.
Q. Now, just go ahead and tell the jury, Mr. Call, what took place while you were there in the bank that morning.
A. Well, I was in the bank and I was met at the door by someone that kind of took ahold of me a little bit. I kind of thought it was a joke.

XII — Tell the Jury What, If Anything, Happened Then

Q. How did he take hold of you?

A. Grabbed hold of me and then I realized and saw there was a gun flashing around there. I thought it was a coal company getting a payroll like they used to do and I still thought it was a joke. And about this time there was a gun came out of this fellow's coat like that *(indicating)* and he said, "This is a stick-up." I said, "I guess it is like that." So, by that time, I was changed over to another fellow and he marched me around the cages to where I found out later Jackson was on the floor. Well, I stumbled over someone [probably Jackson] and he told me if I made a move he'd blow my damn head off and by that time, I was in the rear and he threw me down on the floor face down and told me to stay there.

Q. Now, you say when you went in the bank some fellow got hold of you?

A. Yes.

Q. Look in the room and see if you can identify this man.

A. This man here.

JUDGE WAIT: Well, who is it?

A. This man here, sitting right here in the light suit. [Clark]

Q. He was clear to you?

A. Yes.

JUDGE WAIT: You mean he is one of the defendants in this case?

A. Yes, sir.

Q. You say he turned you over to another man?

A. Yes, sir. This man here. [Detrich]

Q. And he was the one that took you back to the back room and made you lie down?

A. Yes, sir.

Q. In other words, Mr. Call, you recognize both of these two defendants as the ones in the bank there that morning in the bank hold-up?

A. Yes, I do.

Two witnesses from outside the bank testified in the middle of the five witnesses from the bank. The first was C.E. Vansickle, the barber, who was the catalyst for all the mishaps that day. Following him was Elwood Bennett, a witness completely overlooked by the newspapers and one who saw something that no one else saw and oddly did not see something that he should have seen. His testimony is a more fitting lead-in to Vansickle's testimony than the other way around, as the State had it.

Again, it was Homer Ingram doing the questioning.

Q. And whereabouts were you in the city while you were there?

A. Well, I came from home up to Mr. Charley Grant — came to see him and I learned he wasn't there. And I went two doors south and was just standing there looking up the street.

Q. Tell the jury what if anything happened then.

A. Well, while I was standing there, there was a car drove up in front of the State Bank. I wasn't paying particular attention to them. There were three went into the bank — that is what I saw ... three — and I never paid any more attention until there was three fellows come out of the bank and got in the car — a big

Buick sedan. And when they turned in the street and run up on the curbing, why, I kind of thought they were drunk, but, then, I saw they wasn't the way the driver swung the car and they blew a tire. And then they back off of there and when they pulled out in the street, they struck another car and then turned at Vine Street.

Q. How many men were in this car when they turned off Main Street?
A. There were five.
Q. And what direction did you say the car went?
A. Car just turned around in the street and then went north about three-fourths of a block and then went due west.
Q. On Vine Street?
A. Yes.
Q. And I believe that you said at that time there was a tire down on the car.
A. There was a tire busted when they hit the curbing and turned around.

Two things stand out in Bennett's testimony. He saw the bandit's Buick strike a car in the street when it backed away from the curb — no one else did. Secondly, Bennett did not see, or, at least, did not note, the barber with a shotgun. Bennett was not on the list of witnesses drawn up by Prosecutor Ingram on December 22 and presented with subpoenas on the 29th. This may mean that Bennett volunteered to testify. The next witness, C.E. Vansickle, was actually the last of the three witnesses to testify the morning of the first day of the trial. Bennett was the first to testify that afternoon.

C.E. Vansickle was examined by Homer D. Ingram.

Q. Tell the jury whether or not you saw anyone there around the Citizens bank on this morning.
A. I saw two men come up in front of Rosenblatt's store — one dressed a good deal like a hunter, had a leather jacket and cap on. The man on the inside walked up to the door of the bank and walked in and just as soon as he entered or turned in the bank, the other one fellow went in, followed. At that time the street was pretty clear and I could see everybody and a man from Mr. Leed's store attempted to go in the bank and at the time the two men went in the bank, I said to Mr. Curry —

The Defense now objected and the objection was sustained. Conversation outside of the defendants and, especially hearsay, rarely made the record, no matter who made it.

Q. Just tell what you done.
A. I stood there and watched them. I expect I watched them six minutes and at that time, the car pulled up.
Q. What kind of a car was that?
A. Well, I couldn't tell you. It was a dark car — large car — and I watched this car at least two minutes. I watched to see if it was running. Finally, whoever was driving it, stepped on the accelerator and made the smoke come out of the back. As soon as I saw that, I took my gun and two shells and started over that way

and keep going along slow. Pretty soon they began to trail out one at a time, the first fellow getting in the front seat. The car then faced south and he got in the east side. The next one got in the back seat on the right hand side. And then this man [*probably indicating Clark*] came out last and got in the front. I could see him plain. The other two that got in were in the back seat and I could only see their back. They turned right in front of the bank as short as they could and one wheel hit the sidewalk. As they backed off of the sidewalk, I pulled my gun on them. I kept watching the bank to see if there was any alarm coming from the bank. I felt like I ought to shoot the tire. So, finally, somebody hollered, "Shoot them," but then I still thought it was wrong to shoot.

Q. Now, this man you described as walking from Rosenblatt's corner and going to the bank, describe how he was dressed.

A. Rather tall sort of a fellow — light overcoat and overcoat came down to his knees — and he walked erect.

Vansickle is describing Lamm and Clark on the street at Rosenblatt's. Lamm is the tall, erect walking one; Clark is dressed as an outdoorsman. Vansickle saw only two bandits enter the bank but three — or was it four? — come out of the bank. He mentioned a customer entering just before them. That patron may have been Walter Detrich.

Thirty-eight-year-old Harlow Frist, a farmer living 4 1/2 miles northwest of Clinton, was put on the stand after the Clinton policemen, Everett Helms and Walter Burnside. Since his testimony covers less ground than that of the lawmen — about seventy miles less — it may be as well to have it first. He was questioned by Homer D. Ingram.

Q. And just go ahead and tell what happened then.

A. I had gotten well on top of the hill. I was walking on the left hand track in the road and I heard a rushing noise. I looked up and I saw a large, black car coming from the east and it just passed the intersection of the road, probably the length of the big machine or car past the intersection of the north and south road and came to a stop. There was quite a bunch of them got behind this big car and in a very short time. I had probably taken three or four steps. I saw the right part of the radiator on another car just past the corner of the yard, that is, on the east side of the north and south road. At this time, I heard a man's voice say, "Shoot the cops! Get the goddamn cops!"

The Defense now objected to what the witness heard someone say unless he could show that it was one of the defendants who said it or in his presence. The Court overruled the objection.

Q. Go ahead and tell what happened then.

A. Well, about that time I walked up and stood on the bank, out of the road, up near the banks that is on top of the hill from the road. This car that came up second — it started to turn south toward me and there was quite a barrage of rapid gun fire on that car as it made the turn. It came on down probably a hundred and fifty feet towards me and came almost or nearly to a stop again and there was more gun shots. Then the car came down and stopped in the road about even with me and the patrolman got out of the car. The Chief says to me:—

The defense objected to hearing what Chief Helms said unless it had been repeated in front of the defendants. The motion was sustained.

Q. Who do you mean when you say the Chief?
A. Everett Helms.
Q. Chief of Police for the city of Clinton?
A. Yes.
JUDGE WAIT: Mr. Frist, tell what you did and don't say what he told you.
A. I went down the hill towards the car and from there down the side ditch and down the road to my house and telephoned for help.
Q. How many shots would you say was fired there on that corner, Mr. Frist?
A. Probably 35 shots.
Q. And what men did you see that you recognized in this car that came south. Mr. Frist?
A. I didn't recognize any men in the car... Oh, that came south?
Q. Yes.
A. I recognized Patrolman Burnside and Everett Helms.
Q. How was Patrolman Burnside dressed at that time?
A. He had a dark blue uniform and dark blue cap.
Q. And were there any shots fired after the car in which Chief Helms and Burnside were in after they came down the road?
A. And stopped?
Q. Yes.
A. There was.
Q. Did you know where any of those shots took effect down there?
A. I know one bullet went through my coat.
Q. How long was the machine [car] there, if you know?
A. Probably fifteen minutes.
Q. And where, if any place, did they go, if you know?
A. I didn't see anything of their machine after I left to go to the telephone.
Q. And after you went to the telephone, did you come back out on the road?
A. I did.
Q. Where did you go then?
A. I walked part way up the hill, and passed a word or two with the Chief—that was Everett Helms.
Q. And where, if any place, did they go after that?
A. I don't know.
Q. Did you see them leave?
A. I didn't see them leave there. I saw them leave the spot where the other machine had stopped in the first place.
Q. You were up there at the corner?
A. Not at the time they left. I was on top of the hill.
Q. You were on top of the hill south?
A. Yes, sir.

XII — Tell the Jury What, If Anything, Happened Then

Q. And where, if any place, did you go then?
A. I went on up to the corner.
Q. And what, if anything, did you find there, Mr. Frist?
A. I found some empty shells.

The State now offered the empty shells as evidence, labeled as State's Exhibit "F." The Defense objected, saying that the shells could not be shown to have come from any specific person, let alone the two defendants. The objection was overruled.

Q. I will hand you State's Exhibit, marked State's Exhibit "F," and you tell the jury what that is.
A. That is the bullet I found out in a fence post.
Q. Now tell the jury where that fence post was when you got that bullet from it?
A. It was in the north and south fence and the west side of the north and south road and would be between the two cars at the time the coupe was going down the north and south road just after it turned.
Q. Tell the jury which side of that fence post this bullet went into.
A. It went in from the west side of the fence.
Q. Away from the north and south road on the other side?
A. Yes.

The bullet was offered in evidence as State's Exhibit "F." Defense Attorney Colonel C. Sawyer objected to this item being offered in evidence, and cross-examined the witness.

SAWYER AS Q. How did you get that out of that post?
A. I cut very little wood. It was nearly through the post.
Q. Did you examine that post before you went up there this last time when you got that bullet?
A. No.
Q. The day before you hadn't examined it?
A. No.
Q. You don't know when the bullet got in there?
A. No, sir.
Q. Could have been in there a week before that or a month before that?
A. I don't know.

This round sounds a bit like Darrow examining Bryan at the Monkey Trial five and a half years earlier. At any rate, it got the Defense nowhere and the bullet was admitted into the evidence. Sawyer continued with his cross-examination.

Q. When this car came down past you, you said it went south. Which direction did you say the other car went?
A. It was going west.
Q. Did you recognize anybody in that car?

A. I didn't.
Q. Do you know how many men were in the car?
A. I do not.
Q. How far was the car from you?
A. Probably 50 rods, probably that.
Q. Was that the closest you were to that car?
A. Yes, sir.
Q. And the motor was running?
A. I don't know about that.
Q. Well, the car was going or stopped?
A. It wasn't going after it was stopped.
Q. When you first saw it, was the car moving?
A. Yes, sir.
Q. When was it that you heard somebody's voice in the car?
A. I heard somebody say, "Go get the cop!" "Shoot the goddamn cop!"
Q. Where was this car?
A. It was stopped.
Q. Twenty-five rods from you.
A. Probably something like that.

The record doesn't indicate where outbursts of laughter occurred in the courtroom. But "six, two and even" there was laughter during this exchange.

The next witness to testify the afternoon of the first day was Harlow's father, Jediah Frist, a retired farmer living in Dana. He was on his way to the old homestead now occupied by Harlow and his family. He went south past Tillotson corner and had zigzagged a few miles more when he ran into the bandits. He was questioned by Homer D. Ingram.

Q. When you arrived within a mile and a quarter of your home [former home], tell the jury what, if anything, happened.
A. ... I noticed a large machine on the other side of the grade there — there is a vein runs through there with a bridge in it — and I noticed this machine coming down on the other side. I saw they were not going to pull over to the side any and I pulled to the side to let them pass by. They pulled right in front of me, probably two lengths of the machine and stopped. One man hollered, "Get out of that car, old man!" and I didn't move at first. I first thought from the actions that they showed that it was somebody that was looking for me and got the wrong man, but, on second thought, I seen it was the car they wanted. They had a broken wheel — the right front wheel seemed to be crippled. In an instant, there were three men out of the machine, and two of them came to the left-hand door of my machine saying, "Get out of here," and I began to get out. I had a time getting out on my feet because I had on large overshoes and the door fast. I didn't get out quick enough. One man opened the door and reached over to look in. He had a machine gun — came over close to me and held it close to my breast. The other man took hold of my left shoulder and pulled me out of the machine — not rough. Took me out without hurting me and left me standing on my feet. Then they proceeded to get the things out of my car. They said, "Get that sack

of potatoes out of there," but it was a sack of flour. I had a sack of flour and I had a bag of fruit that I was taking to the boys that I had ordered and a bag with a package of sugar in it. I also had a five-gallon oil can that I placed in a sack sitting back there. They proceeded to take those things out. Those two men did that *(indicating)*. They threw the packages with the sugar out and I picked that up. While this was going on, the man that was driving the other car got out from under his wheel, took a few steps to the right door of my car, got right in under my wheel, and there proceeded to turn it around before they got all the packages out. One man turned around towards the other machine and said, "Have you got all the jack?" That is about all that was said. They had the car turned around. The five men were busy taking packages out of their car and putting them into my car. They got my car turned around and went on west.

Q. There were five men there at that time?
A. Five men in action.
Q. How many guns did you see that these five men had?
A. I saw five or six, counting the machine gun.
Q. Did you get a look at these men?
A. I got a real good look at about three. Two of them I didn't get to see very well and the man that was busy in the back end of their car. I didn't get to see his face very well.
Q. Tell the jury whether or not you recognized either of these defendants as being there at that time.
A. I recognized both of them.
Q. They were both there?
A. Yes, sir.
Q. This man here [Detrich], tell the jury what he was doing there.
A. He was the man that took me by the arm and took me out of the car.
Q. And this other man, tell the jury what, if anything, he was doing?
A. He [Clark] was the man that had the machine gun and took hold of the door and opened it, but this man [Detrich] reached around him and took me by the arm. The man also took the packages out of my car.
Q. After your car was gone, did you make any examination of the car that was left there?
Q. I did ... the first thing I found was the first-aid kit. Then we found a stocking with a bunch of bullets — machine gun bullets, I guess — in it ... we found a package with probably a half-gallon of roof nails in it.

The next witness was F.W. Gilbert, whose testimony covers probably no more than twenty minutes of the running fight. For students of Baron Lamm on his final day ever, there is no better source for insights than Wells Gilbert. Lamm was under a great deal of pressure, but he conducted himself like a leader. When Gilbert speaks of "we," he refers to 17-year-old Roy Gritten, his driver, as well as himself. Gilbert was examined by Homer D. Ingram.

Q. Tell the jury where, if any place, you went that morning.
A. I left Mr. Board's garage first. I had put on a new tire and left there and started towards Chrisman on the paved road, 36.

Q. How far did you get on that road?
A. I reckon it was about four miles.
Q. Did you cross the Illinois line?
A. Yes.
Q. Just tell the jury what happened then.
A. I was at the intersection of the road coming south that is near, well, it is near what we call the Roy Wimsett road. It runs north and south but just before we got to that, there was a car. We got right in on the crossing and there was a car dodged right in ahead of us.
Q. Do you know what kind of a car that was that dodged in ahead of you at that corner?
A. I didn't at the time, but I knew it afterwards. It dodged in ahead of us and the first thing I knew, there was five men got out.
Q. Who, if anyone, was with you at that time?
A. A young man named Roy Gritten. He was driving. He was on the left side and this car dodged in ahead of us and it didn't seem to be any more than there [?] when five men were out on their feet. They all had guns in their hands and told us to unload. The boy got out on the south side of the pavement. Of course, we were headed west and I didn't get out very quick. I was a little slow and they kind of got ahold of my arms and kind of helped me out — rather, pulled me up that way. At the time, they had a little argument about who would drive the truck. Seemingly, they didn't want any of them to drive the truck and there was one fleshy fellow said, "Old man, lay down here at the side of that wheel." So I laid down there at the side of the front wheel. It was off of the pavement headed west. They passed several shots there with the boys from the south that was following them. Shot quite a little bit. I think there were three men knelt down right behind me and reloaded their revolvers — took their empty cartridges out and reloaded their revolvers right there behind me. I think this man known as Bell, he said, "This is getting us no place, boys." He said, "Make the old man get in there and drive us." We drove on straight west. Detrich got in beside me. This gentleman that is sitting there *(indicating)* [Clark] stood on the running board and kind of around there. This Mr. Bell.
Q. You mean Detrich, the defendant in this case?
A. Yes, sir.
Q. And the other three, where were they?
A. They was in behind in the cattle rack — it was a stock truck.
Q. Just tell what happened then.
A. Well, we drove west. They were dictating which way I should go, of course, and we drove west to the Scottland Road. Turned directly west on the north side of Scottland. Crossed over on old 36 about 150 yards. There they met a Ford and got changed over to the Ford. Dismissed me and got in the Ford.
Q. Were there any cars following all this time?
A. Yes, sir. There was two cars in sight while I stood there and when they drove ahead, there was two cars just behind me.
Q. Do you know who was driving this Ford that they took?
A. Yes, I know. The Williams boy.

XII — Tell the Jury What, If Anything, Happened Then

Q. Do you know his first name?
A. Fenton Williams.
Q. And what became of Fenton Williams?
A. He started south, walking towards Scottland the last I saw him. He was holding his hands up.
Q. And what, if anything, did you do then?
A. Just stood there until they got out of my sight.
Q. Mr. Gilbert, after they were all gone, was any shots fired then?
A. Yes, sir. They shot a few shots from behind us.
Q. They shot all of the time coming along?
A. Yes, sir, and shot a lot, too.
Q. And did you make any examination of your truck after they were all gone to see what, if anything, was in there?
A. Not at that time.
Q. What did you do then?
A. I was looking for a telephone to call my wife and I drove straight north to the second crossroads, from there directly west. Jogged a quarter north and then west again to my nephew's. Just left my truck and ran in the house to get to the telephone and called my wife to tell her I was all right.
Q. Did you, at that time, examine your truck?
A. I made no examination of my truck outside of the windows — they was both shot out at that time. I made the remark to my neighbors that I thought I had been with the bank gang. My nephew opened up the truck and looked in it and discovered an overcoat with the money in it.
Q. Overcoat?
A. Yes, in the truck there, spread out there, with a lot of loose money piled on top.
Q. Do you know what denominations this money was in?
A. No, sir. They looked like from one to five dollar bills. I got in the truck and threw that overcoat up over it and took it out to his cow barn. I wanted to hide it as quick as I could and my nephew and I took it out there and put it in the straw.
Q. About how large a bundle was that?
A. Oh, it was about a half a bushel, the overcoat and the bills. It looked like there was some papers in it. It looked like there was some papers, notes or something that I could see sticking out at the end. There was a rifle in the truck.
Q. Any other firearms left there?
A. No, sir.
Q. Mr. Gilbert, during the time that you were driving the truck, was there any conversation between these men riding in the truck?
A. Very little. But the gentleman, that seemed to be the leader of the gang, said, "Boys, I believe we are gone." He made that expression.

Neither Jediah Frist nor Wells Gilbert mentions Lamm's accent. In an era just over the "Red scare" and rife with the anti-foreigner Klan, it is curious that Lamm's accent was not noted by either of these individuals, especially Gilbert, who had much more contact with him. Perhaps by 1930, Lamm's accent wasn't as pronounced as his revolver in the minds of those who came into contact with him.

Following F.W. Gilbert on the witness stand was deputy sheriff and railroad conductor Herman J. Kutch, of St. Bernice, Indiana. He was questioned by Homer D. Ingram.

Q. Tell the jury where you went on the morning of the 16th day of December, 1930.

A. Well, about nine twenty-five, I went up to the bank after being notified that there had been a bank robbery in Clinton and got with Doctor Green. We went north from St. Bernice to what you call the Wright Road and then went on and went north to 36. We had to slow down there to let some cars go north. There was an Ohio car there with a man that had just crawled out from under it and he seemed pretty badly worried. I started in to telling him what I was wanting. He said they just went east and the officers went east after them with one man shot. They went in Dana and they had this big car that belonged to Mr. Frist.

Q. And who was the next people that you seen?

A. ... we turned and went north a mile or more and then went west. We observed a truck that was sitting by the side of the barn and two fellows was out and, at the time, they was trying to get in to make Ridge Farm. But it didn't occur to us at the time and the more we studied, the more we felt we ought to go back and we went back and we found Mr. Gilbert. After making out who we was, he said for us to come in and he showed us the rifle the first thing.

Q. Where was the rifle?

A. In his truck.

Q. Did you take the rifle out of the truck?

A. Yes, sir.

Q. I will hand you State's Exhibit marked State's Exhibit "G" and ask you to tell the jury whether or not that is the rifle you took out of Mr. Gilbert's truck. That is the same rifle you took out of Mr. Gilbert's truck?

A. Yes, sir.

Here Colonel Sawyer cross-examined Kutch briefly.

Q. How do you identify this rifle?

A. By the number.

Q. When did you take the number off?

A. As soon as I got it. As soon as I could get an opportunity to look it over. I have been in the business long enough that I knew it was essential to do that.

State's Exhibit "G" was admitted into the evidence.

Mr. Ingram resumed the prosecution.

Q. Tell the Court, Mr. Kutch, what, if anything else, you found in that truck.

A. Well, I found some empty cartridges and some loaded cartridges and I wouldn't be positive but as much as two, if not three, clips of empty cartridges.

Q. What kind of cartridges were those that you found there?

XII — Tell the Jury What, If Anything, Happened Then   177

A. I found some .45 empties and some .38 specials and .32.
Q. What kind of cartridges were the .32s?
A. They looked like they were for a rifle. I think they were rifle cartridges, but I wouldn't be positive about that.
Q. Anything else found in the back of the car?
A. No, that is all that I found in the car.
Q. Tell the jury whether or not there was any money turned over to you there at that time.
A. Yes, sir. While I was busy picking up them empty cartridges, this Mr. Gilbert told us to come in and he pointed to the car ... to the truck ... and, of course, there was part of it. I went up there and I was busy picking up the empty cartridges. I got two for the purpose of evidence, along with the gun. He went around to the north side of the barn and after he went around there, he came back with a big load of something. I couldn't see what it was. I thought it was wheat. He called my attention to it by saying that was the money. He said, if I remember, Mr. Gilbert said he didn't know but he reckoned it was the money. At the time, I didn't have my rifle out of the machine. I just had the revolver. I got to my machine and got my rifle when I seen it was money for fear that we might get held up by somebody else. As soon as we got it fixed to a way that we could travel with it, we took it to the bank — to the Citizens bank in Clinton — and stayed there until they counted it and took a receipt for the money.
Q. How much money was there?
A. $1,000, if I remember correctly.

Much of this is unclear. Kutch seems to have hit 36 in the wake of the Walker shooting. But, in that case, the chase would have led west into Illinois, not east to Dana, Indiana. Possibly Homer Hamm's taking the mortally wounded Joe Walker into Dana before the latter was placed on an ambulance bound for Terre Haute is meant.

Another problem in this testimony is the confusing use of the terms *car*, *truck* and *machine*. Half the time, one wonders whether Kutch's car or Gilbert's truck is meant, though only the latter can be the case.

Harold "Pete" Scott took the stand next. Scott and Homer Hamm, accompanied by Joe Walker, had left Dana to chase the bandits. Scott was there for the long haul. But Dana businessman Homer Hamm's part in the running fight came to an end with the fatal wounding of Joe Walker. Hamm drove Walker back to Dana to be attended by a local physician before being taken by ambulance to Terre Haute. Hamm actually did not testify until the morning of the second day of the trial, but because of his aborted participation in this episode, his testimony should be separated from that of Scott and other members of the posse who remained in the fight until its conclusion.

Homer Hamm was examined by Homer D. Ingram.

Q. I will ask you if you left Dana that morning [the 16th] any time?
A. Yes, sir.

Q. About what time?
A. It was along about nine-thirty.
Q. Where, if any place, did you go?
A. I went five miles south of Dana to the Tillotson corner?
Q. Who went with you?
A. Pete Scott, Joe Walker and myself.
Q. After you got to the Tillotson corner, tell the jury what happened there, if anything?
A. Mr. Scott and Walker stayed at the corner. I went to the telephone to see if they had any news — if they could give us any news which way they were coming.
Q. Go ahead.
A. While I was in the house, there was a car passed and I heard a shot fired. When I came out, they came west and I got in the car and took in west after them.
Q. And where did you go?
A. I went west until we came to the St. Bernice road, turned north to the Randall Electric yards. The first street we took was out to the new pavement at 36.
Q. What, if anything, happened there?
A. This car with five men pulled up on the pavement and Gilbert's truck pulled in from the east there at the same time and they both stopped. We got stopped about a block and a half south of the new pavement.
Q. Just go ahead and tell the jury what happened.
A. There were several shots fired. There is where Joe Walker fell. We were there five to ten minutes. Then these fellows got in the Gilbert car and went on west.
Q. After the car had gone on west, what, if anything, did you do?
A. Got in and drove down there. Got Joe Walker in the car and started to Dana. I got a man to drive this Frist car into town.
Q. Did you make any examination of the Frist car?
A. I did.
Q. I will hand you State's Exhibit, marked State's Exhibit "H," and ask you to tell the jury what that is.
A. That is a sawed-off shotgun.
Q. Did you ever see that shotgun before?
A. Yes, sir.
Q. Where was the first time you ever seen that?
A. In the Jediah Frist car.
Q. Did you take that out of that car?
A. I did.

The State offered Exhibit "H" in evidence. This led to cross-examination by Colonel Sawyer.

Q. How do you recognize the gun?
A. By this stock here on both sides.
Q. You haven't got the number of it?
A. No, sir. I haven't got the number.

XII — Tell the Jury What, If Anything, Happened Then

There followed another round by Homer Ingram.

Q. You had that in your possession some time?
A. I had it a day and a night.
Q. Then what did you do with it?
A. Turned it over to the deputy sheriff.

Now, it was Colonel Sawyer's turn.

Q. Are there any other marks any different from any other gun?
A. Nothing, only the stock. You never see it even like that.

State's Exhibit "H" was admitted in evidence. This exchange was typical of what went down in this trial. Ingram would offer an item in evidence and Sawyer would object, almost always without success.

Homer Ingram now presented another item.

Q. I will hand you State's Exhibit, marked State's Exhibit "I," and ask you to tell the jury what that is.
A. That is a twenty-gauge sawed-off shotgun.
Q. Did you ever see that gun before?
A. I did.
Q. When was the first time?
A. In the Jediah Frist car.
Q. At this time, the State offers in evidence State's Exhibit "I."

Colonel Sawyer had some questions about the shotgun.

Q. How do you recognize or identify that?
A. That fell off when I picked it up.
Q. But you don't know where that gun came from or anything about it?
A. All I know is that it was picked up by me in the Frist car.
Q. Is there any marks that would be different from any other gun of this type?
A. You never see one cut off there so that that handle would drop off. There is a bolt that holds inside and the bolt has been sawed off.
Q. No other shotgun that could be sawed off that way?
A. Not exactly.
Q. It could be, couldn't it?
A. Well, it could be.
Q. You didn't take the number?
A. No.

Sawyer objected to the exhibit as not being definitely identified. Again, the Defense was overruled, and State's Exhibit "I" was admitted in evidence.

Ingram turned to the jury.

"At this time, I would like to have the jury inspect these guns."

"I don't think that is necessary," Judge Wait said. "The jury can see."

Ingram returned to examining Hamm.

Q. State's Exhibit "H" and State's Exhibit "I." These are the two shotguns you have identified here?
A. Yes, sir. There was two shells in the automatic and two shells in the twenty gauge.
Q. Has these shells been fired?
A. No, sir.
Q. Had either one of them?
A. No, sir. There was neither one fired.
JUDGE WAIT: You mean the shells were loaded?
A. ... Yes, sir.
Q. And I believe you said that you had taken Joe Walker to Dana.
A. I did.
Q. And do you know whether Joe Walker died of that gunshot wound or not?
A. I don't know of anything else to kill him.
Q. He died?
A. He did.
Q. Did you find anything else in the Frist car other than these guns?
A. Eighty-six dollars in money in the car and the guns. Two twenty-dollar bills and two one-dollar bills and the rest in quarters and halves.

Roy Haase, a Dana barber, was one of the posse, independent of Joe Walker, Harold "Pete" Scott and Homer Hamm. He was always a step behind the bandits until he caught up with them at the Moody farm. He testified just ahead of F.W. Gilbert the afternoon of the first day of the trial. Haase was examined by Homer D. Ingram.

Q. Tell the jury [where], if any place, you went on that morning.
A. I was in the shop and I heard a woman say that the Clinton bank had been robbed. So I stepped to the door and T. Maddox, a banker of Dana, was going north. I says, "Have you heard where they are?" and he said, "No." I went out the door. I met Maddox and he asked me if I wanted to go and I said, "Yes." He said, "Go to the bank and get a gun." So, I went to the bank and got a gun and got in Mr. Maddox's car.

The testimony led to the Moody farm.

Q. Tell the jury what, if anything, was found in the coal house.
A. This man they call Detrich.
Q. Tell the jury whether or not that is the man that sits right here *(indicating)*.
A. This is the man.
Q. Tell the jury where in the coal house he was found, if you know.
A. Mr. Moody was in the lead and he had made mention that he thought a man was trying to get into the coal shed window. Moody was in the lead of me and just as he looked in the coal shed, he said, "Here is a man," and jumped back to one side. I was to his back and I placed a gun on this man here, Detrich, and he had his hands in this position *(indicating)*. I said, "Stick them up." He said, "Don't shoot. I am unarmed." I said, "Come on out." He walked over coal and by that time Scott met me at the door and put his gun on him. Moody, by

XII — Tell the Jury What, If Anything, Happened Then

that time, put the shotgun[2] to the back of his head. His mother said, "Shoot his head off, Leo." I said, "No, don't shoot." I said, "Search the man. Pete and I will hold the gun on him." By that time, somebody handed me a rope and Pete tied his hands. I took hold of his arm and Scott and I took him to Danville and turned him over to the police at Danville jail.

Q. On your way to Danville, tell the jury whether or not you had any conversation with the defendant, Walter E. Detrich.
A. I did.
Q. Tell the jury what that was.
A. I asked this man what his name was. He said he didn't care to tell or to talk on this subject. I asked this man why as [a] nice-looking man, the education that he had, why he met up with such a bunch as this and took such chances and he just jerked up his shoulders. "Well," I said, "you are better off than your two buddies laying out there in the cornfield at that." I said, "You have got a chance." He said, "Oh, slim."[3] ...When I said the two men were laying out in the cornfield, he sort of asked the description of them and we sort of described them and he just nodded his head.

When Haase said that this was the sum of what Detrich had to say in the car ride to Danville, Prosecutor Ingram begged to differ.

Q. To refresh your memory, Mr. Haase, I will ask you if this defendant, Detrich, didn't say that "we couldn't get a good car or we would have gotten away?"
A. Yes, he made mention of that. He afterwards said he was driving the Ford and he said they never did get a good car or they would have got away. He said it wouldn't run over 55 or 60 miles an hour.
Q. Tell the jury whether or not this defendant, Detrich, said anything at that time about ever being in Clinton.
A. I asked him, I said, "I think I know you," and he said to me, he said like that — shook his head — so, I didn't stop at that. I thought I had saw the man before so I made mention of him being in Clinton before. And he said, "No, you are mistaken." He said, "That is the first time I was ever in Clinton."

The next witness, at least in this survey, is Harold "Pete" Scott, a hardware merchant and, like the previous witness, a Dana man. Along with the weekly *Dana News*, Scott's testimony is the best source we have for the demise of Joe Walker. Scott was questioned by Homer D. Ingram.

Q. Did you leave town that morning?
A. Yes, sir.
Q. And where, if any [place], did you go?
A. Drove south to Tillotson corner.
Q. And just go ahead and tell the jury what you did there.
A. We seen a car coming down the road and Joe said, "Here comes a car." I said, "It can't be them because it isn't a good enough car." We stood out at the crossroads. I said, "Joe," I said, "duck," and we both ducked in the ditch and the car went on past us and we followed it ... them. But, of course, we didn't do any damage.

Q. Just go ahead and tell what happened then.

A. Well, Homer came then and we jumped in the car and started ahead and chief of police and Burnsides was behind us and their car was running so much faster we pulled out to the side. They passed us and went on ahead for a while and then we passed them and we ran on ahead of them for a while. The chief of police pulled up sand said not to get too close. Then we ran behind them for a while and then we passed. The next time he pulled up to the side of our car and he hollered at Joe and Joe hollered at him and said something — I don't know what.[4]

The questioning led up to the next stop, the Roy Wimsett corner.

Q. Well, just go ahead and tell this jury what happened there at the Wimsett corner.

A. Well, we couldn't stop there because our brakes didn't work very quick. Walker was out on the running board. It really seems to be a question whether he really intended to walk straight out or whether he was thrown up when the car was stopped. I was very near out in front of the car when it stopped. They were turned west about thirty — about forty feet west of the crossroad.

Q. And just go ahead and tell what happened then.

A. Well, Mr. Walker had got a way out in front of the car. He had a .25-.20 rifle and I had a .38 gun. I was in the back seat with a lot of ammunition and .25-.20 rifle and a .45 revolver and a .38. When we stopped so quick, it threw me down in between the seat. When I looked up, the boys was out. I opened the door to the left side on the west and I threw my guns and all my ammunition in the ditch. Then I jumped in the ditch myself and before I hardly squared around, I heard Joe holler, "Oh, my God, Pete, they got me," and he went down to his knees. By the time, I had shot all of the shells in my revolver and Joe threw me his and he said, "Give them hell!" I don't know how many shots we fired. I could see the men, but I couldn't see them enough to identify them. A truck came along and that gave them a chance to exchange some of the money from the car to the truck. But the one man I seen was carrying a sack of money and I shot at him. I don't know whether I hit him or not, but he dropped the money on the pavement.... I seen Hamm was there and Burnside and Helms came along and I got in with them. Joe Walker was behind his car, coughing. When he got shot, he went down on his knees, like that, *(indicating)* and Hamm put him in his car and took him on in to Dana and I got in with Burnside and Helms.

Scott went on to describe the action all the way to the Moody cornfield. He mentioned the fusillade his party endured when the bandits took Fenton Williams' Ford near Scottland, Illinois. He told of seeing the bodies of the two dead bandits — Lamm and Landy — being loaded in an ambulance and the capture of Detrich. Much of what he had to say about Detrich's capture and the ride to Danville echoed Haase's testimony earlier. Colonel Sawyer saw fit to cross-examine Scott at the end of his testimony.

XII — Tell the Jury What, If Anything, Happened Then

Q. Calling your attention to your testimony when you drove Hamm's car and stopped and Joe was on the fender, you say you opened the door facing the west and threw your ammunition out in the ditch.
A. I did.
Q. And then you jumped out in the ditch?
A. Yes, sir.
Q. And then you said the next thing you knew Joe Walker was hurt. Then you don't know who shot Joe Walker?
A. Absolutely not.

That bit of cross-examination would have been worth its weight in gold in a murder trial, but, in this case, it was merely academic.

The next witness in our survey had actually testified a bit earlier in the trial but nevertheless on Friday afternoon. Clinton chief of police Everett Helms' testimony took up fifteen pages of the record. Naturally, some of the things he had to say were covered by other witnesses, but Chief Helms is very specific when it comes to locations of the action along the seventy-mile route from Clinton to Sidell. Helms had been police chief for just under a year at this time. Besides his intrepid nature, it didn't hurt his position that he married Mayor Henry Owens' daughter. He was examined by Prosecutor Ingram.

Q. After you received this word, what, if anything, did you do?
A. I got in my car and started out after them.
Q. When you got in your car, who, if anyone, was with you?
A. Patrolman Burnside.
Q. And what firearms, if any, did you have in the car?
A. We had a pistol apiece and automatic shotgun.
Q. Now tell the jury, after you got in the car where you went.
A. I headed north to the Fairview road and turned west to the Fairview schoolhouse. Then north about three miles and back west about three quarters of a mile, where I ran on this car — they were fixing a tire.
Q. I will ask you after you turned north on the Fairview road, whether or not you saw any car ahead of you?
A. I did.
Q. Where was you at that time?
A. I was going through the covered bridge on the Fairview road.
Q. And where was this car at that time that was ahead of you?
A. They were about a half-a-mile ahead, going over the Overpeck Hill.
Q. And did you follow that car?
A. I did.
Q. State whether or not you caught up with that car.
A. I did.
Q. Tell the jury where that was?
A. We caught it at the Jediah Frist corner.
Q. And where is that Jediah Frist corner with reference to the Fairview road?
A. It is just three-quarters of a mile west of the Fairview road.

Q. And when you got up to where this car was just tell the jury what happened then?
A. They opened fire on us with the machine gun and several pistols.
Q. ... How many men at that time did you see?
A. Four.
Q. Tell the jury where these men were.
A. There were three standing to the back of the car and one standing around on the right front side.
Q. What, if anything, were these three men doing at the back of the car there?
A. They were shooting at us.
Q. Tell the jury whether or not you know who these three men were that were back of the car.
A. I did.
Q. Tell the jury who they were.
A. Long [Clark]. Detrich and Bell [Lamm].
Q. And about how long did you stay down on this road south of where these men were?
A. In the neighborhood of about five minutes.
Q. And then what happened?
A. They got their tire fixed and headed on west.
Q. And then go ahead and tell the jury what happened from there.
A. We drove west a little better than a mile and they were changing over and getting into Mr. Frist's car. They left their Buick in the middle of the road. They had turned it around and was just leaving on west.
Q. What Mr. Frist is that?
A. Jediah Frist.
Q. Go ahead.
A. They drove his car west as far as they could go. Turned north as far as they could go, then back west to what they call the St. Bernice road, straight out of St. Bernice.
Q. Tell the jury what, if anything, happened there.
A. At that time, Mr. Joe Walker, Pete Scott and Homer Hamm drove out ahead of us. Before they had went over a hundred feet, I passed them and told them not to get too close. They followed us until we got to the corner and they went around me again and I repeated not to get too close. We followed until we turned back west. I went around them again or pulled to the side of them and told them the third time not to get too close — that I had called for help ahead. We went west in the neighborhood of a mile and a half or two miles and then headed back north where Mr. Walker, Pete Scott and Homer Hamm stopped about a hundred yards back from the corner. Burnside and myself stopped about fifty yards behind them. And then Mr. Boetto and Charley Clark came up and stopped about fifty yards behind us. We were shooting at one another there on that corner.
Q. Where was Joe Walker while you were shooting there at the corner that you described?
A. Well, he got off of the running board of the car and just stopped in front of

the car. He kind of staggered and came back along the right side of the car and fell and lay on the road.

Q. Just go ahead and tell the jury what happened then.

A. They stopped there in the neighborhood of three minutes and headed on west down 36. They kept shooting at us again. They left there and drove on north to Ridge Farm and crossed Number 1 and kept on west and northwest until they got to what is known as Leo Moody's farm.

Q. And then what, if anything, did you do?

A. We started across the field after the three fellows.

Q. How many of you?

A. Pete Scott, Ernie Boetto, Patrolman Burnside and myself.

Q. Where did you go?

A. They [We] cut across the field directly behind those three fellows. I took down the west side of the field and then south and east a little there about a half-a-mile out there in the cornfield. I cut south down the west side of the cornfield. I could see them cut across there and I kept hollering at them and telling Burnside, Scott and Boetto where they were at. By that time, the road was surrounded by automobiles and we just closed in on them.

A. And tell the jury what happened then.

A. We came up to where we found two laying on the ground dead.

Q. Tell the jury who those two men were.

A. Mr. Landley[5] and Mr. Bell.

———————

Q. Was Bell dead at that time?

A. Not quite.

Q. Did he die after that awhile?

A. He did.

———————

Q. And then what else happened?

A. Mr. Long had went on south to where those two men were laying and came down west in an open ditch a little ways and then back south, with his hands up and was waving a white handkerchief. Patrolman [Burnside], Scott and Boetto and several other men were on the south side of the field there.

Helms was followed on the witness stand by Patrolman Walter Burnside. Burnside was with Helms from the get-go, and much of what he had to say had already been covered by Helms. Still, there are some points he raised that deserve our attention because he alone could speak to them, such as his wound and its effect. Burnside was examined by Prosecutor Ingram.

Q. Tell the jury what that call was.

A. About the bank robbery.

Q. Which way did you go after you started?

A. We went north on 8th to the Fairview road and then went over west to the schoolhouse and then went north.

Q. Did you see any car a little after you turned north on the road?

A. We asked that fellow at that gasoline station and he said it just went north.

Q. And you soon saw the car?

A. Yes, we seen the car when we went through the covered bridge. It has[d] passed through there going over the hill.

Q. Well, now, just tell about that firing at the Jediah Frist corner.

A. Well, they shot our car up and one of the bullets came in and hit me here *(indicating)*. I was all right in about five or ten minutes — ready to go again. We went down there I judge in the neighborhood of three hundred yards.

Q. Did you know at the time who was shooting at you?

A. Yes, sir. This is the fellow right here *(indicating)* [Clark] that had the machine gun on us. This fellow here *(indicating)* [Detrich], he had a light coat and hat on and he was shooting the rifle.

Q. And then what happened?

A. Then we went on west ... Joe Walker and Pete Scott and Homer Hamm, they came out there and went along with us.... The chief, he pulled up alongside of them and he told them to not get close. He warned them three — two or three times — and they went on to where 36 comes in there — that cement road.

Q. That new 36?

A. Yes, sir. And they got that cattle truck there.

Q. Who owned the truck?

A. Gilbert. They kept on driving and driving for quite a ways, a good long ways. A Ford came along and they got out and stopped that Ford. Every time they would stop a car, they would get out and hold us back.

Q. How do you mean?

A. They would fire — turn a machine gun on us.

Q. And you just stayed back of them about all the distance?

A. Sure.

Q. You went on until you came to the Moody farm?

A. Yes. They pulled up to the barn there.

Q. And what took place there?

A. They pulled up in there and they ran out and got in behind the building there. We kept coming up on them all together and when we got up there, we seen three crossing the field. Well, we kept shooting at them and they started across the field.

Q. What kind of a field?

A. An open field, nothing on it.

Q. And then where did they go?

A. In the cornfield. It was about ten or fifteen minutes until there was a hundred around there and we just kept getting close in on them. Of course, we seen this fellow right here *(indicating)* [Clark]. He came up from one of the corn rows with his hands up and waving his handkerchief.

Q. What fellow?

A. This Long fellow. The other two fellows, we found them dead.

The last witness on Friday afternoon was Clinton auto dealer Ernest Boetto. Besides selling cars, he was a deputy sheriff, deputized by both the Indiana Bankers' Association and Sheriff Harry Newland. His testimony traces the route he took to catch up with the bank robbers, something that did not happen until the incident in which Joe Walker was killed. From this point until the end of the chase at the Moody farm, Boetto and his driver, Charley Clark, would see plenty of action. Boetto was questioned by Homer D. Ingram.

Q. When did you first hear that the Citizens bank had been robbed?
A. Right around nine-thirty.
Q. Then, where, if any place, did you go?
A. Mr. Prosecutor and the Court please, I would like to explain to this jury just as it really happened. Mr. Clark came down to the garage there and I was in my office there and he said the bank had been robbed.
Q. Just tell the direction you went.
A. ... We went on north and stopped at a couple of farms to find out if a car had passed there and found out that it had. We went on north there.
Q. Where did you go from there?
A. Kept on going and the first thing we found was some pieces of tires and rim where they came on this car at Jediah Frist's.... [We] just kept on going, you know, and going until we came up on the Chief and Burnside on this pavement and we stopped there. I don't know how many miles we drove there, but it was quite a few miles, anyhow.
Q. How many other cars were there?
A. Just the Chief and Joe Walker seemed to be ahead about fifty yards.
Q. Up on the pavement?
A. Yes. I seen this truck up there and there was fellows running back and forth exchanging something. Of course, it was all excitement there.
Q. Just tell what happened there.
A. Mr. Burnside said then, "I am shot," and the Chief said, he said, "They have killed Joe Walker."

These quotes brought an objection from Colonel Sawyer, which was sustained. The jury was instructed to disregard this part of the answer.

A. He said, "They have shot Joe Walker."
Q. Now, Mr. Boetto, don't use any of the conversation.
A. I saw Joe Walker in the back of this car that he was driving, holding his hands over his stomach. I knew that he had been shot.... Understand that is a fact I saw this stuff they were exchanging — this money and all of this stuff. The Chief asked, "Have you got a revolver?" and I said, "Yes."

The Defense objected.

Judge Wait said, "There are some things you can't tell here, Mr. Boetto, and that is what people said outside of the presence of these defendants."

Q. Just tell what you done and seen, not what you heard there.
A. So I got outside of the road there and started firing into this truck as they started to leave four or five times.... We followed them after they got started and they opened up on us with a machine gun.... Understand that I was all that was firing at them at that time. I said, "Let's wait a minute. We want some help here."

The Defense again objected.

A. These men were shooting at us and these bullets were flashing on the pavement.... They pulled this truck across the road — right square across the road there — one fellow with the machine gun, standing there with the machine gun. I seen a car coming towards us, I jumped out and stopped him. He happened to be a bond salesman from Danville. So he had sense enough to turn around right quick and he said, "Where do you want to go?" I left Charley to get some gas and we went on ahead. There was a farmhouse there and when we got up there, these fellows opened up with the machine gun. When they opened up, they had a clean sweep on us. This bond salesman pulled the car in the ditch and stopped there. They went on ahead and turned into this farm yard. The Chief of Police was ahead and I said to this bond salesman, "You go get some help right quick because we haven't got much shells and there is going to be something happen here." ... We seen three fellows going across the open field and the corn was laying low down there and there they was going across there, this fellow, especially *(indicating)* [Clark]. So we called to them to come back, but they wouldn't do it. One fellow turned around that way — that was the fellow that had the machine gun. I fired and one fellow dropped down and lay down, didn't he, Pete?[6] and then got up and staggered and fell down again. We seen this fellow [Clark] was up along the hedge fence. Understand we didn't know who he was and so they wanted to open up fire arms at him — these fellows from Sidell. I said, "No, let's see what he's going to do." Pretty soon he pulled out a handkerchief and waved it.... We found this gentleman right here [a smiling Clark] up along the hedge with his hands over his head. He didn't say nothing. He didn't know nothing about it. He had a pair of overalls on. We tried to question him. We had seen the other fellows, but we didn't know what happened to them and we asked where they were.

We formed a posse around this field about ten feet apart and Mr. Helms was coming down along the fence. He wanted to know what had happened and didn't I holler at you? I said, "If that is you, Pete, be careful," because these fellows was ready to shoot at him.... He came down with me and we formed a circle as we went up after fifteen yards from these two that was laying there. This man [Lamm] had his shirt open and blood was coming out his chest and this other man [Landy] was laying there along the corn row. He made one raise up and fired a shot and then fell back down. Then, we rushed up and this fellow was just dying as we got to him.

The last witness to take the stand was Vermillion County sheriff Harry Newland. He testified on Saturday morning, January 2, 1931. Judging from his statements, he was not involved to any real degree in any phase of the running fight. His remarks are of interest only insofar as they concern Walter Detrich.

He was questioned by Homer D. Ingram.

Q. The first time you ever saw Detrich where was he?
A. When I first saw Detrich, he was in jail in Danville.

Q. And did you have any conversation with the defendant, Walter Detrich, concerning the Clinton bank robbery?
A. Yes, sir.
Q. Tell the jury what he said, if anything.
A. Well, on the 17th of December, I went to Danville with Chief of Police Helms and he came back with us — Detrich did. On the way, back, we discussed the robbery. I asked him if it was their intention to turn around in the street and he said he didn't think it was. I asked him what made them turn. He said he didn't know. And I made the remark to him — I said, "You had tough breaks all the way." He said, "Yes, we did." He said, "We didn't want to hurt anybody. We could have killed all of the officers if we wanted to," he said. "But we didn't want to. All we wanted was to get a good machine and get away."
Q. Do you know whether or not there was any machine gun left at the Sheriff's office in Danville, Illinois, on the 16th day of December, 1930?
A. It was left at the bank on the 16th and taken to the Sheriff's office on the 17th.

Sheriff Harry Newland (courtesy the *Danville* [IL] *Commercial-News*).

Thus, the final witness. All witnesses and all jurors had been examined by Prosecutor Homer D. Ingram. Deputy Prosecutor Willis Satterlee seems to have spent his time gathering evidence here and there with Chief Helms.

In a courtroom where nerves were constantly on edge due to the tight security, an incident occurred that was almost laughable in its inappropriateness. The courthouse elevator got away from its operator, George Wise, and having fallen from the third floor into the basement, reverberated like Vulcan's stithy. Everyone in the building was sure a bomb had gone off. Machine gun–toting guards readied their weapons instantly. For a few minutes there was pandemonium in the packed courtroom, until the source of the disturbance was revealed. Thankfully, no one was hurt in the accident.

The jury was out only fifteen minutes. By 11:02 that morning, jury foreman George Stevenson announced the unsurprising verdict: "We, the jury, find the defendants guilty as charged in the affidavit and that the true age of Walter E. Detrich is 26 years and that the true age of James Clarke [sic], alias William M. Long, is 32 years."

All that remained now was the sentencing. That would come later in the day. Judge Wait purposefully declined to announce a time so that the courtroom would be mostly empty when he did so.

Shortly after one that afternoon, Clark and Detrich, under heavy guard, were brought in to face Judge Wait. Wait looked solemnly down at the men and asked, "Do either of you know why sentence should not be handed down at this time?"

The two responded in unison, "No, sir."

Judge Wait then read the sentence:

> It is considered and adjudged by the Court that said defendant, Walter E. Detrich, be and here is committed and sentenced to Indiana State Prison for and during the term of his natural life and that said defendant be disenfranchised and rendered incapable of holding any office of trust and profit for the same term. It is therefore ... [And] considered and adjudged by the Court that defendant, James Clark, alias William M. Long, be and here is hereby committed and sentenced to Indiana State Prison for and during the term of his natural life, and that he be disfranchised and rendered incapable of holding any office of trust and profit for same term.[7]

The life sentence was to take place in the state prison at Michigan City. The term would begin by the middle of the following week.

As it happened, the two prisoners were on their way to Michigan City by nine that night. There would be one more supper for the prisoners while at Newport. Detrich inquired as to what was on the menu. He was informed that the meal would be beans and bacon.

"In that case, go heavy on the bacon," Detrich suggested.[8]

Sheriff Harry Newland, Deputy "Razz" Foltz, Patrolman Walter Burnside and Chief Everett Helms accompanied the men in two cars. The prisoners would be inducted by the next afternoon.

Detrich's prison packet records, listing what valuables he had on his person when he arrived at the state prison, show no check mark beside the watch chain entry. In September 1993, Margaret Helms, the police chief's widow, explained how that was.

When the group arrived at the prison, Detrich pulled out a silver watch chain and handed it to Chief Helms.

"You might as well have this. Where I'm going, I won't be needing it."[9]

It wasn't long before Detrich and Clark appealed their case. For their appeal, they were somehow able to hire a Lebanon, Indiana, firm—Roscoe Hollingsworth and Carl W. Lambert. The motion to appeal began on January 20, 1931. The attorneys listed some points that they felt made the brief trial unfair. Their judge, they contended, was wrong to overrule their clients' request for a continuance so as to gather witnesses in their defense. The judge's instructions to the jury, the attorneys insisted, were also improperly conducted. The evidence, furthermore, that had convicted Clark and Detrich was insufficient, and the verdict was unfair.

It may not have helped that this motion was presented to the very same

XII — Tell the Jury What, If Anything, Happened Then

judge who had conducted the trial three weeks earlier. To no one's surprise, the motion was turned down. Judge Wait then gave attorneys Hollingsworth and Lambert ninety days to appeal to the state appellate court.

They did.

By the spring of that year, an appeal challenging twelve points about the trial, such as the merging of two separate counts into one and the indeterminate sentence, was prepared.

On October 26, 1932, the Indiana State Supreme Court confirmed the fairness of the trial and upheld the jury's verdict. By this time, however, Clark and Detrich had another avenue of release in motion. His name was John Herbert Dillinger.

XIII

The Greatest Escape

That's one of those things you never know at the time. — Ernest Hemingway, "The Killers"

If anyone should have been worried when Walter Detrich and Oklahoma Jack Clark broke out of the Indiana State Prison at Michigan City on September 26, 1933, it was Leo Moody. After all, Clark was captured on his farm, and it was Moody himself who had rounded up Detrich in the cob house. Nevertheless, if he was worried, neither his widow nor his son-in-law chose to recall it six decades later.

It may have been that Leo got his worrying out of the way early. His friends and neighbors kept a tight vigil on his farm the first few days following the gun battle. Six days after the debacle, a car was seen circling the area repeatedly. Hearing of this, armed men from Fairmount rushed to the Moody farm but found no suspicious vehicles in the vicinity.[1]

As it happened, when Detrich and Clark regained their freedom, they did not exactly exit the Big House alone. There were eight other fugitives along for the ride. Two were killers and nearly all were bank robbers. They were the worst that Michigan City could boast. And a few had tried to get out before.

In fact, a break had been attempted on December 29, 1930, while Detrich and Clark were cooling their heels in the Newport "icebox," perhaps the day after Carroll Williams and his brother-in-law had a little talk with them for the sake of a slow Sunday afternoon's diversion. When Clark and Detrich arrived at the Indiana State Prison, there were 2,365 inmates present. Some of the cell blocks and dormitories were severely overcrowded, harboring almost twice as many prisoners as originally intended. Cell Block D was one such cell block. In addition, those prisoners locked up there were the most desperate in the penitentiary.

Cell Block D housed 530 inmates. It was designed to hold 340.[2] There was great unrest among the prisoners, but there were only five solitary cells in the whole prison to cool troublemakers off. The aborted prison break began with Joseph Burns fashioning a key to his cell block out of a spoon. Burns had murdered a cashier in a bank robbery in 1921, but in prison he was looked up to by the other inmates and would be involved in a number of escape attempts, including the one that succeeded in September 1933. In the 1930 escape attempt, a file was also worked into a knife. The knife was the handiwork of cold-blooded Al Rosenberg, "a man," as Lady Caroline Lamb might have styled him, "mad, bad and dangerous to know."

It was just after midnight when Burns and Rosenberg and ten of their fellow inmates, including two murderers, overpowered two guards and were about to free the adjoining cell block. They had cut through two cell bars, and severing one more bar would have allowed the men in the cell block to enter the prison proper. One of the subdued guards, Guy Barklow, however, alerted the captain in C Dormitory in time and, instead of going to the aid of the two guards, the captain called the prison office. This simple expedient single-handedly prevented the riot from succeeding. Deputy Warden H.D. Claudy (known not-so-affectionately as "I, God" Claudy by the inmates due to his slurring of "My God"),[3] and Clifford W. Craig, chief clerk, rushed to Cell Block D. Finding the door blocked by inmates, Claudy demanded that it be opened immediately.

Rosenberg made a demand of his own.

"Go to hell!"

Within a few minutes, all manner of prison personnel, including Warden Walter H. Daly, fifteen Michigan City cops and an engine house load of firemen were on hand to snuff out the riot with tear gas before it could get up on its hind legs. Besides Burns, three other names that were to figure in the successful prison break three years later made the nation's front pages — James Jenkins, Russell Clark and Harry Pierpont. The aborted break took less than forty-five minutes to quell, but its lack of success did not diminish its luster. It played just like a scene from *The Big House*, the granddaddy of prison pictures, starring Wallace Beery, Robert Montgomery and Chester Morris, a movie released six months earlier.

Burns and the others — Jenkins, Russell Clark and Pierpont — would try again later in a big way.

John Dillinger, though he was inmate no. 13225 at the penitentiary and ever restive, does not seem to have been involved in the failed break. Obviously, he was locked up in a different cellblock, or it may have been, as John Toland suggests, that he was behaving himself in hopes of an imminent parole. Dillinger had been in prison since October 1924.[4] He had been sent first to the reformatory at Pendleton, Indiana, for nearly five years and then by his own request to Michigan City to the state prison. (Most of his hardened buddies were in the state prison by this time.)[5]

By December 1930, the twenty-seven-year-old Dillinger had been in the penitentiary for a year and a half and was as bent on escaping as he was upon entering the Pendleton Reformatory. A thoroughgoing reformation was undertaken by the gray-eyed hard case early in 1932 with the intention of making parole certain and thereby helping his fellow inmates from the outside. The trademark escape attempts of his early incarceration and his unruly behavior throughout ceased altogether, and something approaching model behavior ensued. Back home in Mooresville, a petition soon circulated, which was signed by numerous friends and neighbors of the Dillinger family, including B.F. Morgan, the grocer assaulted by the future public enemy in 1924. In addition, Dillinger's father was getting on in years. As it turned out, it wasn't his father's health that was the real concern; it was his stepmother's. She was the victim of a stroke only a couple of days before the inmate would leave Michigan City.

Dillinger arrived at the family farm in time to see Elmer F. Harvey's hearse leaving the long driveway with his stepmother's body.[6] Making the situation all the more pathetic was the valuable time lost owing to an overheated car on the way home. This, added to the fact that bureaucratic paperwork had kept Dillinger behind bars ten days beyond his scheduled release date of May 12, 1933, made the misery of missing his stepmother alive by just a few hours all the more painful.[7]

Dillinger did not have any idea of going straight now that he was out. He stuck around the family homestead long enough to take his two young sisters to the movies at the Orpheum in Indianapolis and for walks in the woods adjoining the farm. He was good to family and friends, but his grin was broadest when he held a Tommy in his hands. Dillinger was soon in Indianapolis with the White Cap gang, robbing drugstores and ice cream parlors. It is believed that, within three weeks of his parole, Dillinger and young William Shaw, of White Cap notoriety, were among the bunch that robbed a New Carlisle, Ohio, bank of $10,000.

When the White Cap gang was broken up by the arrest of Shaw and two other signature members in mid–July 1933, Dillinger himself narrowly escaped arrest. He was lucky, but he was very much an amateur holdup man. Learning the business did not come easy for him. On June 24, a Saturday, he bungled a payroll robbery at the Marshall Fields thread mill in Monticello, Indiana, but not before he wounded the factory foreman, Fred Fisher. On July 17, he and Harry Copeland hit the Daleville Commercial Bank for $3,500. It was the noon hour and only twenty-one-year-old teller Margaret Good was in the bank.[8] Dillinger, wearing a straw hat and light suit, asked to see the president of the bank.

"The president is no longer active in the bank," Margaret replied. Dillinger wondered about the cashier.

"He's at lunch."

Pushing his boater back from his forehead and flashing a toothy smile, Dillinger pulled out a blue long-barreled revolver and pointed it at the trembling young teller.

"Well, honey, this is a stick-up."[9]

It was an easy robbery, involving only three customers and one bank teller. No shots were fired; no one was hurt.

Two days later, Dillinger and Copeland hit another bank. This time they drove to the Indiana-Illinois line and robbed the Rockville National Bank. Again, it was the noon hour and again only a bare handful of people were present in the bank. But the robbery didn't go nearly as smoothly as the one two days earlier. This time a young cashier had stepped into the lavatory only to emerge and find a bandit pointing a pistol at his father. The young man was armed with a pistol and immediately fired at the bandit. He missed his mark but sent a bullet through the glass in the front door, narrowly missing Copeland.

Coming through the hallway from an insurance office, Dillinger rounded the corner at this moment and punched the young man in the stomach, knocking him to the floor. Taking the pistol in one hand, Dillinger helped the young man to his feet.

"Don't you know you could have killed somebody like that?" he asked in the manner of a Torquemada sizing up a heretic.

Sadly, no scribe or Boswell was on hand to record the answer to the bank robber's query.

Dillinger shoved his charge out the front door of the bank while Copeland followed. The pair of outlaws then drove off in a Plymouth, leaving Indiana's youngest cashier standing at the curb. But that young man's day was not quite complete. He went back inside, grabbed a high-powered rifle, and, running out the door, flagged down a ride. Dillinger and Copeland had tossed some roofing nails on the road to make good their getaway, but these didn't interfere with the pursuit.[10] The volume of traffic on the road did, however, and no shots were fired. After switching cars at Jungle Park and adding a third party to the proceedings, the outlaws got away. They had only been able to obtain one hundred and forty dollars for their pains, because a spherical safe in the bank had proved worthy of its reputation — and cost. The pair had to make do with what was in the drawers and, it is said, overlooked much of that.

Dillinger was learning the business.

The robbery of a bank in Montpelier, Indiana, followed on August 4.[11] Another robbery, this time with an exciting but bloodless shootout, took place ten days later in Bluffton, Ohio. The heist of the Massachusetts Avenue Bank in Indianapolis on September 6 netted Dillinger and two others more than $24,000. At a pretty good clip, Dillinger was accumulating the funds needed for an elaborate prison break. His first attempt to break out his buddies was, however, quite crude and inexpensive. Reminiscent of Laurel and Hardy in *Hoosegow* (1929), Dillinger simply threw three pistols, caked in either plaster or wrapped in newspaper — which, isn't clear — over the wall.[12]

These were quickly found by two inmates, and three other inmates were locked in solitary; they were not the ringleaders of the break, as the warden reckoned, but interested parties, nevertheless. This was some time before September 26.[13] Dillinger and Detrich next arranged to have weapons sent in to the prison in a crate from a Chicago shirt factory. Everything was set for September 28.[14] Then something happened that no one counted on. Dillinger was himself arrested in Dayton, Ohio.

All that summer of 1933, Dillinger, often in a blue serge suit, had been feeling his oats with an unhappy wife named Mary Longnaker. Mary's brother, James Jenkins, had been sent up for the murder of a grocer during a robbery in April 1930, and Mary was interested in getting him out. Whatever she felt for Dillinger, the desire to free her brother was certainly uppermost in the young lady's mind. Dillinger took Mary and her friend, Mary Ann Bucholtz, to the Century of Progress exhibition in Chicago in July, right after the Daleville and Rockville robberies. While there Dillinger snapped pictures of a policeman, and the policeman, not knowing with whom he was dealing, obligingly shot photos of the outlaw and his girl. (These would soon turn up in the hands of two tenacious Dayton police detectives when they arrested Dillinger on September 22.)

Dillinger took Mary to see her brother in the penitentiary on their way back to Dayton from Chicago. Inside a banana he gave Mary to take in with her, he carefully folded up a fifty dollar bill, ten dollars of which were to go to certain characters who might be needed for a favor later on. Mary, furthermore, was to tell Jenkins to "sit tight." When they left, Dillinger told a gatekeeper to give Jenkins fifty dollars for dental care. At this time, Dillinger was not yet a wanted man. Daleville would put him on the map, but it would take weeks for him to be tagged with the robbery.

Meanwhile, Forrest Huntington, operative for the American Surety Company, which covered losses for a number of banks robbed by Dillinger and was mentioned previously in connection with the investigation of Lamm's Lafayette robbery, sent information about the outlaw to the Pinkertons in Indianapolis, which was forwarded to the Cincinnati office. Soon, the latter office contacted Inspector C.E. Yendes of the Dayton, Ohio, police force and told him to be on the lookout for Dillinger, as he was seeing a lady in town.

Yendes assigned two detectives to a stakeout of the boarding house where the outlaw's girl, Mary Longnaker, was staying. After two uneventful weeks, finally a tip came from the landlady of the boarding house. The detectives found Dillinger with his girl looking at photographs from the Chicago World's Fair. When the detectives entered the room, the outlaw almost went for his gun but not quite — fortunately for him, since he was covered by a Tommy gun and a shotgun. He was placed in the Allen County jail for the Bluffton robbery. On his person was found an odd diagram. One of the detectives thought that it was a break-out plan for the Indiana State Prison at Michigan City. Unfortunately, nobody pursued this lead, and four days later, ten prisoners fled the prison.

Just how much Dillinger had to do with the actual breakout is uncertain. Certainly he was in on it. Walter Detrich also had a hand in setting things up, as most likely did Joseph Burns and Harry Pierpont. Once things got rolling inside the prison, it was Pierpont who called the shots. The sandy-haired and blue-eyed Pierpont was thirty-one. He was six-one and nearly half a foot taller than the future leader of the soon-to-be created Dillinger gang. A crate, marked with a red X in crayon, had been sent from the Henry Myer Manufacturing Company in Chicago to the Gordon Shirt Company inside the prison at Michigan City. Inside the crate were at least three pistols. It reached that part of the prison where the so-called "shirt shop boys" worked. Among the shirt shop boys were Walter Detrich, James "Oklahoma Jack" Clark, Harry Pierpont, Russell Clark, John Hamilton and Charley Makley. Walter Detrich knew what was afoot when the box arrived on the 23rd and quickly notified the others. He concealed three .38s in a box of buttons and sent the factory crate on its way.

Fearing prison snitches, Pierpont moved the date of the break up a day. The break would come off on Tuesday, the 26th.

That afternoon, a rainy one, Walter Detrich notified civilian superintendent G.H. Stevens that two men, who wished to buy shirts, had arrived at the prison. Stevens accompanied Detrich to the storeroom.[15] There he was jumped by the whole crew under the leadership of the three cons with pistols — Harry Pierpont, John Hamilton and Russell Clark. Shortly afterwards, the assistant warden, Albert Evans, a man indistinguishable from a bulldozer, was told by Detrich that a jug of wine was in the basement. When Evans investigated, he was greeted by a .38 in the belly. Pierpont growled, "I ought to shoot you, you fat son-of-a-bitch." Charley Makley urged discretion. It would be too noisy to shoot the man. "Besides," said he, "we're going to need his big lard ass." After turning it over in his mind, Evans must have felt some measure of gratitude to Makley for his somewhat qualified concern.

John Hamilton, one of numerous "Three-Finger Jacks" known in criminal annals, put it very simply. "We're going home and you're going to lead us out of here."

When Supervisor Dudley Triplett and five trustees came down, they were locked up in the heating tunnel leading to the prison's power plant. With Evans and Stevens in the lead, the ten convicts marched across the prison yard. All carried bundles of shirts, including the three with guns. Those without guns carried a steel shaft under their shirts. About fifty yards ahead was the administration building. Right behind Evans marched Detrich, gun in hand — a phony gun. Evans turned over his shoulder as the two marched and asked, "How am I doin', Walter?"

Detrich growled, "As soon as we get to the gate, I'm going to shoot you in the ass."

But between the prisoners and the administration building were three steel gates. At the first of these, guard Frank Swanson held the men up.

Evans spoke in a whisper. "They've got guns. Open the gate or they'll kill us."

After Swanson unlocked the gate, he was quickly added to the procession. At the second gate, guard Guy Burklow did not offer any resistance either. During the break attempt three years earlier, however, it had been his alarm that prevented the break from getting out of hand. This time it was different. There would be no accolades for Burklow on this day. The attempt would not fail.

Just the same, young Jimmy Jenkins wanted to put a hole in Burklow for his role in foiling the break three years before. Jenkins needed Pierpont's .38 to exact even the most cursory revenge, but protocol demanded that he ask the prison kingpin for it.

"We're out of here," Pierpont said. "Why kill anyone?"

It was one of those rare moments when Harry Pierpont wasn't quite himself.[16]

At the third gate, guard Fred Wellnitz went after the hero's badge. He reached for his rifle and was knocked unconscious. Evans objected to such treatment of a comrade-in-arms and was immediately given a dose of the same medicine. The keys to the gate were in Wellnitz' pocket and the prisoners helped themselves to them.

They now entered the administration building. Here they encountered Lawrence Mutch, the superintendent of prison industries. He was taken without slugs or slugging and urged back to the prison storehouse where all manner of weaponry was to be had. But Mutch was not about to open the door, possibly because he didn't know the combination. His obstinacy brought on a good drubbing.

The inmates next poured into the large office of the administration building, rounding up eight clerks. One of these, the seventy-two-year-old Finley

Carson, apparently did not move fast enough and was cursed and shot in the stomach by one of the cons. Carson survived, but the senseless act outraged all who heard of it or read of it.[17] The other clerks were rounded up and placed in the vault. One of the prisoners inside the vault was none other than the warden, who, fortunately for him, was not recognized.

At this point, the ten inmates were well on their way to upgrading their status to that of fugitives. They burst through the front door of the administration building, encountering Harrison County sheriff Charles Neel,[18] of nearby Corydon, and a dentist, Lee B. Wolfe. The pair had just dropped off a prisoner, James Whitman, who was about to begin a sentence of one to ten years for killing his father. Neal, an older man about to retire, was quickly subdued by Detrich.

"Have you got a car?"

"Hell, yes," snapped the curiously belligerent lawman.

After taking the lawman's car keys, Detrich motioned to three other convicts to join him at this point.

The three, Oklahoma Jack, Joseph Fox and Joseph Burns, hopped in, stuffing Neal back in his Chevy, while Wolfe was thrust down in the mud— a small price to pay for his freedom. The last man to get in the car, Walter Detrich, is said to have thumbed his nose at the guard tower as they drove off.[19] This gang of four, commandeering Neel and the Chevy, composed one group of cons.

The other group, under the leadership of Harry Pierpont, left the prison in similar fashion. This second group comprised six felons — Harry Pierpont, John Hamilton, Charles Makley, Russell Clark, Edward Shouse and James Jenkins. The latter group took two tries to get on the road, the first attempt going awry when a gas station proprietor defied the men and ran off with his car keys. For his recalcitrance, the man was fired upon, but he emerged unscathed.

Detrich and Clark's movements, after the break, are not always easy to trace. Clark's trail, however, was a short one, lasting only three days. He was constantly accompanied by Sheriff Neel, whose health, as well as his own, Clark was concerned about. For more than two years, the ten escapees would be hunted. Four would be killed and the rest would receive long prison terms. Oklahoma Jack would be the first to have the cuffs back on. His unquiet stomach, plagued with ulcers, did not allow him to participate with the usual vim and vigor demanded of an outlaw on the run and determined to stay that way. This, in addition to being on foot most of the time, kept him within reach of the long arm of the law.

Detrich's trail is much more knotty and problematic and would last more than three months.

In a bizarre incident, Gary radio station WIND sent five announcers to a wooded area eight miles southwest of Chesterton, Indiana, on the night of September 27. Between 11 and 12 o'clock, they set up a broadcast purportedly covering a gun battle between the escaping cons and Indiana state troopers. The broadcast came out of the studios of Columbia Broadcasting and was carried by WIND and its sister station, WBBM, in Chicago. Listeners in the area heard items such as this: "Here we are, folks, on the scene of a gigantic manhunt.... Listen close, folks, and you can hear the shots, as a deadly patter of lead is rained all about."

The frantic sound of sirens filled the air. A cluster of machine gunfire and small weapons fire followed — amazingly, the weapons were provided by local officers.

Hearing a report that a group of cons were seen in the area, five hundred vigilantes had converged on the woods and provided the weapons used in the broadcast.

Among the concerned listeners in the immediate vicinity was Captain Matt Leach of the Indiana State Police, who heard the broadcast over a radio at a filling station. He raced to the scene only to discover that he had been much imposed upon. Cook County, Illinois, sheriff William D. Meyering also heard the broadcast and was just as alarmed as Leach. He alerted scores of county highway patrolmen to throw up roadblocks on roads leading into Chicago from northern Indiana. For his part, Matt Leach wanted to prosecute the broadcast team for the hoax but settled for a retraction of the story over the airwaves the next day (the 28th).[20]

With Detrich at the wheel racing along and the murky weather a factor, Sheriff Neal's Chevy went into a pond and got stuck. Soon after, Detrich, Clark and the two other convicts, with Sheriff Neal in tow, came to a farmhouse of a man named Cecil Spanier and his family. Spanier was asked to assist in getting the sheriff's Chevy out of the muck. Spanier demurred, saying that he was too tired. The next, somewhat predictable, movement in the getaway symphony, according to Sheriff Neal, went this way — "They put guns on him."

The four cons forced the farmer to drive them in his car. Spanier was to drive the four to Gary, keeping on dirt roads and bypassing Chesterton and Valparaiso. The farmer was able to ditch the convicts when they crossed a stream in the rain, or it may have been that he just ran off when the gang stopped for gas at a Deep Valley filling station, having lifted twenty dollars from the sheriff. How Spanier really made his exodus isn't clear.[21] In any case, Spanier got away with his life. He presented no major problem to the wanted men, since what was needed was his car, not him. They drove off but after another road mishap found themselves on foot in the vicinity of Hobart,

XIII — The Greatest Escape

Indiana. The weather was wet and cool and the fugitives were forced to sleep in a wooded area by day while foraging for food at night. This routine soon lost its charm, and the men began to ponder what to do with their prisoner, Sheriff Neal. Clark volunteered to stay with the officer while the others went their way. At this point, then, Detrich and Clark separated. Detrich joined Joseph Fox and Joseph Burns in their flight. They separated on foot, though not before the trio of escapees threatened to murder Sheriff Neel's family in Corydon if he revealed that the men were on foot and not driving.

That flight probably led to Chicago, though by what means and how soon is unknown. What is known, however, is that Detrich and Burns had set up an appointment with an ex-con to give them a ride to New Orleans for fifteen hundred dollars. The rendezvous was set for the corner of Sheridan Road and Ainslee Avenue in Chicago on the evening of Thursday, September 28. The ex-convict informed on the pair but to no avail. The two fugitives did not show.

Although the meet on the 28th didn't work out, a Detrich doppelganger, as well as a Burns one, showed up at 10:20 the night before at an Ottawa, Illinois, gas station about seventy-five feet from the police station and a block from the sheriff's office. Of course, the outlaws, if such they were, did not know anything more about where the sheriff's office or police station in Ottawa were than the Methodist Church there, where lecturer Mark Twain once wondered if he ought to be funny in church. The man thought to be Detrich bore a facial scar and had an eye twitch, attributes not usually mentioned in connection with Detrich (though granted to just about every other outlaw of notoriety). The deputy warden (H.D. Claudy) at the Indiana State Prison confirmed Detrich's scar and the identification. The two men were riding in a 1929 or 1930 green Buick sedan with sidemounts and wire wheels. The car was without license plates.

The Detrich double was wearing gray trousers with badly stained kneecaps; one wore a blue jacket, the other a brown one. Detrich was the car's driver. When he pulled into the Johnson filling station on La Salle Street, Detrich immediately got out and ran to the curb, watching up and down the street. The Burns lookalike sat in the front seat keeping an eye on attendant Andy Claus as he put five gallons in the tank. Claus didn't like the looks of the men, especially those suspicious trousers that looked like prison issue, so he took a look at the back seat the first chance he got. There he saw a machine gun and a sawed-off shotgun. The pair had been seen earlier that evening eating supper at Marseilles, Illinois.

The men declined to have their oil and radiator checked but did ask for directions to Peoria. They then departed at a high speed. About this time, two men fitting the descriptions of Oklahoma Jack Clark and Walter Detrich stopped at a filling station in Lincoln, Nebraska. As with Dillinger's Crown Point breakout some months later, once a big story breaks nearly every community, big and little, has something to say about it.[22]

The next afternoon a green Chevy with five desperate-looking men in it drove through Ottawa, again not far from the police station. The car had "Police" in white letters on one side. Four of the men were unshaved. According to a witness walking his dog, the driver matched Detrich's description and the man next to him was Charlie Makley. The witness took six hours to deliver this information to police, imparting it when visiting his son in jail. This sighting, unlike the first Ottawa sighting, sounds farfetched.

In the midst of such goings-on, real or imagined, ex-president Herbert Hoover and his wife stopped at a service station and restaurant in nearby Mendota. Hoover had been out of office for less than seven months. With the Hoovers were a chauffer, an armed guard and the governor of Missouri, Guy Brasfield Park, a Democrat, oddly enough. The group was headed to Missouri before returning to the Hoovers' home in California. They had just come from the Century of Progress exhibition in Chicago. If anyone in the quintet was concerned about the breakout in Michigan City the day before, they did not show it. Hoover asked the attendant how the National Recovery Act was going. The attendant said that people seemed to be going back to work. Mrs. Hoover had a simple lunch at the counter, refusing to sit at a table and be fussed over.

That Detrich was one of the Ottawa men is a possibility, since everything about him is a blur at this point and for the next few months in his life. He may have sought to tie up with Handsome Jack Klutas in Peoria. Why Burns would be traveling around with Detrich and not Clark is anybody's guess; that is, if there was anything to the sighting. It just may be that the two men in Ottawa on the night of the 27th were Detrich and Joseph Burns striking out on their own after entertaining second thoughts about the intended rendezvous in Chicago the next night.[23] If so, it contradicts the tale told by Sheriff Neal as to the movements of the fugitives in the time he was with them. But, then, that wouldn't be hard to do.

It should be mentioned that Sheriff Neel's account cannot always be trusted. After Clark was arrested, he changed some things in it. This divergence seems to have been based on two things — his gratitude to Clark for looking out for him through some desperate hours and also the fear he had for his family's safety if he told too much to the authorities and the newspapers. Bear in mind, most of the fugitives at this time were yet on the loose in parts unknown. Furthermore, these desperate men had been assisted in their bid for freedom by persons unknown. There was no telling how big an organization was behind the break. All of this must have sped through Neal's mind just as soon as he regained his freedom.

Oklahoma Jack, now separated from the other three cons and carrying a pistol loaded with gas pellets, made his way on foot with the hostage sheriff across open country, eating raw corn and green tomatoes. The latter, whatever their effect on the lawman (if he ate at all), did not agree with Clark's stomach ulcers. He needed medical attention badly. Clark and Sheriff Neel made their way to a nearby highway, Route 6, and caught a ride to Hobart, Indiana, where on the morning of Friday the 29th the sheriff bought Clark a handsome breakfast. He also gave the con a topcoat. After taking a streetcar to Gary, the two men split up.

Clark took the interurban to Hammond, Indiana, and then hired a cabbie, Vernon Moats, to take him to Joliet, Illinois. The cabbie, getting a gander at Clark's clothing, called the police under the pretense of seeking authorization for such a long drive from his boss. Clark's freedom was at an end soon after. Four policemen pulled alongside Clark's cab and that was that.[24] The ailing con didn't seem to mind too much. He later explained that the only reason he had gone along with the prison break was to get proper medical attention on the outside — for an unspecified number of years, of course.

Clark was taken to the Hammond police station, where he was reunited with Sheriff Neal after a lapse of several hours. The two men were photographed shaking hands, and then Neel handed Clark five dollars. The convict had only joined the break at the last minute. He would soon be on his way to Michigan City for the rest of his life. But not quite. Apparently, the impetus for Clark's parole was his petition for a new trial in February 1949. Only a year later, in March 1950, he was paroled by Governor Henry F. Schricker. Clark was to keep out of Indiana altogether and live in Kansas with his brother. It was the last that was heard of Oklahoma Jack.

For a man sometimes said to have been the brains behind the Denver Mint robbery, Clark seems a very passive participant in the Michigan City break eleven years later.

The other six fugitives, under the leadership of Harry Pierpont, grabbed another car and forced the driver and his two female passengers out. They did this after stopping another car and threatening to kill the driver if he disobeyed their wishes. He did, and they shot at him as he ran away. Somehow, all three shots fired in his direction missed. Just as miraculously, no one had been killed in the breakout itself, though three people suffered gunshot wounds.

Before his arrest, Dillinger had visited Mary Kinder, Pierpont's girl, and sister to one of the inmates who didn't make it out. He told her to get things in readiness for Pierpont and the others who would soon be coming to Indianapolis. He gave her money to assist the men in buying something to wear instead of the regulation blue prison issue.

Pierpont and the others went to Indianapolis, where they were outfitted by Mary Kinder. They were spotted by police in Indianapolis and had to make a chase of it. Jimmy Jenkins fell out of the bandit auto when a door flew open. He was fired upon by a jeweler who sized up the situation, but young Jenkins managed to avoid any flying lead at this point. He commandeered a car and headed south out of Indianapolis. The young driver played a ruse on Jenkins by telling him that the car had run out of gas and he was going to have to get some. When Jenkins stepped out of the car to check the gas tank, the youth drove off.

On foot, Jenkins made his way into Bean Blossom in the heart of scenic Brown County, Indiana. He was spotted loitering and when cornered, wounded a vigilante. He was immediately blown away by another vigilante's shotgun. Jenkins was the second escapee accounted for — his death coming just one day after Clark's arrest.

The fugitives, with the help of Harry Copeland, set up in Hamilton, Ohio, and by early October had robbed a bank for funds to help spring Dillinger, who was now residing in the Allen County jail at Lima, Ohio. On Columbus Day, the gang struck, killing Sheriff Jess Sarber in freeing Dillinger. Dillinger was becoming nationally known at this point, and the gang itself took on the appellation of "the Terror Gang."

On December 20, 1933, gang member Edward Shouse, one of the ten fugitives from the penitentiary, was captured in Paris, Illinois. Shouse was thought to be meeting up with Dillinger. Unfortunately, an Indiana state trooper was accidentally killed by his superior in making this arrest. By then Shouse was not likely to rendezvous with Dillinger, since a month previously he had been expelled by the gang for becoming too chummy with Dillinger's girl.

Three others were arrested in Tucson on sabbatical, along with Dillinger on January 25, 1934. They were Harry Pierpont, Charley Makley and Russell Clark.

Dillinger's incarceration was merely a temporary inconvenience as he escaped the Crown Point, Indiana, jail on March 3, 1934, with the famous wooden gun. Pierpont and Makley were restless prisoners themselves. On September 22, 1934, two months to the day after Dillinger's death at the Biograph and mindful of Dillinger's wooden-gun opus, they carved guns out of soap and tried to break out of the Ohio State Penitentiary. The artifice got Makley killed on the spot. The following month, Pierpont went to the chair. As for Russell Clark, his prison stay was a long one — the longest of any "Terror Gang" member. He was finally paroled in August 1968, terminally ill with cancer. He died at the end of the year.

A third casualty from bullet wounds of the Michigan City Ten was John "Three-Finger Jack" Hamilton, who died following the shootout at Little

XIII — The Greatest Escape

Bohemia in April 1934. With the arrest in Chicago of Joseph Burns in December 1934, the total of escapees killed or captured was nine. Only Joseph Fox made it into 1935 as a fugitive from justice. His arrest came in June of that year.

The break — the largest ever in Indiana — was, according to John Toland's view, a result of petty politics. Somehow, H.D. Claudy, the deputy warden, became aware that something was up but didn't figure on anything for at least two days. He was a Republican, and the warden, Louis Kunkel, like 69 of the 120 guards, was a Democrat and new on the job, having arrived in June. Claudy, a Republican, did not wish to ruffle any feathers by giving the alarm when he had little to go on. Many of the old guards had been fired because they were Republican appointees. Because of a lack of communication between officials of different political persuasions and because Harry Pierpont was not a patient man, the break came off one day early without a hitch.

Former governor Harry Leslie had been discussing this precarious situation only that Tuesday morning. That experienced guards had been let go because of politics could only bode ill. He predicted that a riot or prison break was imminent. What he probably did not predict is that the break would be the largest in Indiana history.

An investigation following the prison break, ordered by Governor Paul V. McNutt, found that the main factors involved in the break were overcrowding and a crew of only 120 guards to watch over 2,500 inmates. Antiquated structures, such as guard towers and the quarter-inch plywood wall that separated the prison library from the trustees' mess hall, also needed renovation. When Harry Copeland was arrested in Chicago on November 20, McNutt was still interested at this late date on any light he could shed on the breakout.

Between the day of the prison break — September 26 — and the end of 1933, Detrich almost vanishes from the record completely. He may have been at one or other of the police station robberies committed by the Dillinger gang in Auburn and Peru, Indiana, in October. He may also have been among the bunch with Dillinger that cleaned out the Central National Bank in Greencastle, Indiana, on October 23. We simply don't know. The next month, he was reported by Dillinger himself to be in St. Louis accompanied by John "Three-finger Jack" Hamilton. The snitch obtaining this information from Dillinger — Art McGinnis, to be exact — did not elaborate on what the two men were doing in St. Louis. As for Dillinger, he would shortly after have his hands full leading the police on a merry chase down Irving Park Boulevard — without gunfire (either from him or his moll, Evelyn Frechette) and without casualties, which would add some to the legend that he was fast creating. The following month, Detrich would make the list of Illinois public enemies, weighing in at number six, just ahead of Terrible Tommy O'Connor and well ahead of Baby Face Nelson, who was still relatively unknown. John Dillinger headed the list.

Detrich's days were numbered after the New Year—1934—began. The bungalow occupied by Handsome Jack Klutas and his associates in Bellwood, a Chicago suburb, was watched with great interest by neighbors. Men and women were seen coming and going at all hours, something of an occupational hazard for gangsters. In an effort to divert suspicion, Klutas had given out information to neighbors to the effect that he was a Secret Service agent. Neighbors didn't think so and called the police with their concerns. The police in turn handed the matter to the state attorney's police. The house was soon staked out.

Klutas was away when state attorney's police arrived. A number of other hoodlums, however, were present. None of these characters are today known to anyone but Klutas students, except for Walter Detrich. These operatives performed kidnappings under Klutas' guidance and planning. The fact that Handsome Jack had majored in commerce at the University of Illinois (without taking a degree) was not lost on his cohorts or the press.[25]

When Klutas came to the bungalow, he was told by police to throw up his hands. Instead, he reached for a pistol and was riddled with machine gun fire.[26] With Klutas out of the way, Detrich, being one of the ten escaped inmates in Indiana's most notorious prison break, was the focus of attention. He was the fourth of the ten Michigan City fugitives to be accounted for.

Under the auspices of the Indiana State Police and its head, Captain Matt Leach, Indiana had Detrich extradited to the State House in Indianapolis for questioning two days after his capture. There, Detrich unfolded a tale that blasted the prison administration for barbarous treatment, namely, beatings in the "hole" (solitary confinement).

Detrich boasted of having, quite against the rules, a portable shower for use any time he or anyone else wanted it and surmised that he could get anything smuggled into the prison that he wanted, including an elephant, possibly for emergencies when the portable shower ran short of water.

Whatever the specific aftershocks of Detrich's revelations, an investigation into prison management was undertaken by order of Governor Paul V. McNutt.

A photo appearing on the back pages of the *Indianapolis Star* on January 11, 1934, shows Detrich seated in the company of Captain Matt Leach of the Indiana State Police. The two men look fairly relaxed, though well short of amicable. Oddly enough, Detrich would be released to Leach's custody when it came time for his parole two decades later.[27]

Detrich was quite open about conditions at the state prison and the details of how the ten-man crash-out was consummated. It was his opinion that Dillinger provided the three pistols used in the breakout.[28] According to Detrich, Harry Pierpont was the planner of the break with assistance from Joseph Burns.

Detrich's life in prison appears to have been an uneventful one. In 1944, he was taken to court, probably for a 1929 Los Angeles theater robbery. The decision went against him. However, the L.A. authorities dropped the matter subsequently, settling for Detrich's indeterminate sentence as adequate. The bandit would serve less than another decade in prison. On December 11, 1952, Indiana governor Henry F. Schricker commuted Detrich's life sentence to time served. After three years of good behavior, a different governor of a different political party, George N. Craig, allowed him an unconditional release — or at least, with only one condition. As with Clark three years before, Detrich was not to come back to Indiana. In 1964, he married a second time, his first wife having left him. He worked in St. Louis as a pipe fitter for the rest of his days, apparently without any wrongdoing. He had spent twenty-two years in prison. He would be fortunate enough to spend the remaining twenty-six years of his life out of prison. He died April 11, 1979, at the age of 74.

Upon reflection, something undoubted emerges from all this: the only way a gangster could attain old age was to go to prison for life.

XIV

Laid at His Doorstep

> It's a frame, I tell you. A frame.
> Yeah, and you're the picture for it. — *She Done Him Wrong* (1933)
>
> Just name anything — I've done it. — *Bringing Up Baby* (1938)

One of the most notorious crimes of the first decades of the twentieth century took place at the Denver Mint on Monday morning, December 18, 1922. Just after 9, a pickup truck with wire mesh over the bed, belonging to the Federal Reserve Bank of Denver, pulled up in front of the mint on Colfax Avenue. The truck was about to withdraw money from the Denver Mint because the Federal Reserve branch in town, not having enough space to store all its cash, had deposited the surplus in the mint.

A sizable bundle of five-dollar bills amounting to $200,000 was being taken from the mint to the bank's pickup truck when a black Buick touring car pulled up behind the pickup. A bandit shouted, "Hands up!" and the packages of money were seized. Then all hell broke loose. For the next minute and a half shots were exchanged between mint guards and the robbers. Guard C.T. Linton was killed instantly in the fray, and a robber was seen to be slumped over in the front seat when the Buick pulled away.

The gang had planned the job at the Altahama apartments down Colfax Avenue from the mint, and it was at that place that they were seen assembling around noon. They split up the take, the whole $200,000. Nothing more was heard of the gang for almost three weeks. Then on January 5, 1923, the Buick was found inside a rented garage on Gilpin Street. A body was found in the front seat. The dead man was identified as Nicholas Trainor, alias J.S. Sloane, a member of Harvey Bailey's gang.

The next month the manhunt moved to St. Paul. No robbers were captured, but $80,000 of the Denver loot was found in the cellar of a local banker. From this point on, downright optimism flourished only to be succeeded by absolute bafflement. The robber band grew in number from a mere handful to perhaps a dozen, with as many as three gangs implicated. In 1924, the names of the bandits were at least known to the authorities, even if they were still at large. Ten years later, Denver police chief A.T. Clark stated that all the robbers were dead or in prison.

And that is pretty much the disposition of the case at the present day.

Harvey Bailey was connected with this job. We have his word for it. But he wasn't on the scene when the robbery occurred. He was in Detroit at the bedside of his dying brother. Those that were involved had operated counter to his instructions — or so he wanted the authorities to believe.[1]

According to Kerry Ross Boren, Baron Lamm was also involved with the Denver Mint heist.[2] This hypothesis is much less certain than Bailey's involvement. But if Dow Helmers is right in believing that as many as a dozen men were in on the job, there's room for Lamm and several other big-timers.[3] All that can safely be said about Lamm's ties to the Denver Mint robbery is that the Department of Justice did not mention it among the crimes that he was wanted for at the time of his death.[4]

Denver authorities, however, were interested in James "Oklahoma Jack" Clark, known to them as Mike Burke. He was the master mind of the operation — at least as far as they knew in 1930. Interesting, considering that Clark was no more than a busted horse thief early in 1922. When Clark went to Michigan City in 1931 for life, Denver pretty much lost interest in him.

Much more probable than either Lamm or Clark's participation in the Denver Mint robbery is the involvement of Jake and Ralph Fleagle. Ralph was reported to have taken a room in Denver just a few days before the robbery.[5] In 1930, both Fleagles paid for their transgressions by the hangman's noose in the one case and by a postal inspector's bullet in the other.

In Toledo, Ohio, Eva Zientara had just remarked to a neighbor what a beautiful spring day it was when she got the tragic news. Her husband, patrolman George Zientara, had been killed that morning following an express car robbery. Zientara didn't know what he was getting into. He had a partner with him. He should have had a heavily-armed company of Texas Rangers ready to earn their twelve dollars a month. Less than three years after Chicago inaugurated the fashion, George Zientara was Toledo's first machine gun victim.[6] He was two days short of his thirty-fifth birthday.

It was around nine on Monday morning, April 16, 1928, when residents living near the intersection of Bancroft Street and Upton Avenue reported a car driving recklessly with broken glass flying out of it onto the pavement at each turn. Officers George Zientara and John Bispkupski raced to the neighborhood to check out what they thought were bootleggers. They parked in an alley off Upton Avenue and Milburn Street. An assortment of garages fronted on the alley. Some of the occupants of the speeding car had gone into a garage while the rest entered a rented house nearby. Officer Zientara was going up the alley when a suspect came out of the house. He quickly got the drop on the man and told him, "Stick 'em up." The man was in the act of complying when a group of men came out of the house armed with machine guns and pistols. Zientara went down in a hail of lead, one bullet striking him in the head. He would expire at 11:40 that morning.

As it happened, officers Zientara and Bispkupski were after the robbers of an American Express Company truck, not bootleggers. At 8 A.M. in downtown Toledo, a Packard sedan got in line behind the American Express truck and followed it to the intersection of Knapp and Broadway. When the truck stopped for the traffic, two men got out of the Packard and entered the truck — one in front, the other in back. The American Express agents found themselves looking down the barrels of sawed-off shotguns. They were quickly disarmed and tape was put over their eyes. The driver was told to drive another three miles to a lonely spot on University Boulevard, just off Nebraska Avenue. The Packard followed the truck to its new destination. Three safes were unloaded from the truck, but not before young John White, a student at the University of Toledo, saw the truck, got in his car and drove to the scene to investigate. White's father was the general agent of American Express in Toledo.

White was quickly scooped up by the bandits and shoved in the back of the truck with the guards and driver. The bandits took White's car and abandoned the Packard. Other bandits pulled up in a touring car and the two cars drove off, bearing three safes from the American Express truck. One of these was a small strongbox containing ten thousand dollars in cash and payroll checks.

For no sensible reason, the bandits drove away with great speed, attracting the attention of bystanders, especially when the screeching tires and swerving led to a safe's busting out a window in the touring car. No chase had been mounted.

The bandits drove to their hideout at 2304 Upton Avenue, a neighborhood where they had been living since January. The neighbors found their all-hours-of-the night behavior suspicious. A woman, giving her name as Mrs. Hill, opened up a charge account at the neighborhood grocery. A little girl from the same house as Mrs. Hill said her name was Anna May Baker and at the grocery proudly proclaimed, "Daddy doesn't have to work."

When Zientara and Biskupski arrived at the alley off Upton Avenue, the bandits had already unloaded two large safes and a small strongbox. After shooting Zientara, they fired on Biskupski. Biskupski feigned death, as FBI agent William Smith would do under similar firepower five years later in the Kansas City Massacre. One of the bandits ran up to Biskupski and relieved him of his police automatic .38. The scout car driven by the two patrolmen was also taken.

The bandits made a hurried departure, whether for another part of

Toledo, Lansing, Detroit or Chicago isn't certain. They left behind young White's car and their own Chrysler touring car, as well the Packard sedan, merely going with the scout car. This, too, was abandoned when they stumbled on another car of the same make and promptly stole it. They took with them the small strongbox containing ten thousand in cash and payroll checks.

From photographs left in the Upton Avenue residence, police were able to pick up the two women living with the gang — Mrs. Joseph Baker, 27, and Loretta "Pooch" Ryan, 35 — and young Anna May Baker, 6, and Martin Baker, 5.[7] A man whose picture was also found in the house was well-known to Toledo officers and he, too, was picked up in a Toledo flophouse.

One of the first suspects brought in by a police dragnet was rumrunner William Daly. He seemed to know who did in Zientara. He was booked for transporting liquor and "being a suspicious person."

Mrs. Thomas Round lived next door to the gangster hideout on Upton Avenue. She and her husband had been in Toledo five weeks when the shooting incident occurred. Her husband worked for a railroad in India and his employer had given the couple six months to tour England and America. Mrs. Round had heard about America's big-time crime but had to wonder if it was exaggerated. From her window, she saw the shooting of patrolman Zientara. She told a reporter that she couldn't wait to go to Canada and that a stop in Chicago beforehand was definitely out.[8]

Chicago's reputation was already in the tank at this time, with hundreds of gang-related deaths reported since 1924. In ten months, with the St. Valentine's Day Massacre of more than local notoriety, Chicago's place in criminal annals would be firmly entrenched. And Chicago, as it turned out, was just the place where the Toledo police should have been looking. The very men who had killed Patrolman Zientara would be involved in the killing of seven of Bugs Moran's bunch in Chicago the next St. Valentine's Day. At Toledo, phony press cards were found at the scene of the patrolman's death. They had been dropped by the gang in their flight. The cards bore two names and were issued by a correspondence school. Obviously, the gang had thought the cards would get them out of a tight situation, in case their car was stopped.

Such subterfuges would be employed in the St. Valentine's Day Massacre. Two police uniforms would be worn by killers masquerading as cops so as to catch victims and bystanders off guard.

The five men who held up the American Express truck were almost certainly Shotgun George Ziegler, Fred "Killer" Burke, Gus Winkler, Byron Bolton and Toledo's own Ray "Crane-neck" Nugent. It had been Nugent's place that the gang was staying at in Toledo.

From the robbery of an American Express truck and the St. Valentine's Day Massacre to Baron Lamm is something of a reach, viewed at the distance of more than eight decades. But, at the time of Lamm's death, the killing of Patrolman Zientara was still unsolved, or, at least, still on the books, for Toledo police had a pretty good idea of the identity of some of the culprits immediately. When Lamm was killed, along with Landy and Hunter, word got out that Fred "Killer" Burke had been killed at Sidell. The Ohio Bankers' Association quickly asked that shell casings from the cornfield on the Moody farm be matched with those found in the alley off Upton Avenue in Toledo when Zientara was killed. This theory soon exploded when it was learned that Burke and Ziegler were not involved at Sidell.

The crime would go unsolved another four months before justice began to be meted out. Fred "Killer" Burke was arrested in Missouri in March 1931. A few months later, the word among the underworld was that Ray "Crane-neck" Nugent had been bumped off. Gus Winkler was the next to go, slain apparently by his friend and business associate, Shotgun George Ziegler in October 1933. Six months later Shotgun George would himself be slain in Cicero, quite possibly by his friends and business associates, the Barker gang. By 1935, with the arrest of Byron Bolton, the Toledo American Express truck robbery and murder of Patrolman Zientara would finally be atoned for.[9]

Almost exactly a year later, on April 18, a bloody robbery took place at Columbia City, Indiana, a town not far from Ft. Wayne in Whitley County. Since assistant cashier R.R. Ferry was kind enough to grant an interview to a staff correspondent of the local paper shortly after the robbery of the Columbia City State Bank detailing how matters stood on the inside of the bank during the robbery, it will be as well to begin with that account.

> At 11:30 o'clock, I and Elmer Bump, the bookkeeper, were the only ones in the bank. W.H. Carter, president, H.A. Beeson, the cashier, and Adrian Everhard and Roscoe Brumbaugh, the assistant cashiers, were at lunch.
>
> Bump was up in the front of the bank waiting on a woman.... I stepped to the rear of the bank, into our telephone booth, to put in a call. While I was in, Bump finished waiting on the customer, who left. Bump heard a noise behind him, turned around and one of the bandits stuck a gun in his face, telling him to "Stick 'em up."
>
> About that time I came out of the telephone booth and the bandit also turned the gun on me. He marched both of us back to the vault and made us lie down with our faces to the floor. Our alarm, however, had been turned in.
>
> The bandit then told Bump to get up and open the money chest in the vault. Bump said he didn't know the combination. He protested that he was a new man and didn't know how to open the chest. Just then, Fred Clark, a mail messenger, entered the bank. Another bandit in the vestibule grabbed him and marched him back to the vault and made him also lie down on the floor, face downward. The bandit in the vault then ordered me to open the chest.
>
> I fumbled with the chest twice and then turned to get a look at the bandit's face. He knew my intent evidently for he said:

"Don't look me in the face. Turn around and open that chest. If you fumble again, I'll bump you off."

I stalled a few seconds, knowing the sheriff and his deputies were on their way. Just as I opened the chest, shots were heard at the front door and the bandit ran from the vault to the front of the bank. I then snapped off the light in the vault and reached for a gun but I didn't get a chance to use it.

As far as I can figure it out, there was a bandit in the vault with me, another in the vestibule on guard, another behind the counter, the one who scooped up the money out of the drawers and the fourth on guard in the car outside.[10]

Mail carrier Fred Clark was pulled into the bank by the bandits. As so often happened in those days, Clark thought that he was the butt of a joke. He actually grabbed the bandit's pistol and tried to take it out of his hand before he was shoved in back with Bump and Ferry.

Things now were heating up outside. Sheriff Alvin Haney and his deputies, along with a number of vigilantes, closed in on the bank. The bandit by the car was armed with a Tommy gun and began firing at the men. A firefight soon erupted in which a hundred shots were fired. Sheriff Haney took a slug in his face but survived. A lady across the street in the kitchen of her apartment was not so fortunate. She was killed instantly by a stray shot.

The bandits were able to make it to the getaway car and drive off. The bandit guard, who wielded the Tommy gun and fought with three officers and a vigilante, while hiding behind the blue Buick getaway sedan was hit grievously and had to be helped into the car. He had blood streaming from his face. The trail led to Pennsylvania, where the next day three members of the gang were stopped by a Pennsylvania state policeman for a traffic violation. They opened fire and the officer was killed. But the outlaws were captured afterwards. Some of the money from Columbia City was found in their car as well as newspaper accounts of the robbery. The robbers hailed from Minnesota and were not big-time operators. They were put away for life.[11]

The fourth outlaw may have been mortally wounded in the shootout at Columbia City.

Though quickly solved, the Columbia City job has been charged erroneously over the years to both Baron Lamm and Fred "Killer" Burke. The first bet was also dead wrong. Kirby Davis, an outlaw well-known in Indianapolis and wanted for murder, had been locked up once by Sheriff Haney and vowed vengeance in a big way. That Sheriff Haney was hit seemed proof that Davis was the brains behind the Columbia City robbery and that Davis was settling an old score with the officer just as much as pulling a heist. Perhaps the power of suggestion explains why someone thought they saw him on the scene.

Peru (pronounced "PEE-roo" by the locals) is the county seat of Miami

County, Indiana. Its minor league ball club is said to have bested the Chicago Cubs in the days of Grover Cleveland Alexander in an exhibition game.[12] More certainly, Peru was the hometown of Cole Porter. In the old days, it was the winter quarters for a number of circuses, including the Ringling Brothers and Barnum and Bailey's circuses. Cowboy star Tom Mix spent part of his winters in the late twenties in Peru under contract to the Sells-Floto Circus. Screen icon James Dean got his start as a performer here, when he won the state speech contest in dramatic reading in the spring of 1949. Peru is one of those small towns that live in the memory as ever sunny and always beautiful.

Friday, October 18, 1929, was just such a bright, sunny day in Peru. At 11:30 that morning, a car bearing seven men, coming from the east, pulled up on Main Street in front of the First National Bank. One man got out and took a position on the sidewalk in front of the bank. Another man went over to a side door and stood guard, hand in coat pocket. Four men went inside the bank while the seventh man remained at the wheel.

Because it was the start of the lunch hour, several key bank personnel were away from the bank. The bank president and cashier were absent on business and the vice president was visiting a doctor in Indianapolis. Two assistant cashiers were present in the bank — and they had their limitations.

The four "inside men" commanded everyone in the bank to lie down on the floor behind the counters. They were not to look up for any reason. In the ten minutes that the robbery occupied there were no more than ten people in the bank, excluding the four robbers. One employee somehow entered the bank from the side door — probably arriving just as the bandits were setting things up — and, seeing what was going down from the cloakroom, pressed the burglar alarm. One of the inside men caught him but merely ordered the man to join the others on the floor. The bandits were fully aware of the new situation.

The four bandits went into the tellers' cages, scooping up cash into sacks. One of the bandits jerked up Gordon Smith by the collar and ordered him to open the safe in the vault. Another bandit nearby said, "Shoot his ears off if he don't open it for you." The telephone now began to ring. Martha Endicott, a stenographer, was told to answer it. Suspecting that the police were calling, one of the bandits told her to tell them that everything was all right. She did. Nevertheless, as far as the gang was concerned, everything was not all right.

"They've turned in the alarm. Let's go," one of the men announced. Meanwhile, the street was coming to life. A policeman, who happened to be in the vicinity, was shot in the foot either by the man in front or the driver. Another man, fresh out of the hospital, thought he'd go downtown that day. He no sooner arrived at the bank than he was plugged in the calf.

Ruth Knott, an employee of an insurance company housed in the basement of the bank building, heard the shooting and deemed that she knew what it was all about. She ran for help to a nearby shop. The shopkeeper went to a lawyer's office across the street to get a rifle, but the rifle was unavailable just then. Had it been around, the Peru robbery might well have been one of the bloodiest of this bank-robbing era.

The lawyer peered out his second-story window only to have a bullet ricochet off the building near his head. By this time, the bandits were getting into the getaway car.

As the car, described by the lawyer as a seven-passenger open car, made its exit down Main Street, it was followed by music store employee Sam Clark when it reached the Miami Street intersection. He followed the vehicle to Canal Street and then over to Second, Third, Benton and Main and back east out of town. The bandits were going at a pretty good clip and left Clark in the dust. Clark did get a good look at the license plates, however. They were Michigan plates — 63-944. A farmer saw the gang going past Erie and that was the last glimpse anyone had of them.

Before noon, news of the robbery was flashed all over the Midwest by the Associated Press. A posse, consisting of such brass as the prosecuting attorney of Peru and a deputy sheriff in a Ford/Lincoln dealer's car, complete with hired driver, went in pursuit of the bandits. They headed north to Warsaw. They apparently made good speed — a little too good. Near Claypool, Indiana, they were fired on by another posse in ambush. No one was hurt, but in the resulting confusion, word got around that the bandits had been seen at last.[13]

Some remarkable things occurred in this robbery. They were all the more remarkable perhaps because they did not go unremarked. None of the safety deposit boxes were molested. Only the bank's money was wanted by the robber gang. Both of the wounded men were wounded on purpose; the intent being, like Jack Crab's when he put two arrows in the Pawnee, not to kill but to distract. The lawyer who gazed at the bandits from aloft also was missed on purpose.[14]

Whoever did this robbery were not amateurs, nor were they the type to commit a St. Valentine's Day Massacre on the side. The Michigan plates put the robbery more in Burke's corner than Lamm's, but the Indiana Bankers' Association charged this one to Lamm's account, and they quite possibly knew whereof they spoke.[15] Certainly the AP report carried in the *Frankfort Morning Times*, October 20, 1929, which mentions that the apparent leader of the outfit was 6'2" and the others were around 5'10", suits Lamm, Landy and probably Clark and Detrich.

The take at the Peru robbery was at first said to have amounted to $68,000. In time, the loss would be reported at upwards of $90,000.

Three suspects were picked up within a few days at a garage in Michigan City. All three were armed and all three lived in Lafayette. Nothing much could be found on two of the men, but a third seemed like a good prospect for a bank robbery/murder rap at Mishawaka. This is how matters stood until Lamm's death a little over a year later.

There was some question about the response of the police to the bank raid. One officer was exonerated, at least in the press, for his seeming reluctance to engage the bandits in their getaway. Another question had to do with the mysterious phone call to the bank in the middle of the bank robbery.

At an investigation by the police board and the Clearing House Association into the robbery on October 21, chief of police D. Elbert Brown was asked by a police board member if he or any member of the force phoned the bank during the robbery. He replied, "No."

Martha Endicott, the bank employee who answered the phone, however, thought otherwise.[16]

The meeting resulted in some recommendations. Parking was prohibited in front and at the side of the bank. The police department was to be equipped with machine guns and riot guns to adequately combat gangs who were invariably better armed than officers. This last recommendation is especially interesting in view of what took place almost four years to the day after this bank robbery. On October 14, 1933, John Dillinger, Harry Pierpont and, perhaps, Walter Detrich, dropped by the Peru police station and helped themselves to as much of the arsenal as time and reason permitted. There was a big high school football game going on, so the circumstances must have seemed congenial to the robbers.

In any case, the meeting between the police board and Clearing House Association resulted in the police department's being exonerated. This announcement was posted on the front page of the *Peru Republican* (October 25):

> At the meeting of the police board held last evening it was learned that the officers on duty had acted without delay when the alarm was given, despite the numerous criticisms to the contrary.
>
> The bank officials were present at the investigation and showed no disposition to place the blame on the officials for the fact that a group of desperate men had completely outwitted the entire community.
>
> The records of the meeting are opened for inspection to any one desirous of learning the exact facts.

XV

Who Else?

> I'm very interested in that body.—*The Thin Man* (1934)
> That's another one I can't answer right now.—*The Thin Man* (1934)

Were the reports of Baron Lamm's death greatly exaggerated?

On the one side, there was the dead certainty that the corpse wasn't Fred "Killer" Burke.[1] On the other is the likelihood that he could have been just about anybody else. Most likely, Baron Lamm is dead and has been moldering in a pauper's ditch these seventy-five years and more.

He was identified by his mug shot and presumably by his fingerprints.[2] Fingerprints don't lie — though they have told stories out of school, such as that of a print on a beer bottle in a basement, which a year after it was left, proved conclusively that Pretty Boy Floyd was the machine gunner at the Kansas City Massacre, June 17, 1933. It may have been so, but that fingerprint (actually, that of Floyd's partner, Adam Richetti) has cocked a few brows in recent years and did so back then as well. Yet, there is a fine line between mislabeling a dead man's fingerprints and creating a false set.

For some, John Dillinger's death, even with two sets of the outlaw's fingerprints to match the dead man's killed at the Biograph and the innumerable physical correspondences between the outlaw and the shooting victim, has become quite an issue. The Dillinger controversy has been around since July 22, 1934. It is not likely to go away any time soon.[3]

If we assume that the Milwaukee authorities and Chauncey Manning knew their man when they saw him (as the Ohio Bankers' Association did not — they were looking for Fred "Killer" Burke, not Lamm) and if we assume that Lamm's fingerprints equaled those of Bell and Tommy Wyatt and George Barney and Herbert Madsen and other sundry Joe Doakes floating around, which had as their common denominator one Herman K. Lamm, then it would seem that we are on pretty firm ground when we believe that Baron Lamm died as history records.[4]

But if there is just a bit of doubt about the fingerprints, real or inferred, or the on-the-spot identification of the unclaimed body at McCauley's, then the scales tip the other way. That's because there are plenty of things to put in.

The first thing that comes to mind is the number of bandits who participated in the Clinton robbery. Hardly any of Lamm's robberies lend themselves to exact numeration.[5] From the amount of loot taken to the number of bandits participating, there are often discrepancies in the statements from those who know or should know. Supposedly, there were five robbers at Clinton. Most reports said so. In other words, there were five bandits, at the least. Less than two weeks earlier, at Frankfort, Indiana, six men and one woman — or was it eight men? — were involved in the bank robbery at the Farmers' State Bank. If, as seems likely, Baron Lamm and his gang perpetrated both robberies, one has to wonder what happened to the extra man (men) and the woman who took part in the Frankfort robbery.

As mentioned in Chapter VIII, Clinton telephone operator Hazel Haase alerted authorities that six men were in the gang. Her report must have been the earliest of all concerning the robbery, and it was obtained, it must be recalled, from a customer in the bank. Reading the testimony from some of those in the bank at the time of the robbery, few were sure about how many bandits were in the bank. No more than three were ever observed by a single witness. Yet four seems to have been the case. With all those pistols around, nobody saw too much. As we have seen, Arthur V. Hedges and Pete Voto couldn't even identify Clark and Detrich, both of whom were certainly in the bank that morning.

Hazel Haase's initial report was in line with other early reports, which also mentioned six robbers. In its second extra edition on the 16th, the Indianapolis *News* in its subheads specified six robbers in the Clinton robbery that morning.

In addition to this is the report in the *Paris* (IL) *Daily Beacon-News* for December 16, which reads: "The bandits attempted to use the machine gun as they had before to stand off the posse, but a withering gun fire from the Danville authorities swept the truck, wounding *three* of the men. The other *three* took cover in a field. The posse kept at a safe distance while reinforcements were summoned from Danville" (italics mine).

This, of course, was written when things were yet sketchy; the "Danville authorities" had about as much to do with the actual gunfire involved as Marie Dressler. But even as late as December 19, the *Terre Haute Tribune* ran this misleading caption under photos of Landy, Detrich and Bell/Lamm: "Three of five bandits who robbed the Citizens State Bank at Clinton Tuesday shown here. Bell and Landry [*sic*] were killed in a battle with officers and volunteer possemen, and Detrich was captured, *along with three companions*, one of whom, E.H. Hunter, of Terre Haute, died Thursday morning at Danville, Ill" (italics mine).

Then, too, when one recollects the testimony of Harlow Frist in the trial of the two bandit survivors, it almost sounds as if Frist saw the bandit car in close proximity with another car. You have to read the testimony more than once to get the idea that he means Helm's Oldsmobile in its approach to the scene. But neither the Prosecution nor the Defense was thrown by Frist's vagueness, so no matter as to that. His testimony also referred to "quite a bunch of them," rather than a specific number of bandits, such as the five one might have expected. "Bunch" sounds rather more numerous than the handful that a mere five is. Again, the extra car and the odd choice of words were left hanging to tantalize future students of the testimony.

And what on earth did Jediah Frist mean in his testimony by "five men in action," when asked how many men there were in the gang? Why not just five men? Why add "in action?" Probably, he was just playing to the court reporter, but adorning frill or not, the expression is confusing.

Pitted against the early reports of six outlaws in the robber band and the cruxes found in the testimony of both Frists is the fact that in their testimony at Clark and Detrich's trial, both Jediah Frist and Wells Gilbert explicitly stated that there were five bandits who waylaid them to get their "machines." These two men had plenty of time to count noses and guns. If there were six robbers that morning, one must have fled the scene before Frist was pulled over by the gang. Nevertheless, though Jediah Frist was sure that he was stopped by five men, he could identify only three. Apparently, Dad Landy and E.H. Hunter were sensed by Frist rather than seen.

Now, it is obvious that no more than five individuals would fit into Fenton Williams' Model-A coupe on its wayward course to oblivion, but that does not mean that more than one car wasn't involved in the bank robbery at Clinton initially or at some point afterward.

In fact, two cars were reported coming to the aid of the stricken Buick when it stopped a short distance outside of Clinton that morning.[6] Even if this report was only half right, some of the bandits may have gotten away. Coupled with this report is an interesting, if defiant, remark made by Walter Detrich soon after his capture. "If we had a fast car, we would have gotten away." Did he imply that others in a fast car did, indeed, get away?

Moreover, in an *Indianapolis News* article, either Chief Helms or Patrolman Burnside — which, isn't clear — specified more than one bandit car: "We drove north out of Clinton and then swung west towards Fairview [a suburb of Clinton]. At that point we saw the bandit *cars* and we gave chase. As we closed in on *them* they opened fire with a machine gun" (italics mine).[7]

Bear in mind, too, that the posse was ready to call it quits after just three of the bandits were rounded up. Hunter and Detrich were somewhat tardily apprehended, the latter perhaps as much as an hour after the former.

No one seemed to know just how many bandits they were after. Once Hunter was captured, most of the posse departed, with only a few officers hanging around, together with a throng of curiosity seekers. Any number of fugitives might have gotten away, if only they could have squeezed into the Model-A in their hour of need.

The question arises: What if they didn't have to squeeze into the Model-A? Another car on the scene seems possible, almost probable. But if there was such a car, it did not take part in the long flight of the fugitives. It must have made itself scarce early in the action before there was much of a posse in pursuit of the bandits. Like the much-mooted Dalton gang's sixth rider, the extra car did not pull its weight, unless, as seems unlikely, someone actually got in it. How many people might have hopped into this hypothetical car cannot now be determined, but two seems a good guess.

Somebody may well have gotten away. They might even have been in the Ford coupe that furnished the last leg of the death ride, but that seems most unlikely. As speculated above, someone in the gang might have been driving another car that morning and scuttled away altogether unnoticed by the posse. They would have had to exit in the early going, probably when the five commandeered the Frist Buick. They may have grabbed their share and taken off, judging that with the bandits in a late-model Buick, they would be in the clear. Support for something of the sort having taken place was provided by Henry Myers, an Illinois highway patrolman.

While cleaning debris from a culvert on U.S. 36 (formerly, State Road 121) outside Camargo, Illinois, on January 10, 1931, more than three weeks after the Clinton robbery, he noticed a bundle of papers in the weeds. The papers were abstracts, deeds and other legal documents taken from the Citizens State Bank during the robbery. These papers were inspected by assistant cashier Pete Voto and confirmed as coming from the Citizens State Bank. Something, however, was not among the papers—the twenty-five hundred dollars (not immediately divulged), which was unaccounted for after the robbery.[8]

Camargo is twenty-five miles from the farthest point west that the bandits reached.

Giving emphatic credence to reports of six bandits in the gang is the testimony of an unnamed farm woman who mentions six men changing a tire. If she had seen six men in the McWethy yard, it might be that the extra man was Jediah Frist, having just then been pulled over by the gang. But this doesn't really make sense. The men were not looking to repair their disabled vehicle at this point; they were looking to take another car. Moreover, whatsoever we make of this, other unnamed parties saw six men in the gang as they fled Clinton at the beginning of their long flight.

How does one figure all this?

Two possibilities seem likeliest.

The first likelihood is hard to gainsay — that the bundle of legal papers and the missing two grand or so was absconded with by some Gatewood of the Prairie State among the vigilante element. How much attention was paid to the loot, how carefully watched over it was, the report doesn't indicate. It sure got around. Some was in Jediah Frist's Buick, some was found in Wells Gilbert's cattle truck. That found by Leo Moody was taken to Fairmount, Illinois, shortly after the fracas was over. The money in each case was handled by responsible persons, so nothing is likely to have happened to it in its roundabout route back to Clinton. We know that a billfold, replete with names and addresses, whatever it held of money, disappeared soon after it was discovered on the person of one of the fallen bandits. Weapons, too, went missing, including the unwieldy machine gun, which most newspaper and oral accounts mentioned. Someone at various points along the trail or in the barn lot just might have had his way with a portion of the loot.[9] Five hundred dollars in gold was given to Frist by the bandits for the use of his Buick.[10] This munificence, not mentioned in Frist's testimony, was recovered in full — if, indeed, there was anything to it in the first place.

The bit of money found in Wells Gilbert's truck — just enough to make him fearful of being held up for it — also found its way into the proper hands. The loot, over fifteen thousand dollars strong, was reported to have been found, for the most part, in a satchel in the barn lot of the Leo Moody farm. But someone spoke too soon. The money wasn't all recovered. Whether the satchel was tampered with or whether some bandit's clothing carried more money than was reported in the newspapers, no one can say. The sure fact is that the books afterwards came up somewhere between eighteen hundred and twenty-five hundred dollars short, a fact strangely overlooked in the trial of Clark and Detrich.

It is almost inconceivable to think that a vigilante could have pocketed so much money when others were around. And if he was seen to do it, how did he keep others off his back so successfully for so long? No one ever mentioned such chicanery connected with the aftermath of the fight on the Moody farm. But such there might have been. The idea covers all the bases.

The more colorful and much more likely option is that some member or members of the gang got away cleanly. This theory is the only one mentioned by the local dailies, apparently never imagining the possibility that some vigilante or vigilantes weren't altogether on the up-and-up. Camargo is twenty-five miles from Sidell, very near Tuscola, and situated on the intersection of Routes 36 and 130. The bandits in their flight came nowhere near it, except, perhaps, in their wildest dreams. Yet part of the contents of the little safe in the Citizens State Bank got there.

As reported earlier, shortly after the Frankfort robbery, chief of police Arthur G. Eversole of Lafayette saw a Plymouth carrying six men followed closely by two coupes on the road just before he was alerted to be on the lookout for a black Buick bearing six desperadoes. (As usual, the number of suspects differs in reports. Two men and a woman rode in the Plymouth in one report, although two coupes followed the Plymouth.) The suspicious Plymouth played on Eversole's suspicions. If his instincts as a lawman were true, the Frankfort job was a large-scale operation. It may be that the Clinton robbery was, too. There just may have been two automobiles—perhaps two coupes—coming to the assistance of the crippled Buick outside Clinton, as some witnesses said. Harvey Bailey planted an extra car on a side street during a Cincinnati robbery. He also sometimes had an extra car follow the getaway car in case the first car ran into trouble. Lamm may well have done the same thing—both at Frankfort and Clinton.

At the very least, six men and a woman were in on the robbery of the Farmers' State Bank at Frankfort. The extra man and woman didn't immediately figure in the Clinton robbery, unless they had something to do with those two mysterious autos mentioned above. Do they show up otherwise?

Possibly.

A man and a lady of interest stopping by the McCauley undertaking parlor at some point in the week-long wake for the three dead bandits were seen by Merrel Chew, who was eight at the time. In 1992, he recalled the moment:

> I know one time I was coming by [McCauley's funeral parlor in Sidell, where the bodies of Lamm, Landy and Hunter lay] and I was all by myself that day out in front of the undertaking parlor they have there and this big, ol' yellow Packard convertible drove up. And it just looked like something right out of the movies, you know. This guy got out with a blue suit and pearl gray hat and a beautiful blonde gal was driving the car, you know. And he rushed in—wasn't anybody around—I was just kind of standing there on the corner watching them. He dashed back out and shook his head "no" to her and, boy, away they went. What I figured out was they were checking to see if they were members of their gang.[11]

What they were looking for is anybody's guess. That the results proved negative raises the question of who wasn't present at the funeral parlor.

Now, if this visit took place soon after the battle—and Merrel Chew couldn't be precise as to the number of days after the 16th that he saw the pair—it may be that they were looking for E.H. Hunter. Hunter died in the early morning hours of the 18th and his body, therefore, would not have been placed alongside his fellow bandits until that afternoon at the earliest. Had the man and the woman looked for Hunter on the morning of the 17th or 18th, they would have met with disappointment. That might explain the head shaking and the couple's apparent haste to leave town.

The natural inference is that the pair had some ties to the dead men, probably underworld ties rather than as blood relations. An even stronger inference presents itself. Were these two the man and the woman in Frankfort parked in the alley in back of the bank in the getaway Buick on December 3?

But if these two people were the ones in the Buick, who drove that day? Hunter, according to Detrich and Clark, was the gang's usual driver (at this time, anyway), and while there's no law that says that a rumrunner/racetrack driver, of questionable reputation, can't be friends with comely young ladies, Hunter cannot have survived his own death. He was dead, as dead as one frontier judge could wish Billy the Kid when he sentenced him to hang by the neck until he was "dead, dead, dead." If the man and woman were the same as the two spotted at Frankfort, then Hunter either was not driving the getaway car that day or he did double duty as an inside man and driver. Either way, who the extra man was and what he was supposed to be doing at Frankfort are both good questions.

Then, too, this head-shaking naysayer may have been Lamm.

After all, Lamm's thick Teutonic accent, noted by John Nolan at Clinton, was not mentioned in connection with the Frankfort robbery. Lamm could have been incommunicado while looting the bank or he simply may have sat this one out — out back in the alley in the Buick with a lady. That would be robbing a bank with style and going the Lamm method one better.

What if the man and the woman weren't looking for Hunter but were looking for Baron Lamm instead? And what if the man, by shaking his head, signified to the lady that the ever-elusive Lamm was not in that day? Or might the man have even been Lamm himself seeking someone in particular amongst the fallen and not finding him?

Or could the man have been lying when he suggested to the lady that whomever they were looking for wasn't present at the mortuary? Perhaps he wanted to spare her. Perhaps he wanted to keep up Lamm's image of elusiveness. Who knows?

Other questions pop up. Could the well-dressed man have been Walter Detrich's good friend, Handsome Jack Klutas? Here again, there is plenty of reason to wonder.

Around nine on the evening of the 17th, a man showed up at a garage in Danville, Illinois. He said his name was James Ward, which meant that he was Al Capone's so-called Rum King, and he was looking for a ride back to

Chicago Heights. He hired a taxi and at Hoopeston, twenty-five miles north of Danville, he phoned Danville police to inform them that he had been missing since the 15th and had just then been released. Or did he? Many questions arose after the "Rum/Bootleg King" returned to Chicago Heights. For one: Did he really call the Danville police? They had no record of such a call. Did he call the *Commercial-News* immediately after his release by the gang, shortly after 9 at night on the 17th? The *Commercial-News* was open till 1:30 A.M., but no call from Ward was received there. This was news to the *News*. Furthermore, Ward said that he had chartered a Yellow Cab at Danville for the trip to Chicago Heights. The cab company had no record of it.[12] Ward was one of Al Capone's favorite bootleggers, and he had just been ransomed for fifty thousand dollars by his family. A few years before, Ward had been abducted and ransomed in similar fashion for twenty thousand dollars. It was rumored that Capone himself had paid the ransom on that occasion.

Abducting someone like James Ward was in Handsome Jack Klutas's line. This was the snatch game as played by the College Kidnappers. Like Verne Miller, the mastermind of the Kansas City Massacre, Klutas dared to mess with Capone. He may even have kidnapped Ward both times. If, as an informer later asserted, Klutas was responsible for the second kidnapping, he was in the same precise area as Lamm and his gang at almost the same time. He, therefore, might well have been the well-dressed person of interest, accompanied by a lady companion, that Merrel Chew saw one December morning on his way to school. Unfortunately, Merrel Chew did not give any clear indication of the man's age, but the inference is that Klutas' thirty years would have fit the unidentified man just fine. As we have seen, Klutas had ties to Detrich, and it should not surprise anyone that, if not an actual satellite of the gang, Klutas, at least, was in touch with it.[13] That December morning—the bodies of the three bandits were kept in Sidell until their burial on the 24th—Klutas may have wanted to see who was dead and who wasn't. No doubt, he was looking for Walter Detrich, in particular. The two may have had a past and certainly would have a future.

This Klutas business introduces a monkey wrench into a situation already replete with monkey wrenches. Was Klutas' presence in the Danville area connected with the Clinton robbery? After all, the gang had stayed overnight on December 15/16 at a Danville hotel, possibly the Carleton on West Harrison Street.[14] Dealing with Ward must have been enough for Klutas in itself, but he may have wanted to do some celebrating with Detrich at Danville after the Clinton job and after Ward had been ransomed. That Detrich and Klutas were in Danville at almost the same time or exactly the same time seems more than coincidental.

The written record presents us with further anomalies. E.H. Hunter was wounded on the morning of the 16th. He was first taken to the Danville police station by Deputy Mace Smoot and others of the posse.[15] Then Hunter went to the county hospital, where he later died. The Poor Farm records of Vermilion County indicate that he was a bank bandit and that he had died as the result of being shot in the abdomen. Other than these two things, there is only one other detail worthy of notice. Under the heading of birthplace is the notation, "Germany." This seemingly minuscule item upsets the apple cart when it comes to what is known or noised abroad concerning Hunter. No one among the old-timers on the scene of the battle at the Moody farm, nobody in the posse and certainly no newspaper reporter mentioned anything about Hunter's having a German accent.

Hunter's history, as far as anyone knew, was rather pedestrian and provincial. He grew up not far from where he was killed. An unidentified posseman had him a rumrunner from Terre Haute. A later assessment thought him a Danville, Illinois, taxi driver.[16] If Hunter spoke with a thick Teutonic accent, someone would have noted it. Instead, there is this lone notation in the Vermilion County Poor Farm records (which, in turn, was based upon Hunter's death certificate).

If he came over from Germany, Hunter should have sounded German to somebody interviewing him. If he came to this country from Germany as a child or infant, it is hard to see how his speech would have wholly escaped the influence of his parents' native tongue. He might well sound like Lawrence Welk, ending every other word with an "uh." If he had no German accent, there should not have been this entry in the record. Surely, the normally taciturn Hunter didn't tell anyone that he was from Germany, unless, of course, he was lying. But prevarication, while on one's deathbed, is bad form, even in the case of an outright outlaw. Hunter isn't likely to have talked about Germany in his last moments with so much else to think about. He knew that he wasn't going to make it, and that seems to have been what he dwelled on. Moreover, it is quite inconceivable to think that anyone would have entertained the idea that Hunter was from Germany if someone from Tennessee, with an Irish surname, had him pegged as his brother.[17]

Germany, as a fatherland, just doesn't suit what we know of Hunter, any more than it does that assuredly native-born road agent, Jesse James. And the initials "E.H.H." are a good fit for the Anglo surname "Hunter."[18]

Germany, as a fatherland, does, of course, fit Baron Lamm to a "T."

So where did the idea that Hunter was German come from? The simplest and most feasible answer is that the listing is a mistake — a scribal error, so to speak.[19] Perhaps some of Lamm's information found its way into Hunter's record. There may have been a conflation of two separate records, in this instance, the death certificates of Hunter and Lamm/Bell. Lest this likelihood

STATE OF ILLINOIS)
) SS
COUNTY OF VERMILION)

I, Lynn Foster, County Clerk of Vermilion County, State of Illinois, do hereby certify that this is a true and complete copy of the Certificate on file in the Office of the County Clerk, Vermilion County, Illinois.

FILED FOR RECORD: Dec 22, 1930
DATE: June 11, 1996
COUNTY CLERK: Lynn Foster

THIS IS NOT A VALID CERTIFIED COPY WITHOUT THE EMBOSSED SEAL AND SIGNATURE OF THE COUNTY CLERK OF VERMILION COUNTY.

Lamm's death certificate.

seem to be reaching too much, it might be well to take a close look at Baron Lamm's death certificate.

The death certificate lists Baron Lamm as Thomas Bell. In fact, Bell wasn't Coroner John D. Cole's first choice for the name of the deceased, as one can tell from the tremendous pen pressure it took to make the name appear as Thomas Bell. What was originally set down cannot now be made out, but a couple of vestigial letters can. They are "W" and "L." Was G.W. Landy the original name?

That the obliterated name may well have been G.W. Landy is attested by the age and the date of birth on the death certificate. Again, there has been fudging. An original date of circa 1860 has been overwritten with a date of 1885. The age of Bell, therefore, undergoes a sea change. It is now 45. Judging by the obvious shading, it originally was something else. What it was can no longer be deciphered. If Chauncey Manning's statements in the newspapers had been heeded about the outlaw, the age would not have been 45 but 42. Bell's residence, furthermore, instead of being unknown, would have been Pittsburgh.[20] It is incredible, too, that, while Hunter's birthplace was given as Germany, Baron Lamm's birthplace was unknown, that is, according to their death certificates. Coroner Cole seems to have been flying by the seat of his pants when it came to Baron Lamm. He leaned on his informant, Sheriff F.W. Ward, for information about the dead outlaws, and Ward knew even less about the men than the coroner did.

If Hunter really was from Germany, what then? How does that alter what is known about Baron Lamm?

It probably doesn't, much. It would mean nothing more than that Hunter and Lamm, both of similar age, had a similar background. It might suggest that the two had worked together before Clinton — but this would be no more than the barest inference.

This business about Hunter coming from Germany looks like simple carelessness at best. Germany is entered on a record where it shouldn't be and doesn't appear on the one record that it should. The authorities must have suspected that somebody in the gang was German, and Hunter came away with the prize. Physical and ethnic traits seem to have been passed around from record to record, as though interchangeable. It wasn't quite a case of one size fits all, but it was working up to it. After all, there were some who thought of Dad Landy as someone named Ziegler, perhaps Capone's "American boy," Shotgun George Ziegler, real name, Fred Samuel Goetz.

The coroner's inquest was all done quickly. Almost with a dismissive wave of the hand, Coroner Cole made it known to reporters that he wasn't going to take a whole lot of time getting to the bottom of the bandit deaths. Only four witnesses were called upon at the inquest. Nobody from Indiana was summoned, even though these members of the posse had been in the pursuit of the gang from start to finish. All of those interviewed arrived on the scene only in the last stage of the game. With but one exception, they were not law enforcement personnel. Of course, Coroner Cole can be excused for some of the half-baked findings. He waited a whole week before burying the fallen bandits so that loved ones might claim their bodies and throw some light on their backgrounds. Even though the graves were unmarked, Cole wanted their location noted should any relative later wish to claim the bodies. Despite E.H. Hunter's dead-certain protestations of familial devotion upon his death, no one ever showed up to claim his body. So, probably, Coroner Cole did the best he could under the circumstances, apart from, apparently, not talking with Chauncey Manning or anyone else from the Indiana Bureau of Criminal Identification and Investigation.

One thing for sure, Lamm's many aliases have caused plenty of trouble for researchers. His foremost alias, Thomas Bell, is just common enough that any number of outlaws could have been confused with him. Certainly, that was the case with James "Oklahoma Jack" Clark. There was a James Clark (an alias), who died in the St. Valentine's Day Massacre. Nobody ever worried about him after 1929, but they reported Oklahoma Jack dead as well. Oklahoma Jack Clark was supposedly killed in the aftermath of a Seminole, Oklahoma, bank robbery in 1928. It is not known that there was any connection between the Chicago gangster's very real death in 1929 and the erroneous report of Oklahoma Jack's death.

There was, moreover, another James Clark who was a bank robber in the Depression years. He broke out of the Kansas State Penitentiary at Lansing in 1933 and 1934, robbed several banks, and planned to rob several more before being recaptured. He never made the big time, but he knew three who did — John Harvey Bailey, Wilbur "the Tri-State Terror" Underhill and Big Bob Brady, the last most particularly. It may have been this James Clark who was associated with the Seminole, Oklahoma, bank robbery and in the aftermath of which Oklahoma Jack was mistakenly reported killed.

Oklahoma Jack used the alias William Long when captured after the Clinton robbery. He was still using it throughout his trial. It was only when he got to the Big House in Michigan City that he was booked under his real name and logged in as prisoner 14352 — if James M. Clark was, indeed, his real name.[21] When authorities in Moberly, Missouri, heard about Clark's arrest, they were interested. They had a drug trafficker named William Long that they were looking for. What happened to Moberly's William Long doesn't appear, but the Clinton version went to jail for a long, long time — not including a self-imposed three-day furlough in September 1933.

Walter Detrich was a different matter altogether. In his case, it wasn't a phony name that caused confusion. It was his real name that was the problem. General W.F. Rhinow, head of the Minnesota State Bureau of Criminal Apprehension, knew of a Walter Detrich locked up in a South Dakota prison and warned Vermillion County authorities that their Walter Detrich was likely an impostor using the South Dakota inmate's name. What with all the Bells and Martins and Longs running around and deceased Clarks and purportedly-deceased Clarks, things were getting murky to say the least. Obviously, the authorities had some sorting out to do.

When it came time to put Clark and Detrich on trial at the beginning of the New Year, Clark was still referred to as William Long most of the time, with James Clark as his alias when mentioned at all, while Baron Lamm was usually Thomas Bell. Lamm, in any case, was never called Baron Lamm but always Herman K. Lamm.

Shortly before the two surviving bandits went on trial, they were served a fine Christmas dinner. It certainly wasn't the county that arranged for the meal, even if it was disposed to be charitable in keeping with the season — keep in mind that this was one year into the Great Depression and everyone knew a depression was on. Clark and Detrich were indigent, with a court-appointed attorney who didn't wish to handle their case until they could get their hands on some money. Someone from Chicago, however, found money no object. For whatever reason, he stayed clear of the pair's legal costs, but he did interest himself in their stomachs. He signed himself either "Uncle Ed" or "Uncle Ben"[22] (which, isn't clear) when he paid for the lavish Christmas dinner. He was never heard from again. One wonders just who he was and what connection he had with the gang in general and with Baron Lamm in particular.

"Uncle Ben" doesn't ring a bell, but "Uncle Ed" may. Ed, short for Edward, suggests Jonathan Edward — Jonathan Edward Klutas, "Handsome Jack" Klutas — a man connected to Walter Detrich in the last phase of his career as the leader of the College Kidnappers. As we have seen, Klutas was certainly in the Danville area when Detrich and Clark were captured following the Clinton raid, dropping off "the rum king," James Ward, reportedly one of Capone's favorite bootleggers. And as we also have seen, he may even have been glimpsed paying a visit, perhaps with Detrich's sweetheart, at McCauley's mortuary in Sidell.

Apart from his identity, the foremost question about this mysterious benefactor arises: why was he afterwards forever incognito and incommunicado?

Or was he?

In September 1933, ten men broke out of the Indiana State Prison at Michigan City. Now, it has been batted back and forth just how much of the responsibility for this was to be laid at John Dillinger's door or whether the break was altogether somebody else's handiwork. Detrich is sometimes said to have denied that Dillinger was responsible for smuggling in the guns that led to the break, and this statement is usually taken as his effort to sidestep any connection that he had to the Dillinger gang and its crimes.[23] But what if Detrich was telling the truth about the prison escape? Might his old avuncular benefactor — and Clark's, for both men broke out — have been behind the delivery of the ten prisoners?

Whatever his role or lack of it in the crash-out of 1933, the benefactor's presence on the scene in the waning days of 1930 makes us uneasy, even at this late date. Who was "Uncle Ed" or "Uncle Ben"? Did some gangland kingpin get away scot-free — if not Lamm himself, perhaps someone even bigger in stature than Lamm?[24]

After all, $2500 was never accounted for in the Clinton robbery. Quite possibly some gang member got away. The man was not likely to have been Baron Lamm, but he could have been Dan Morgan or Handsome Jack Klutas. Whoever he was, his presence with the gang was, like the hypothetical sixth rider of the Dalton gang, worse than useless. He provided no firepower to the gang in their getaway. He did not even fool half the posse into following him in the getaway. All he did was relieve the gang of some of their loot, though much of it was worthless.

But it is that figure which must give us pause, which must tip the scales in trying to decide how to account for the missing $2,500 — vigilante or bandit. The overall take in the robbery of the Citizens State Bank came to roughly $15,000. That amount split six ways comes to $2,500 each. But to assume that a sixth bandit got his share and ran off is a big assumption. The gang would have had to know how much the haul came to and then have to divvy it up evenly. There simply wasn't time for arithmetic that morning — what with National Guard airplanes flying overhead and posses shooting at them and stolen vehicles acting up at every turn. Yet that figure jumps out at us in neon lights. It is precisely the amount a sixth man would have made off with — that is, if there was a sixth man. And, in the early stages of the getaway, there could have been. Question is: what did the sixth man do in the robbery? As far as anyone now knows, nothing.

All kinds of questions surround the incarnate mess that is Baron Lamm. Did some other outlaw hide in the coal/cob shed besides Detrich? When Detrich was caught, did the forces of law and order let their guard down long enough for this other to escape? After all, Detrich was not spotted in the coal/cob shed when Moody's mother and sister went in around noon. Goodness knows how many others visited that shed before Leo Moody and others finally went in and captured Detrich.

Furthermore, might Thomas Bell have been something more substantial than an alias for Baron Lamm or vice versa? Might Bell have been a separate individual from Lamm, hailing from Pittsburgh? The question perhaps needs to be addressed once and for all. Here it can only be mentioned as a topic for further research. In Danville, Illinois, there is a death certificate that records little more of an individual's identity than the name "Thomas Bell." This suggests merely that Bell=Lamm or was someone just as mysterious.

Thomas Bell and Baron Herman K. Lamm may have been two different people. Bell may have died by his own hand or somebody else's when surrounded by a posse, as the death certificate has it. Lamm may have been the sixth man who vanished ever afterwards, visible just long enough to be counted when somebody thought to count.

The fingerprints taken from the corpse at McCauley's undertaking parlor in Sidell satisfied some that Bell was dead and others that Lamm was dead. Barring a fiendish plot of outrageous proportions, this establishes that both identities belonged to the same individual. Nevertheless, the questions about Baron Lamm, whether he survived his death or not, keep coming. When so little is positively known about a man, it is only natural that sensationalism enters to flesh out the picture.

The sixth man, if a viable entity, need not be anyone so high profile as Handsome Jack Klutas or Dan Morgan. He is more likely to be a non-descript, like E.H. Hunter and, like Hunter, likely working on his first job. He may have been just green enough to commit some stupidity that saved his life, as, for instance, pulling off the road and hiding in one of those innumerable thickets that line S.R. 63 all the way from Clinton to U.S. 36. According to one of Helms' reports, Patrolman Burnside and he did not catch sight of the bandits until they got to the covered bridge on Ninth Street. A parting of the ways may have occurred among the bandits by that time.

That Chauncey Manning, head of the Indiana Department of Criminal Identification and Investigation, judged Lamm dead through the use of mug shots only is most unlikely. Reports indicate otherwise. And even should this have been the case, is it likely that the detective sent by the Milwaukee Police Department especially to confirm Lamm's death would not have fingerprinted the deceased bandit in Sidell?

Even so, that Christmas dinner from whomsoever it was — "Uncle Ben" or "Uncle Ed" or another — whether Baron Lamm or Handsome Jack Klutas or some unknown incorrigible — puts the Lamm conspiracy theory on a par with more celebrated conspiracy theories. In short, it gives the Lamm conspiracy theory a warm body. Brushy Bill Roberts was the poster boy for the Billy-the-Kid-is-not-so-dead as-all-that urban legend, and a character based on him even makes an appearance in the film *Young Guns II* (1990). J. Frank

Dalton did almost as much for Jesse James. If hardly bona-fide apostles of veracity, these two emblems of the conspiracy movement have nevertheless made for some lively discussions among theorists.[25] Baron Lamm could catch onto the same phenomenon with a little bit of luck. But whatever year he died in, his name does not yet cast much of a shadow. If some Lamm-like wraith had performed an act of grand larceny after 1930, bankrupting a bank or two, perhaps we would be hearing much more about Lamm today.

But, then, that wouldn't be like Baron Lamm at all. Keeping a low profile—"hide thy life," as Epicurus would have it—was the one thing he took to his grave.

Chapter Notes

An Unarmed Prologue
1. John Collings Squire, ed., *If; or, History Rewritten* (New York: Viking Press, 1931).
2. John Toland, *The Dillinger Days* (New York: Random House, 1963).
3. Toland has a map of Dillinger robberies on the endpapers of his book and Rockville appears on it. But there is not one word about Rockville in the text.
4. The most thought-provoking books about the Kansas City Massacre, in my opinion, are Robert Unger, *The Union Station Massacre: The Original Sin of Hoover's FBI* (Kansas City, MO: Andrews McNeel, 1997) and Bryan Burrough, *Public Enemies: The War on Crime and the Birth of the FBI, 1933–34* (New York: Penguin, 2004), pp. 49–50, 521.
5. Richard Gid Powers, *G-Men: Hoover's FBI in American Popular Culture* (Carbondale, IL: Southern Illinois University Press, 1983), pp. 51–73, esp. 55–56.
6. Burrough, *Public Enemies*, pp. 539–41.
7. For Hoover's relationship with organized crime, see Richard Gid Powers, *Secrecy and Power: The Life of J. Edgar Hoover* (New York: Free Press, 1987), pp. 332–6, 365–7; Anthony Summers, *Official and Confidential: The Secret Life of J. Edgar Hoover* (New York: Putnam's, 1993), pp. 12–13; 242–45; for Hoover's reputed homosexuality and cross-dressing, see Summers, *Official and Confidential*, pp. 91–95, 254–58; for a differing view of Hoover's sexuality, see Athan Theoharris, *J. Edgar Hoover, Sex and Crime: A Historical Antidote* (Chicago: Ivan R. Dee, 1995), pp. 23–55; for his passing for white, see Millie L. McGhee, *Secrets Uncovered: J. Edgar Hoover — passing for white?*, 2nd ed. (Cucamonga, CA: Allen Morris, 2000).

Chapter I
1. Kerry Ross Boren, "The Man Who Taught Dillinger," *South Point Magazine*, September 1992. More accessibly, it's on the Web at www.prospector.utah.com/dill.htm.
2. *Danville* (IL) *Commercial-News*, December 29, 1930, p. 3, col. 8; December 30, 1930, p. 5, col. 3.
3. Toland, *Dillinger Days*, pp. 29–31. See also his *Captured by History: One Man's Vision of Our Tumultuous Century* (New York: St. Martin's, 1997), pp. 175–183.
4. Jay Robert Nash and Ron Offen, *Dillinger: Dead or Alive?* (Chicago: Henry Regnery, 1970), p. xi. Interestingly, Dillinger's first biographers skirt the South Bend robbery, though, apparently, co-author Joseph Pinkston later changed his mind about Dillinger's non-complicity in the robbery (Robert Cromie and Joseph Pinkston, *Dillinger: A Short and Violent Life* [McGraw-Hill, 1962; Evanston, IL: Chicago Historical Bookworks, 1990]; citations are to the 1990 edition). Dary Matera's *John Dillinger: The Life and Times of America's First Celebrity Criminal* (New York: Carroll and Graff, 2004) is based on working notes by Pinkston. The South Bend robbery is covered on pp. 306–318.
5. Summers, *Official and Confidential*, p. 73.
6. Jay Robert Nash, *Bloodletters and Badmen: A Narrative Encyclopedia of American Criminal from the Pilgrims to the Present* (New York: M. Evans, 1995 reprint, originally published 1973), p. 209. Paper bags were used at the start of the robbery, but typewriter covers were later substituted when the loot grew too cumbersome.
7. Warren Weith, "The Getaway Car: Step on the Pedal and Go," in *Murder Ink: the Mystery Reader's Companion*, Dilys Winn, ed. (New York: Workman, 1977), pp. 227–29.
8. Raymond Chandler's friend Eric Partridge

dates the expression "on the lam" to ca. 1935 (Partridge, *A Dictionary of Slang*, 8th ed. [London: Routledge, 2000], p. 663), but Christine Ammer dates the expression back to the nineteenth century (Ammer, *The American Heritage Dictionary of Idioms* [Boston: Houghton Mifflin, 1997], p. 469).

9. Nash, *Bloodletters and Badmen*, p. 209.

10. Burrough, *Public Enemies*, pp. 17–18.

11. John McCarthy, *Hollywood Gangland: The Movies' Love Affair with the Mob* (New York: St. Martin's, 1991), p. 95.

12. Harry M. Warner was a generous donor to and active member of FDR's 1932 presidential campaign (Jean Edward Smith, *FDR* [New York: Random House, 2007], p. 354).

13. Unger, *Union Station Massacre*, pp. 225–31.

14. In the film "*G" Men*, Brick Davis (James Cagney) accidentally shoots and kills his friend and mentor, "Mac" McKay (William Harrigan), at the latter's North Woods lodge in Wisconsin. The scene may be based on an incident that happened in Paris, Illinois, seventy-five years ago as this is written. At a hotel in town, the Indiana State Police set up a trap for what was supposed to be a Dillinger rendezvous. Dillinger was not there, and when troopers rushed the car of former Dillinger gang member Edward Shouse one trooper shot and killed another by accident. I am the more convinced that this incident was portrayed in the film when I recollect that Cagney's G-man boss goads him, "And Collins got away with it." For Collins, read Dillinger—and court is adjourned.

15. Bogart gets shot by Errol Flynn's buddy, legendary stuntman Buster Wiles. Wiles not only shoots Bogie/Earle off the top of a cliff, he also takes the subsequent ninety-foot slide for him (A.M. Sperber and Eric Lax, *Bogart* [New York: William Morrow, 1997], p. 127).

16. I talked with Mrs. Patzke in the summer of 1991, about a year after location shooting for *Dillinger* (1991) was wrapped up in Milwaukee. She showed me her copy of the film's script and the black dress that she wore for her cameo in the picture. She furthermore told me about a fine luncheon, provided by the Wolper Organization, Bernard Sofronski and Warner Brothers, on the set. The main course was either barbecued ribs or barbecued chicken and so irresistible was it, she wanted to lay her fork aside and eat with a will using her fingers alone. But she didn't dare in such exalted company. (I am reminded of what Huck Finn says about how you can always count on getting an itch when it won't do to scratch it). Incidentally, Dillinger had some curiosity about Mrs. Patzke's own culinary acumen as he dropped her off in rural Wisconsin, having held her and the bank president hostage all afternoon. Jesting, Dillinger wanted to know if she could cook and would not stay for an answer. But I got an answer all those years later. Mrs. Patzke, who died in 2001 at the age of 95, was a fine cook, and I very much enjoyed eating a piece of her cherry cake.

(Mrs. Patzke's maiden name was James. I can't believe that after she told me this, I did not ask her if she was related to Jesse. Granted, a saner interviewer would not have dreamed of asking such a question, but we are as we are. Had Mrs. Patzke been a relative of the Missouri brigand, a subplot of the Racine robbery would then involve a James being held up by a Dillinger!)

17. During the early stages of my research on Lamm, when I had no photograph to rely on, this odd little man colored my whole image of Baron Lamm. *Call this a bank r-r-r-r-obbery?*

18. Lamm's near contemporary Clyde Nimerick (aka Charles Norman) correctly listed his race as Caucasian on his draft card. Lamm listed his race as German. As Lamm misunderstood this question, he may have misunderstood the other question as well.

Nota bene: In this survey of gangster films, I have omitted *Young Dillinger* (1965), starring Nick Adams as Dillinger, a negligible film in all aspects. I have not seen it in many years, but my recollection of it does not bring to mind a Lamm prototype, nor does my reading of its plot summary. For a lively digest of more Dillinger and Dillinger-related films than even I have looked at, see McCarthy, *Hollywood Gangland*, pp. 128–35.

Chapter II

1. *Frankfort Evening News*, June 3, 1924, p. 8.

2. *Frankfort Morning Times*, December 17, 1930, p. 3, col. 2. Landy had to move very quickly and very stealthily, if he really did go to Logansport. Federal agents came to Newport looking for him the day he was released from custody. What the agents wanted with him is not clear, but it likely had some connection with Lamm or the Denver Mint robbery. Landy was released in early November (*Frankfort Evening News*, November 10, 1924, p. 1, col. 2; November 11, 1924, p. 1, col. 4; December 12, 1924, p. 1, col. 5). Indeed, the Pennsylvania line went through Logansport. Whether or not Landy went to Logansport, the legendary Nellie Bly certainly did upon the conclusion of her famous around-the-world trip in early 1890. She took a Pennsylvania Railroad carrier at Chicago and

shortly after passed through Logansport, spurring considerable romantic speculation (Brooke Kroeger, *Nellie Bly: Daredevil, Reporter, Feminist* [New York: Random House, 1994], p. 169).

3. *Frankfort Evening News*, June 23, 1924, p. 8, col. 3.

4. For a second possible Landy arrest and acquittal in Kentucky, see the *Indianapolis Star*, December 17, 1930, p. 1, col. 8. According to the *Danville Commercial-News* for December 17, 1930 (p. 5, col. 3), Landy had been arrested at some point for having stolen goods. The case was still pending at the time of his death. This may refer to the 1924 charge of having safe-blowing equipment in his possession when arrested at Frankfort. The equipment had belonged to a Kokomo, Indiana, man. Or the case mentioned in the Danville paper may have had something to do with the Kentucky incident — or something else altogether. Landy was wanted for gas station robberies and bank heists, but nothing seems to have stuck.

5. *Frankfort Evening News*, May 24, 1924, p. 2, col. 1.

6. That Norman/Nimerick's picture did not appear in the next day's paper, along with those of Landy and Morgan, is deeply to be regretted (perhaps).

7. *Frankfort Evening News*, May 21, 1924, p. 1, col. 2. Yet Morgan took the three dollars that was on attendant Fred Baker in the Frankfort robbery (*Frankfort Evening News*, May 19, 1924, p. 1, col. 5). Both Fred Baker, of Frankfort, and John Robertson, of Lebanon, identified Morgan as the man who robbed them.

8. *Frankfort Evening News*, May 23, 1924, p. 1, col. 5.

9. Ibid., May 26, 1924, p. 8, col. 1.

10. Ibid., July 3, 1924, p. 1, col. 7. For Lamm as Herman Williams, see the *Danville-Commercial News*, December 17, 1930, p. 1, col. 8.

11. *Frankfort Evening News*, June 25, 1924, p. 6, col. 3.

12. *Frankfort Morning Times*, December 17, 1930; *Frankfort Evening News*, July 8, 1924, p. 1, col. 4; p. 8, col. 3. Encapsulating coverage by the *Newton* (KS) *Evening Kansan Republican* makes it clear that Norman was back in safekeeping at least as late as July 8, 1924, thereby overriding the *Clintonian* report. Norman/Nimerick was still locked up in November 1924 (*Frankfort Evening News*, November 10, 1924, p. 1, col. 2). It appears that Charles Norman was born in St. Clair County, Illinois, on November 23, 1894. His real name was Clyde Hamilton Nimerick. He was part of a bank-robbing syndicate led by Dressed-up Johnny Gardner, operating out of Vandalia, Illinois, and covering the whole country. He may have had ties with both Egan's Rats in St. Louis and later with Al Capone in Chicago. He married Lenora Woodruff (known to the authorities as Ona) on December 20, 1923, a month before he robbed a bank in Walton, Kansas, of $140,000. He apparently went by his wife's maiden name on occasion — thus, James Woodruff. He ended up as no. 648 AZ (escape risk) in Alcatraz (in 1944?) He died on June 11, 1959, and is buried at the Jefferson Barracks Cemetery in St. Louis.

13. *Frankfort Evening News*, June 30, 1924, p. 8, col. 2.

14. *Daily Clintonian*, April 11, 1924, p. 1, col. 1.

15. The first robbery was a burglary at the same bank (then under a different name) in December 1920. No one was charged with the crime, but one can certainly hazard a guess or two as to just who may have committed it. The latter robbery was a payroll job whereby a railroad payroll (not the same company as in 1924) was lifted en route from Clinton to the American State Bank in St. Bernice on August 25, 1925. Again, no one was charged with the holdup (as far as Laura Wilson of the Indiana Bankers' Association could find), and it may possibly have been Lamm's work. Though successful, it was an intricate but clumsy job, and one of the gang appears to have been badly wounded by one of the guards in making the getaway.

16. *Daily Clintonian*, April 10, 1924, p. 1, col. 7; p. 8, col. 1; and April 11, 1924, p. 1, col. 1.

17. *Frankfort Evening News*, May 22, 1924, p. 1, col. 3.

18. Ibid., June 11, 1924, p. 8, col. 3. I'm reminded, in view of how Morgan's trial turned out, of the Mae West film *I'm No Angel* (1933). When Mae berates her maid for her testimony in a trial, the maid protests that she was only telling the truth, as Mae had requested. Mae rejoins, "Yeah, but you're telling too much of it."

19. *Frankfort Morning Times*, January 15, 1927.

20. *Frankfort Evening News*, July 15, 1924, p. 1, col. 7.

21. Matera, *John Dillinger*, p. 27; Cromie and Pinkston, p. 14; Jeffrey S. King, *The Rise and Fall of the Dillinger Gang* (Nashville, TN: Cumberland House, 2005), p. 10; Toland, *Dillinger Days*, pp. 19ff.

Chapter III

1. A book should be written about all those robberies in which the amount of money overlooked was vastly greater than that taken by the

robbers. Jesse James and his gang missed $2,000 in Northfield and got shot up for a lot less — about fifty dollars. When I first learned of the amount overlooked by Dillinger at Racine, I hurriedly called Harold Graham, a cashier at the bank at the time, to ascertain the truth of the matter. In the Racine holdup, Graham heard someone approach him with a demand to "hand over that dough." Graham replied that the man must be joking. The man, Fat Charley Makley, fired his automatic, and Graham was hit by a bullet that penetrated his arm and hip. He dropped to the floor. Makley stepped up and said, "That'll show you I ain't joking." The joke, however, was on Makley. The outlaw had less than a year to live. Graham lived another six decades. I learned from Graham that Dillinger had missed a whopping $50,000 that day due to Makley's hair trigger.

2. Talking to Gordon Sayers in 1992 about the Greencastle robbery, I was struck by the fact that he mentioned Dillinger only to say that he had seen him vault the railing at the beginning of the robbery. Gordon said that Handsome Harry Pierpont was his "commander" that day. About all that Gordon got out of Handsome Harry on this occasion was "Yeah," in response to his query about whether he should open a gate in the back of the Central National Bank.

Some DePauw University students in Greencastle got a kick out of this situation and made up a song about it. Addressing the fears the bank personnel dreaded most in such robberies, Gordon said, "We always heard that they stepped on your hands when they made you lie down in back." Gordon said that Pierpont rubbed his nose a lot, which indicated to him that he took drugs. It was also obvious to him that Pierpont was wearing a bullet-proof vest — "His coat didn't fit just right."

3. *Milwaukee Journal*, December 10, 1924, p. 1, col. 7.

4. Ibid., December 8, 1924, p. 1 A photo of a beaming Gertrude Hahn appears at the bottom of page 1 in the *Milwaukee Journal* for December 8, 1924. As her attire is summery, the picture must have been taken earlier that year. Nevertheless, her interview by the *Journal* comes off as decidedly light-hearted.

5. In December 1991, I phoned Don Steele of Racine about the 1933 robbery of the American Bank and Trust Company in that city. He told me that when he was caught scrutinizing Dillinger too keenly during the robbery, he received a swift kick and a pointed reprimand while he lay on the floor. Lamm, apparently, was even more sensitive on this point than Dillinger.

6. According to the newspaper account, at one point, Digman told the bandit leader that he did not know the combination of the strongbox. At another, he said that the vault had a time lock in place and that he was made to try it anyway. The vault is where the securities were kept, and Lamm somehow got these. Digman's statements about what he was asked to open and what he actually did open are confusing. The explanation may be that there was more than one vault, as Digman indicates at one point. But, then, who opened this other vault and for whom? (*Milwaukee Journal*, December 8, 1924, pp. 1–2).

7. Ibid., p. 2, col. 3.
8. Ibid., p. 2, col. 5.
9. Ibid.
10. Girardin and Helmer, *Dillinger: The Untold Story*, pp. 321–2.
11. Jack Cejnar, "The Jinx That Stalked the Outlaws" (Jack Cejnar papers, Indiana Historical Society, Indianapolis, Indiana), part 2, pp. 29–30.

Chapter IV

1. Bruce Smith, *Rural Crime Control* (New York: Columbia University Press, 1933), 75–102.
2. Ibid., p. 111.
3. Cejnar, "Jinx," part 1, p. 11.
4. Paul Musgrave, "A Primitive Method of Enforcing the Law: Vigilantism as a Response to Bank Crime in Indiana, 1925–1933," *Indiana Magazine of History* 102, no. 3 (September 2006): 187.
5. Bruce Smith, "Rural Police Protection," *Illinois Crime Survey, 1929*, eds. John H. Wigmore and Arthur V. Lashly (Chicago: Slakly Printing Company and Illinois Association of Criminal Justice, 1930), pp. 342–3; AP dispatch, *Bloomington* (IL) *Daily Pantagraph*, September 19, 1930, p. 1, col. 3.
6. Roland Goheen, telephone interview, October 26, 1991. Though Roland Goheen did not take part in the action that day, his good friend and fishing companion, Harry Berg, a South Bend jeweler, did. Berg shot Baby Face Nelson in the chest with his pistol. Nelson escaped any real danger because he wore a bullet-proof vest. Still the gesture enraged him, and he unloosed a volley from his submachine gun at Berg and his general vicinity. The jeweler was not hit, but two pedestrians were wounded.
7. *Bloomington Daily Pantagraph*, October 19, 1930, sec. D, p. 1, col. 8.
8. *Frankfort Evening News*, September 3, 1925, p. 3, cols. 4–5.
9. *Des Moines Register*, article in the *Bloom-*

ington Daily Pantagraph, September 19, 1930, p. 1, col. 2.
  10. *Frankfort Evening News*, September 3, 1925, p. 1, cols. 4–5.
  11. *Chicago Daily Tribune*, March 16, 1925, p. 4, cols. 1–3.
  12. *New York Times*, May 5, 1926, p. 41, col. 3.
  13. Ibid.
  14. Ibid.
  15. Illinois Crime Survey, 1929, pp. 342–3.
  16. Cejnar, "Jinx," part 2, p. 26. *Frankfort Evening News*, September 3, 1925, p. 1.
  17. *Milwaukee Journal*, December 20, 1924, p. 1.
  18. *Lafayette Journal and Courier*, November 9, 1927, p. 1, col. 3.
  19. It is significant, in this respect, that the film *Little Caesar* (1931) opens with the robbery of a filling station.
  20. *Daily Clintonian*, December 13, 1930, p. 1, col. 4.
  21. It just may be that the Clinton robbery was the last bank robbery committed by either Oklahoma Jack Clark or Walter Detrich. Certainly, it was Clark's.
  22. I talked to Margaret Haines, the former Margaret Good, a number of times in 1991. I interviewed her because Dillinger had robbed her bank, but I learned that she had been robbed by somebody named Clevenger. James Clevenger, of Yorktown, had been one of the Albany State Bank bandits. He, along with another man, had dropped in on Margaret Good at the Daleville Commercial Bank on December 19, 1930, three days after Baron Lamm hit the Citizens State Bank at Clinton. Clevenger scared the daylights out of Miss Good and Mrs. Barnard, the cashier's wife, because he had been drinking and was probably hopped up as well.
  23. Musgrave, "A Primitive Method of Enforcing the Law," p. 202.
  24. Matera, *John Dillinger*, p. 367. Matera also includes Pennsylvania in this statement, although Dillinger was a strong suspect in a September 1933 Farrell, Pennsylvania, robbery.
  25. AP dispatch, the *Bloomington Daily Pantagraph*, November 21, 1930, p. 22, col. 2.
  26. *Frankfort Morning Times*, March 29, 1927, p. 1, col. 4.
  27. Girardin and Helmer, *Dillinger*, p. 284.
  28. *New York Times*, May 5, 1926, p. 41, cols. 3–4.
  29. Saunders, "Organized Protection," p. 804.
  30. "The Hold-Ups of Banks Increased 50% This Year," *Hoosier Banker*, December 17, 1931, p. 19.
  31. Burrough, *Public Enemies*, pp. 517–552, esp. 517–21; the quote is from p. 545.

Chapter V

  1. Boren, "The Man Who Taught Dillinger."
  2. Described as "tacks" by the *Winston-Salem Journal* (February 21, 1927, p. 1), the nails are described more formidably as "big-headed" and able to stand upright when dropped on the highway by the *Charlotte-Observer*, February 22, 1927, p. 1.
  3. *Winston-Salem Journal*, February 21, 1927, p. 13.
  4. Ibid., March 2, 1927, p. 9.
  5. The weapons charge carried the most weight: two years in prison or on the chain gang.
  6. *Winston-Salem Journal*, March 2, 1927, p. 9.
  7. Ibid., March 7, 1927, p. 1.
  8. Ibid., March 9, 1927, p. 2, col. 2.

Chapter VI

  1. The *Frankfort Morning Times* in its coverage of the robbery does not mention the last, most telling part—"we know who you are"—nor does the *Lafayette Journal and Courier* consistently (only November 1, p. 4, col. 5). In all the crazy bank robberies that I have studied, from Jesse James at Columbia, Kentucky, in April 1872 to Jake Fleagle at Lamar, Colorado, in May 1928, none is as bizarre as this one. It just doesn't add up—unless and until we find the missing pieces of the puzzle. In the aforesaid Lamar robbery, incidentally, a revolver once belonging to Jesse James played a role in the shootout. The gun was in the hands of the bank president, of all people, and put a hole in the jaw of one of the robbers. Sadly, the bank president and three others were killed as a result of the robbery (Betz, *The Fleagle Gang*, pp. 20, 213). The latter page states that Jesse James was the pistol's owner at one time; the earlier entry isn't quite definitive as to whom among the James gang the gun belonged.
  2. *Lafayette Journal and Courier*, November 1, 1927, p. 2, col. 1; *Frankfort Morning Times*, November 2, 1927, p. 2, col. 1.
  3. Helen Cheney heard perhaps ten shots exchanged in the robbery. Her sister, Margaret Cheney, heard at least eight. Half the shots fired were those by Captain Arman (*Frankfort Morning Times*, November 2, 1927, p. 2, col. 1). A third Cheney sister, Mrs. Walter Spencer, lived in Frankfort, but, contrary to my first impression, she did not impart any new information gathered from either or both sisters to the local

paper (*Frankfort Morning Times*, November 2, 1927, p. 1, col. 7).

4. For the wounded bandit leaving the bank needing assistance in getting to the getaway car, see the *Frankfort Morning Times*, November 2, 1927, p. 1, col. 7.

5. *Frankfort Morning Times*, November 2, 1927, p. 2, cols. 1–2; *Lafayette Journal and Courier*, November 1, 1927, p. 4, col. 1.

6. *Frankfort Morning Times*, November 2, 1927, p. 2, col. 1; *Lafayette Journal and Courier*, November 1, 1927, p. 2, col. 1. The mention of the Hupmobile makes one think back to the St. Bernice burglary three and a half years earlier in which a Hupmobile may have been involved. It will be remembered that Dan Morgan was one of the burglars.

7. *Lafayette Journal and Courier*, November 2, 1927, p. 11, col. 6.

8. Ibid., November 1, 1927, p. 2, col. 2.

9. Ibid.

10. Taylor Pensoneau, *Brothers Notorious: The Sheltons, Southern Illinois' Legendary Gangsters* (New Berlin, IL: Downstate Publications, 2002), pp. 115–18. This robbery was an even wilder free-for-all than these pages chronicle as the lady postmaster got into the action with a revolver: "Mrs. Nora Aull, postmistress and wife of the assistant cashier, opened fire on the bandit car, not knowing her husband was a hostage therein. Upon being informed of the robbery by the bookkeeper at the bank, who was the only bank employee to escape during the holdup, she ran to the bank, taking with her a .45-calibre revolver, part of the post office equipment, and in spite of assurance from a friend that the bandits could not possibly escape, upon seeing the Cadillac appear in the street in front of the bank building, she ran into the street through a rain of bullets from [the] outlaw car and emptied the contents of her gun at the speeding machine. It was the first time she ever shot a gun in her life" (*Bloomington* [IL] *Daily Pantagraph*, September 30, 1924, p. 2, col. 6).

11. Michael Wallis, *Pretty Boy: The Life and Times of Charles Arthur Floyd* (New York: St. Martin's, 1992), pp. 283–85.

12. *Frankfort Morning Times*, November 2, 1927, p. 2, col. 2.

13. *Lafayette Journal and Courier*, November 2, 1927, p. 4, col. 4. Forrest Huntington's work on the Dillinger case is most extensively covered in Cromie and Pinkston's *Dillinger: A Short and Violent Life*, pp. 41ff., esp. pp. 99–103.

14. *Lafayette Journal and Courier*, November 2, 1927, p. 1, col. 2.

15. Ibid.

16. For the West Baden tip, see the *Lafayette Journal and Courier*, November 4, 1927, p. 1, col. 4.

17. Ibid., November 5, 1927, p. 1, col. 1.

Chapter VII

1. *Frankfort Morning Times*, December 4, 1930, p. 1, col. 6.

2. *Daily Clintonian*, January 6, 1931, p. 1, col. 2.

3. The International News Service correspondent was certainly impressed by the professionalism of the bandits. Most likely, this was Jack Cejnar, INS bureau chief at Indianapolis. See the *Lafayette Journal and Courier* for December 17, 1930, p. 1, and the *Indianapolis Star* for December 17, 1930, p. 1.

4. For the relevance of cigars to gangsters and gangster movies see "End of Rico, Beginning of the Antihero," special feature, *Little Caesar*, DVD, directed by Mervyn LeRoy (1931; Warner Home Video, 2005).

5. One of those givens that Depression-era bandits could take to the bank, even in an age before cell phones, was the likelihood that someone inside the bank would be on the phone when the gang entered the bank. Dillinger found this to be the case when he robbed the First National in East Chicago.

6. What would the Depression have done without those nifty, one-size-fits-all expressions, "You're telling me" and "It'll be just too bad?" The former, employed by Baby Face Nelson at Mason City, Iowa, found service as the title of a 1934 W.C. Fields comedy. The latter, uttered by Lamm at Frankfort, can be found in the film *Little Caesar* (1931). Both expressions turn up in the film *42nd Street* (1933) — twice.

7. Thus, the *Lafayette Journal and Courier* for December 4, 1930, p. 1. The *Indianapolis News* for December 4, 1930, p. 2, has Sheriff Eversole seeing two men and a woman (not six men) in the sedan, followed by two coupes, but not specifying the number of occupants or makes of the latter two vehicles.

8. Ironically, Kin Hubbard was then very much in his own last days. This column was among the last that the humorist would write. He died on December 26, at the age of 62.

9. Found at www.babyfacenelsonjournal.com/fred-burke.html, taken from William J. Helmer and Rick Mattix, *Public Enemies: America's Criminal Past, 1919–1940* (New York: Facts on File, 1998).

10. This, according to Grover C. Garrett, chief of the Indiana State Police, in the *Daily Clintonian*, December 4, 1930, p. 1, col. 2; *Indianapolis News*, January 10, 1931, p. 13, col. 5.

11. *Frankfort Morning Times*, December 5, 1930, p. 1.
12. *Lafayette Journal and Courier*, December 7, 1930.
13. Thus, Helen Hamilton. Her father, Oscar Hamilton, described "Smitty" as about fifty, with dark eyes, black hair and a small mustache. *Indianapolis News*, December 8, 1930, p. 1, col. 2.
14. *Chicago Daily Tribune*, December 7, 1930, p. 3, col. 1; December 8, 1930, p. 5, col. 7; December 24, 1930, p. 1, col. 7. Two things told against Lamm's presence in this robbery. First, the submachine gun in the hands of the leader. According to Cejnar ("Jinx," part 2, p. 30), Lamm preferred the long-barreled pistol in his robberies. Second, a safe deposit box in this robbery yielded $50,000. Lamm did not bother safe deposit boxes in any of his likeliest robberies, apparently taking pride in himself as a robber of banks and not the banks' customers.
15. *Danville Commercial-News*, December 24, 1930, p. 4, col. 8.

Chapter VIII

Much of this chapter relies on the account written by Jack Cejnar, based on the recollections of Chief Everett Helms and others, housed at the Indiana Historical Society in Indianapolis. The account, which runs to 71 pages, is called "The Jinx That Stalked the Outlaws."

1. *Indianapolis Star*, December 17, 1930, p. 9, col. 2.
2. This is John Nolan's recollection of how the robbery opened. I garnered this bit from Nolan's friend, Harold Frist, in a telephone interview on April 14, 1997.
3. The *Paris* (IL) *Beacon-News*, January 3, 1931, p. 2, col. 4, has Detrich striking Jackson according to Jackson's testimony at the trial of Detrich and Clark. The court transcript, however, makes it clear that it was Lamm who struck Jackson.
4. I follow Cejnar in having Harry Call as the man upon whose shoulders the fate of Baron Lamm and his gang was placed. In the telephone interview with the aforesaid Harold Frist (who, by the way, was a grandson of Jediah Frist), the name of the man so instrumental to Lamm's downfall was Marshall Frist, Harold's father. As Harry Call was subpoenaed to testify at the trial of the two surviving bandits, I have gone with the Cejnar account (Cejnar, "Jinx," part 1, pp. 2, 8). But, possibly, both Harry Call and Marshall Frist played their parts that day. In an account of Vansickle's role in the thwarting of the bandit getaway in the *Paris Beacon-News* for January 3, 1931, Vansickle says that he was going rabbit hunting the day of the robbery, as does the *Danville Commercial-News* (January 2, 1931, p. 1, col. 2). No mention is made of Marshall Frist, but Frist may have been slated to go hunting with him. Call's routine was certainly the deciding factor in the episode, regardless of whether the barber was about to go hunting with Marshall Frist or not. The *Daily Clintonian*, in a retrospective on the robbery for November 20, 1972, does, indeed, state that Vansickle was waiting on a friend to go hunting (*Vermilion County, Indiana: History and Families* [Paducah, IN: Turner, 1990], pp. 92–4).
5. The name is sometimes spelled Van Sickle. Cejnar spells it thus, but since court documents spell it as above, as do the 1920 and 1930 U.S. censuses, I have gone with that spelling. Yet another rendering of the name — Van-Sickle — can be found in the *Paris* (IL) *Beacon-News* for December 18, 1930, and the *Daily Clintonian* for January 2, 1931, p. 1, col. 7. The same paper later spells it Van Sickle (January 3, 1931). There must be a hyphenated version out there somewhere, too. Confusion also existed over Patrolman Burnside's surname (Burnsides for Burnside) and Roy Gritten's (Gritton for Gritten), both in court documents. Nothing, nothing at all, about the Clinton robbery was straightforward, it seems.
6. I sometimes think that half of Indiana's male population in the old days worked as auctioneers, at least part of the time. James Dean, the legendary actor, came from the Marion-Fairmount area, two hours' drive to the northeast of Clinton. His grandfather and great grandfather on his father's side both worked as farmers and auctioneers, as did a cousin of that great grandfather. There is a priceless clip of Dean's grandfather doing his auctioneer bit in front of Dean in the film *The James Dean Story* (1957) and did Dean enjoy it! Ditto Dennis Stock, Dean's friend and Boswell.
7. Cejnar mentions that Vansickle had recently broken his arm and, for this reason, he was not able to hoist the weapon up to his shoulder and fire — this, in addition to his uncertainty at this point about the motives of the men in the car.
8. *Daily Clintonian*, December 22, 1930, p. 1, cols. 3–6, esp. col. 5.
9. I first came by this information in interviews with Chief Helms' widow, Margaret, on September 8 and November 6, 1993. It also appears in the *Daily Clintonian* for November 20, 1972, and in *Vermilion, Indiana: History and Families*, p. 93.
10. As far as the type of rifle Boetto used to

fire on the bandits, two seem likeliest. Harold Frist believed that Boetto used an M-1. Whenever newspapers got more specific than the usual "high-powered rifle," they designated the weapon as a .30–30 rifle (see, for example, the *Danville Commercial-News* for December 17, 1930, p. 4, col. 1). M-1s had not come into general use at this time, so the weapon was probably a .30–30.

11. *Daily Clintonian*, December 22, 1930, p. 1, col. 4. In his testimony two weeks later, Helms spoke of the covered bridge on the Fairview road, outside of Clinton.

12. *Danville (IL) Commercial-News*, December 16, 1930, p. 1, col. 8. Cejnar does not mention the gold, but merely says that a bunch of silver was left behind in the original Buick by the outlaws in their haste. Nor does Frist specifically mention the gold in his testimony at Detrich and Clark's trial.

13. Toland (*Dillinger Days*, p. 30) also states that the top speed that the Frist automobile could make was 35 miles per hour — more confirmation that he knew the Cejnar account.

14. *Dana News*, December 18, 1930, p. 1, col. 3. "Reckless courage" is the exact wording.

15. Interview with Margaret Helms, September 8, 1993.

16. *Dana News*, December 18, 1930, p. 1, col. 1.

17. Van Daily's account of the Walker shooting comes from the *Terre Haute Tribune*, December 20, 1930, p. 1, col. 3. It is told in the third person or I would have printed it word for word. Van Daily, curiously, was not subpoenaed to testify at Clark and Detrich's trial. Art Hockett mentioned an incident similar to the Van Daily account, although, regrettably, I did not tape this interview. If memory serves, a farmer pulling a load of corn came between the bandits and posse during a shooting scrape. According to Art, all shooting stopped until after the farmer cleared the area. It may be that Art had the Van Daily episode in mind and I did not get the details straight in my recollection of it, or it just may be that a second incident occurred in which all gunfire ceased during a momentary truce.

18. *Dana News*, December 18, 1930, p. 1, col. 1.

19. Telephone interview with Art Hockett, December 26, 1992.

20. According to his own statement at the trial of the two surviving bandits in the *Danville Commercial-News*, he followed the bandits with the posse after Walker was shot (*Danville Commercial-News*, January 2, p. 3, col. 7). Actually, Hamm's testimony indicates that he took Walker back to Dana.

21. Art Hockett in conversation with Carroll Williams and myself in Williams' ranch-style home in rural Scotland, Illinois, on June 4, 1996. *Nota bene*: Cejnar ("Jinx") places the Williams' carjacking at Woodyard. For once, I disagree. I place the carjacking just northwest of Scotland, several miles to the east of Woodyard. The *Danville Commercial-News* for January 10, 1931 (p. 3, col. 5) specifically states that the bandits went through Chrisman, Illinois, then went north to Woodyard before turning west. It does not say exactly where Fenton Williams' Ford was seized by the gang. The *Daily Clintonian* (December 22, 1930, p. 1, col. 5) states that the bandits crossed Illinois 1 at Woodyard, making it sound as though the bandits were headed west at that point and not north. Many newspapers and Art Hockett placed the incident nearer Scotland than Woodyard, e.g., the *Danville Commercial-News*, December 16, 1930, p. 1, col. 8. Cejnar (part 2, p. 9) says that Bell/Lamm wanted to fire the machine gun on the posse from the road — but only as a passing thought. Clark, in this same account, actually did fire the machine gun at the posse from the road (Cejnar, part 2, p. 9).

22. Carroll Williams interview at Scotland, Illinois, June 4, 1996.

23. Carroll Williams said that Fenton was coming from the north when he was intercepted by the bandits. Cejnar has Fenton coming from the west going east. This may have been the case if Fenton was a rural Ridge Farm resident and he was coming down a side road — or if he was headed toward Scotland. But, as coming from the north would have been the most straightforward course for a resident of Ridge Farm going to Woodyard, I follow Carroll Williams' account.

24. Interview with Virginia Gilbert at Chrisman, Illinois, June 4, 1996. This was Art Hockett's "Auntie Virginia," whom I met exactly once in my life and only briefly, but whom I shall never forget. In the old days, she carried candy mints in the pocket of her white sweater and little Art would tug at her sleeve to see if she would part with any.

25. Vermilion County, Illinois, in its overall history, certainly led the state and may have led the country in one-room schoolhouses. Telephone communication from Vermilion County Historical Society to Amy Richard of the Bloomington, Illinois, Public Library, April 7, 2009.

26. Interview with Charlie Lyons at Sidell, Illinois, October 30, 1993.

27. Undated conversation (probably in 1993) with librarian Mary Tate at Sidell.

28. Undated conversation with Art Hockett at Sidell, Illinois.
29. Undated conversation with Art Hockett at Sidell. See also the *Danville Commercial-News*, December 21, 1930, p. 3, sec. 1.

Chapter IX

1. *High Sierra* was the first film to mention Dillinger's name. In fact, the screenplay just refers to the outlaw as "Johnnie," owing to the Hollywood code against gangsters, particularly Dillinger. The line quoted is part of an observation by actor Henry Hull to Humphrey Bogart's Roy Earle. "Do you remember," Hull says, "what Johnnie Dillinger said about guys like you and him? He said that you were just rushing towards death. Yeah, that's it. Just rushing towards death."
2. The farm is sometimes referred to as the Morehouse farm or the Clyde Witherspoon farm (*Danville Commercial-News*, December 16, 1930, p. 4, col. 5).
3. Interview with Dorothy Moody Winland (Mrs. Leo Moody) at Tilton, Illinois, January 16, 1993.
4. Interview with Stan Hayes, Moody's son-in-law, at Catlin, Illinois, October 30, 1993.
5. An early report in the *Danville Commercial-News* mentions that Walker may have shot Hunter (December 16, 1930, p. 1, col. 7).
6. These were Baron Lamm's last reported words.
7. It's hard to believe that Lamm could have been marching around issuing orders while suffering a gunshot wound in or near the heart. Surely, he was not the man hit in the barnyard.
8. *Chicago Daily Tribune*, December 17, 1930, p. 12.
9. Both Hunter and Detrich buried their guns and their ammo in either straw or corn cobs. The thinking seems to have been that if caught — or when caught — they would be able to say they were just passing by when the shooting started. This elementary school naïveté, handy for throwing spit wads, would little avail in a grown-up world where tough questions demanded convincing answers. For his part, Hunter actually did play the innocent bystander to the hilt, claiming to be kidnapped by the gang to drive their cars (Cejnar, "Jinx," part 2, p. 33; *Terre Haute Star*, December 19, 1930, p. 5, col. 5). One is reminded of Jake's hard fate in *Lonesome Dove*.
10. *Danville* (IL) *Commercial-News*, December 17, 1930, p. 2, col. 3. See also the *Daily Clintonian*, December 17, 1930, p. 1, col. 6.
11. According to the *Terre Haute Tribune* (December 16, 1930, p. 2, col. 8), a member of the posse came upon the wounded Landy in the cornfield. The prostrate bank robber rose up from where he lay, huge revolver in hand. The posseman quickly pulled the trigger of his pistol, only to hear that daunting clicking sound of a firing pin striking an empty chamber. Landy now lifted his revolver and pulled the hammer back. Suddenly, he turned the pistol to his head and fired the round into his right temple. This account is so near what Cejnar heard from Chief Helms that one feels that Helms or Boetto was the member of the posse mentioned (Cejnar, "Jinx," part 2, p. 30).
12. *Danville Commercial-News*, December 17, 1930, p. 5, col. 3.
13. Ibid., p. 5, col. 3. The structure is sometimes spoken of as a cob house. The reason for the confusion is that the building served as both a coal shed and cob house with a bare section in between (Stan Hayes interview, 1993). More confusingly, the outbuilding is sometimes placed on a different farm, one near Fairmount, Illinois. See United Press report in, among other papers, the *Bloomington* (IL) *Daily Pantagraph*, December 16, 1930, p. 1, col. 7.
14. Interview with Stan Hayes at Catlin, Illinois, October 30, 1993. I talked with the late Robert Volk on three occasions in 1992–3. He found himself in a situation with John Dillinger (77 years ago as this is written) that can only be described as a Mexican standoff. Volk witnessed the legendary wooden-gun jailbreak, March 3, 1934. Young Volk carried an ancient horse pistol in a shoulder holster, and Dillinger saw it as he was stealing Sheriff Lillian Holley's car in the Main Street garage that morning. The outlaw said nothing to Volk, who was a mail carrier carrying a pistol by mandate of his insurance company. Dillinger was carrying a submachine gun at the time, as was his compeer, Herbert Youngblood.

"Do you mean to tell me that Dillinger didn't say a word about the pistol you were carrying?" I asked Volk.

"Why should he? Hell, he had the drop on me."

(Interview at Volk's yellow-frame home — built in 1887, as a sign there proudly announced — on Joliet Street in Crown Point, October 9, 1993.) Volk admitted that he couldn't have hit the broad side of a barn with that old weapon. He later became a Crown Point policeman.

15. Stan Hayes interview.
16. Interview with Margaret Helms, November 8, 1993. According to the *Daily Clintonian*, November 20, 1972 (quoted in *Vermilion*

County, Indiana: History and Families, p. 94), Mrs. Walter Burnside had a similar shock. Unlike Chief Helms, her husband really was wounded when a bullet bounced off the passenger door handle and through his Sam Browne holster into his ribs. It was the noon hour, and Mrs. Burnside was preparing charity meals for school children at the First Baptist Church in Clinton when she heard her husband had been shot. How badly he was hurt went unresolved for the next few hours.

Chapter X

1. *Urbana Evening Courier*, December 16, 1930, p. 1, col. 1; *Danville* (IL) *Commercial-News*, December 17, 1930, p. 2, col. 6; *Indianapolis Star*, December 17, 1930, p. 9, col. 3. This was the first time — in Indiana history, anyway — that bandits were chased by airplanes (*Lafayette* (IN) *Journal and Courier*, December 17, 1930, p. 13, col. 5). Altogether, four planes may have touched down on the Moody farm — two from the Indiana National Guard, one piloted by an Ogden, Illinois, man named Harvey (surname), and Andy Tate's plane out of Champaign. The National Guard planes were sent by Adjutant-General Manford G. Henley and were piloted by Lieutenants Matt G. Carpenter and Robert N. Taylor. It is not clear whether Harvey actually landed on the Moody farm.

2. In the 1930s, there were 114 lynchings in the U.S. Of these, 103 were of blacks and 11 were of whites, of which probably the most famous were the two men in San Diego whose deaths inspired the Fritz Lang film *Fury* (1936) (William Tucker, *Vigilante: The Backjash against Crime in America* [New York: Stein and Day, 1985], p. 29).

3. *Danville* (IL) *Commercial-News*, December 19, 1930, p. 4, col. 1.

4. *Daily Clintonian*, November 20, 1972; *Danville Commercial-News*, December 21, 1930.

5. Interview with Stan Hayes at Catlin, Illinois, October 30, 1993.

6. Sgt. Frank Reynolds, of Chicago's famed "Dillinger Squad," had twelve notches on his pistol handle. Toland, *Captured by History*, pp. 175–76.

7. *Danville* (IL) *Commercial-News*, January 4, 1931, p. 5, sec. 1, col. 2.

8. Ibid., December 16, 1930, p. 1, col. 8.

9. Ibid., December 17, 1930, p. 3, col. 5. Miss Brookbank was most reticent and retiring and, apparently, had no wish to be interviewed. She did, however, stand still long enough for her picture to be taken by the Associated Press. According to the *Indianapolis News* (December 18, 1930, p. 1), Miss Brookbank was Mrs. Brookbank, of undetermined age, and the former head of the Driver's Bureau (DMV) in Clinton. Her livelihood at the time of the robbery was not given. Furthermore, according to this account, she was accompanied, not by a lad of fourteen, but by three members of the posse. The lady was quoted in the *Danville Commercial-News* as saying that her arms were so tired during that wild chase that she almost had to pull over.

10. At least one member of the posse recognized Hunter as a rumrunner from Terre Haute (*Paris* (IL) *Beacon-News*, December 16, 1930, p. 1).

11. Besides the account book with its one name and address, a billfold was found bearing several names. The billfold disappeared shortly after its discovery, to the everlasting regret of researchers. The billfold, if it did indeed exist and was taken by a vigilante or spectator, may yet turn up. If this billfold belonged to Baron Lamm, it might well be the most important significant single artifact connected with his life *Danville* (IL) *Commercial-News*, December 17, 1930, p. 5, col. 3.

12. Telephone interview with Harold Frist, April 14, 1997. Mr. Frist referred to Landy as Ziegler in the interview, perhaps having Shotgun George in mind. Fred "Killer" Burke went to the Michigan State Prison for the murder of a Michigan policeman and died there in July 1940. Fred Samuel Goetz, a.k.a. Shotgun George Ziegler, was a World War I flyboy, who parlayed that service for five hours' credit at the University of Illinois. He was an Illini freshman in 1919, along with John Thomas Scopes of Monkey Trial fame, and John Edward "Handsome Jack" Klutas, of "College Kidnappers" infamy. He majored in business, managing somehow to ace consecutive courses in Goethe and Schiller while doing so (thus, his transcripts). In 1925, he was charged with the attempted rape of a seven-year-old girl in Chicago. He paid the bond but jumped bail. He was on the run until his death in Cicero in March 1934. Ziegler was associated with the Barker/Karpis gang and is sometimes said to have engineered the St. Valentine's Day Massacre in Chicago, February 14, 1929 (William J. Helmer and Arthur J. Bilek, *The St. Valentine's Day Massacre* [Nashville: Cumberland House, 2004], pp. 231–2).

13. *Danville* (IL) *Commercial-News*, December 18, 1930, p. 1, col. 2.

14. Ibid., December 18, 1930, p. 1, col. 2. Doubts about Hunter's identity surfaced on December 19 when the *Terre Haute Star* (p. 2, col. 5) revealed that his tattooed initials were actually "E.K.," a point also made by Jack Cejnar in his

retrospective on the Clinton robbery ("Jinx," part 2, p. 33).

15. Ibid., December 17, 1930, p. 1, col. 8.

16. Ibid., p. 1, col. 8. It is interesting how often the name *Burke* comes up as an alias. Oklahoma Jack, in one of his nefarious incarnations, was reputedly Mike Burke. Detroit mobster Frank Wright, gunned down in March 1927, went by the name of Frank Burke. Thomas Camp, the most famous of the phony Burkes, took as his handle Fred Burke, to hide behind while committing his vile deeds in the late '20s and early '30s. By an odd coincidence, Fred "Killer" Burke was one of the triggermen that mowed down Frank Burke and two others in Detroit's Millaflores Massacre on March 28, 1927. Nor should we forget the Frank Burke of the Harvey Bailey gang, who was really Alvin T. Johnston (Haley, *Robbing Banks Was My Business*, p. 46).

17. *Daily Clintonian*, December 19, 1930, p. 2, col. 3; January 5, 1931, p. 1, col. 2.

18. *Danville* (IL) *Commercial-News*, December 26, 1930, p. 1; December 30, 1930, p. 3, col. 3; *Daily Clintonian*, December 19, 1930, p. 2, col. 4; January 5, 1931, p. 1, col. 2.

19. For the color of the bandit's clothing, I have relied on interviews with Merrel Chew (Dec. 26, 1992) and Charles Lyons (October 30, 1993), both at Sidell, Illinois. "The shorter one — the baldheaded one [Hunter], I can remember he had a brown ... tan-brown ... suit on. I heard when they went through some of their belongings, they found tennis shoes. They all wore tennis shoes, I guess, to muffle their sounds" (M. Chew interview, Sidell, December 26, 1992). A remarkable detail, this last, and one not sufficiently picked up on by the present writer or anybody else at all! In any case, Lamm, as his morgue shot shows, did not wear that brown-checked suit that he wore to his death. The bit about the cardboard in Landy's shoes came from a telephone conversation (my only such) with Art Hockett in Sidell on December 26, 1992.

20. M. Chew interview.

21. *Danville* (IL) *Commercial-News*, December 21, 1930, p. 1, col. 4. Maybe so, but there is still so much doubt about how Lamm met his fate that the matter will never likely be settled. He was shot through the heart — whether by his own hand or someone else's, we don't know. Also, it would be interesting to know whether he was wounded before he was shot in the heart. The death certificate does not indicate that he was. But Moody and Chief Helms both thought that someone fell — Lamm possibly — when the shooting started at the Moody farm. Nobody doubts that there were powder burns on Lamm's body, but Helms said that the shot passed clean through as though he was hit by a high-powered rifle. A gaping wound in the chest would indicate to me at least that Lamm was shot from behind. The evidence as to Lamm's death is fraught with caveats.

22. There may yet be some record of the lot number. Coroner Cole requested the grave's whereabouts be recorded by the cemetery authorities so that should any relatives of the deceased claim the bodies, they could readily be disinterred.

23. *Daily Clintonian*, December 17, 1930, p. 2, col. 6.

24. *Chicago Daily Tribune*, December 17, 1930, p. 12, col. 2; *Daily Clintonian*, December 17, p. 1, col. 7.

25. *Danville (IL) Commercial-News*, December 17, 1930, p. 5, col. 3.

26. Interview with Carroll Williams at Scottland, Illinois, June 4, 1996.

27. *Daily Clintonian*, December 22, 1930, p. 1, col. 7.

Chapter XI

1. It is little short of amazing that Jack Cejnar, the foremost authority on the Clinton robbery, kept calling Clark by his alias, "William H. Long," long after Clark had been enrolled at the Indiana State Prison as James M. Clark, inmate no. 14253. More astounding still, Lamm was always Thomas Bell to Cejnar. For more about Cejnar see Elliott J. Gorn, *Dillinger's Wild Ride: The Year That Made Public Enemy Number One*.

2. For "Uncle Ed," see the *Danville* (IL) *Commercial-News*, December 29, 1930, p. 3, col. 8; for "Uncle Ben," see the *Danville Commercial-News*, December 30, 1930, p. 5, col. 2. See also note 2, chapter 2. For more about

3. Something of bank-robbing syndicates and their ways can be found in R.C. Saunders, "Organized Protection Against Organized Predatory Crime," *Journal of Criminal Law and Criminology*, vol. 23, no. 5, Jan.–Feb. 1933, pp. 797–805. Saunders makes the interesting point that bank robberies were primarily burglaries, not bold daylight bank robberies, until after the First World War.

4. *Terre Haute Star*, December 19, 1930, p. 2, col. 5; Cejnar, "Jinx," part 2, p. 32.

5. For Sawyer's hire and salary, see the *Danville Commercoal-News*, December 31, 1930, p. 4, col. 6. The ill-fated Major Crowson, killed in January 1934 during a prison farm break engineered by Bonnie and Clyde, was no more a

major than young Sawyer was a colonel (honorary or otherwise) (Jeff Guinn, *Go Down Together: The True, Untold Story of Bonnie and Clyde* [New York: Simon & Schuster, 2009], p. 247).

6. *Danville Commercial-News*, December 30, 1930, p. 5, col. 3. Two days before, however, the same paper (December, 28, 1930, sec. 3, p. 1, col. 1) carried a communication from the Lafayette (IN) Police to the Danville police chief, Robert H. Swift, saying that three bandits had been identified in the fatal shooting of Lafayette police captain Charles Arman on November 1, 1927 — James Clark, Walter Detrich and Herman Lamm. Landy was not mentioned at this time.

7. As with the Etna Green bank robbers, John Pfeffer and Russell and Garland Ives, in their sentencing in January 1931.

8. *Indianapolis News*, December 23, 1930, p. 3, col. 7.

Chapter XII

All quotations in this chapter, unless otherwise indicated, are from the trial transcript. Grammatical errors, except for misspellings and run-on sentences, have not been corrected.

1. Dad Landy's presence in the bank is a real problem. No one in the bank or out of it saw more than three men, with barber Vansickle seeing only two enter, probably missing Detrich's entrance. Pete Voto, a cashier at the bank, was interviewed by Jack Cejnar in the days following the robbery, as was virtually everyone else involved in the episode, save for the wrongdoers. I follow Cejnar in placing Landy in the bank.

2. That Moody had a shotgun is questionable. His widow, his son-in-law and the newspapers all spoke of him always using a rifle. He apparently was a rifleman on all other occasions — such as slaughtering livestock. He could, of course, have borrowed the shotgun from some member of the posse.

3. I have no idea what "Oh, slim" was supposed to convey — at least, not in polite society.

4. Almost certainly Scott chose to forget what Margaret Helms recalled for me sixty-three years later, and that was Joe Walker shouting, "Come on, you yellow sons of bitches, follow me!"

5. Landy is meant. He was often called Landley and Landry at this time.

6. This certainly looks as though Boetto put a slug in Lamm. But maybe not. He got either Lamm or Landy, if he got anyone, and there's nothing to say that it wasn't Landy. The inquest and death certificate mention only the fatal wound to the temple in Landy's case. He may have been shot in the leg or foot by Boetto early on. All we know is that he was in a prone position when he fired the shot into his temple. The "Pete" in this remark could have been either Harold "Pete" Scott or Chief Helms, both of whom were with Boetto at the time of this shot. Most likely, Helms is meant, since Scott was a Dana man.

7. I can think of only one outlaw sentenced to life in prison who was paroled and later ran for office. Al Jennings, long rider, train robber and prison bunkmate of O. Henry, ran for governor of Oklahoma in 1914 and lost.

8. *Daily Clintonian*, January 5, 1931, p. 1, col. 3.

9. Interview with Margaret Helms at Clinton, Indiana, September 8, 1993.

Chapter XIII

1. *Danville Commercial-News*, December 24, 1930, p. 4, col. 8.

2. Horace M. Coates, *Indianapolis Star*, December 29, 1930, p. 1.

3. Toland, *Dillinger Days*, p. 25.

4. Ibid., pp. 25–6.

5. In a letter to his half-brother, Hubert, Dillinger maintained that he went to Michigan City because he was a hand at baseball in Pendleton Reformatory (ibid., p. 26).

6. "What does the 'O' stand for?" Eve Kendall inquires of Roger O. Thornhill in the film *North By Northwest* (1959). "Nothing," Thornhill replies. It was a little bit that way with Elmer F. Harvey, the undertaker who handled both Dillinger's and his stepmother's funerals. Since Harvey is always referred to as Elmer F. Harvey, I wondered about it to his son when I talked with him in 1992. The "F" was not Harvey's middle initial. He had none. He adopted the initial, so to speak, because of his fascination for Friday in Robinson Crusoe. The "F" in Elmer F. Harvey thus stood for Friday (interview with Dr. Robert Harvey at Greencastle, Indiana, September 26, 1992).

7. One has to wonder what Dillinger would have been had his stepmother lived beyond May 22, 1933. It is sometimes said that Dillinger did not get along with her. When I talked with his half-sister, Frances, in 1992, I heard a much different slant. Of course, by the time of his parole, Dillinger had long had his mind made up to go bad. His stepmother, Elizabeth, would have had an uphill fight to subdue his baser nature, whatever their relationship.

8. Margaret Haines interview at Alexandria, Indiana, July 24, 1991.

9. This was at the height of Dillinger's "blue period" — blue-barreled revolver period, that is.

He later made the switch to automatics, much to his own surprise since he didn't trust them initially. The revolver may have been a Lamm touch via Walter Detrich and Oklahoma Jack Clark. The observation about Dillinger's antipathy to automatics came from the late Lisle Reedstrom, a fine researcher, writer and artist, in March 1993, at St. John, Indiana. He wrote about Dillinger's aversion to automatics in the September number of *Guns and Ammo* magazine in 1979. Reedstrom garnered the information from Dillinger's first crime partner, William Shaw, either in manuscript form or audiotape or both, as he told me that he had both formats.

10. Roofing nails were a staple of virtually every outlaw gang of the era needing to make a hasty exit to stay one jump ahead of the law. I remember that when talking with Carroll Williams, Fenton's brother, upon hearing how Lamm and company tossed roofing nails on the road after taking a Model-A coupe from Fenton, my jaw dropped, as it seemed to me, novice that I was, that Dillinger had picked up this artifice from Detrich and Clark while all three were in Michigan City. But this need hardly have been the case. The tactic was a common one among bandit gangs — just like jumping over the counter in a bank robbery. And its effectiveness may be questioned. Only at Sioux Falls, South Dakota, did the tactic do Dillinger any good, whatever its efficacy or lack thereof for Lamm. Lamm, incidentally, had been using the ploy at least since his arrest at Winston-Salem, North Carolina, in February 1927. Talking with Darwin Hagan in 1993, I got a laugh out of one such incident as reported by him. It involved Dillinger. While the outlaw and four others were cleaning out the Central National Bank in Greencastle, Indiana, teller William Stiles beat it out the basement door. He went across the street to a hardware store and acquired some roofing nails. (Responding to my playful query about whether he paid for the nails, Stiles, with a grin, couldn't quite remember.) He hurriedly scattered piles of the nails under the tires of the getaway Studebaker, which was unguarded and parked at the side of the bank on Jackson Street. As Dillinger's cars always had good rubber on them, the roofing nails had no effect. But a few moments later, when Darwin Hagan's wife parked in the same spot, all four of the world-weary tires of the family Oldsmobile went flat.

11. On August 5, 1995, sixty-two years and a day after the Montpelier robbery, William Chaney, who was nine at the time of the robbery, told me of hearing the bell at the fire station ringing frantically to sound the alarm that day. I was timely as a June bug when I interviewed Gordon Sayers at Greencastle, Indiana, on October 23, 1993. This date was sixty years precisely after the Dillinger robbery in that town, wherein Gordon had witnessed Dillinger's vault over the bank railing. When I reminded Gordon of the significance of the day, he smiled patiently as if to say, "Is this all you have to do?" I sometimes wonder the same thing.

12. The *Chicago Daily Tribune* (September 27, 1933, p. 2, col. 1) merely says that the guns were wrapped in soundproof material.

13. Girardin and Helmer (*Dillinger: The Untold Story*, p. 27) have this day on or about August 10.

14. Toland (*Dillinger Days*, p. 113) says that the break was planned for the 27th. Matera (*John Dillinger*, p. 83) has it set for the 28th. G. Russell Girardin and William J. Helmer (*Dillinger: The Untold Story* [Bloomington, IN: Indiana University Press, 1994], p. 28) and Cromie and Pinkston (*Dillinger: A Short and Violent Life*) do not mention the change in date except that the former duo says that the original date was the 20th. For no reason but a gut feeling, I have gone with Toland.

15. Cromie and Pinkston (*Dillinger: A Short and Violent Life*, p. 61) state that it was Russell Clark and Harry Pierpont who lured Stevens into the basement storeroom. They also have the pistols of the botched escape attempt wrapped in newspaper (p. 58). I have no new information on these matters, merely going with Walter's Dillinger biography, which, by the way, is based on an unfinished manuscript by the late Joseph Pinkston.

16. In 1991, I talked with Ursula Patzke, who experienced two of those moments when Pierpont wasn't quite himself. She worked at the American Bank and Trust when the Dillinger gang robbed it and abducted her and the bank's president. She was in the backseat of the getaway car when, for some reason, Charley Makley began swearing. Pierpont then spoke up, "Cut it out, Mack. We've got a lady in the car." He also loaned her his coat during the getaway. Later, when the gang had deposited her and the bank president in the woods and was about to drive off, Pierpont returned with a dangerous look in his eye, He walked over to where the two hostages were tied to a tree with a brand new pair of shoelaces. "I need this," he said as he lifted the hat off the president's head. He had given it to him in the getaway car when the latter complained that his head was cold. In the 2009 film *Public Enemies*, Dillinger replaces Pierpont in the chivalry bit. Mrs. Patzke, moreover, is Barbara, instead of Ursula.

17. Toland (*Dillinger Days*, p. 116) suspected

the shot was accidental, caused by a con jumping over a counter with a gun in his hand. But, if as Matera has it (*John Dillinger*, p. 84), Carson was shot twice, it was no accident. The *Chicago Daily Tribune* (September 27, 1933, p. 2, col. 1) supports Matera's take on the matter, stating that Carson was shot twice — in the abdomen and thigh.

18. The *Chicago Daily Tribune* has the name as "Neel" in the early going of its coverage of the break as does the 1930 U.S. census. The name in several accounts appears as Neal.

19. Toland, *Dillinger Days*, p. 118. Toland knows far more about Detrich than any of Dillinger's other biographers. One suspects the assistance of Jack Cejnar, INS Indianapolis bureau chief. Toland, perhaps not coincidentally, knows far more about Baron Lamm than other Dillinger biographers, too.

20. I don't know whether or not 18-year-old Orson Welles was stateside at the time of this incident, but one feels certain that he must have gotten wind (pun intended) of it owing to its uncanny similarity to his War of the Worlds broadcast five years later. Welles was a Kenosha, Wisconsin, native and was supposedly in Chicago taking in a picture when Dillinger was killed at the Biograph the following year (Simon Callow, *Orson Welles: The Road to Xanadu*, vol. 1 [New York: Viking, 1995], p. 175).

21. Matera (*John Dillinger*, p. 87) says the former; Sheriff Neel, in the *Chicago Daily Tribune* for September 29, 1933 (p. 2, col. 1), says the latter.

22. *Lasalle Daily Post-Tribune*, September 28, 1933, pp. 1–2.

23. *Bloomington (IL) Daily Pantagraph*, September 28, 1933, p. 1, col. 2 (AP dispatch).

24. Clark's arrest could have passed for a meeting of the U.N. Security Council. The surnames of the four arresting officers were Kelley, Wilson, Dimitroff and Mroz (*Chicago Daily Tribune*, September 30, 1933, p. 1, col. 8).

25. Upon hearing of his life and career and the end result of both, the university's newspaper, the *Daily Illini*, trenchantly disavowed him. Unfortunately, it would have to do the exact same thing less than three months later when Fred Goetz, Shotgun George Ziegler, was gunned down in Cicero.

26. Toland (*Dillinger Days*, p. 351) says that the gun Klutas reached for when he was killed was bought in Hammond, Indiana, by Dillinger and presumably given to Handsome Jack by Detrich. Toland's source for this bit appears to have been Joe Healy, a detective who was in on the kill.

27. Detrich's name is spelled thus in the caption beneath this picture. Elsewhere in the same paper at this time, he is mostly Dietrick. The surname appears as Detrich on his tombstone. The information about his parole to the custody of Matt Leach was provided by Vicki Casteel of the Indiana State Archives (e-mail to author, dated February 29, 2008).

28. Toland (*Dillinger Days*, p. 112) makes it four, though he only accounts for three fake guns (p. 114). He goes counter to other Dillinger biographers in moving the breakout one day ahead of schedule, rather than two (p. 113). See also note 14.

Chapter XIV

1. J. Evetts Haley, *Robbing Banks Was My Business: The Story of J. Harvey Bailey, America's Most Successful Bank Robber* (Canyon, TX: Palo Duro, 1973), p. 35.

2. Boren, "The Man Who Taught Dillinger."

3. Dow Helmers, "The Denver Mint Robbery," *Denver Post*, December 7, 1975.

4. INS dispatch, datelined Indianapolis, in the *Lafayette Journal and Courier*, December 16, 1930, p. 1, cols. 4–5.

5. N.T. Betz, *The Fleagle Gang: Betrayed by a Fingerprint* (Bloomington, IN: Author House, 2005), p. 303.

6. *Toledo Blade*, April 16, 1928, p. 1.

7. Ibid., April 17, 1928, p. 7, col. 4.

8. Ibid.

9. Helmer and Bilek, *The St. Valentine's Day Massacre*, pp. 85, 219*ff.*

10. Undated clipping from the *Columbia City Post*, probably from page 2 of the April 19 edition. A similar statement from Ferry appears in the *Fort Wayne News-Gazette*, April 19, 1929, p. 10, cols. 4–5. The latter statement lacks the bandit's order not to look at him.

11. Officer Down Memorial Page (www.ODMP.org), Pennsylvania Highway Patrol, Harrisburg, PA, Patrolman Russell T. Swanson, April 19, 1929.

12. I remember walking into the Miami County Historical Society at Peru one pleasant July day in 1991 and being assailed (as I thought) with the gratuitous information that the local minor league team had once bested the Chicago Cubs, led by the great Grover Cleveland Alexander in an exhibition game back in the '20s. I guess people can tell by looking at me that I bleed Cubbie blue. On that same day, I also saw a submachine gun in a glass case in the lobby of the Peru City Hall. Dillinger and two others helped themselves to just such a weapon October 21, 1933.

13. *Peru Republican*, October 25, 1929, p. 1, col. 2; *Frankfort Morning Times*, October 19, 1929, p. 1, col. 7.

14. *Peru Republican*, October 25, 1929, p. 1, cols. 1–3.
15. "Clinton Bandits Killed by Posse, Buried in Pauper's Ditch," *Hoosier Banker*, January 16, 1931.
16. *Peru Daily Tribune*, October 22, 1929, p. 1, col. 6; *Peru Republican*, October 25, 1929, p. 1, col. 3. For Ms. Endicott's response, see the *Peru Daily Tribune*, October 20, 1929, p. 2, col. 4.

Chapter XV

No one has ever said that Baron Lamm was not killed in the aftermath of the Clinton robbery. One feels that someone by now would have said so were it not for the fact that Lamm has not been much written about. His story is not well known. An evil genius — even if only a reputed one — tempts such a fate. With far less justification, other outlaws have had colorfully mooted resurrections — Jesse James, Billy the Kid, Butch Cassidy, Dillinger and even this last's close associate, Three-Fingered Jack Hamilton. The likelihood is all against Lamm surviving his only known death, but the evidence doesn't always stack up that way.

1. Baron Lamm's mug shot (from Winston-Salem in 1927?) and the photograph of the dead man in the McCauley funeral parlor do not at first blush look that much alike. Apart from the fact that one photo shows a dead man and the other a living man, the facial shape and weight of the two appear to be different, with the dead man looking like a heavier, more compact version of the living desperado. To be blunt about it, the dead man looks healthier than the living man. He even appears younger. Life has been harder on the living man than a bullet through the heart has been on the dead man. Also, the man in the mug shot has ears, but it is questionable if the dead man has — at least to the same degree. The dead man's ears appear to be set very close to the head, indeed. Countering these discrepancies is the deviated septum shared by both. (But then, Fred "Killer" Burke — with whom Lamm was confused in the course of the last two or three years of his existence — also sported a deviated septum. Burke, apparently, was a much smaller man than Lamm.) Both pictures also show the same right eyebrow in both men. Nevertheless, without other evidence, comparing the two photographs can hardly prove conclusive to my unprofessional eye. Recently, two other mug shots have come to hand. The first appeared in the *Indianapolis News*, December 17, 1930, p. 8 — and it contrasts dramatically with the other two known photographs of Lamm — that from the *Danville Commercial-News* (December 22, 1930, p. 12) showing him in the morgue and one from the *Terre Haute Tribune* (December 18, 1930, p. 2, col. 4). In the new photo, his nose lacks the deviated septum and even flourishes a little pointed tip. His hair is very much graying, in marked contrast to his morgue shot. The second popped up recently on the Internet (www.outlawhistory.com/Herman%20K.%20Lamm.html ; also in Wikipedia's take on Baron Lamm, at http://en.wikipedia.org/wiki/Herman_Lamm). This fourth photo, subscribed "Is this the 'Baron'?" is most definitely Lamm, around age 30, possibly taken at Utah State Prison or some subsequent arrest, of which there were a handful. The nose is more massive than usual, but the right eyebrow is the same as ever. This is Lamm at his most sinister. No one need try to rehabilitate this man. So, in my opinion, four shots claiming to be Lamm are known. Three of these are more or less certainly him and one definitely isn't. In the end, one is left wondering if a true likeness of Lamm can be obtained only by conflating the three genuine photographs in order to arrive at the original Baron Lamm.

2. Unger, *Union Station Massacre*, pp. 120–31. Lamm, according to the *Milwaukee Journal* (December 19, 1930, p. 1), was identified by his fingerprints. But the *Terre Haute Tribune* for the same date has him identified by photographs. Oklahoma Jack Clark and Walter Detrich were identified by fingerprints and Bertillion measurements. Hunter apparently wasn't identified by any trustworthy method. He seems to have been identified by a member of the posse who knew him by the tattoo on one forearm. Landy was fingerprinted at Frankfort in May 1924 and was identified in death by Indiana State police lieutenant Rex Resser (or Reeser or Risher).

3. For a highly entertaining, if not altogether convincing, look at the Dillinger controversy, see Nash and Offen, *Dillinger: Dead or Alive?* and the former's *The Dillinger Dossier* (Evergreen Park: December Press, 1983). The Dillinger conspiracy theory certainly has legs. Besides making it into the bestselling *People's Almanac* (three editions, 1975–1981), it even finds its way into a recent biography of Clark Gable (Warren G. Harris, *Clark Gable: A Biography* [New York: Harmony Books, 2002], p. 121).

4. A report in the *Terre Haute Tribune* for December 19, 1930 (p. 14, col. 5) states that Lamm was identified not by fingerprints, as Clark and Detrich were, but by photographs. Given the discrepancies outlined above between his mug shot(s) and morgue shot, I would say that, if this was so, his identification rests on somewhat tenuous evidence, indeed. The *Terre Haute Star* for December 17, 1930 (p. 1, col. 8)

mentions that Lamm/Bell was identified by fingerprints.

5. In *1 Henry IV*, even Shakespeare had trouble counting his thieves (John Jowett, "The Thieves in 1 Henry IV," *Review of English Studies*, New Series 38, no. 151 [August 1987]: 333). That Shakespeare knew intimately the ploys and devices of the "stand-up men" of his day is a point made in Alan Stewart's fascinating article "Shakespeare and the Carriers" (*Shakespeare Quarterly* 58, no. 4 [Winter 2007]: 431–64). This wasn't Shakespeare's fault. It was the era of the popular rogue pamphlets.

6. *Danville* (IL) *Commercial-News*, December 16, 1930, p. 4, col. 4. Again, an early report in an afternoon daily.

7. *Indianapolis News*, December 17, 1930, p. 8, col. 6. This account is special to the *Indianapolis News*. It should be noted that in his account of this episode given to Associated Press wire service, Chief Helms did not mention any other cars besides the original getaway Buick and those vehicles commandeered by the gang in their flight. But Chief Helms' account, at least in this context, is not only sketchy but inaccurate in places. For instance, Helms states that the gang took S.W. [*sic*] Gilbert's car and drove it to Sidell, all of which is wrong (*Frankfort Morning Times*, December 17, 1930, pp. 1, 3, esp. 3). Helms' as-told-to account, reported by Jack Cejnar ("Jinx," part 1, p. 3), mentions only one original getaway car—a 1931 black Buick. The first take by the *Danville Commercial-News* on the robbery (December 16, 1930, p. 4, col. 4) mentions that "two other machines" came to the aid of the stricken getaway car on the outskirts of Clinton.

8. *Indianapolis Star*, January 11, 1931, p. 8, col. 1; *Paris Beacon-News*, January 13, 1931, p. 2, col. 1; *Danville Commercial-News*, January 12, 1931, p. 1, col. 3.

9. Cejnar ("Jinx," part 2, p. 28) says that vigilantes combed the cornfield in search of gang members and loot after the bodies of Lamm and Landy had been carried off. The *Danville Commercial-News* (December 17, 1930, p. 5, col. 3) states that the clothing on the dead bandits had been removed before the authorities (apparently, Coroner John D. Cole) arrived.

10. Cejnar ("Jinx," part 1, p. 22) says that the bandits merely left that amount lying in their haste to get away, moreover demoting the specie as merely silver and paper.

11. Interview with Merrel Chew at Sidell, Illinois, December 26, 1992.

12. *Danville Commercial-News*, December 19, 1930, p. 13, col. 1.

13. According to Cejnar ("Jinx," part 2, p. 33), who got his information from Clinton Chief of Police Everett Helms and E.L. Osborne, head of the Indiana Bureau of Criminal Identification and Investigation, Lamm was wanted by Washington, Iowa, authorities. They were interested in Lamm/Bell in connection with the deaths of two officers there on June 25, 1930. These killings were undoubtedly the work of Klutas, but who helped in his getaway is the question.

14. *Danville Commercial-News*, December 23, 1930, p. 1, col. 7.

15. Mace Smoot—what W.C. Fields would have given to have thought up this name!

16. Telephone interview with Harold Frist, April 14, 1997.

17. Two days after the Clinton robbery, Clinton police received word from G.M. McKee, of Memphis, Tennessee, that his brother John McKee went to Terre Haute in September and stayed at a hotel there. He was never heard from again. McKee wondered whether E.H. Hunter, the mortally-wounded Clinton bandit, might be his missing sibling. Nothing seems to have come of this lead, but if there was anything to this McKee/Hunter identity, it raises serious questions about the entry in the Poor Farm records, perhaps giving it the good-bye altogether. Hunter, on his deathbed, expected plenty of people to claim his body; whether Tennesseans or Teutons, he didn't indicate (*Daily Clintonian*, December 18, 1930, p. 1, col. 7). The *Terre Haute Tribune* (December 19, 1930, p. 14, col. 3) reported that the description of the missing McKee by G.M. McKee all but matched Hunter. In any case, Hunter was buried in the potter's field, along with Lamm and Landy.

18. Cejnar ("Jinx," part 2, p. 33) says that the initials were "E.K." Cejnar further describes additional tattoos of a sailor and an anchor and a dagger to one side of the sailor.

19. Something just doesn't add up. Hunter seems to have taken on some of Lamm's identity, as Lamm for a time on his death certificate took on some of Landy's identity. Hunter is said to have been "born in Germany," the only one of the deceased outlaw trio so ascribed.

20. *Bloomington* (IL) *Daily Pantagraph*, December 17, 1930, p. 1, col. 2; *Dana* (IN) *News*, December 18, 1930, p. 1, col. 1; *Danville Commercial-News*, December 17, 1930, p. 1, col. 8.; *Daily Clintonian*, December 17, 1930, p. 1, col. 6; *Paris (IL) Beacon-News*, December 17, 1930, p. 1, col. 2.

21. He was incarcerated and paroled under that name (*Chicago Daily Tribune*, March 10, 1950, p. 1, col. 3).

22. See note 2, chapter 2; note 2, chapter 11.

23. Girardin and Helmer, *Dillinger*, pp. 280–81. Dillinger is mentioned numerous times by Detrich as a source for contraband pistols but not necessarily the ones leading to the escape. Pierpont is given credit for planning the break (*Chicago Daily Tribune*, January 11, 1934). In the write-up in the *Indianapolis Star* of the same date, Detrich could not say "positively" that Dillinger had smuggled in the guns that led to the break in a thread box.

24. In the heyday of syndicated bank robbery, as Lamm's heyday assuredly was, it is very likely that some big shot remained free after the gang's Waterloo. As to just who "Uncle Ed" or "Uncle Ben" may have been, understood in the context of syndicated bank robbery, Dressed-up Johnny Gardner might be the place to look.

25. They were apparently good friends. At least two photographs show them together. What's more, Dalton seems to have led investigators to Brushy Bill (Jannay P. Valdez and Bobby E. Hefner, *Billy the Kid, "Killed" in New Mexico, Died in Texas* [Palo Alto, TX: Outlaw Publications, 1995}, pp. 190–91). For Dalton and Brushy Bill's relationship, see C.L. Sonnichsen and William Vincent Morrison, *Alias Billy the Kid: "...I want to die a free man..."* (Albuquerque: University of New Mexico Press, 1955), pp. 3–4, 11.

Bibliography

Books and Articles

Ammer, Christine. *The American Heritage Dictionary of Idioms*. Boston: Houghton Mifflin, 1997.

Barrett, Paul W. and Mary H. *Young Brothers Massacre*. Columbia: University of Missouri Press, 1988.

Betz, N.T. *The Fleagle Gang: Betrayed by a Fingerprint*. Bloomington, IN: Author House, 2005.

Boren, Kerry Ross. "The Man Who Taught Dillinger." *South Point Magazine*, September 1992. www.prospector.utah.com/dill.htm.

Buel, J.W. *The Border Outlaws: An Authentic and Thrilling History of the Most Noted Bandits of Ancient or Modern Times, the Younger Brothers, Jesse and Frank James and their Comrades in Crime*. St. Louis, MO: Historical Publishing, 1882.

Burrough, Bryan. *Public Enemies: The War on Crime and the Birth of the FBI, 1933–34* (New York: Penguin, 2004).

Callahan, Clyde C., and Byron B. Jones. *Heritage of an Outlaw: The Story of Frank Nash*. Hobart, OK: Schoonmaker, 1979.

Callow, Simon. *Orson Welles: The Road to Xanadu*. New York: Viking, 1995.

Cejnar, Jack. "The Jinx That Stalked the Outlaws." Jack Cejnar papers. Indiana Historical Society, Indianapolis, Indiana.

Cromie, Robert, and Joseph Pinkston. *Dillinger: A Short and Violent Life*. Evanston, IL: Chicago Historical Bookworks, 1990. Originally published by McGraw-Hill in 1962.

DeNeal, Gary. *A Knight of a Different Color: Prohibition Days and Charlie Birger*. Danville, IL: Interstate Printers and Publishers, 1981.

Donald, Jay. *Outlaws of the Border: A Complete and Authentic History of the Lives of Frank and Jesse James, the Younger Brothers, and Their Robber Companions, Including Quantrell and His Noted Guerillas*. Cincinnati: W.E. Dibble, 1882.

Ewing, Steve. *Fatal Rendezvous: The Life of Edward "Butch" O'Hare*. Annapolis, MD: U.S. Naval Institute Press, 2004.

Gash, Donna, Brenda Davis, and Burma K. Thomas. *Songer Cemetery, Catlin Township, Vermilion County*. Danville, IL: s.n., 1978.

Girardin, G. Russell, and William J. Helmer. *Dillinger: The Untold Story*. Bloomington, IN: Indiana University Press, 1994.

Gorn, Elliott J., *Dillinger's Wild Ride: The Year That Made Public Enemy Number One*. New York: Oxford University Press, 2009.

Guinn, Jeff. *Go Down Together: The True, Untold Story of Bonnie and Clyde*. New York: Simon & Schuster, 2009.

Haley, J. Evetts. *Robbing Banks Was My Business: The Story of J. Harvey Bailey, America's Most Successful Bank Robber*. Canyon, TX: Palo Duro, 1973.

Harris, Warren G. *Clark Gable: A Biography*. New York: Harmony Books, 2002.

Helmer, William J., and Arthur J. Bilek. *The St. Valentine's Day Massacre: The Untold Story of the Gangland Bloodbath That Brought Down Al Capone*. Nashville, TN: Cumberland House, 2004.

_____, and Rick Mattix. *Public Enemies: America's Criminal Past, 1919–1940*. New York: Facts on File, 1998.

Horan, James D. *Desperate Men: Revelations*

from the Sealed Pinkerton Files. New York: Bonanza Books, 1949.
Kelly, Charles. *The Outlaw Trail: A History of Butch Cassidy and His Wild Bunch*. New York: Devin-Adair, 1959. First published in 1938.
King, Jeffrey S. *The Rise and Fall of the Dillinger Gang*. Nashville, TN: Cumberland House, 2005.
Kirchner, L.R. *Robbing Banks: An American History, 1831–1899*. Rockville Centre, NY: Sarpedon Books, 2000.
Kroeger, Brooke. *Nellie Bly: Daredevil Reporter, Feminist*. New York: Random House, 1994.
Martin, Floyd. *Record of Inmates, 1926–1936, Vermilion County Home (the Poor Farm)*. Danville, IL: Illiana Genealogical Society, 1995.
Matera, Dary. *John Dillinger: The Life and Death of America's First Celebrity Criminal*. New York: Carroll and Graff, 2004.
McCarthy, John. *Hollywood Gangland: The Movies' Love Affair with the Mob*. New York: St. Martin's, 1993.
McGhee, Millie L. *Secrets Uncovered: J. Edgar Hoover — Passing for White?* 2nd edition. Cucamonga, CA: Allen Morris, 2000.
Musgrave, Paul. "A Primitive Method of Enforcing the Law: Vigilantism as a Response to Bank Crimes in Indiana, 1925–1933." *Indiana Magazine of History* 102 (September 2006): 197–219.
Nash, Jay Robert. *Bloodletters and Badmen: A Narrative Encyclopedia of American Criminals from the Pilgrims to the Present*. New York: M. Evans, 1995.
_____. *The Dillinger Dossier*. Evanston, IL: December Press, 1983.
_____, and Ron Offen. *Dillinger: Dead or Alive?* Chicago: Henry Regnery, 1970.
Nickel, Steven, and William J. Helmer. *Baby Face Nelson: Portrait of a Public Enemy*. Nashville: Cumberland House, 2002.
Partridge, Eric. *A Dictionary of Slang*. 8th edition. London: Routledge, 2000.
Pensoneau, Taylor. *Brothers Notorious: The Sheltons, Southern Illinois' Legendary Gangsters*. New Berlin, IL: Downstate Publications, 2002.
Powers, Richard Gid. *G-Men: Hoover's FBI in American Popular Culture*. Carbondale: Southern Illinois University Press, 1983.
_____. *Secrecy and Power: The Life of J. Edgar Hoover*. New York: Free Press, 1987.

Saunders, R.C. "Organized Protection Against Organized Predatory Crime." *Journal of Criminal Law and Criminology*, vol. 23, no. 5 (January–February 1933).
Sifakis, Carl. *The Encyclopedia of American Crime*. New York: Facts on File, 1982.
Smith, Bruce. *Rural Crime Control*. New York: Columbia University Press, 1933.
Smith, Jean Edward. *FDR*. New York: Random House, 2007.
Smith, Robert Barr. "The Dalton Gang's Mystery Rider at Coffeyville." *Wild West* 8, no. 3 (October 1995).
_____. *Daltons! The Raid on Coffeyville, Kansas*. Norman, OK: University of Oklahoma Press, 1996.
Sonnichsen, C.L., and William Vincent Morrison. *Alias Billy the Kid: "...I want to die a free man..."* Albuquerque, NM: University of New Mexico Press, 1955.
Sperber, A.M., and Eric Lax. *Bogart*. New York: William Morrow, 1997.
Squire, John Collings Squire. *If; or, History Rewritten*. New York: Viking, 1931.
Stewart, Tony. *Dillinger, the Hidden Truth: A Tribute to Gangsters and G-Men of the Great Depression Era*. Philadelphia: Xlibris, 2002.
Stiles, T.J. *Jesse James: Last Rebel of the Civil War*. New York: Alfred A. Knopf, 2002.
Summers, Anthony. *Official and Confidential: The Secret Life of J. Edgar Hoover*. New York: Putnam's, 1993.
Swiercybski, Duane. *This Here's a Stick-up: The Big Bad Book of American Bank Robbery*. Indianapolis: Alpha Books, 2002.
Theoharris, Allen. *J. Edgar Hoover, Sex and Crime: A Historical Antidote*. Chicago: Ivan R. Dee, 1995.
Toland, John. *Captured by History: One Man's Vision of Our Tumultuous Century*. New York: St. Martin's, 1997.
_____. *The Dillinger Days*. New York: Random House, 1963.
Tucker, William. *Vigilante: The Backlash against Crime in America*. New York: Stein and Day, 1985.
Unger, Robert. *The Union Station Massacre: The Original Sin of J. Edgar Hoover's FBI*. Kansas City, MO: Andrews McNeel, 1997.
Valdez, Jannay P., and Bobby E. Hefner. *Billy the Kid, "Killed" in New Mexico, Died in Texas*. Palo Alto, TX: Outlaw Publications, 1995.
Vermilion County Historical Society. *Vermil-*

ion County, History and Families. Paducah, KY: Turner, 1990.

Wallechinsky, David and Irving Wallace, eds. The People's Almanac. Garden City, NY: Doubleday, 1975.

Wallis, Michael. Pretty Boy: The Life and Times of Charles Arthur Floyd. New York: St. Martin's, 1992.

Winn, Dilys, ed. Murder Ink: The Mystery Reader's Companion. New York: Workman, 1977.

Newspapers and Newsletters

Bloomington (IL) Daily Pantagraph
Champaign (IL) News-Gazette
Charlotte (NC) Observer
Chicago Daily News
Chicago (IL) Daily Tribune
Columbia City (IN) Post
Daily Clintonian
Daily Illini
Dana (IN) News
Danville (IL) Commercial News
Denver Post
Des Moines (IA) Register
Fort Wayne (IN) News-Gazette
Frankfort (IN) Evening News
Frankfort (IN) Morning Times
Hoosier Banker
Hoosier State
Indianapolis (IN) News
Indianapolis (IN) Star
LaFayette (IN) Journal and Courier
Lasalle-Peru (IL) Daily Post-Tribune
National Police Officer
Paris (IL) Beacon-News
Peru (IN) Republican
Peru (IN) Tribune
Terre Haute (IN) Star
Terre Haute (IN) Tribune
Toledo (OH) Blade
Tuscola (IL) Review
Urbana (IL) Courier
Winston-Salem (NC) Journal

Interviews

Barnes, Edith (Dana, IN)—telephone interview, April 10, 1997.
Botten, Sue (Sidell, IL)—December 18, 1993.
Chew, Merrel (Sidell, IL)—December 26, 1992.
Crays, Irma (Rockville, IN)—September 5, 1992.
Dixon, Norval and Patricia (Rockville, IN)—September 5, November 7, 1992.
Frist, Harold (Dana, IN)—telephone interview, April 14, 1997.
Gilbert, Virginia (Chrisman, IL)—June 4, 1996.
Goheen, Roland (South Bend, IN)—telephone interview, October 26, 1991.
Graham, Harold and May (Racine, WI)—telephone interview, May 30, 1992.
Hayes, Stan (Catlin, IL)—October 30, 1993.
Helms, Margaret (Clinton, IN)—September 8, 1993; November 6, 1993.
Hockett, Art (Sidell, IL)—numerous times between December 26, 1992 and June 4, 1996.
Ingram, Hubert (St. Bernice, IN)—October 1, 1996.
Lyons, Charles (Sidell, IL)—October 30, 1993.
Meyers, Harold (St. Bernice, IN)—October 1, 1996.
Patzke, Ursula (Racine, WI)—July 6, 1991.
Sayers, Gordon (Greencastle, IN)—many times from September 19, 1992, to April 1995.
Steele, Don (Racine, WI)—telephone interview, December 21, 1991.
Stout, Walter (St. Bernice, IN)—October 1, 1996.
Volk, Robert (Crown Point, IN)—November 14, 1992; March 20, 1993; October 9, 1993.
Williams, Carroll (Scottland, IL)—June 4, 1996.
Winland, Dorothy (Mrs. Leo Moody) (Tilton, IL)—numerous times between January 16, 1993 and July 23, 1996.

Online Resources

Ancestry. Draft Registration Cards, 1917–1918; census records. http://www.ancestry.com/.
"Clinton." Trip Trivia. http://www.triptrivia.com/IN/Clinton.
"Dillinger Gang." ICPR. http://www.in.gov/icpr/2830.htm.
"The Man Who Taught Dillinger." http://www.prospector-utah.com/dill.htm.
The Officer Down Memorial Page. http://www.odmp.org/.
Outlaw History. http://www.outlawhistory.com/Herman%20K.%20Lamm.html.

Videos

"G" Men. DVD. Directed by William Keighley. Original release, 1935. DVD release, Warner Home Video, 2006.

Little Caesar. DVD. Directed by Mervyn LeRoy. Original release, 1931. DVD release, Warner Home Video, 2005).

Public Enemies. DVD. Directed by Michael Mann. Original release, 2009. DVD release, Universal Studios Home Entertainment, 2009.

Court Transcripts

State of Indiana vs. Walter E. Detrich and James Clark, alias William M. Long, case #26100.

ID# Index

Numbers in **bold italics** indicate pages with photographs.

Ackerson, Joe 149
Adams, Sheriff Carl 35
Alexander, Grover Cleveland 204
Allen, "Nervy" 63
Allen, Deputy Ron 36
Allen, Woody 13, 27
American Bankers Association 20
American Experience 31
American National Bank (Frankfort, IN) 48
American State Bank (St. Bernice, IN) 41–45, 47
American Surety Company 89, 94
Arman, Charles 80–81
Austin, Hart 64

Bailey, Harvey 17, 21, 44, 68, 71, 74, 83, 100, 208, 222, 228
Baker, Anna May 211
Baker, Fred 41, 235n7
Baker, Mrs. Joseph 211
Baker, Martin 211
Balwin, Erwin 55
Barker, Freddie 72
Barker, Ma 72
Barker-Karpis gang 56
Barnes, George 45
Barrett, Helen M. 34
Barrow, Buck 66
Barrow, Clyde 59, 66, 243n5
Barry, Lt. Andy 141
Baum, James E. 63
Bean Blossom, IN 204
Beatty, Warren 119
Beck, Ed 73
Beery, Wallace 193
Beeson, H.A. 212

Beisel, Ben 38
Beloc, Hilaire 5
Bennett, Elwood 167, 168
Benton, Robert 25
Bentz, Edward Wilhelm 16, 17, 21, 73
Bertillon measurements 18
The Big House (1930) 193
Billy the Kid 212–213
Billy the Kid: "Killed" in New Mexico, Died in Texas 249n25
Biograph Theater 19
Birger, Charlie 21
Bishop, Ray 152
Bishupski, John 208
Bloodletters and Badmen 19, 22, 233ch1n6
Bluffton (OH) bank robbery 197
Bly, Nellie 234n4
Boetto, Ernest ***109***, 112, 118, 120–121, 128, 130–132, 143–144, 151, 184–185, 244n6
Bogardus, Adam 129
Bogart, Humphrey 234n15
Bolivia 33
Bolton, Byron 211–212
Bonnie and Clyde (1967) 6
Boren, Kerry Ross 21, 22, 73–74, 209
Brady, "Big Bob" 222
Branch, Emmett Forrest 42
Brazil (IN) 65, 71
Bright, John 25
Broadwell, Dick 4
Brookbank, Mildred 2, 143, 242n9
Bryan, William Jennings 171
Bump, Elmer 202
Burghby, Sgt. Frank 83
Burke, Fred "Killer" 83, 133, 144, 211–212, 217

255

Burklow, Guy 193, 198
Burnett, W.R. 23
Burnette, Smiley 119
Burns, Joseph 99, 183, 202, 205, 207
Burnside, Walter **108**, 110, 114, 116–118, 121, 128, 130, 132, 142, 169–170, 231
Burnside, Mrs. Walter 241–2n16
Burrough, Bryan 23, 29, 72

Cagney, James 11, 23–24
Cain, James M. 88
Caldwell, Ray 94
Call, Harry 104, 106, 166–167, 239n4
Calloway, George M. 75
Calumet City, IL 83
Capone, Al 71, 95, 224
Capote, Truman 4
Captured by History 233chIn3
Car and Driver Magazine 20
Carroll, Pat 36
Carson, Finley 198–199
Carter, W.H. 212
Cassell, Germany 2, 33
Cassidy, Butch 21–22, 33
Catlett, Kemp C. 147
Catlin, IL 28
Cayuga (IN) 44
Cejnar, Jack (John A.) 18, 29, 30–31, 131, 243n1, 248n9, 248n10
Cejnar, Mrs. Jack (Esther Jones) 30
Central National Bank (Greencastle, IN) 205
Chadwell, Bill 5
Chandler, Raymond 88
Chaney, William 245n10
Charleston (S.C.) 5, 15
Cheeks, Herschel 108
Cheney, Helen 80, 82, 237n3
Cheney, Margaret 82, 237n3
Chesterton, G.K. 5, 15
Chew, Merrel 1, 2, 9–10, 29, 222, 229, 243n19
Chicago and Eastern Railroad 44
Chicago World's Fair 197, 202
Chrisman (IL) 8, 30
Church, E.A. 145
Clark, Chief A.T. 201
Clark, Charles 109, 112, 118, 121, 123, 143, 184, 187–188
Clark, Fred 212, 213
Clark, James "Oklahoma Jack" 8, 10, 19, 21, 24, 26, 28–29, 31–47, 48, 50, 57, 67, 69, 73, 75–77, **81**, 93–94, 96–97, 104, 106, 110, 112, 122, 129–133, 138–140, 145–146, 151–161, 163, 184, 186, 189–192, 197, 199–203, 209, 215, 223, 228–229, 244n6, 246n24
Clark, Russell 193, 197, 199, 204, 224
Claudy, Deputy Warden H.D. 193, 215
Claus, Andy 201
Clinton Co. (IN) Bankers Association 94
Clinton (IN) bank robbery 56, 60, 99–107, 218, 237n4
Cloutier, Louise 100, 165
Cole, Coroner John D. 145, 148, 151, 227, 228
Columbia City (IN) 212–213
Copeland, Harry 17, 26, 194–195
Cosner, Harry 90
Cotton-Top Walker gang 17, 87
Craig, Clifford W. 193, 201

Daily, Van 116, 149, 240n17
Daleville (IN) bank robbery 26, 194
Dalton, Emmett 6
Dalton, J. Frank 232, 249n25
Dalton gang 4, 17, 22, 158
Daly, Warden Walter H. 193
Dana (IN) 28
Darrow, Clarence 171
Davis, Bill "Lop-eared" 63
Davis, Kirby 213
Dawson, Ernest 89
Dean, Harry "Canada Yellow" 63
Dean, James 239n6
Dempsey, Jack 87
Denver Mint robbery 21, 24, 203
Depp, Johnny 26
Detrich, Walter 8–9, 16, 19, 26, 28–29, 31, **81**, 87, 92–93, 101–102, 104, 106–107, 110, 115, 117, 121, 130, 134–136, 139–143, 145, 147, 151–161, 163, 165–166, 169, 181–182, 184, 186, 188–192, 201–202, 205–206, 223–224, 228–230, 244n6, 246n27, 249n23
Deventer, Louise 82
Digman, Henry A. 47, 236n6
Dillinger (1945) 25
Dillinger (1973) 29, 92
Dillinger (TV-movie, 1991) 26
Dillinger, Elizabeth 244chXIIIn7
Dillinger, Frances 1
Dillinger, John 1, 2, 7, 10–13, 18, 20, 22, 24, 26, 28, 33, 41, 47–48, 56, 59, 61, 66, 69–70, 84–85, 191–195, 203, 206–207, 216–217, 230, 236n1, 236n2, 238n5, 244chXIIIn9, 246n12, 247n3, 249n24
Dillinger: A Short and Violent Life 238n13

Index

The Dillinger Days 6, 18, 25
Dillinger: Dead or Alive? 19, 233*ch*I*n*4
Dorsey, John 34
Drummond, Hattie 123
Drummond, Martin 149
Duerr, W.L. 97

East Chicago (IN) 19
Emmanual, Louis 65
Endicott, Martha 214
Eubank, Richard 40
Evans, Albert 197
Everhard, Adrian 212
Eversole, A.G. 91, 222, 238*n*7

Fairmount (IL) 10
Farmers State Bank (Frankfort, IN) 89–94, 218, 272
Federal Bureau of Investigation 44
Ferguson, Gov. Miriam "Ma" 47
First National Bank (Clinton, IN) 100
First National Bank (Peru, IN) 214–216
Fisher, Fred 194
Fleagle, Jake 62, 72, 209, 237*n*1
Fleagle, Ralph 209
Fleagle gang 17, 74
Floyd, Charles Arthur "Pretty Boy" 10–11, 24, 59, 71
Foltz, Raymond "Razz" 122, 133, 155, 162, 190
Ford, John 16, 26
42nd Street (1933) 102
Fox, Joseph 199, 205
Frechette, Evelyn "Billie" 26, 205
Frederick, Pauline 39
Freese, Woody 138
Frist, Harlow 110, 112, 169–171, 218
Frist, Harold 28
Frist, Jediah 28, **111**, 113, 172, 175, 178
Frist, Marshall 239*n*4
Fuller, Anne 65
Fundamentalism 38
Fury (1936) 242*n*2

"*G" Men* (1935) 11, 23–24, 72, 234*n*14
G-Men (Powers) 233Pro*n*5
Gardner, "Dressed-up Johnny" 249*n*21
Garrett, Grover C. 238*n*10
Gaulke, Walter 53
The General (1926) 35
Gilbert, F. Wells 3, 118, **114**–115, 117, 120–121, 141, 173–178, 180, 219
Gilbert, Virginia 30, 240*n*24
Girk, Chief Joseph A. 147

Goddard, Rowland 146
The Godfather (1972) 84
Goheen, Roland 61, 236*ch*IV*n*6
Goldman, Emma 10
Good, Margaret 194, 237*n*2
Goodman, Fred 82
Graham, Harold 236*n*1
Grey, Judd 88
Gritten, Roy 23, 115, 173–174

Haase, Hazel 109, 111, 140, 218
Haase, Roy 2, 135, 180
Hagan, Darwin 245*n*10
Hahn, Gertrude 55–56, 236*n*4
Hamilton, Helen 95–96, 239*n*13
Hamilton, John "Three-Fingered Jack" 71–72, 137, 100, 204
Hamilton, Oscar 94, 239*n*13
Hamm, Homer 2, 113, 177, 180, 182–184, 186, 240*n*20
Hammond, IN 95, 203
Haney, Sheriff Alvin 213
Hankin, Hank 63
Harmon, Mark 26
Harvey, Elmer F. 194, 244*ch*XIII*n*6
Hawley, C.N. 104, 108
Hayes, Stan 3, 29, 136, 140, 147, 149
Healey, Joe 246*n*26
Hecht, Ben 23
Hedges, Arthur V. 100, 103, 164, 218
Helms, Everett "Pete" 28, 30, **108**, 110, 112, 114, 116–118, 121, 128, 130–131, 169–170, 183–184, 186, 248*n*7
Helms, Mrs. Everett (Margaret Owens) 1, 28, 113, 136–137, 190, 239*n*9
The Henriad 3
Henry, Lydia 54
High Sierra (1941) 24
Hillaire, Marcel 27
Hilliard, Nicholas 22
Hockett, Alice 66
Hockett, Art 1, 8–10, 29, 118–120, 123
Hogan, "Scar-faced" 63
Hollingsworth, Roscoe 190–191
Hollywood Code 22
Holton, Wade 133, 149
Homer, Leslie "Big" 92
Hoosegow (1929) 196
Hoosier Banker 10
Hoover, Pres. Herbert 202
Hoover, J. Edgar 10, 11, 12, 19
Hope, Bob 30
Houghton, Roy 149
Hubbard, Kin "Abe Martin" 91, 238*n*8

Hunter, E.H. 143, 145, 147, 149, 151, 219–220, 223, 225, 231, 242n14, 248n17, 248n19
Huntington, Forest 84, 196

If, or History Rewritten 5
Illinois Bankers Association 60
In Cold Blood 5
Indiana Bankers Association 20, 186, 215
Ingram, Homer 160, 163–168, 172–173, 176, 180–183, 185
Ingram, Roy 162
International Police Chiefs Association (IPCA) 23
Irvine, A.C. 39

J. Edgar Hoover 233Pron7
Jackson, Lawrence 101, 103, 165
Jacksonville (IL) 4
James, Jesse 1, 5, 33, 232, 236n1, 237n1
Jenkins, James 193–194, 197–198, 204
Jennings, Al 244chXIIn7
Jennings, James 47
"The Jinx That Stalked the Outlaws" 27
Jones, Ed "Pardner" 129

Kanner, Dutch 57
Kansas City, MO 3
Kansas City Union Station Massacre 11, 23
Kansas State Penitentiary 43
Karpis, Alvin "Old Creepy" 12, 71–72
Kelley, Rev. Harmon 149
Kelly, Paul 87
Kimes, Matthew 87
Kincaid, IL 104
Kinder, Mary 203–204
King, Dr. A.C. 59–60
King, Martin Luther 12
Klutas, John Edward "Handsome Jack" 223–224, 229–231
Kokomo, IN 42
Koon, Raymond F. 150
Kramer, Sheriff 162
Kunkel, Warden Louis 205
Kutch, Herman J. 176–177

Lafayette (IN) 2
Lamb, Lady Caroline 193
Lambert, Carl W. 190–191
Lamm, Herman K. "Baron" **145**; aliases of 2, 41; death certificate 227; draft card 15, 94; Prussian ancestry 15–16, 30, 33; rap sheet 44
Lamm Method 17–18, 20, 26

Landisch, Marian 56
Landy, G.W. "Dad" 8, 17, 19, 22, 36–38, 40, 42, 45, 47–49, 74, 76, 82, 93–94, 102–103, 107, 111, 122, 129, 131–132, 139, 144–**145**, 147, 149, 151, 156, 158–159, 182, 188, 215, 219, 234n2, 235n7, 241n11, 244n6, 244chXIIn1
Lansky, Meyer 12
Leach, Capt. Matt 26, 86, 200, 206, 246n27
Leopold, Nathan 35, 37, 51, 84
Leslie, Gov. Harry 205
Lincoln, Pres. Abraham 125
Lindbergh, Charles 35
Linton, C.T. 208
Little Bohemia 23
Little Caesar (1931) 23
Loeb, Richard 35, 37, 51, 84
Loger, Jake 68
Loger, Mrs. Jake 68
Longabaugh, Harry "Sundance Kid" 33
Longnaker, Mary 196–197
Love's Labor's Won 4
Lusitania 35
Lyons, Charles 29, 122

MacArthur, Charles 23
MacLane, Barton 23
Maddox, Roy 135
Makley, Charlie 197, 199, 204, 236n1
Malory, George Leigh 34
Maltese Falcon (1941) 24
Mann, Michael 29
Manning, Chauncey A. 84, 145, 228, 231
Margolis, Janet 13
Mason County (IL) Bankers Association 62
Massachusetts Avenue State Bank robbery (Indianapolis) 26, 196
Masters, Clarence 90–93, 157
Masters, Freddie "the Kid" 63
Mazzon (IL) 96
McCafferty, J.H. 78
McCarty, Lew 21
McCauley, F.W. 149, 151
McGinnis, Art 205
McKee, G.M. 248n17
McKellar, Sen. Kenneth 12
McNeil Matt 56–57
McNutt, Gov. Paul V. 85, 205–206
McVeigh, Timothy 15, 87
Merchants National Bank (South Bend, IN) 61
Michigan City (Indiana) 24, 28
Milius, John 26

Millaflores Massacre 243*n*16
Miller, Verne 224
Milwaukee (WI) 2
Minnesota State Prison 51
Mix, Tom 32, 214
the Mob 12
Monogram Pictures 25
Montgomery, Robert 193
Monticello (IN) 194
Montpelier (IN) 195
Moody, Leo 4, 10, 13, 125–*126*, 127, 130, 134–136, 192, 221, 230, 243*n*2
Moody, Mrs. Leo (Dorothy) 1, 28, 125, 138–139
Moody, Mary 128, 134, 181
Moore, John 101, 103
Mooresville (IN) 1
Mooresville (NC) 21
Moran, George "Bugs" 93, 211
Morgan, Dan 21, 35–48, 74–79, 106, 230–231, 235*n*7
Morgann, Maurice 10
Morris, Chester 193
Murder Ink: The Mystery Reader's Companion 20
Murray, Edna "the Rabbit" 72
Mutch, Lawrence 198
Myers, Henry 220
Myers, Dr. W.C. 117

Nash, Frank 11
Nash, Jay Robert 19–20, 22
Neel, Sheriff Charles 199–203
Nelson, "Baby Face" (Lester Gillis) 10–11, 56, 61, 71–72, 74, 206
Newland, Sheriff Harry 112–113, 122, 133, 138–139, 152, 162, 186, 188–*189*, 190
Newman, David 4, 25
Nichols, Glen 97, 132, 140
Niersteimer, Sheriff Walter 62
Nolan, John 2, 27, 100, 165, 223, 239*n*3
Norman, Charles (Clyde H. Nimerick) 35, 37, 40, 45, 49, 74, 106, 158, 234*n*18, 235*n*12
Northfield (MN) 5
Northwestern National Bank (Milwaukee, WI) robbery 48, 51–57
Nugent, Ralph "Crane-neck" 217

Oates, Warren 19
O'Bannion, Dion 56
O'Connor, "Terrible Tommy" 36, 42, 204
O'Connor, William 84

Offen, Ron 19
Official and Confidential 19, 233*n*7
101 Ranch 64
Owens, Mayor Henry 183

Paramount Pictures 23
Paris (IL) 204
Park, Gov. Brasfield 202
Parker, Bonnie 59, 243*n*5
Patzke, Ursula 26, 234*n*16
Pendleton Reformatory 47, 75
Peoples Savings Bank (Grand Haven, MI) 74
Peru (IN) 213, 246*n*12
Peterson, Paul 27
Petrified Forest (1936) 26
Pierpont, "Handsome Harry" 2, 6, 31, 37, 47, 92, 193, 197–199, 203–205, 216, 236*n*2, 245*n*16
Pinkston, Joseph 233*ch*I*n*4
Pontiac (IL) 62
Porter, Cole 214
Power, Sheriff Dan 36, 39, 45, 75, 158
Pryor, Frank 43
Public Enemies (2009) 17, 26–27, 245*n*16
Public Enemies (Burrough) 22, 26, 233Pro*n*4
Public Enemies program 11, 71
Public Enemy (1931) 23, 25
Purvis, Melvin 9, 10, 72

Randolph, John 83
Resser, Rex 2, 247*n*2
Reynolds, Sgt. Frank 242*n*6
Roberts, "Brushy Bill" 232, 249*n*25
Rockville (IN) 7, 195
Rogers, Winchester W. 123, 132
Roosevelt, Franklin Delano 23
Rose, Mickey 27
Rosenberg, Al 193
The Rubaiyat 2
Ruth, Babe 34, 87
Ryan, Chief William 141

Sacco and Vanzetti 88
St. Bernice (IN) 28
St. Joseph Valley Bank (Elkhart, IN) 69
St. Louis (MO) 20
St. Valentine's Day Massacre 211
San Antonio (TX) 47
San Francisco (CA) 3
Sarber, Sheriff Jess 25
Satterlee, Willis 154, 160, 189
Saunders, Roscoe C. 62, 243*n*3

Index

Sawyer, C.C. 156, 160–161, 171, 176, 178–179, 182, 187, 243n5
Sayers, Gordon 236n2, 245n10
Scarface (1932) 23
Scarrat, Sheriff J.L. 62
Schmitz, Herman 83–84
Schofield, Albert 84
Schricker, Gov. Henry P. 203
Scott, Harold "Pete" 113, 118, 134–135, 178, 180–186
The Searchers (1956) 3
Secrecy and Power 233Pro$n$7
Secrets Uncovered 233Pro$n$7
Seward Bank of Burdet (IN) 69
Shakespeare, William 248n5
Shaw, William 194
Shouse, Edward 1, 100, 204
Sidell (IL) 4, 8–10, 28, 30
Sims, Grover 90–91
Smith, Mrs. Claude 81
Smith, Eddie 123
Smith, Gordon 214
Smith, Henry 59, 61
Smoot, Mace 133, 143
Snyder, Deputy Jack 36, 42
Snyder, Ruth 87
South Bend (IN) 19, 233ch1n4
South Point Magazine 21
Spanier, Cecil 200
Starr, Henry 6
Startling Detective 20
State Bank of Clearing (IL) 96–97, 239n14
State Bank of Lenore (IL) 67
State Bank of Mundelin (IL) 97
state police radio system 70
Steele, Don 236n5
Stege, Capt. John 69
Stevens, G.H. 197
Stockwell (IN) 94
Stoner, Peter G. 78
Stout, Walter 28
Straw, John 43
Summers, Anthony 12
Superior (WI) 3
Swanson, Frank 198
Swift, Chief Robert A. 140

Take the Money and Run (1969) 18, 27, 98
Tate, Mary 9
Teapot Dome Scandal 38
Ten Most Wanted List (FBI) 13
Thew, Harvey F. 25
Thomas, Chief J.A. 76
Thompson, Carl 1

Thompson, Mark L. 84
Tierney, Lawrence 25
Tilton (IL) 28
Tiomkin, Dimitri 25
Toland, John 6, 13, 18, 20, 22, 25, 30–31, 193, 205, 240n13, 246n19
Toland, Toshiko 18
Towne, Robert 6
Trainor, Nicholas 208
Triplett, Dudley 198
True Detective Mysteries 20
Tunney, Gene 87
Tuscola (IL) 8
Tuscon (AZ) 24
Twain, Mark 4, 201
Tym, State's Attorney Charles 154–155

Underhill, Wilbur "Tri-state Terror" 222
Underworld (1927) 23
Union Station Massacre 233n4
Utah State Prison 31

Van Meter, Homer 56, 61
Vansickle, Clarence Edward **105**–107, 167–169, 239n5, 239n7
Vermillion County Bankers Association 150
vigilantism 4, 60–72
Volk, Robert 241n14
Voto, Pete 101, 123, 218

Wait, Judge William 156, **159**–161, 170, 180, 187, 189–190
Walker, Florence Jones 150
Walker, Deputy Joe 28, 112–**113**, 115–116, 119, 139, 143–145, 149–150, 154–155, 161, 163–178, 182–183, 244n4
Walton (KS) 35
War Dept. (US) 62
War on Crime 11–12
Ward, Sheriff F.W. 131, 140, 151, 227
Ward, James "the Rum King" 223–224, 229
Warner Brothers 23
Washington, Gen. George 34
Wayne, John 125
Weaver, Charles 83
Weaver gang 22
Webster, Harry 84
Weinhart, William 84
Weith, Warren 20
Welles, Orson 246n20
West, Mae 235n18
Wheel of Fortune 1
White, John 210

White Cap gang 194
Wild Bunch 21, 33
Wilder, Billy 88
Wiles, Buster 234n15
Williams, Carroll 28, 120, 151–152, 240n21, 240n23
Williams, Fenton 28, 120, 143, 174–175, 240n21, 240n23
Williams, James 40
Winkler, Gus 211–212
Winston-Salem (N.C.) 159
Wise, George 189
Woodford County (IL) Bankers Association 60

Worley, Chief Claude 88
Wright, G.P. 84
Wright, Ollie 93

Yendes, C.E. 196
Yordan, Philip 25
Young Brothers 70
Young Guns II (1990) 232
Younger Brothers 5

Ziegler, "Shotgun George" (Fred Goetz) 133, 144, 211–212, 227, 242n12, 246n25
Zientara, Eva 209
Zientara, George 209, 212